AMERICANS IN LONDON

An anecdotal street guide to the homes and haunts
of Americans from John Adams to Fred Astaire

BRIAN N. MORTON

Macdonald
Queen Anne Press

Macdonalds Americans in London

A Queen Anne Press BOOK

© Brian N. Morton 1986

First published in Great Britain in 1988 by
Queen Anne Press, a division of
Macdonald & Co (Publishers) Ltd
3rd Floor
Greater London House
Hampstead Road
London
NW1 7QX

A Pergamon Press plc company

Front cover illustration: Rita Wüthrich
Back cover photographs: *left* Mary Pickford and Douglas Fairbanks
Snr (Popperfoto)
right Louis Armstrong (Popperfoto)

All rights reserved. No part of this publication may be reproduced,
stored in a retrieval system, or transmitted, in any form or by any
means, without the prior permission in writing of the publisher, nor be
otherwise circulated in any form of binding or cover other than that in
which it is published and without a similar condition including this
condition being imposed on the subsequent purchaser.

British Library Cataloguing in Publication Data

Morton, Brian
    Americans in London. — (A Queen Anne Press book).
    1. London (England) — Description — 1981 — Guide-books
    I. Title
    914.21'04858'0240313   DA679

    ISBN 0-356-15558-7

Reproduced, printed and bound in Great Britain
by Hazell, Watson & Viney Ltd,
Member of BPCC plc, Aylesbury, Bucks.

Contents

Introduction

When Americans come to England it is a family affair. There is an inevitable mixture of anticipation and anxiety rather like that of meeting new relatives. Some Americans seek approval, some seek to prove themselves, some are defensive, few are indifferent. The first encounter is rarely easy. Self-assured English men and women with their clipped British accents tend to make even the most intelligent American feel ill at ease, if not inferior. Abigail Adams, as quietly self-confident as anyone, admitted to her "apprehension" upon first meeting London society. James Fenimore Cooper, much aware that he was one of the first American writers to face London critics, adopted a defiant and brash air. Already famous in England thanks to the success of *The Last of the Mohicans*, he had come to finish *Notions of the Americans*, an assault on British prejudices toward the United States. He was quite taken aback when he found himself received with many invitations and much kindness. "The Johnny Bulls," noted Mrs. Cooper, "are so civil to him that I am afraid that he will not be able to abuse them, and so the piquancy of his book will be much spoiled." Almost a century later T.S. Eliot's desire to be accepted translated itself into a punctiliousness which became a family joke with Virginia and Leonard Woolf. "Come to dinner," wrote Virginia to her brother-in-law, "Eliot will be there in a four-piece suit." A few years later John Barrymore arrived in London for the supreme challenge—to play Hamlet on the English stage. No English producer would back an American performing Shakespeare, so he financed his own production. It was not the ten thousand pounds profit which Barrymore pocketed that was so important, rather it was the satisfaction of knowing that he had succeeded in London and that the critics, beginning with the *Sunday Times,* had found his performance to be "magnificent." *Americans in London* traces the joys, anxieties, hopes, setbacks and achievements of those who passed through the city and others who chose to live there.

London began to fill with Americans soon after the first rumblings of the Revolution. By 1777 more than five thousand loyalists had arrived in England. Although the mother country continued to pay their salaries and pensions, these officers of the Crown found themselves snubbed by London society. Their dress and accents were considered provincial. As the war dragged on, they became a sad, lonely group. Day by day they learned that everything they had represented was collapsing. Their enforced idleness and their increasing impecunity became an embarrassment to themselves and to the British government. After the war, haunted by the idea of dying abroad, many loyalists returned home to an uncertain welcome. Others left London and faded into the English countryside.

Representing a new, young and independent America, John Adams settled in Grosvenor Square in 1785. He soon discovered that although the British army had surrended at Yorktown, the news had reached but few in London. The British navy went on seizing and impressing American-born seamen into service in the very port of London. British officials continued to treat their "former subjects" with arrogance and condescension. Adams was to suffer through what became a difficult and sometimes humiliating relationship with the officials in Whitehall, one which would not improve for well over a century. The chief reason was that the British government resented an ever growing and more powerful America. They were not displeased to see the Civil War break out, a war in which they favored the South until it became expedient to change sides. Even when General Pershing arrived in London in 1917, leading the vanguard of the American Expeditionary Force, the British High Command proposed that American troops be split up and used in British units to replace those killed and wounded. Pershing politely refused and left with his men for France.

On a personal level, however, most Americans felt at home in London. Painters such as Benjamin West, Gilbert Stuart, John Copley and Charles Peale enjoyed honors and patronage, earning sums which would have been unthinkable in Boston or Philadelphia. For American writers, 19th-century England offered a much bigger, wealthier and sophisticated reading public than did America. Large publishing houses were concentrated in London which led to competition and higher royalties. In 1820 Washington Irving moved to London and signed a contract with John Murray, whom he termed as the "Prince of Booksellers." Nine years later he received an honorary degree from Oxford University. He was followed by Longfellow, Melville, Emerson, and Henry James, who told his mother on Christmas Eve 1876, "I must be a born Londoner." Mark Twain, living in Chelsea, enjoyed nothing better than calling on his American neighbors, John Singer Sargent and James McNeill Whistler. The 20th century saw Ezra Pound and Hilda Doolittle followed by Robert Frost, Archibald MacLeish, Sinclair Lewis, Conrad Aiken, Edmund Wilson and Sylvia Plath.

The London stage drew American actors and actresses early in the 19th century. Edwin Forrest, Charlotte Cushman, Edwin Booth, the Barrymores, all performed at Drury Lane or the Haymarket. Early in this century Tallulah Bankhead, in her twenties, earned $2,500 a week, lunched at the Houses of Parliament with Ramsay MacDonald, the prime minister, and bought a Bentley and a house in Mayfair. Fred Astaire and his sister took London by storm. Ruth Draper, Helen Hayes, Paul Muni, Paul Robeson, Duke Ellington and Louis Armstrong were all applauded.

Early in World War II, Britain, desperate and fighting alone, asked for American aid. By 1944 over one million GIs crowded the island. London was packed. Eisenhower and Churchill even grew to like one another. Americans recognized the courage of Londoners during the bombing, while Londoners noted the GIs distributing candy and chewing gum to cockney children and public school boys alike. As the Allied forces prepared to embark for the beaches of Normandy, American troops received touching farewells and genuine invitations to return when the fight was over. Ever since, Americans have been welcome in England.

Among the many librarians who were so helpful in London, I would particularly like to thank the reference staff at the British Museum and at the Guildhall library. Ben Weinreb, coauthor of *The London Encyclopedia,* was a genial host and advisor. My thanks also go to Miss Wiggins of the Greater London Council and to the staff of the Peabody Trust. My appreciation goes to Peter McWilliams and to the Kaypro Corporation for the use of a portable computer.

About the Author

Brian N. Morton was born in London, England. He did his graduate studies at Columbia University, New York. He taught at Williams College, Massachusetts, and since 1969 has been teaching French literature at the University of Michigan, Ann Arbor. His forthcoming book, *Beaumarchais and the American Revolution*, deals with secret French aid to America from 1776 to 1778. Together with his French wife and two children, he divides his time between Ann Arbor, London and Paris.

Subsequent editions would be enriched by readers sharing their interests and knowledge with the author. Any corrections or suggestions for additional entries will be gratefully received and fully acknowledged whenever possible. Please write to Professor Brian N. Morton, 4220 MLB, University of Michigan, Ann Arbor, Michigan 48109.

About the Guide

This guide is organized by streets in alphabetical order. House numbers or house names in bold face indicate that the original building is still standing, even though its use may have changed and the front may have been modernized. House numbers in parentheses indicate the site where the original building once stood. The symbol ⚘ separates entries at the same address. Street names in capital letters within the text indicate that the story continues at that location.

You can choose someone of interest from the *List of Americans* (p. xiii). This list identifies by profession most of the Americans appearing in the guide and gives the address or addresses linked to their stay in London. When there is more than one address, they are listed in chronological order. For example:

Henry James Morley's Hotel, 4 Trafalgar Square
      7 Half Moon Street
      3 Bolton Street
      34 De Vere Gardens

Thus you may begin at Morley's Hotel, overlooking Trafalgar Square, sharing with James his arrival in London in February 1869. After a week in a musty bedroom you may accompany him to his first flat in London, on Half Moon Street, where he found dark rooms decorated with wax flowers. He soon left for France but returned seven years later to settle permanently in England. First on Bolton Street, a stone's throw from Piccadilly, where he achieved fame with *Daisy Miller* followed by *Washington Square*. Famous and financially secure, James then moved to 34 De Vere Gardens, where from his desk he could see the Palace Gate leading into Kensington Gardens. There is a blue plaque commemorating the fifteen or more years he spent here.

Street Names

London street names change. The popularity of the Duke of Wellington after his defeat of Napoleon at Waterloo in 1815 led to no less than seventeen streets and squares bearing his name. Few survived. There used to be several Norfolk Streets. The last and probably the oldest ran from the Strand down to the Victoria Embankment. At present there is no Norfolk Street in London. Street names in no ways correspond. Under no circumstances should you expect to find Chandos Street, for instance, near Chandos Place. They are three miles apart.

A map reference follows for streets appearing on one of the area maps to be found at the end of the book. Sites of buildings which no longer exist or which are far from central London have no map references.

House Numbers

Eccentric might be the best term with which to characterize the numbering system of buildings along the streets of London. Bond Street goes northward from Piccadilly, the numbers run from 1 to 24 on the eastern side of Old Bond Street till breaking off at Burlington Gardens where they turn back on the western side running from 25 to 50. Old Bond Street continues north but becomes New Bond Street with numbers 1 to 86 on the eastern side and 87 to 180 on the western. Actual house numbers along an entire street are changed sometimes when a building is added or torn down. Thus, when you read in a biography published in 1870 that Washington Irving lived at 21 Edward Street in 1821. There is little way of knowing whether number 21 today corresponds to number 21 of his day or whether the biographer, aware of the changes of the street numbers between 1821 and 1870, simply gave the number of Irving's house as it appeared in 1870. In cases, where the original house is still standing and can be identified, there is less confusion. In Grosvenor Square, for instance, the house where John and Abigail Adams lived is number 9; it was number 8 in their day. I have spent long hours in the archives of the Greater London Council in Middlesex House trying to establish present house numbers. The numbers given in this guide have been checked against the original street plans of London and may differ from those given in published correspondence or in present day biographies. As with Adams, I have used today's house numbers. Nevertheless errors undoubtedly still exist for which I can only apologize.

List of Illustrations

List of Americans

Addresses for each American are listed in chronological order.

Actors, actresses, playwrights and producers

Bankhead, Tallulah	Shaftesbury Avenue, Shaftesbury Theatre Farm Street, 1
Barrymore, Ethel	Bedford Street, 21
Barrymore, John	Cheyne Walk, 2
Booth, Edwin	Berkeley Street, 3 Wellington Street, The Lyceum
Cushman, Charlotte	New Bond Street, 92 Haymarket, 6 Baker Street, 1
Draper, Ruth	Pall Mall, 80 Ebury Street, 120 St. Leonard's Terrace, 20 Knightsbridge, 66
Fairbanks, Douglas & Mary Pickford	Piccadilly, Ritz Hotel
Forrest, Edwin	Catherine Street, Theatre Royal Drury Lane Covent Garden, St. Paul's
Frohman, Charles	Henrietta Street, 5 St. Martin's Lane, Duke of York's Theatre Waterloo Place, 11
Gordon, Ruth	Brook Street, 51 Waterloo Road, Old Vic Theatre
Hayes, Helen	Park Lane, 97
Jefferson, Joseph	The Strand, Adelphi Theatre
Muni, Paul	Charing Cross Road, 10
Payne, John Howard	Catherine Street, Theatre Royal Drury Lane Rosebery Avenue, Sadler's Wells Ludgate Hill, Fleet Prison
Williams, Tennessee	The Strand, Savoy Hotel Haymarket, 6

Art critics and patrons

Berenson, Bernard	Lord North Street, 13
	Old Bond Street, 14
Guggenheim, Peggy	Cork Street, 30
Norton, Charles Eliot	Queen's Gate Terrace, 18

Composers, musicians and singers

Armstrong, Louis	Temple Place, Howard Hotel
	Argyll Street, Palladium
Bechet, Sydney	Buckingham Palace
Berlin, Irving	Cranbourn Street, Hippodrome
	Argyll Street, Palladium
Ellington, Duke	Argyll Street, Palladium
Gershwin, George	Leicester Square,
	Empire Theatre
Homer, Louise	Bow Street, Royal Opera House
Miller, Glenn	Sloane Court West, 25
	Portland Place,
	Broadcasting House
Robeson, Paul	Catherine Street,
	Theatre Royal Drury Lane
	The Strand, Savoy Theatre

Diplomats and statesmen

Adams, Charles Francis	Mansfield Street, 5
	Portland Place, 98
Adams, John & Abigail	Buckingham Palace
	King Street, 43
	Adam Street, 6
	Throgmorton Street, 27
	Catherine Street,
	Theatre Royal Drury Lane
	Piccadilly, 156
	St. James's Palace
	Grosvenor Square, 9
	Downing Street, 10
Bancroft, Edward	Rathbone Place
Bancroft, George	Eaton Square, 90
Burr, Aaron	Craven Street, 30
	Clerkenwell Close

Choate, Joseph H.	Carlton House Terrace, 1
Deane, Silas	Fleet Street, 135
Donovan, William J.	Brook Street, 51
Franklin, Benjamin	Craven Street, 36 Westminster, Houses of Parliament
Fremont, John Charles	New Bond Street, 169-174
Goldberg, Arthur	Brook Street, 51
Grant, Ulysses S.	Cavendish Square, 17
Hay, John	Carlton House Terrace, 5
Hoover, Herbert	Hyde Park Gate, 39 Hornton Street, The Red House The Strand, Savoy Hotel
Hopkins, Harry	Brook Street, 51
Houghton, Alanson B.	Curzon Street, Crewe House
Jay, John	Buckingham Palace
Jefferson, Thomas	Golden Square, 14
Kellogg, Frank B.	Curzon Street, Crewe House
Kennedy, Joseph	Princes Gate, 14 Grosvenor Square, American Embassy
Laurens, Henry	Tower of London
Lee, Arthur	Garden Court, Middle Temple, 2
Mason, James M.	Devonshire Place, 54
Morris, Gouverneur	King Street, 43 Catherine Street, Theatre Royal Drury Lane Wellington Street, The Lyceum Westminster Bridge Road, Astley's Amphitheatre
Roosevelt, Franklin & Eleanor	Dover Street, 21
Roosevelt, Theodore	Dover Street, 21
Seward, William Henry	Adam Street, Wright's Hotel
Sumner, Charles	Vigo Street, 2
Van Buren, Martin	Stratford Place, 7

Webster, Daniel	Hanover Square, 10
Weed, Thurlow	St. George Street, 12A
Wilson, Woodrow	Southampton Street, 22-25 Buckingham Palace
Winant, John	Aldford Street, 7

Doctors and nurses

Baynham, William	St. Thomas's Street, Guy's
Gibson, William	St. Thomas's Street, Guy's
Holmes, Oliver Wendell	St. Paul's Churchyard, 6
Howe, Samuel G.	Baker Street Caledonian Road, Pentonville Prison
Jackson, James	St. Thomas's Street, Guy's
Physick, Philip	Hyde Park Corner, St. George's
Reynolds, Edward	St. Thomas's Street, Guy's
Sanger, Margaret	Torrington Square, 67
Stevens, Alexander H.	St. Thomas's Street, Guy's
Wagner, John	St. Thomas's Street, Guy's
Warren, John C.	St. Thomas's Street, Guy's

Entertainers

Astaire, Fred	Shaftesbury Avenue, Shaftesbury Theatre Haymarket, Carlton Hotel
Barnum, Phineas T.	Buckingham Palace Piccadilly, 170
Cody, William "Buffalo Bill"	Northumberland Avenue, Metropole Hotel Pool of London Earl's Court Exhibition Hall
Houdini	Leicester Square, Alhambra
Thomas, Lowell	Bow Street, Royal Opera House
Thumb, Tom	Buckingham Palace Piccadilly, 170
Ward, Artemus	Piccadilly, 170

Inventors and scientists

Ames, Oakes	Northumberland Avenue, Metropole Hotel
Burroughs, John	High Holborn, 270
Conant, James B.	Downing Street, 10 Bedford Street, 21
Edison, Thomas	Russell Street, Hummums Hotel Queen Victoria Street, 11
Fulton, Robert	Charlotte Street, 84 Margaret Street, 67 Newman Street, 18 Bedford Street, 9
Morgan, Lewis Henry	Bury Street, 15
Morse, Samuel	Vauxhall Gardens Cleveland Street, 141

Journalists

Bierce, Ambrose	Old Mitre Court, 5
Brooks, Van Wycks	Old Compton Street, 16
Davis, Richard H.	Albany Court Yard, The Albany
Lippmann, Walter	Suffolk Street, 15
Miller, Joaquin	Old Mitre Court, 5
Murrow, Edward R.	Hallam Street, 84 Portland Place, Broadcasting House
Sherburne, John	Piccadilly, 170

Loyalists

Curwen, Samuel	Brompton Road, 23
Hutchinson, Thomas	New Bond Street, 149
Quincy, Samuel	Brompton Road

Merchants and businessmen

Barlow, Joel	Litchfield Street, 18
Bates, Joshua	Portland Place, 46
Bingham, William	Harley Street, 62 Manchester Square, Hertford House

Depew, Chauncey	St. Paul's Cathedral
Hughes, Howard	Hamilton Place, Inn on the Park
Peabody, George	Eaton Square, 80 King Street, 26 Peabody Avenue
Selfridge, Gordon	Oxford Street, 400
Vanderbilt, Cornelius	Jermyn Street, 76
Yerkes, Charles Tyson	Lots Road

Military officers

Arnold, Benedict	Gloucester Place, 18
Eisenhower, Dwight D.	Brook Street, 51 Grosvenor Square, 20 Grosvenor Square, 47
Patton, George	Tower of London
Pershing, John	Whitehall, War Office

Novelist, poets and writers

Aiken, Conrad	Great Ormond Street, 37 Brunswick Square, 1
Alcott, Louisa May	Aubrey Road, Aubrey House Westbourne Grove Terrace, 6
Atherton, Gertrude	Cork Street, Hall's Hotel
Brooks, Van Wyck	Old Compton Street, 16
Burroughs, William	Egerton Gardens, 44
Cather, Willa	North Road, Haringey, 17
Cooper, James Fenimore	Adam Street, Wright's Hotel St. James's Place, 33 Holland Park, Holland House Regent Street, 264 Westminster Abbey
Crane, Stephen	Baker Street, 82
Dana, Richard H.	Regent Street, 19 Covent Garden The Strand, 100
Doolittle, Hilda	Kensington Church Walk

Eliot, T.S.	Crawford Street, 18
Emerson, Ralph Waldo	The Strand, 142
	Pall Mall, 107
	Kew Gardens
	Lincoln's Inn Fields, 58
Ferber, Edna	The Strand, Savoy Hotel
Fitzgerald, F. Scott & Zelda	Brook Street, 51
Frost, Robert	Bloomsbury Street, 6
	Devonshire Street, 35
	Woburn Walk, 5
Gunther, John	Gower Street, 104
Harland, Henry	Cromwell Road, 144
Harte, Bret	Portland Place,
	Langham Hotel
	Lancaster Gate, 109
Hawthorne, Nathaniel	St. George Street, 24
	Mansion House Street,
	Mansion House
	Tower of London
Irving, Washington	Royal Exchange,
	New York Coffee House
	Norfolk Street, 35
	Edward Street, 21
	Great Malborough Street, 46
	Chandos Street, 3
	Westminster Abbey
James, Henry	Trafalgar Square, 4
	Half Moon Street, 7
	Bolton Street, 3
	De Vere Gardens, 34
	King Street, St. James's Theatre
	Pall Mall, 107
Kerouac, Jack	Coventry Street, 39
Krutch, Joseph	Guilford Street, 62
Lewis, Sinclair	Sloane Street, 75
	Bury Street, 10
	Temple, 1 Crown Office Row
	Henrietta Street, 15

Longfellow, Henry W.	Princes Street, 8 Portland Place, Langham Hotel
Lowell, Amy	Berkeley Street, 3
Lowell, James Russell	Lowndes Street, 37 Radnor Place, 2
MacLeish, Archibald	Great Russell Street, British Museum
McCullers, Carson	St. Leonard's Terrace, 25
Melville, Herman	Craven Street, 25
Millay, Edna St. Vincent	Hertford Street, 41
Mumford, Lewis	Belgrave Road, 65
O'Hara, John	Chelsea Manor Street, 52
O'Neill, Eugene	Berkeley Street, 3
Plath, Sylvia	Borough High Street, St. George the Martyr Chalcot Square, 7 Fitzroy Road, Primrose Hill, 23
Pound, Ezra	Regent Street, 309 Kensington Church Walk, 10 Holland Place Chambers, 5
Saroyan, William	The Strand, Savoy Hotel Cheltenham Terrace, The Whitelands House
Stanton, Elizabeth Cady	Great Queen St, 59-60
Stein, Gertrude & Leo	Bloomsbury Square, 20 Knightsbridge, Knightsbridge Hotel
Steinbeck, John	Piccadilly, 116 Park Lane, Dorchester Hotel
Stowe, Harriet Beecher	Stable Yard, St. James's
Tarkington, Booth	Henrietta Place, 21
Thurber, James	Albany Court Yard, 5 St. James's Place, 16
Ticknor, George	Piccadilly, 139

Twain, Mark	Old Mitre Court, 5
	Tedworth Square, 23
	Wellington Court, 30
	Dover Street, 21
Van Doren, Mark	Guilford Street, 62
Wharton, Edith	Berkeley Street, 3
	Jermyn Street, 81
Wilder, Thornton	Northumberland Avenue,
	Metropole Hotel
	Charlotte Street, 16
	Whitehall Court, 2
Wilson, Edmund	Knightsbridge, 66
	Half Moon Street,
	Green Park Hotel
	Basil Street, 8
Wolfe, Thomas	Russell Square, 62
	Wellington Square, 32
	Hanover Square, 25
	Sherwood Street,
	Regent Palace Hotel
	Jermyn Street, 81

Painters, sculptors and architects

Abbey, Edwin A.	Tite Street, 42
Allston, Washington	Great Titchfield Street, 132
	Maple Street, 49
Audubon, John	Great Russell Street, 55
	Regent's Park
Borglum, Gutzon	Mortimer Road, Kilburn,
	Harlestone Villa
Brown, Mather	Cavendish Square, 20
Catlin, George	Piccadilly, 170
	Waterloo Place, 6
Copley, John Singleton	Panton Square
	Leicester Square, 28
	Spring Gardens, Great Room
	St. George Street, 25
Dunlap, William	Charlotte Street, 84
Hood, Raymond	Argyll Street, 1

King, Charles Bird	Cleveland Street, 2
Leslie, Charles Robert	Cleveland Street, 141
Peale, Charles Willson	Castle Street
Peale, Rubens & Rembrandt	Pall Mall, 118
Pennell, Joseph	Buckingham Street, 14
Sargent, John Singer	Tite Street, 31-33
Stuart, Gilbert	Buckingham Street, York Bldgs Gracechurch Street, 30 Villiers Street, 27 Newman Street, 7 New Burlington Street, 3
Sully, Thomas	Cleveland Street, 2
Trumbull, John	Buckingham Street, York Bldgs Newman Street, 14 Pall Mall, 125 Tothill Street, Prison
West, Benjamin	Bedford Street, 19 Hyde Park, The Serpentine Castle Street Buckingham Palace Panton Square Pall Mall, 118 Newman Street, 14 Pall Mall, 125
Whistler, James McNeill	Sloane Street, 62 Newman Street, 70 Cheyne Walk, 96-100 Princes Gate, 49 Westminster, Court of Exchequer Tite Street, 35 Cheyne Walk, 74
Wright, Frank Lloyd	Suffolk Street, 15 Portland Place, 66

Publishers and booksellers

Putnam, George P.	Waterloo Place, 6
Stevens, Henry	Trafalgar Square, 4
Weed, Thurlow	St. George Street, 12 A

Miscellaneous

Coburn, Alvin Langdon

Guilford Street
Lower Mall, Hammersmith,
Thameside

King, Martin Luther, Jr.

St. Paul's Cathedral

Lindbergh, Charles

Dover Street, 21

Simpson, Wallis

George Street, 5
Cumberland Terrace, 16

Streets of London

Cornhill and Lombard Street from the Poultry, 1829

STREETS
OF
LONDON

Adam Street

(6)   Adelphi Family Hotel. Abigail Adams, accompanied by her daughter Nabby, took accommodation here on 20 July 1784. That evening she wrote to her sister: "We have a handsome drawing-room, genteelly furnished, and a large lodging-room. We are furnished with a cook, chambermaid, waiter etc., for three guineas a week; but in this is not included a mouthful of victuals or drink." Here she hoped to be reunited with her husband and their son John, neither of whom she had seen for five years. A few days after her arrival she told her sister: "The city of London is pleasanter than I expected; the buildings more regular, the streets much wider, and more sunshine than I thought to have found.... At my lodgings I am as quiet as at any place in Boston." As for clothes, the gentlemen were "very plainly dressed, and the ladies much less so than with us. You must put a hoop on and have your hair dressed, but a common straw hat, no cap, with only a ribbon upon the crown, is thought dress sufficient to go into company. Muslins are much in taste; no silks but lutestrings worn."

Abigail went shopping on Cheapside but found everything more expensive than at home. A week later, she took her first walk accompanied by an American friend, Charles Storer. She wrote: "I had never been out before but in a coach. Mr. Storer advised me to walk as it was a fine morning and the sides of the streets here are laid with flat stone as large as tile. The London ladies walk a vast deal and very fast. I accordingly agreed to go out with him, and he led me a jaunt of full four miles." She returned exhausted, "unable to walk across the room," but this was largely due to her having just spent five weeks on board ship. She resolved that if she were to live in London, she would take a walk every day. While she was resting, Mrs. Copley, the wife of the American painter John Copley, called upon her. To her sister she explained: "The servant came up and asked me if I was at home? The replie ought to have been no, but Ester not being accustomede to London Stile, replied yes. Fortunately Nabby was near dresst, so we past off Miss Adams for Mrs. Adams, one being at home, the other not." Nevertheless, the London practice of not being in for callers bothered Abigail.

Her social life was full; dining out every day, she declared, "I am in love with what I have seen of the London Stile of entertaining company." One simple dinner, she wrote, consisted of "a table neatly set, fish of a small kind, at the head; a ham in the middle, and a roast fillet of veal at the foot, peas and collyflower, an almond pudding and a pair of roast ducks were brought on. When the fish was removed, cherries and goosberries." Only one servant for the seven guests, but he was "a thorough master of his business."

Finally, at the end of July, one long awaited reunion took place. Whilst she was writing to her sister, "a servant in the family runs puffing in ... young Mr. Adams is come. O Where where is he, we all cried out? In the other house, Madam, he stoped to get his hair drisst." When John Quincy Adams, 17, finally appeared, his mother drew back, not believing her eyes, until he cried out, "Oh my Mamma and my dear sister." His appearance, his mother wrote, "is that of a Man, and in his countenance the most perfect good humour." From the Hague, John Adams requested that his family join him there. Their last days in London were spent visiting Drapers' Hall, the Foundling Hospital and seeing the paintings of John Trumbull and fellow Bostonian John Copley. As Abigail admitted to her sister, while strolling with her children she felt herself "exceedingly matronly with a grown up son on one hand, and daughter upon the other, and were I not their mother, I would say a likelier pair you will seldom see in a summers day." In her last paragraph, she confessed: "I have a partiality for this country."

Wright's Hotel. James Fenimore Cooper and his wife arrived in London on 1 March 1828. They had come from Dover along "beautiful roads, at the rate of ten or eleven miles the hour in perfect security." Cooper, 39, was already known in England through *The Last of the Mohicans*, which had been published two years earlier. He intended to stay six weeks and finish *Notions of the Americans*—an almost belligerent assault on British prejudices toward the United States and an answer to her critics. He did not expect any favors from London society, and was somewhat taken aback when he received many invitations and kindnesses. "The Johnny Bulls," noted Mrs. Cooper, "are so civil to him that I am afraid he will not be able to abuse them, and so the piquancy of his book will be quite spoiled." One English host, the writer Barry Cornwall, reported that on telling Cooper that his books pleased the English, the American replied, "It wasn't what I intended then." Cooper seemed, Cornwall added, "to have 'meant nothing but fighting,' as they say in the ring."

Cooper enjoyed the street music of London. "Respectable artists," he wrote, "such as would be gladly received in our orchestras, walk the streets and play the music of Rossini, Mozart, Beethoven, Meyerbeer and Weber." On their second evening in London, a party of street musicians began to play under their hotel window. Cooper remained on the sofa reading until they played "Yankee Doodle." This cost him half-a-crown and the comment: "It is something, at all events, to have taught John Bull that we take pride in that tune." After five days in Wright's Hotel, the Coopers took a house in ST. JAMES'S PLACE.

William Henry Seward and his father arrived by stagecoach in London at the famous Saracen's Head posting house at Snow Hill in July 1833. (It was here, five years later, that Dickens's Nicholas Nickleby was introduced to the schoolmaster, Wackford Squeers, who had but one eye although "popular prejudice runs in favor of two.") The two Sewards took a hackney to "Mrs. Wright's Hotel, Adam Street, Adelphi, just out of the dust and smoke of the city proper." The younger Seward, future secretary of state under Lincoln, spent most of his time in London in the galleries of the House of Commons. As usual, the subject under debate was Ireland and Seward wondered whether the Irish would ever acquiesce to British rule as long as the United States would provide asylum for Irish exiles. He was struck by the earnestness and attention paid to debates by the members of Parliament, and thought that it was because they sat "in close proximity to one another." In the House of Representatives, members were seated at desks spread out over a broad area which, he felt, frequently led to listlessness. But Seward left after two weeks with few regrets: "It seemed to me then that little as we loved the English nation, they loved us still less."

Albany Court Yard Map C

The Albany. Built in 1770, the house was converted in 1802 into sixty-nine sets of chambers for bachelors, yet another reminder that London was a city designed for men. Safely protected from the bustle of nearby Piccadilly, everyone lived here from Gladstone to

Edward Heath. Richard H. Davis, 33, a leading journalist, settled here in June 1897. His rooms were cluttered with Hogarth prints, old silver, blue and white china, Zulu weapons, fur rugs, and easy chairs covered with Indian silk. Davis had come to cover Queen Victoria's Jubilee for *Harper's Weekly*. His description of Buckingham Palace began with himself:

> Dear Family,
> I was a beautiful sight at the Levee. I wore a velvet suit made especially for me but no dearer for that and steel buttons and a beautiful steel sword and a court hat with silver on the side and silk stockings and pumps with great buckles. I was too magnificent for words...I saw beefeaters and life guardsmen and chamberlains with white wands and I gave one my card and he read out "Richard Harding Davis of the United States by the American Ambassador" and then I bowed to the Prince and Duke of York, Connaught and Edinburgh and to the American Ambassador.

Alas, no one knew Davis, so he ended up going to Cox's Hotel where he showed himself in his velvet suit "to Miss Groves and Miss Wather," the two room clerks. He gave a lunch at the Savoy for Ambassador John Hay and his daughter, Mr. and Mrs. Asquith and a bevy of socialites. For dessert the hotel sent in "an American Eagle of ice, decorated with American flags and dripping icy tears from its beak. It cost me five shillings a head," he told his mother, "and looked as though it cost that in pounds." The scenes of the Jubilee are to be found in Davis's *A Year from a Reporter's Note-Book* (1898).

(5)   Formerly the Storran Gallery. James Thurber and his wife arrived in London in May 1937. Their year in Europe began with a one-man show of Thurber's drawings here at the Storran Gallery. Thurber was already well known in England, all his books having been published by Hamish Hamilton. "The hallmark of sophistication is to adore the drawings of James Thurber," said the *Daily Sketch* for 25 May 1937. Most of the London reviewers were struck by the Freudian, surrealistic quality of his drawings. The *Daily Sketch* spoke of the "wild nonsense through which gleams of nightmare logic" in cartoons such as "That's my first wife up there, and this is the *present* Mrs. Harris." Matisse happened to be in London at the time of the exhibition and the gallery owner, anxious to obtain his endorsement, invited the master to meet

Thurber. Matisse's secretary, declining the invitation, informed the owner that Matisse had never heard of Thurber, the *New Yorker* or its editor Harold Ross. Thurber evened the score for his editor later by remarking that "Ross had never heard of Matisse." The success of his art show in London was confirmed for Thurber when two of his drawings were stolen. In the *Observer,* David Garnett made the English publication of *Let Your Mind Alone* the occasion for a general assessment of Thurber, describing him as "the most original and humorous writer living."

Aldford Street Map C

7   John Winant took a third-floor furnished flat next door to the embassy in February 1941; his five years as ambassador were difficult ones. The importance of his arrival was evident. When his plane landed at Bristol, the Duke of Kent welcomed him and on the way to London the private train stopped at Windsor, where Winant found the king waiting for him on the platform—the first time in Britain's history that a king had gone to meet an ambassador. After an hour's talk at Windsor Castle, Winant declined the invitation to stay the night and continued on to London. Three days later he dined alone with Winston Churchill, and was frequently at Downing Street over the next two months. He and Churchill signed the agreement for the British to lease bases in the Caribbean to America in exchange for fifty old U.S. destroyers. A warm friendship developed between Winant and Anthony Eden, the 44-year-old foreign secretary, brought about partly because both men were similarly overshadowed. As the war went on, Roosevelt and Churchill took increasingly to dealing directly with one another by phone, leaving both Winant and Eden excluded. As the number of American missions to England increased dramatically, Winant felt he was no longer being consulted or being properly informed by Washington. When Averell Harriman arrived in London to run the Lend-Lease Program, he was received by Churchill far more frequently. With Grosvenor Square almost entirely taken over by American military missions, OSS groups and FBI representatives, by late 1943 Winant was complaining bitterly to Washington that the business relegated to him could be done by any efficient foreign service officer. He was also upset by rumors in the British press that he

was about to be replaced by Averell Harriman as ambassador.

Lonely in London, Winant was delighted to meet five American graduates who had joined Anthony Eden's old army unit, the 60th King's Royal Rifle Corps. When the five got a weekend pass, they came to supper in his flat here in Aldford Street and talked until the early hours of the morning before dropping off to sleep on the floor. Winant learned a lot from them about daily life in the army. When two of them were killed in North Africa, Winant labored over letters to their families. He enjoyed entertaining British socialists and intellectuals, such as R.H. Tawney, the economic historian, H.G. Wells, Harold Laski and Sir William Beveridge, the father of the British social security system. When the Labour party came to power in 1945, President Truman kept their friend Winant at his post. After having shared five years of danger and austerity with the British, Parliament, press and people were unanimous in praising him when he left. He returned to America in 1946.

Argyll Street Map C

1   Palladium House was built in 1928 by Raymond Hood. Its impressive facade of black sheer granite and rich gilt with lush floral motifs reflects the architecture of the Paris exhibition which Hood had visited three years earlier. He returned to New York city to become one of the principal architects of Rockefeller Center.

London Palladium. Louis Armstrong began a two-week engagement here on 18 July 1932. He had arrived unexpectedly and without a band and so a group was sent over at the last moment from Paris which included trumpeter Charlie Johnson, saxophonist Joe Hayman, tenorman Fletcher Allen, guitarist Maceo Jefferson and a few others. They shared the bill with a number of other acts and appeared toward the end of the evening playing four numbers: "Them There Eyes," "When You're Smiling," "Chinatown, My Chinatown" and "You Rascal, You." For the many musicians who made up part of the audience, the young American trumpeter was a sensation. Aged 32, Louis Armstrong was at his peak. But for the Palladium regulars it was just a lot of noise. They did not know the songs, did not understand the improvisation and did not stay long enough to appreciate the sweating, strutting figure in the spotlight hitting endless high notes. Even his supporters admitted that half the regulars walked out before Armstrong had ended. The British music paper *Melody Maker* wrote:

> top Fs bubble about all over the place, and never once does he miss one. He is enormously fond of the lip-tree, which he accomplishes by shaking the instrument wildly in his right hand.... He works with a microphone and loud speakers— except for his trumpet playing which varies from a veritable whisper to roof-raising strength, mostly the latter.

The following year, 1933, Duke Ellington and his band played for two weeks at the Palladium while on a tour arranged by the English bandleader, Jack Hylton. They were number thirteen on the program and enjoyed a triumph. "Stormy Weather," sung by Ivie Anderson, was followed by "Rockin' in Rhythm" with shake-dancer Bessie Dudley performing in front of the band, who were dressed in cream suits, orange ties and brown shoes. The newspaper magnate, Lord Beaverbrook, gave a special party for the band at his house, The Vineyard (76 Hurlingham Rd.), in Fulham. Here Duke Ellington drank gin with the Prince of Wales who later played on Sonny Greer's drums while Prince George (the future Duke of Kent) played the piano. Over the years, on his return visits to England, Duke Ellington counted among his friends Queen Elizabeth II, the Duke of Edinburgh and Princess Margaret.

By 1943 the resentment by British tommies of American troops in England had begun to alarm the Allied High Command. American soldiers were paid six to seven times as much as their British counterparts, which meant that they could afford to give the girls a better time. Fights in pubs had become more and more common. In 1944, a popular joke in England asked what were the three things wrong with Americans? Answer: "They're oversexed, overpaid and over here." It was a joke which American soldiers did not find funny. When the musical *This is the Army* was about to open at the Palladium with one third of the seats to be given free each evening to Allied soldiers on leave in London, Irving Berlin was asked to add a song which might soothe some of the bitterness. Berlin wandered through the streets of the West End in the blackout, sat in a pub, went back to his hotel here on Argyll Street and took a long, hot bath. "By the time I was through with the bath, I had it all worked out," he wrote. Adopting the voice of the GI, the result was "My British Buddy." Recognizing that the American and the British soldiers were as different as could be, the second line ran: "He thinks he is winning the war and I think it's me."

Both the musical and the song became top hits.

Aubrey Road, Kensington Map G

Aubrey House. Louisa May Alcott spent the first ten days of June 1865 in Aubrey House; built in the 1690s, it is the last surviving country house in Kensington. Thanks to an introduction from Ralph Waldo Emerson, she was the guest of Peter Alfred Taylor, M.P. for Leicester. Taylor was involved in English political movements for the promotion of freedom and had already entertained Frederick Douglass, a former slave who had escaped from Maryland. A whole new world opened here for the future author of *Little Women* (1868). She listened to William Gladstone and to the Italian patriot and revolutionary Mazzini talking about Margaret Fuller, and she heard Charles Dickens read from his stories. Taylor took her to the Houses of Parliament to hear John Stuart Mill and Benjamin Disraeli speak on the Second Reform Bill which was passed two years later and enfranchised one million men, largely from the urban working classes. Louisa Alcott was at home with these English liberals and intellectuals, having grown up with their New England counterparts. On 11 June she moved to lodgings in WESTBOURNE GROVE TERRACE.

Baker Street

(1)   Charlotte Cushman took a four-story brownstone house here overlooking Portman Square, where the gracious elm trees and broad walks reminded the 29-year-old actress of her childhood in Boston. It was in 1845, and it was a big step up from her previous modest chambers on NEW BOND STREET. Her success at the HAYMARKET THEATRE in the role of Romeo was complete, and her confidence, force and self-possession drew many young women admirers toward her. Among them was Jane Carlyle, who invited herself one day at 1 p.m. and stayed until 8 p.m. "Such a day I have not known!" Cushman recorded, describing her as "clever, witty, calm, cool, unsmiling, unsparing, a *raconteur* unparalleled, a manner inimitable, a behaviour scrupulous, and a power invincible." Yet sometimes even these qualities did not enable Jane to put up with her husband, Thomas Carlyle, who expected to be "treated with the respect due to genius." Jane Carlyle found refuge and company with her new American friend. But it was the English poet, Eliza Cook, 27, who became Cushman's close companion.

In her high-ceilinged rooms, playing and singing at her grand piano, Charlotte Cushman entertained George Putnam, Monckton Milnes, John Ruskin, Ralph Waldo Emerson, the American minister and historian George Bancroft, Thomas Carlyle and their wives. At the Princess Theatre, she played Lady Macbeth opposite the greatest English actor of the day, William Macready, followed by Henry VIII's Queen Katharine to Macready's Cardinal Wolsey. She had deliberately asked to play Queen Katharine in order to invite comparison with Sarah Kemble Siddons's favorite role. In 1849, when she had been in England almost five years, she was finally invited to perform before Queen Victoria at Drury Lane. She had come from America an actress of promise, and returned one of the leading actresses of her time.

(82)   The Mortuary. The body of the writer Stephen Crane lay here on 11 June 1900 so that friends might say farewell before it was taken back to America for burial in the family plot in Hillside, New Jersey.

Crane, accompanied by Cora Taylor, had settled in England in the summer of 1897. The couple took a house in Oxted, Surrey, where Crane worked on a short story, *The Open Boat*. In October, Crane met Joseph Conrad at a luncheon given by the publisher William Heinemann. The two writers took to each other immediately and spent the afternoon tramping through Kensington Gardens and Hyde Park, stopped for tea, continued through Green Park, and ended up sharing a late night supper at Monico's, discussing Balzac and his *Comédie Humaine*. Conrad remembered that they parted "with just a handshake and a goodnight—no more—without making any arrangements for meeting again, as though we had lived in the same town from childhood and were sure to run across each other next day." Crane, 26, was already famous for *The Red Badge of Courage,* whereas the 40-year-old Conrad was still struggling with the problems of language and form. He sent the manuscript of *The Nigger of the Narcissus* to Crane who immediately told him that the work was outstanding. Conrad replied, "When I feel depressed about it I say to myself, 'Crane likes the damned thing,' and am greatly consoled. What your appreciation is to me I renounce to explain. The world looks different to me now, since our long powwow." In 1898, Crane left for Cuba to report on the Spanish-American War. When he returned to England, Cora had taken Brede Place, a 14th-century manor house on the south coast of England, close to Henry James who used to drop in. It was here that Crane spent the last full year of his short life.

Dr. Samuel G. Howe and his wife Julia Ward spent their honeymoon in June 1843 in a house somewhere on Baker Street. Dr. Howe, 42, was organizer of the New England Asylum for the Blind (which later became the Perkins Institution) and was known in England for the education of a young woman who was blind and deaf. Julia, 18 years his junior, wrote poetry and later worked on social reform, abolitionism and women's suffrage; she wrote "The Battle Hymn of the Republic." Accompanied by their friends Horace Mann and his wife Mary Peabody Mann, they called on Thomas Carlyle, were guests of the Duke and Duchess of Sutherland at Stafford House, dined at Lansdowne House and attended balls. Julia Howe, who had grown up in Boston and had never been permitted to go to the theater before, was delighted with the London stage. When she saw the beautiful and sensuous Fanny Elssler dance she recalled the dialogue between Margaret Fuller and Emerson when, in 1811, they had seen Elssler dance in America: "Margaret, this is poetry." "Waldo, this is religion." During the day, their guide who knew London better than anyone else, Charles Dickens, showed them schools, asylums, workhouses and Pentonville Prison in the CALEDONIAN ROAD. There were night visits to witness the harlots and to see the seamy side of Victorian England—but only Dr. Howe and Horace Mann went on these expeditions, set up by their friend Dickens who obviously

feet wide, intended to sustain a crew of six at sea for twenty days and to be anchored while submerged. An illustrious commission was appointed to examine his plans. Headed by Sir Joseph Banks, president of the Royal Society, it included Sir Home Popham, a distinguished naval officer, John Rennie, the designer of London Bridge, Henry Cavendish, a leading chemist, and Major William Congreve, inventor of the rocket whose "red glare" during the 1814 British bombardment of Fort McHenry at Baltimore was immortalized in "The Star-Spangled Banner." The committee quickly determined that while the submarine was probably technically feasible, it would most likely prove impractical in combat. This ended Fulton's work on the submarine, but not his perseverance. Next, he tried to interest them in his "torpedo." After a series of letters and appeals, he was received at the prime minister's country estate near Dover on 20 July 1804. With the navy represented by Sir Home Popham, Fulton explained his "torpedo" to William Pitt. Both men were impressed and a contract was drawn up in which Fulton agreed to supervise the production of his "submarine bombs" and to assist in the carrying out of the operations. He was to receive £200 a month salary and up to £7,000 for "the payment of his mechanical preparations," while "His Majesty's Dock, Yards and Arsenals" were to furnish all materials. He was to receive £40,000 for every decked French vessel destroyed by his weapons.

The first chance to try out his submarine bomb came quickly. Napoleon was busy amassing warships and troops at Boulogne in order to invade England. On 2 October 1804 Fulton was on board HMS *Monarch* when the British attack against the French fleet at Boulogne began. It lasted from 9 p.m. until dawn. Two mines attached to either end of a line were pulled by cutters to within five hundred yards of the enemy, then the timers were set and it was hoped that they would drift with the tide and attach themselves to the enemy ship's anchor cable. It was a scheme fraught with dangers and difficulties, but one French ship was sunk. The rest of the mines either failed to explode or were washed ashore.

For the next few weeks, the British navy argued the merits of Fulton's invention. In a final attempt to convince them of its excellence, Fulton procured a brig which he intended to blow up in front of their eyes. At 3 p.m. on 15 October 1805, before a group of skeptical British naval officers, Fulton gave the signal for a mock attack on the *Dorothea,* a small warship about 100 feet in length and weighing some 250 tons. This time the mines were kept buoyant by cork-filled boxes. Fifteen minutes later a tremendous explosion took place, lifting the whole body of the vessel almost out of the water. The brig had been blown into two pieces and "in one minute nothing of her was to be seen but floating fragments." The era of modern naval warfare had begun. There were no longer doubts concerning Fulton's invention, the floating mine. Ironically, only six days later, Nelson defeated the French decisively at Trafalgar and Fulton's mines were no longer needed. Fulton was awarded £14,000 and salary due to him of £1,640. He wrote to his friend and financial backer Joel Barlow in Connecticut that he would be sailing for home in October, adding "and be with you, I hope, in November, perhaps about the 14th, my birthday—so you must have a roast goose ready." Thus Robert Fulton departed from Europe for even greater fame, and a rendez-vous with a roast goose.

(19)　　Benjamin West arrived in London on Sunday, 21 August 1763, and the following day took lodgings in this fashionable street off the Strand. Aged 25, he had just spent three years studying in Italy and had come to London on his way home to Pennsylvania. He enrolled at St. Martin's Lane Academy, and let it be known that he would take commissions. During the winter he did a full-length portrait of General Robert Monckton, a hero of the Battle of Quebec. He was introduced to Joshua Reynolds who, having looked at his work, urged him to exhibit the following April in the show of the Society of Artists at the Spring Gardens gallery. West began to consider staying in London, but there was the problem of his fiancée, Betsy Shewell, who had been waiting for him for almost four years in Philadelphia. He decided to invite her to London where she arrived in August 1764, chaperoned by her cousin, Matthew Pratt, a young Philadelphia painter, and John West, her future father-in-law. During his year here in Bedford Street, Benjamin West began to establish himself as a leading portrait painter. He made enough money to be able to afford a house for his bride in CASTLE STREET, Leicester Square.

21　　Ethel Barrymore and fellow actress Suzanne Sheldon took the two upper floors, above the publisher William Heinemann, in the fall of 1897. Miss Barrymore opened at the Lyceum Theatre in *The Bells* with Sir Henry Irving and Ellen Terry and was soon engaged to Irving's son, Laurence. She cabled the news to her father, who replied: "Congratulations Love Father." A few weeks later, she cabled him again saying that she had broken off the engagement, and received the reply: "Congratulations Love Father." Her 15-year-old brother John had been sent by their father to attend King's College School, Wimbledon, but spent most of his time here in Bedford Street before being accepted at the Slade School of Art. When not performing, the 20-year-old Ethel was busy going out in London, where she became good friends with James Barrie, with 25-year-old Winston Churchill and with an older Henry James who said that she was rather "Gothic" and reminded him of a cornice on a Gothic building. It was fashionable during that season to wear tiaras and, since her weekly salary of £10 at the Lyceum was not enough to buy one, she wore oak leaves in her hair instead. Someone called her Daphne and the name stuck. Her next fiancé was Gerald Du Maurier, the son of the artist and illustrator. Although this engagement was also broken off, this time by Barrymore, the two remained good friends and Du Maurier later named his daughter Daphne after her. Ethel Barrymore played many seasons in the West End under the producer Charles Frohman.

The tailors Moss Brothers, famous for their hire of dress clothes for weddings, coronations and special occasions, took over the entire corner building at New Row and Bedford Street in 1917. James B. Conant, in London on a secret wartime mission, stopped here on 12 March 1941 to rent a tuxedo. (In England, gentlemen own their tuxedos—others rent them.) On the rental card, under employment, he wrote down: "President of Harvard University," and gave his address as Claridge's Hotel. The clerk was polite but firm. Had he no job in England? No. Had he any personal references? Well, he had just been dropped off by A.V. Alexander, the first lord of the admiralty. A pause. Anyone else? Well, the first lord had picked him up at Buckingham Palace. Where he had seen the king? Yes, replied Conant, they had spent a very pleasant fifteen minutes chatting together. Why did he need a tuxedo? Because he was on his way to a country home called Chequers. To have a chat with Winston Churchill? the clerk asked with a slight smile. No, replied Conant, to spend one or two days with him. The British are not to be easily fooled by Americans with wild tales like this one. Moss Bros. requested a full cash deposit before "Mr. Conant" was allowed to leave with his rented suit.

Belgrave Road Map F

65   Lewis Mumford arrived in England in May 1920 and settled in a small room on the top floor of the headquarters of the Sociological Society. The building, LePlay House, Mumford recalled, "was a New York brownstone with an English basement, newly done over with a coat of muddy stucco," reeking of soft coal fires. The 25-year-old graduate of City College of New York and Columbia University had been invited to London by Victor Branford and Patrick Geddes to become the acting editor of the newly founded *Sociological Review*. It was early recognition for the future American social philosopher.

One of the purposes of the founders of LePlay House was to give academic status and influence to sociology, an area of science that was still being questioned (at Oxford University on the grounds that its very name was a miscegenation of a Greek and Latin root). The Sociological Society sought to reconcile diverse schools and break down partisanships, but Mumford soon found that their aim of peaceful unity in order to further social analysis engendered even more bitterness than had originally existed. Furthermore, he discovered that he had been brought to London in the naive hope that a bright young American might serve as a catalyst in this transformation. Were not all Americans energetic and hopeful? Mumford quickly realized that probably no one could fill this role, least of all a young American alien to the British scene. Yet his six months in London were intellectually rewarding. He met men such as Frederick Soddy, the physicist, whose theory on isotopes was to win him the Nobel Prize the following year. He lunched regularly with Edward Westermarck, the Finnish social philosopher and anthropologist, professor of sociology at London University, whose three-volume *History of Human Marriage* was already in its fifth edition by 1920. He became friends with Ramsay MacDonald, the future Labour party prime minister, and Sidney and Beatrice Webb, socialist economists. But such intellectual excitement could not compensate for the absence of Sophia Wittenberg in New York—and Mumford returned there to marry her a year later.

Berkeley Street, Mayfair

(3) Berkeley Hotel, formerly the St. James Hotel. Very fashionable in the 1930s, it was taken down in 1970. The Bristol Hotel now stands on the original site.

Edwin Booth, accompanied by his wife and his 19-year-old daughter Edwina, took rooms in the St. James Hotel on 1 October 1880. He opened his London engagement as Hamlet at the Princess's Theatre on Oxford Street on 6 November. The critics were polite but not enthusiastic. As Booth wrote, they "damned me with faint praise." It was inevitable that his Hamlet be compared to that of the famous English actor Henry Irving who was also in town. But on this score the critics were divided and decided to wait and see Booth in other roles. Two weeks later, Booth played the lead in Lytton's *Richelieu,* which the *Standard* critic—who had labeled Hamlet as disappointing—found "from the first to the last ... striking and effective." The second week of *Hamlet* grossed £686; the second week of *Richelieu* took in £845. At Christmas, the manager proposed a six-week extension of the contract, but Booth refused what he called these "cheap jew" managerial tactics, and finished in March as King Lear. The conservative *Sunday Times* wrote that his Lear was "a brilliant illustration of method and capacity ... seldom, if ever, seen on our stage." Booth finished in triumph at the Princess's Theatre. In November, he had written to Irving who was managing and performing at the Lyceum Theatre. As he told a friend, "they tell me Irving (who, by-the-by has not yet deigned to notice my existence) has a kitchen & French *chef* in his theatre & cooks a jolly repast while the play is on for the entertainment of his critics *et al* after the show. I can't afford such luxury *yet."* Irving took his time to reply, but when the two actors met the Englishman proposed that they play in *Othello* together. Booth was delighted and they opened at the Lyceum Theatre, on WELLINGTON STREET, in May 1881.

At the hotel, however, a real tragedy was taking place. Mrs. Booth was dying of tuberculosis. Sir William Jenner, physician to Queen Victoria, advised Booth not to reveal the cause of her illness to her as it would simply "hasten the end." Booth would return late at night, exhausted from playing King Lear, to be prevented from sleeping by her constant coughing. It kept him, he wrote, "in a semi-craze all the while." Both were helped by his daughter, Edwina, who had been born in London in 1861 during Booth's first visit. "Edwina," he wrote, "breathes her native fog & is well." At the end of March 1881, the family moved to 23 Weymouth Street, a spacious apartment off Portland Place. But Booth's parents-in-law arrived and accused him of retaining their daughter in London and aggravating her illness. He moved out of the apartment with his daughter and took rooms at the Brunswick Hotel. He finished at the Lyceum in June, cancelled a tour of the English provinces and immediately sailed home with his family. His wife died the following winter.

Edith Wharton and her friend Walter Berry took rooms at the Berkeley Hotel on 8 November 1909. Mrs. Wharton, 37, was becoming increasingly well known in England thanks to her short stories and her novel, *The House of Mirth*. For the next month, escorted by Henry James, she launched upon her first major social whirl in London. When she called upon the 80-year-old George Meredith, he approached her with outstretched hands exclaiming, "My dear child, I've read every word you have written." After staying at Clivedon, the 300-acre estate of William Waldorf Astor, she moved to Lady St. Helier's house in Portland Place. To entertain her American guest, Mary St. Helier invited the painter Sir Philip Burne-Jones, and the writers Thomas Hardy and John Galsworthy to dinner. Mrs. Wharton was the guest of James Barrie for dinner at the Savoy Grill. Afterwards they went to see Gerald Du Maurier in Barrie's *What Every Woman Knows*. She lunched at the House of Lords with its librarian, Edmund Gosse, a gossip-loving old friend of Henry James. Gosse, whom Wharton found "quick and flashing," introduced her to Max Beerbohm, the incomparable caricaturist. As a novelist, she was lucky in catching the Edwardian age in full flower before its disappearance in 1914.

Amy Lowell took a top-floor suite at the Berkeley Hotel in the summer of 1913. She had come to London to learn about the Imagist poets and began by inviting them to dinner. "Figure to yourself a young man arrayed as 'poet'," she wrote to Harriet Monroe of their leader, Ezra Pound, "and yet making the costume agreeable by his personal charm; a sweep of conversation and youthful enthusiasm which keeps him talking as many hours as you please." Other Imagist poets that evening included a tall, willowy blonde American girl, "H.D." or Hilda Doolittle, Richard Aldington, whom H.D. would marry, and John Gould Fletcher, another American poet. Eleven years older than Pound, intelligent, domineering, wealthy, overweight and a member of the Boston clan, Amy Lowell nevertheless thought that "all sorts of developments" might be expected from Pound once he had gotten over his "chip-on-the-shoulder attitude." For his part, Pound found her "pleasingly intelligent," and took her along to meet Yeats, to whom she later devoted a two-volume biography. Before leaving for America, she talked with an aged and ill Henry James. Depressed by his drop in popularity, he confessed to her: "I have cut myself off from America, where I belonged, and in England I am not really accepted...don't make my mistake."

The following summer, Lowell returned to the same suite at the Berkeley. She began her stay by going to see George Macmillan, head of the publishing house, and got him to agree to distribute a hundred copies of her *Sword Blades and Poppy Seed.* But when she met Pound she discovered that his tiny flat in KENSINGTON CHURCH WALK had become the cradle for another literary movement, Vorticism. Pound, the painter and writer Wyndham Lewis, and Henri Gaudier-Brzeska, a young French sculptor, were contributing to a new publication, *Blast,* to the partial neglect of the Imagists. At a dinner to celebrate the publication of the first number of *Blast,* she asked for a precise definition of Imagism. Pound left the table and came back with an old-fashioned tin tub on his head like the helmet of a knight-errant. Since Ford Madox Ford had just said that he, Pound, was an authority on all schools of poetry, he wished to say that henceforth there would be a new school, no longer called the "imagiste" but the "nagiste" school—Miss Lowell, he continued, had inaugurated this new school with her poem which concluded with the lines, "Night, and the water, and you in your whiteness, bathing." Everyone laughed and Amy Lowell, a good sport, joined in. At the end of the evening she discreetly paid the bill.

She organized another dinner at the Berkeley on 30 July 1914, to which she invited H.D., Richard Aldington, John Gould Fletcher (whose mistrust of Pound equalled hers), and another writer of whom she had heard but never met, D.H. Lawrence. His entrance was dramatic. He announced that he had just met a friend, the private secretary to Prime Minister Asquith, and that England was going to war. Miss Lowell was not one to permit the foolishness of nations to spoil her plans, and she maneuvered the conversation back to Imagism. By the time dinner was over, she had proposed to edit their contributions to the next volume of the Imagists. That evening began the long friendship between Lawrence, the son of a coalminer, and Lowell, sister of the president of Harvard. Lawrence was well dressed, belonged to no group, was considerate and knew how to listen. He seemed to be the opposite of Pound.

Lawrence's news about the outbreak of war was true, and even a Lowell could not get a berth back to Boston. So she offered her services to the American Relief Committee, headed by an American engineer living in London named Herbert Hoover. She worked at a desk set up on the platform at Victoria Station helping direct more than 100,000 Americans, frequently bewildered and penniless, to find temporary rooms in London while awaiting passage home. Before leaving herself, she contributed $10,000 to the Relief Committee. She reached Boston in September, where she signed a contract with Houghton, Mifflin & Company for the publication of three anthologies. They duly appeared, in 1915, 1916 and 1917, under the title *Some Imagist Poets.*

Eugene O'Neill took a room at the Berkeley with Carlotta Monterey, his future wife, in February 1928. The couple was traveling incognito, since the New York newspapers were already talking about O'Neill's separation from his wife Agnes. O'Neill loved London where no one, he wrote, could intrude upon his bliss. "I wander about foolish and goggle-eyed with joy," he told his friend Kenneth Macgowan, "in a honeymoon that is a thousand times more poignant and sweet and ecstatic because it comes at an age when one's past—particularly a past such as mine—gives one the power to appreciate what happiness means." O'Neill, 40, had already written *Desire Under the Elms;* his nine-act drama, *Strange Interlude,* was to win him his third Pulitzer Prize. After a week in London, he set off with Carlotta for France to begin work on the play *Dynamo.*

Bloomsbury Square Map B

20   Gertrude Stein and her brother Leo took rooms here in September 1902. They spent the first weekend with Bernard Berenson at Fernhurst, in Surrey, where they found the countryside so beautiful that they rented a cottage there for a month. In *The Autobiography of Alice B. Toklas,* Stein recalled: "They settled in lodgings in London and were not uncomfortable. They knew a number of people through the Berensons, Bertrand Russell, the Zangwills, then there was Willard (Josiah Flynt) who wrote *Tramping with Tramps* and who knew all about London pubs but Gertrude Stein was not very much amused." Leo returned to Paris in December and Gertrude began spending her days in the British Museum "absorbed in Elizabethan prose." It was probably about this time, at the age of 29, that she decided that her path to fame, or "la gloire" as she called it, lay in writing, and she prepared for this by reading. In her free time "she wandered about the London streets and found them infinitely depressing and dismal."

Bloomsbury Street

(6)   Robert Frost arrived in Buckinghamshire, England, with his family in September 1912. Once settled, he began to choose poems for inclusion in a first book of poetry. The selection made, his next problem was to find a publisher. He had been reading the English poet William Ernest Henley and, seeing on the title page the imprint of David Nutt, publisher, he called on the firm on Bloomsbury Street. He was received by a sad little woman dressed in black, who spoke with a French accent and told him that she represented David Nutt. With certain misgivings, Frost left her his manuscript of *A Boy's Will.* What he did not know was that David Nutt was dead, that the business had been run by his brother Alfred Nutt, who was also dead, and that he was dealing with the widow of Alfred Nutt. Nevertheless, a week later Frost was elated to receive a letter promising publication. He returned to London and quickly signed a contract which gave the firm of David Nutt the first right to publish his next four books of poetry or prose. Frost, 38, was soon to regret his naivety in giving up his future rights so quickly.

Reviews of *A Boy's Will* ranged from outstanding to lukewarm and certainly did not bring the overnight recognition for which he had hoped, but over the next six months some encouraging and even flattering reviews appeared in the quarterly issues of British and American periodicals, and Frost's confidence in his writing began to return. He set to work on what was to become his second book. Ironically, homesickness drove his memory back to the Derry farm in New England which he had been so glad to leave. Years later, he said, "I wrote the poem 'Mending Wall' thinking of the old wall that I hadn't mended in several years and which must be in terrible condition. I wrote that poem in England when I was very homesick for my old wall in New England." When he told English friends that he intended to call this new collection "North of Boston," they objected that English readers would associate it with Boston in Lincolnshire. But Frost kept his American readers in mind and stuck to the title. When *North of Boston* appeared, the prestigious *Times Literary Supplement* wrote: "Poetry burns up out of it... the simplest of Mr. Frost's poems—'The Wood Pile'—has this clear strangeness throughout, and in its last line the magic of intensest insight." Other reviews were equally enthusiastic. In 1915, after three years in England, the Frost family returned home where Frost found himself finally recognized as a poet.

Bolton Street, Piccadilly

(3)   "I take possession of the old world—I inhale it—I appropriate it," wrote Henry James to his family and in December 1876 he embarked upon that conquest. He had given up France, where he had felt a stranger, for England, where he would penetrate the Victorian world, its drawing rooms, its clubs, its country homes. From now on London was to become the center and focus of his art. Here in Bolton Street, a stone's throw from Piccadilly and Green Park, his dusky lodgings included a housemaid with a dark face but "a divine expression and the voice of a duchess." With a sooty blank wall facing the window at which he wrote, there was nothing to distract his imagination, and he soon achieved fame with *Daisy Miller,* followed rapidly by *The Europeans* and *Washington Square.*

James had come to the conclusion at the age of 34 that he would probably never marry, and least of all have "an English wife!" Marriage, he argued, hindered the "addicted" artist, but he thoroughly enjoyed being thought of as an eligible bachelor. "No man is more popular in London dining-rooms and drawing-rooms than Henry James," a British member of Parliament recorded. According to James's engagement book, he dined out 140 times during the 1878-79 winter season. The success of *Daisy Miller* had made him the most talked-of American writer in England. More important, it gave him an increasing financial independence and allowed him to plan a "great novel"—a work he would write slowly, *The Portrait of a Lady*. He enjoyed meeting fellow Bostonians such as Henry Adams and James Russell Lowell, in spite of the latter being "morbidly Anglophobic."

After two years of constant work in London, he spent September 1879 in Paris, where he called on Flaubert and Turgenev. Paris he found to be most agreeable in its way, but he was glad to have given up trying to live there: "London is worth five hundred of it," he wrote. As he told Grace Norton, his interest in London was chiefly that of "an observer in a place where there is the most in the world to observe." In December 1882, upon hearing of his father's illness, James hurried back to Boston. He was too late and, within the year, his mother also died: "She held us all together, and without her we are scattered reeds." The family house in Cambridge was sold and James felt himself "orphaned" and adrift. He was glad to get back to the "glutinous" fog of London and his "little shabby furnished apartment" in Bolton Street.

James's next work, *The Bostonians,* reflected his loneliness and his attempt to come to terms with his native city. Fortunately he had made two new and important friends: John Singer Sargent and Robert Louis Stevenson. He had seen Sargent's work in Paris and told the young artist that it was time that he settled in London. "I want him to come here and live and work—there being such a field in London for a *real* painter of women." Sargent came, not because of James's urging, but to escape a dropping-off of interest in his own work in Paris. On Sunday, 29 March 1884, he came to lunch here on Bolton Street with James and in the afternoon the two Americans visited artists' studios to see pictures being readied for the spring exhibitions. As for Stevenson, he had known James before achieving fame in 1883 with *Treasure Island;* now dying of tuberculosis, his illness gave an intensity to their friendship. Stevenson appreciated to the full James's artistry, while James enjoyed Stevenson's flair for story telling.

Henry James was joined in 1885 by his sister Alice who had moved from Cambridge to London. Suffering from neurasthenia, she remained in bed as long as there was someone to nurse her. Reluctantly, James found her rooms two doors up the street at number 7. While her presence reminded him of his family, it was a mixed blessing. The following year, James took a larger apartment in DE VERE GARDENS.

Borough High Street, Southwark Map E

Church of St. George the Martyr. Sylvia Plath married the English poet Ted Hughes here on 16 June 1956. The 24-year-old Plath was about to study at Cambridge on a Fulbright grant. At the end of the year, the young couple returned to America where Sylvia Plath taught English for a year at Smith College, while her husband taught at the University of Massachusetts. In January 1960 they returned to England and settled in London in CHALCOT SQUARE.

Bow Street, Covent Garden Map D

Royal Opera House. Louise Homer sang here for the first time on 9 May 1899 in *Cavalleria Rusticana*. She had a modest role, Lola, but she was immediately noticed and *Punch* found "Homer-Sweet-Homer a fascinating Lola." More important, her voice drew the attention of Nellie Melba, who told her after her first performance, "We will talk later, there is much I can tell you." Her real debut was four days later in *Aida* when, she told her mother, the audience burst into an ovation "in the *middle* of the act." Reviews said that her voice was "fresh and brilliant" and that she possessed on stage "true dramatic fire." The 28-year-old contralto was fortunate in being joined at Covent Garden by a new young Italian baritone, Antonio Scotti. Her contract was for eleven weeks at $100 a week. She also received an invitation to Windsor Castle to sing for Queen Victoria. The following year she joined the Metropolitan Opera Company in San Francisco.

Lowell Thomas had just finished showing his travelogue film on the last night of his engagement at Madison Square Gardens when a stranger came to the dressing room. He was Percy Burton, a British impresario, who said that he had been "thunderstruck" by the film about a British hero in the Arabian desert whom he had never heard of, a man called Lawrence. He proposed that Thomas leave immediately for London to show his film. Thomas agreed, and decided to rewrite his script for the British audience while on board ship. He hired a back-country young man who was teaching public-speaking at a YMCA in New York to help him. His name was Dale Carnegie. Seven days later they reached Southampton with the script ready.

At Covent Garden, Burton had persuaded Sir Thomas Beecham to lend them the scenery from Hilding Rosenberg's opera *Joseph and His Brethren.* In August 1919, with a background of moonlight on the Nile and the Royal Welsh Guards Band in scarlet uniforms providing the music, Lowell Thomas introduced Lawrence of Arabia to London. At the end of the two-hour presentation the audience stood and applauded for ten minutes. The most widely read drama critic in London at the time, Alder Anderson, wrote in the *Daily Telegraph:*

> I can conceive of no more invigorating tonic than two hours spent in the company of Lowell Thomas. This illustrated event is a triumphant vindication of the power of moving pictures, accompanied by a spoken story, to charm the eye, entertain the spirit, and move to its very depths the soul of the spectator.

The *Strand* magazine called it "the greatest romance of real life ever told." Within a week people were queueing all night in the hope of getting standing space to see "The Last Crusade." Celebrities included the prime minister Lloyd George with a young aid Winston Churchill, George Clemenceau, Rudyard Kipling, and George Bernard Shaw. The two-week engagement was extended into the fall. Thomas cancelled his West Coast tour and instead moved into the 6,000-seat Royal Albert Hall. But problems soon arose. The acoustics were poor, and the London fog moved into the theater so that on some days it looked as if Lawrence had driven the Turks from the Holy Land through a smokescreen. Giving six two-hour evening shows a week and two matinees with poor acoustics took its toll and, one evening, the 27-year-old Thomas collapsed. A doctor advised an immediate holiday, but Thomas felt that he could not give up this chance of a lifetime. He moved with his wife from their flat in Albemarle Street to a house overlooking Wimbledon Common and moved the show to the more compact Queen's Hall in Langham Place, where it alternated with the "proms." Thomas was driven up to London each evening in a Daimler limousine and enjoyed every minute of it.

Adelphi Family Hotel
in 1904.
(See page 1.)

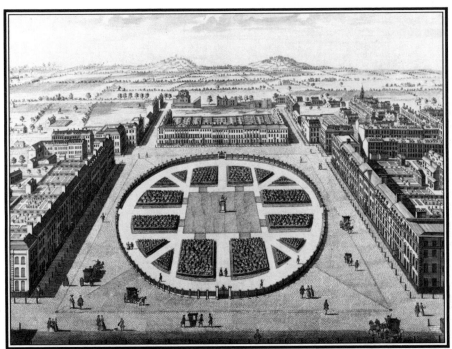

Above: Grosvenor Square in 1754.
Below: Grosvenor Square in the 18th century.
(See page 123.)

Above: Vauxhall Gardens in the 18th century.
Below: A concert in Vauxhall Gardens.
(See page 267.)

Above: The Thatched Tavern in the 18th century. (See page 231.)
Below: The American School *painted in London in 1765*
by Matthew Pratt. (See page 47.)

One evening after the show he received a brief note from a spectator. It was signed T.E. Lawrence. The 32-year-old Lawrence complained that ever since Thomas's film his life had become impossible. He was stopped on the street by strangers then swiftly surrounded by a crowd. He was receiving as many as a hundred letters a day, many from women proposing marriage and others proposing briefer relationships. He took refuge at Oxford where he had accepted a fellowship, but regularly visited Thomas at Wimbledon where the two men would go for long walks on the Common. It was there one day that a distraught Lawrence told Thomas that he had put down his briefcase at a train station while buying a newspaper and it had been stolen. It had contained the only copy of his manuscript of *The Seven Pillars of Wisdom*. To Thomas's question, would he rewrite it, Lawrence said that he hadn't thought about that yet. (He rewrote it over the next seven years.) As a result of his friendship with Lawrence, Thomas was constantly badgered for stories about him. Once when he wanted to check an anecdote, Lawrence simply laughed and said, "Use it if it suits your needs. What difference does it make if it's true—history is seldom true."

Lowell Thomas returned to America in December 1919 and came back a year later to Covent Garden to present "Through Romantic India and into Forbidden Afghanistan." The film was a success, but nothing would ever taste as sweet, he wrote, as his first evening in London.

Brompton Road, Knightsbridge

Known as Brompton Row in the 18th century, stretching today from number 132 opposite Yeoman's Row to number 186, this neighborhood became home to some twenty Massachusetts loyalist families beginning in late 1775. One of them described Brompton Row as "country altho only 3/4 of a mile from Hyde Park Corner." Like all exiles, they tended to stay together and rarely frequented the English. They tried to obtain American foods, kept informed on American affairs, attempted to live "as much in the New England way as ever we can," and awaited the day they would return home in triumph. On Brompton Row, Jonathan Sewell lived at number 1, John Randolph at number 4, Robert Auchmuty at number 7, Thomas Hutchinson, Jr. at number 11, John

Plenderleath at number 14, Elias Ball at number 17, and John Murray at number 18. Nearby lived Thomas Fluckner, John Graham, Colonel John Chandler from Worcester, Massachusetts, and John R. Grymes from Virginia. The Brompton group used to meet to play cards at one another's lodgings every third evening. The solicitor general of Massachusetts, Samuel Quincy, often walked to Brompton Row to talk with "the whole circle" there, or called upon other American friends closer to his lodgings in Parliament Street. As most loyalist refugees lived in rented lodgings and many left London for the countryside in the summer, they changed addresses frequently. They used London coffee houses as places to meet, to receive their mail, to read the latest newspapers from home, and to greet the latest arrivals. Southerners established their headquarters at the Carolina Coffeehouse, 25 Birchin Lane in the City; men from the middle colonies assembled at the New York Coffee House opposite the Royal Exchange, and northerners frequented the New England Coffeehouse on Threadneedle Street.

(23)   Samuel Curwen settled here in 1777 and five years later moved to nearby 1 Yeoman's Row (now occupied by the pub The Bunch of Grapes). He owes his place in history to the journal which he kept from the day of his arrival in London in July 1775 until his departure in August 1784. Born in Salem, Massachusetts, graduating from Harvard in 1735, Curwen became a merchant and served as a deputy judge of the admiralty, dealing with customs and import duties. Married, active in the civil and social life of Salem, he described himself as "a Gentleman of considerable property and fortune." A loyalist with no particular devotion to the king or the monarchy, he was a law-and-order man who had property to lose in the event of civil disturbance. When he refused to join in the public cry that the British were the aggressors at Lexington and Concord, he was threatened with violence and, believing that his life was in danger, he fled. (Charles Dickens, who read his journal, commented aptly: "He does not indeed appear to have been of the heroic stuff of martyrs.")

Curwen, then, was not unlike the other 100,000 loyalists who left America during the revolution, of whom some 5,000 came to London while the rest settled in Canada. He was different, however, in that he was one of the few refugees whose sympathy for America grew as the war dragged on. In his petition to the

Crown for financial relief, he described himself as having been early distinguished for his attachment "to the Authority of the King and the Parliament of Great Britain." His petition was granted and his previous salary of £100 per annum by the Crown was continued for the nine years which he was to spend in exile.

Curwen was well read, with scholarly and refined tastes, a freemason, a good critic of what he saw, and obviously a pleasant companion. His *Journal* provides us with an intimate day-by-day account of life in London covering the theater, debates in Parliament, coffee house gossip, fairs, law courts, public executions, and the changing fortunes of the American colony of loyalists. His journal also reveals his gradual disillusionment with the British ruling class, their arrogance and ignorance of America. A typical entry is that of Sunday, 3 December 1780:

> Air mild for the season, sky cloudy. Sunday at usual place of worship, Mr. Lindsay preached, text *"And these were more noble than those of Thessalonica, in that they received the word with all readiness of mind."* A large assembly. After service, I walkt up the Strand when to my surprize I found myself all alone, not a single person within sight on either side, nor a coach to be seen, or even heard ratling over pavements, which considering the hour, just after 5 o'clock P.M., was a singular circumstance. In this situation, or rather predicament I walkt an 100 or more yards never expecting to see or to hear of its paralel or like again. Arriving at the doors of room, late Coxes Musaeum, now employed, as in this Eve, for theological disputations not yet open, proceeded on to Park. Two females accosted me for lewd purposes, as usual with me rebuffed them by neglect, circuited by horse guards through parliament street and at 2nd arrival not yet opened, entered Spring Garden Coffee House. Drank a dish, reading, hearing post, containing letters of General Washington, Carleton, Arnold and Major Andre the latter though pitied here, perhaps justly, is doubtless to be ranked in the class of spy, and which, however answered here, was in my mind a punishment not undeservedly inflicted, and to be justified by the universal proof of all nations civilized and uncivilized, on persons of that character.

The "usual place of worship" was the Essex House Church on Essex Street in the Strand. Cox's Museum on Spring Gardens had once served as a Huguenot chapel, then a concert hall where Mozart made his London debut, and later as a museum of mechanical works of art in precious and semi-precious stones. The collection was sold in 1775 and the hall was hired out for meetings. The Spring Garden Coffee House was located "on the right hand in the entrance going into Spring Garden and St. James's Park" and was well known during the 18th century. Newspapers were available in coffee houses and during the American Revolution they frequently contained copies of letters from American commanders intercepted by British agents. John André, a major in the British army, had been hanged as a spy two months earlier on 2 October 1780 for his role in Benedict Arnold's treason. The decision to hang the 29-year-old officer had created a storm of protest in England, but Curwen, like other Americans, did not share this sentiment.

In July 1784 Curwen packed his belongings in preparation for his long-awaited return to Salem. He was to sail on the *Union* under the command of Captain Ingersoll. Having paid his passage money, 20 guineas, he made his will. As usual there was a delay in the sailing and Curwen was forced to spend his last nights in London in the New England Coffee House, where he "supped and lodged in a miserable stinted room, on a fourth floor as at this present writing." On his last morning, he strolled to the Horse Guards in Whitehall where he regulated his watch "by that clock which is reckoned the truest timekeeping in London being carefully attended and every day corrected if needful." That afternoon he took one of his favorite strolls, the ramparts of the Tower of London, where on the river Thames he caught "a view of the American 13 stripes flying on 7 or 8 vessels lying in one tier, the first view I ever distinctly had of their independent naval glory."

Brook Street, Mayfair Map C

51   Claridge's. London's most exclusive hotel was begun early in the 19th century by William Claridge, a former butler in a noble household who saved enough money to buy a small hotel in Brook Street. By 1860 Baedeker was describing it as "the first hotel in London."

Scott and Zelda Fitzgerald stayed at Claridge's during the last week of June 1921. When they had first come to England in May, they had stayed at the less exclusive Hotel Cecil (86, the Strand), where they had received a dinner invitation from John Galsworthy.

He gave explicit instructions as to how they should take the tube from the Strand to Hampstead before walking up Holly Hill to Grove Lodge. But a premonition perhaps led Galsworthy to add a post-scriptum: "By taxi-cab it is about 20 minutes from the Hotel Cecil." The Fitzgeralds did not travel by tube. Besides Mrs. Galsworthy, the other guest that evening was the Irish playwright and novelist St. John Irvine. Fitzgerald was disappointed in Galsworthy, telling a friend, "I can't stand pessimism with neither irony nor bitterness." The problem was in part one of generation—the author of *The Forsyte Saga* had just lived through the World War, and Fitzgerald was in many ways still juvenile.

It was probably inevitable that, having discovered that Claridge's was the most exclusive hotel in London and catered to European royalty, the Fitzgeralds should stay there rather than the Cecil upon their return to London. They were entertained by Lady Randolph Churchill and ate "strawberries as big as tomatoes," and by Charles Kingsley, Scribner's London agent, who supervised the publication of *This Side of Paradise* in England. To Maxwell Perkins, his editor in New York, Fitzgerald wrote, "The most beautiful spot in the world is Oxford, without a doubt."

Ruth Gordon lived at Claridge's for four weeks in October 1936 while playing the role of Mrs. Pinchwife in William Wycherley's *The Country Wife* at the Old Vic. Under Old Vic regulations her salary could not exceed £20 a week, so all her expenses, including the round trip from New York on the *Queen Mary,* were paid. She was thrilled with her suite on the second floor at Claridge's, "a beautiful old-fashioned big square sitting room with French windows looking out onto Davies Street"; the bedroom contained a grey marble fireplace, while the bathroom was bigger than her stage bedroom had been at the St. Martin's Theatre. Most of all, she enjoyed "the grand doorman" at the Brook Street entrance of the hotel summoning a taxi for her every evening and announcing in a sergeant major's voice: "Old Vic, WATERLOO ROAD."

William J. Donovan, one of Franklin Roosevelt's early confidential envoys to England during World War II, arrived at Claridge's on 17 July 1940 in the midst of a bitter German air attack. The president had no faith in his ambassador Joseph Kennedy, who kept prophesying Britain's surrender, and he had not informed him of Donovan's mission—to give an unbiased appraisal of England's chances of surviving. Were the British really prepared to fight as Churchill had claimed? The answer was crucial, for the month before 335,000 British troops had escaped to England from Dunkirk abandoning all their equipment in France. There was a great danger for the U.S. in supplying Britain with planes such as the B-17 if they risked falling into the hands of the Germans. All the intelligence which Roosevelt was receiving on Britain's ability and will to continue fighting was contradictory.

Donovan's first call was upon the king at Buckingham Palace. After the customary five minutes of polite conversation, the king showed him a deciphered message from Hitler to his field commanders. Dated 16 July 1940, it announced the impending invasion of England and stressed that first the Royal Air Force had to be destroyed to prevent it from attacking German landing craft. Donovan had arrived in time for the Blitz; Britain at least had a few more weeks to survive. What the message also revealed was that the British had succeeded in cracking the top secret German code, what Churchill was to call "my most secret source." To his dismay, Donovan discovered that British defenses after the debacle in France consisted only of 786 field guns, 167 antitank guns and 259 tanks, each far inferior to the German Panzer. All told, it was enough to equip two divisions, while across the channel there were forty German divisions being assembled. Donovan spent a week listening to key Americans in England. Lieutenant Colonel Carl Spaatz, who had been inspecting the Royal Air Force bases, said that he thought the young RAF pilots with their excellent fighter planes and their incredible morale could hold off the German Luftwaffe for three months. Donovan visited an RAF base in Kent, where he watched Spitfires in a dog fight with German fighter planes and learned that, thanks to radar, the British could track the incoming German planes, saving both time and petrol. CBS news reporter Ed Murrow said that the British would never surrender and would fight for every foot of soil; their morale, since Churchill had taken over, he said, was incredibly high.

Before leaving England, Donovan met with Churchill and spent his last night talking until 2 a.m. with Rear-Admiral John Godfrey, one of the heads of British Intelligence. Donovan told him that his first advice to Roosevelt would be to appoint a new

American ambassador. (Kennedy resigned in October 1940 and was replaced by John Winant.) As to the question, "Were the British earnest about the war and were the British worth supporting?" the answer would be "definitely yes." He would recommend the immediate dispatch of fifty U.S. destroyers, squadrons of Flying Fortresses with technical maintenance staff, new Sperry bombsights, as many surplus guns as possible, the use of American airfields for training British, Canadian and Australian pilots, etc. On 5 August he was back at the White House. Donovan, who was to head the Office of Strategic Services (the precursor of the CIA), made many subsequent trips to England during the war and stayed in London at Claridge's.

Harry Hopkins settled in his suite at Claridge's on Thursday evening, 9 January 1941. The personal representative of Franklin Roosevelt had had a tiring wartime crossing—from New York to Bermuda, then to the Azores and Lisbon, in neutral Portugal. He then boarded a Dutch plane which made a wide swing out over the Atlantic to avoid the German airforce, before finally landing in Poole in southern England. He was met by Brendan Bracken, Churchill's personal assistant, and boarded a private train for London. The following morning he was escorted to 10 Downing Street where "a rotund, smiling, red-faced gentleman appeared— extended a fat but nonetheless convincing hand and wished me welcome to England." He lunched alone with Churchill on soup, cold lamb, salad, cheese and coffee, a light wine and port—he did not take enough mint sauce for the lamb to suit Churchill who served him some more. Hopkins began by saying that Roosevelt was anxious to meet with Churchill, which delighted the British leader. The only problem was where and when. Hopkins then said that there was a feeling in some quarters that he, Churchill, did not like the Americans or Roosevelt. The prime minister denied it vigorously and cited Ambassador Joseph Kennedy, who had just served for two years in London, as the source of that total misrepresentation.

During Hopkins's stay in England, Churchill promised him full access to all military installations, secret operating centers and communications. He was received briefly by the king before joining Churchill and his advisers on a three-day visit to see the British fleet in Scapa Flow, off north Scotland. There he caught a severe cold and spent two days in a bunk in a battleship, while the indefatigable Churchill, sixteen years his senior, clambered aboard ship after ship.

Often privy to secret military cables, Hopkins was intrigued by the British habit of quoting poets and the bible. When referring to the sending of military supplies to the Middle East, Churchill's telegram to the commander of the region read: "Ask, and it shall be given you; seek, and ye shall find; knock, and it shall be opened to you" (Matthew 7:7). Hopkins was delighted to read one top secret cable containing a quote from Walt Whitman. There was nothing like literate allies.

In his report to Roosevelt he noted that "the people here are amazing from Churchill down and if courage alone can win—the result will be inevitable," but he was perturbed by the British assumption that now that Roosevelt had been reelected for a third term he could easily declare war on Germany if he wished. Hopkins did his best to explain the limitations on the president's power, but they seemed incredible to the British, especially in view of the extraordinary influence possessed by Churchill. Hopkins's list of recommendations for aid to Britain included 50 destroyers, 250,000 Enfield rifles and 50 million rounds of ammunition, an increase in the number of B-17 bombers already serving in England, and American pilots to ferry bombers to England in order to release RAF pilots for bombing missions.

Hopkins, the British discovered, had no concept of security. His room at Claridge's was strewn with highly classified documents. He had given a suit to be dry cleaned at the hotel and top secret cables were discovered in the inner pocket. Since he was returning to America with Britain's most important technical secrets which were now to be made available to the U.S. Armed Forces, the British provided him with a security officer to accompany him and his many files all the way back to Washington. Hopkins said goodbye to Churchill on 8 February 1941. The following month, he was appointed to administer the Lend-Lease program, which provided $31 billion of aid to Britain and the Commonwealth over the following four years.

Generals Eisenhower and Clark arrived in London on 24 June 1942 and were assigned suites at Claridge's. Eisenhower had just been named commander-in-chief of the American forces in Europe and spent the first month meeting with British leaders. He was soon to discover that he could not play a social role and also run an army. At the insistence of Ambassador John Winant he went to the American embassy on the Fourth of July and shook hands with over 2,000 guests—the following day his right hand was so swollen that he could not even initial memos. He accepted a luncheon invitation from King Haakon of Norway and learned that protocol prohibited guests from leaving before royalty. Soothed by the many toasts, the king sat and chatted until after 4 p.m., by which time Eisenhower was furious. It was the last of his social engagements. When he called on General Montgomery, the famed British general promptly informed him that he did not permit smoking in his headquarters. Eisenhower, a chain smoker, put out his cigarette, but his dislike of the Englishman began that day; over the years, as he suffered Montgomery's perpetual self-righteousness, his dislike grew.

On 20 July 1942 he was joined at Claridge's by General George C. Marshall, chief-of-staff. The Allies had promised the Russians that they would start a second front in 1942; the question was where. The Americans favored an invasion of France; the British refused it as too risky. After six days of discussions, the decision was taken to invade North Africa, and Marshall returned to Washington. Eisenhower went to work on Operation Torch in his offices in GROSVENOR SQUARE.

Eisenhower disliked Claridge's Hotel. His suite was done in black and gold and looked, he thought, like a Hollywood set; his bedroom he described as "whorehouse pink." He moved to the Dorchester, which was still luxurious but closer in style to the Waldorf Astoria. He left for North Africa in November 1942.

Arthur Goldberg, future associate justice of the Supreme Court, served in the Office of Strategic Services in World War II as contact man with the European underground labor movements. Early in May 1943, Goldberg met Samuel Zygelbojm, representative of the Jewish Board in the Polish government-in-exile in London, who provided him with the first fully documented proof of the existence of Nazi concentration camps. Photographs of the camps and affidavits of a few prisoners who had escaped proved the reality of the horrors which, up until then, had been but rumor. Zygelbojm requested that Goldberg have Donovan forward these documents to Roosevelt and ask to have the railroads leading to the camps bombed. He told Goldberg that Allied bombers were already attacking targets within five miles of some of the camps. Such an attack would show the Germans that the Allies knew about the camps and would hold them accountable when the time came. On 11 May 1943, Goldberg invited Zygelbojm to dine at Claridge's, when he told him that Roosevelt had refused his request. The next day, Zygelbojm committed suicide.

Brunswick Square

1   Conrad Aiken, separated from his wife Jessie and their three children in January 1927, went back to Harvard where he tutored for a year and then returned to England and settled in London. Jessie, living in their home in Rye, Sussex, was preparing to marry British author Martin Armstrong, whose novel, *All in a Day,* was making him "pots of money," wrote Aiken half bitterly and half humorously. "Was anything ever so monstrous?" he asked a friend. The answer was yes, London in December. "My beard is hung with icicles, my eyes are as hard as stones, and thank God I don't feel my feet anymore." It was so cold that he "had to keep drunk to keep warm." Aiken attended the Criterion Christmas dinner where he got "tight as a tick" in the company of poets John G. Fletcher and John Freeman, Harold Monro, owner of the Poetry Bookshop in London, and Herbert Read. The dinner was given by T.S. Eliot, editor of the quarterly *Criterion* and an old Harvard friend. "Tom is a lost man. He's unsure of himself, more dependent than he used to be, wary, and now faced with a growing opposition and a shrinking following," Aiken confided to Bostonian editor, Robert N. Linscott. He invited his 26-year-old friend, Theodore Spencer, who had just begun teaching at Harvard, to come to London for a year or two. Despite "the physical misery," London was a "profound, wonderful, and horrible place; rich inferno; death and transfiguration if it isn't plain suicide." Spencer stayed at Harvard.

The following year, Aiken's *Selected Poems* won the Pulitzer Prize and he married Clarissa Lorenz, musician and part-time journalist. They shared their time between Rye and London where, besides poetry, novels and short stories, Aiken wrote the London letter for the *New Yorker.* In January 1936, when he reported on the deaths of King George V and Rudyard Kipling under the title,

"Kiplings and Kings Depart," the English were so angry that Aiken lost his job. "I still remember walking the two miles over Vauxhall Bridge to the Houses of Parliament with the mourners," he recalled. "But they didn't appreciate my mentioning the knitting needles that clicked as people waited to pass the King's bier." In 1950 Aiken was appointed to the poetry chair at the Library of Congress.

Buckingham Palace Map C

Originally known as "Buckingham House," it was built in 1702-5 for the Duke of Buckingham, and was purchased by George III in 1762 as a private home. George IV engaged the architect John Nash to build a new palace, but the estimate of £500,000 upset the British government. The result was a series of enlargements of the original building. The east front, built in 1847, encloses the courtyard and faces the Mall and is familiar to the public today. A ballroom was added a few years later but, other than renovations, the 600-room palace with its 45-acre garden has changed little over the past 150 years.

Benjamin West had every reason to feel nervous as he walked through St. James's Park on his way to Buckingham House one fine July morning in 1768. News of the success of his recent painting, *The Landing of Agrippina at Brundisium with the Ashes of Germanicus,* had reached George III, who had summoned the young painter for a private audience. Having passed the guards, he was shown into an anteroom where he carefully unwrapped the painting which he had carried under his arm. As he waited, he went over the etiquette to be followed in the presence of the king. His Majesty was always to speak first and to choose the topic of conversation. One began with, "May it please your Majesty." Having said "Your Majesty" several times, one was then permitted to say "Sir." The queen was also to be addressed as "Your Majesty" and then as "Ma'am." One never disagreed with or contradicted their Majesties. They were never to be touched unless they extended a hand to be kissed. One remained standing. If there was a crowd in the room, all conversation was to cease when the king entered and was then to be conducted in a whisper. The king decided the length of the audience and would then bow or say, "I will not detain you any longer." When leaving, one bowed and retreated, never turning one's back upon the king.

The-king entered and after a brief greeting studied *The Landing of Agrippina* in silence, but with apparent satisfaction the painter felt. The king was a tall man, West noted, weighing almost 200 pounds, with a ruddy complexion, blond eyebrows, and an open expression. Was there sufficient light? he asked. West agreed that the light was insufficient and the king led him through several apartments until they found better light. Here the king again examined the painting and then left the room to return with the queen. Having explained the story of Agrippina to her, the king asked if the final departure of Regulus from Rome might not make a fine picture? West, who had almost certainly never heard of Regulus, agreed that it certainly would. "Then," said the king, "you shall paint it for me." A valet brought in the 17th volume of Livy's *History of Rome* and the king translated the epic story of Roman courage and heroic martyrdom. He then showed West an empty panel measuring 7 feet by 10 feet in what was called the Warm Room; the painter must have noticed two other empty panels nearby. An hour later, a jubilant West was back in his home in CASTLE STREET where his American assistant, Charles Peale, immediately began to pose as Regulus, the Roman general. Benjamin West from Springfield, Pennsylvania, was on his way to becoming historical painter to King George III.

John Adams and John Jay, accompanied by Benjamin West, visited Buckingham House on 8 November 1783. The royal family, away at Windsor, had given West permission to show "the whole house" to the two American diplomats. In the queen's bedchamber lay her German bible and, in the king's library, "the books were in perfect order, elegant in their editions." Adams noted that the books had been chosen with "perfect taste and judgment; every book that a king ought to have...maps, charts etc. of all his dominions in the four quarters of the world, and models of every fortress" in his empire. "We gazed," wrote Adams, "at the great original paintings of our immortal countryman, West, with more delight than on the very celebrated pieces of VanDyck and Reubens." The three Americans found "the same taste, the same judgment, the same elegance, the same simplicity" throughout the building. Adams, for once, was delighted with his visit.

The most popular American visitor at Buckingham Palace during the 19th century was the midget General Tom Thumb. His show had barely opened at Egyptian Hall on PICCADILLY when his manager Phineas T. Barnum received a visit from the master of the queen's household. Both were invited to the palace. Barnum received the usual instructions as to how to conduct himself in the presence of royalty, but Tom Thumb was given none since Queen Victoria desired "to see him act naturally and without restraint." Their first visit in March 1844 took place in the queen's picture gallery. The queen and Prince Albert, the Duchess of Kent and some twenty members of the court stood at the far end of the gallery awaiting their arrival. The doors were thrown open and the general, recorded Barnum, "advanced with a firm step and, as he came within hailing distance, made a graceful bow, and exclaimed, 'Good evening, ladies and gentlemen!' " This greeting drew a burst of laughter. The queen promptly took Tom Thumb's hand and led him about the gallery asking him questions. The general assured the queen that her picture gallery was "first-rate," and asked to meet the Prince of Wales. The queen regretted that the prince had already retired for the night but promised that he would see him upon another occasion. Tom Thumb then performed his songs, dances and imitations, including one of Napoleon, and finished by chatting with Prince Albert and others for almost an hour. Before leaving the palace they were escorted to an apartment where "fine refreshments" were provided. Immediately after the visit, Barnum asked to see the gentleman in charge of the "Court Journal" which appeared each day informing the British public of the activities of the royal family. He was anxious that the journal contain more than a mere line on their visit. The official, obviously unaccustomed to good old American promotion, found himself provided with a paragraph prepared by Barnum who recorded, "I was pleased to see afterwards, that he had inserted my notice *Verbatim.*"

Their second visit to the palace took place two weeks later in what was called the "Yellow Drawing-Room," on account of its gold panelling. Tom Thumb shook hands with the queen and promptly told her that he found the drawing room prettier than the picture gallery. He was introduced to the Prince of Wales and, after his performance, the queen presented him with an elegant present made expressly for him. On their third visit to the palace, the king and queen of Belgium were also present. After half an hour of questions, Queen Victoria asked Tom Thumb to sing a song. He chose "Yankee Doodle." This visit was equally successful and was fully recorded in the "Court Journal." The result of all this publicity was that Barnum had to rent a larger showroom at the Egyptian Hall, thanks, he recorded, to "the force of the Court."

Sidney Bechet, saxophonist with a black quartet, gave a Command Performance here in August 1919. In his auto-biography, *Treat It Gentle,* Bechet recalls walking into the palace: "It was just like Grand Central Station with a lot of carpets and things on the walls. By the time we got to play I was thinking I'd gone through enough doors to do me for a month." After the performance, King George V told the quartet that the piece he liked the most was *Characteristic Blues.* Bechet had come to England with the Southern Syncopated Orchestra and they played at the Rector's Club in Tottenham Court Road for three years.

President Woodrow Wilson and his second wife Edith were guests of King George V and Queen Mary beginning on 26 December 1918—the first non-royal heads of state ever to stay at the palace. After being met by the king and queen upon their arrival at Charing Cross Station, they were escorted to the palace in royal coaches with outriders and footmen in crimson liveries. It was a cold but sunny day and the streets were lined with cheering crowds of women, children and old men. They turned in the Albert Gate and discovered the courtyard to be filled with American troops, with the foreground reserved for those on crutches or in wheelchairs. A great shout went up as Wilson got out of his carriage to greet them. Among the American press who had managed to "crash" the arrival ceremony were Arthur Krock, Walter Lippmann and William A. White.

Inside the palace the king and queen escorted their guests to their rooms, the Belgian Suite overlooking the garden in the back. The large living room, with windows reaching to the floor, was adorned with fresh flowers everywhere. "My husband's bedroom had a large alcove cut off by heavy red curtains. His Majesty lifted one of these to disclose a well-equipped bath and a small electric heater," recalled Edith Bolling Wilson in *My Memoir.* "My room was enormous, with the largest bed I ever saw. It contained no heat at all.... My bath, at the end of our hall, had a marble tub, beside which stood a high-backed chair as big as a throne." They were then invited to the balcony of the palace where they waved small Union Jacks while their Majesties waved small American flags. Dinner that night was small and informal. The king began with a story of his visit to British troops in France where American soldiers were also billeted. As he had moved down the reviewing line of the British soldiers, he had overheard one of the American onlookers ask his buddy, "Who's that bug?" The other replied, "Why, man, that's the King of England!" The first shrugged his shoulders and said, "Hell! Where's his crown?" The evening was a success.

At the official banquet the following evening, Wilson spoke on the obligation of governments to obey "the great moral tide running in the hearts of man." It was a speech in favor of his fourteen points. He made no mention of the immense British losses in the war and Lloyd George, sitting at a nearby table, noted coolness in the applause. American aides warned Wilson, and the following day at luncheon in the Guildhall, the American president paid lip service to the "prowess and achievements" of England and her allies. On their third and last day, King George V, having learned that it was Wilson's birthday, offered him a set of books on the history of Windsor Castle. Their Majesties accompanied the Wilsons to the train station for their trip to Rome. The visit was judged a success, in spite of Edith Wilson's refusal to curtsy to the queen and Wilson's use of "Sir" rather than "your Majesty" to the king. But Wilson's professorial approach and his tendency to moralize were found tiring by the British governing class.

Buckingham Street Map D

York Buildings. Gilbert Stuart took a modest room here upon his arrival in London in November 1775. With the outbreak of the American Revolution, his loyalist family had abandoned Rhode Island for Nova Scotia, while the 20-year-old Stuart came to England determined to become a painter or a musician. A born storyteller, he was standing one day in the local ale house when his listeners asked him in what part of England he was born. He told

them he was not born in England, Wales, Ireland or Scotland.
"Where then?" he was asked.
"I was born in Narrangansett."
"Where's that?"
"Six miles from Pottowoone, and ten miles from Poppasquash, and about four miles from Conanicut—not far from the spot where the famous battle with the warlike Pequopts was fought."
"In what part of the East Indies is that, Sir?"
"East Indies, my dear Sir! It is in the state of Rhode Island, between Massachusetts and the Connecticut River."

If such tales amused his neighbors, they did not amuse his landlord when Stuart was unable to pay the rent. Happily he was saved by the sudden appearence of a boyhood friend, Benjamin Waterhouse, a medical student, who helped him move to GRACECHURCH STREET.

✦

John Trumbull, 24, late colonel in the American rebel army, arrived in London on 13 July 1780. He took lodgings "near the Adelphi" and moved to York Buildings a few months later, sharing rooms with a former American army officer, John Steel Tyler. Trumbull brought with him from Paris a letter of introduction from Benjamin Franklin to Benjamin West. He was well received but, having none of his own work with him, he chose to copy Raphael's *Madonna della Sedia*. Three days later, West examined the finished copy and announced: "Mr. Trumbull, I have now no hesitation to say that nature intended you for a painter. You possess the essential qualities; nothing more is necessary, but careful and assiduous cultivation." Trumbull then set to work in the large painting room on NEWMAN STREET.

On 15 November 1780 news reached London of the hanging of the British spy Major John André. Playing upon British indignation, American loyalists denounced Tyler and Trumbull as spies and traitors. Tyler was forewarned and escaped to the continent but Trumbull was arrested and taken to the Brown Bear, a lock-up house opposite Bow Street Magistrate's Court. Trumbull had originally received permission to study art in England under the general amnesty offered to all rebels by the British Peace Commission in October 1778. Two supposedly incriminating letters were found in his desk: one from his father, the rebel governor of Connecticut, and another from William T. Franklin from Paris. He was taken before three examining magistrates and found guilty of "the Crime of High Treason committed within His Majesty's Colonies and Plantations in America." On 20 November he was committed to Bridewell Prison on TOTHILL STREET.

14 Joseph Pennell rented this house in February 1892. Illustrator, etcher, lithographer and author, Pennell was greatly influenced by Whistler who became a frequent guest here. Elizabeth R. Pennell, his wife, wrote articles for the New York *Nation* and other magazines. The couple held open house on Thursday evenings, which were attended frequently by impecunious and struggling young artists who could be sure of a good meal. Pennell, in an article in *Studio* (April 1893), was one of the first to recognize the genius of a 21-year-old illustrator called Aubrey Beardsley. In 1905, two years after Whistler's death, Pennell organized the Whistler Memorial Exhibition held at the New Gallery on Regent Street. For the first time in Europe the extent of Whistler's creativity was recognized. The exhibition contained 200 paintings, including *The Mother* and *Carlyle,* 500 different prints and over 300 etchings. Rodin came from Paris and gave a seven-word opening speech: "Ladies and Gentlemen, the exhibition is open." The Pennells returned to America in 1908 after finishing their celebrated two-volume biography of Whistler.

Bury Street, St. James's Map C

10 Georgian House. Sinclair Lewis took a service flat here in January 1922 for four months while he continued to work on *Babbitt.* He told his father that he had left his wife in Rome with friends and had returned to England to write, but in reality they were experimenting with a separation. He worked each day until tea-time and then met writers such as John Galsworthy, George Moore, H.G. Wells, Lytton Strachey, dramatist John Drinkwater and drama critic John Archer. He enjoyed his own rising literary reputation in England and was invited to dinner several times by Somerset Maugham, but he spoiled any meaningful intercourse in society by monopolizing every conversation and by heavy drinking. By May he had finished *Babbitt,* his wife arrived from Rome and they sailed to New York together.

In March 1923 Lewis was back in England with Paul De

Kruif, a 33-year-old bacteriologist and author of *Our Medicine Men*. Lewis was working on *Arrowsmith* and De Kruif got him introductions to scientists and entry into laboratories and clinics in London. At the Brompton Hospital, Lewis watched Dr. Inman doing blood tests for tuberculosis and lunched with Sir Walter Fletcher, professor of physiology at Cambridge. During his previous stay in London he had met a new young publisher, Jonathan Cape, who republished *Main Street* and brought out *Babbitt* with a glossary of 125 Americanisms for the British public. Before leaving, Lewis had told Cape that he wanted to see his name in lights, by which he meant promotion. Cape misunderstood him: when the book came out he had the name "Sinclair Lewis" and "Babbitt" put up in lights at Piccadilly Circus. This, of course, was seen by British writers not merely as vulgar but typically American. *Babbitt* was a sensation in England and brought even greater prestige to Lewis, but unfortunately his manners did not improve. George Jean Nathan, New York drama critic, recalled being at a dinner in London when a fellow guest leaned across the table and said, "You are an American and I have a message for you. If your country doesn't recall Sinclair Lewis at once, there will be a war between England and the United States." Lewis had been drinking and giving speeches delivered in different dialects on the shameful neglect of American literature by British critics. During the daytime when he was sober, he debated with the British novelist, Ian Hay, in the London School of Economics on the subject "Main Street and High Street," for the benefit of London hospitals. He left for France in June.

By the time he was back in England in early 1927, he was considered the most successful writer in America. He returned to his service flat and immediately decided to round up his old friends by giving a dinner party. He telephoned Lady Sybil Colefax, Lord Thomson and half a dozen others. When his guests arrived he was already drunk. Seated at the head of the table, he would leap up and move around behind the chairs making unpleasant and sometimes highly offensive remarks to his guests, the literary and newspaper powers of London. Before dessert he collapsed and was put to bed. He left for Paris a week later.

Lewis returned here in January 1931 from Stockholm where he had been the first American to receive the Nobel Prize for literature. He was bitter with his friend and publisher, Alfred Harcourt, whom he accused of losing interest in his books. The failure of Harcourt Brace & Company to rise to the occasion of the Nobel Prize had made their indifference only too evident. The decade through which they had helped make an international reputation for Lewis, and become wealthy in return, was over. Lewis's sense of reality was no longer central to American history, which was changing and leaving the 45-year-old writer behind. Alfred Harcourt knew that Lewis's important writing lay behind him. His novels continued to sell and to make money, while their author drifted around in London, drinking and turning out a story or two for the *Saturday Evening Post*.

Sinclair Lewis stayed in Bury Street for the last time in 1933. The sales of his latest novel *Ann Vickers* had been enormous, especially in England where the newspaper reviews were almost all enthusiastic. He was joined here by his new American publisher, Nelson Doubleday, who was delighted with his new author. But his former English friends were no longer interested in being the butt of his practical jokes or putting up with his drinking, while Lewis knew enough to realize that his new admirers merely wanted a Nobel Prize winner at their dinner table. To his wife, the journalist Dorothy Thompson who had recently left him, he wrote, "I am staying here in England sort of vaguely...but I think I shall go in just a few days."

(15)   Lewis Henry Morgan, the "Father of American Anthropology," took rooms here on 1 August 1870, in "a miserable dingy lodging house, unfit for human habitation." Nevertheless he stayed for almost two months. Morgan had studied the Iroquois tribe which led him to world anthropology. His *League of the Ho-de-no-sau-nee or Iroquois* (1851) is considered the first scientific account of an Indian tribe. He was already known to the scientific community in England, and met Charles Darwin, the biologist Thomas Huxley (father of Julian), and the naturalist Sir John Lubbock, among others. Together with Jeffrey Wyman, professor of anatomy at Harvard, he visited the Henry Christy Collection of Prehistoric Antiquities and Ethnography at 103 Victoria Street before it was moved to the British Museum. Morgan's visit to England is of interest in part because he represents a scientific community whose members could now travel to Europe on relatively modest funds. By 1870, steamships from New York to Liverpool took only seven or eight days, the weekly service was reliable, safe and getting cheaper and cheaper. Indeed, in his journal Morgan mentions running constantly into American friends in London. Besides scientific displays, Morgan was fascinated by the signs of merchants in London claiming the patronage of the royal family. An ambitious baker, Morgan noted, would print on his paper bags: "Francis Stewart, 46 Old Bond St. Piccadilly, by Special Appointment to H.R.H. The Prince of Wales, H.R.H. The Duke of Edinburgh, Purveyor of Biscuits, Rusks, Oat Cakes and Tops and Bottoms to the Royal Family," with a vignette of the coat of arms of the Prince of Wales for good measure. Like most Americans, Morgan was struck with the "roar of the London streets." Oddly enough, he felt that the noise was due to their cleanliness. "Throughout the day boys may be seen with a brush and pan taking up horse manure as it is dropped, there is no litter therefore on the stone pavements to break the incessant roll of vehicles." It was the clatter of the iron shoes of the horses and the ring of the wheels on the clean stones which made the noise so deafening. "Broadway is noisy enough," Morgan concluded, "but it does not compare with London."

Caledonian Road

Pentonville Prison. Built in 1842 as a model prison, it was based on John Haviland's Pennsylvania Eastern State Penitentiary and was characterized by light, airy cells occupied by single inmates. In the summer of 1843 Mr. and Mrs. Horace Mann, Dr. Samuel Howe and his new wife, Julia Ward Howe, all involved in social reform, visited the prison where they were shown around by the Duke of Richmond and Lord Morpeth. The system relied on total solitary confinement and the duke, Julia Howe recalled, "interested himself in showing us how perfectly it was carried out. Neither at meals nor at prayers could any prisoner see or be seen by a fellow prisoner. The open yard was divided by brick walls into compartments, in each of which a single felon, hooded, took his melancholy exercise." Dr. Howe approved of the solitary discipline; his wife had her doubts. Among the prisoners there were no doubts whatsoever. Within a short time, there was, a report stated, "an unusually large number of cases of mental affection among the prisoners." As a remedy the authorities merely decided to increase the amount of exercise with a new method of "brisk walking."

The Manns and the Howes also visited the old prison of Bridewell where their guide was Charles Dickens. Mrs. Howe continued:

> We found the treadmill in operation. Every now and then a man would give out, and would be allowed to leave the ungrateful work. The midday meal, bread and soup, was served to the prisoners while we were in attendance. To one or two, as a punishment for some misdemeanor, bread alone was given. Dickens looked on and presently said to Dr. Howe, "My God! if a woman thinks her son may come to this, I don't blame her if she strangles him in infancy."

Carlton House Terrace Map C

Consisting of two magnificent terraces overlooking the Mall and St. James's Park, built by John Nash in 1827, this is perhaps the most prestigious address in London.

1 Carlton House Terrace was purchased by Levi Leiter of Chicago for his daughter Mary upon her becoming Lady Curzon. Her husband, an M.P., was under-secretary of state for India and foreign secretary from 1919 to 1924.

❧

Joseph H. Choate, American ambassador, rented this house just down the street from the court of St. James from 1899 to 1905, while Lord Curzon was in India. Relations between America and England had improved enormously by 1900. England had been forced to recognize the increasing economic strength of its former colony, while some Americans in London realized that they could still learn something from their former mother country. Choate, a brilliant lawyer who helped arouse New York city to defeat Tammany Hall, was just such an American. From the English he concluded that government could function well without the omnipresence of lawyers:

> Of the nineteen members of the present government, only two, the Lord Chancellor and Lord James of Hereford, were bred to the bar. In fact the study of law instead of being, as with us, almost the only avenue to public office and affairs, seems here to be regarded as not only unnecessary for that purpose, but as a positive hindrance.

He also discovered a civil service where corruption was "practically unknown," and where patronage played but "a very small part"—unimaginable for anyone from New York city. Like other ambassadors at the turn of the century, Choate led a leisurely life: March and April on the French Riviera with his family, August in Switzerland, and October in Scotland hunting grouse. During his six years in London he contributed strongly to Anglo-American friendship.

5   John Hay, appointed ambassador to the court of St. James by President McKinley, arrived in London on 21 April 1897 and moved to Carlton House Terrace a few days later. The event of the summer was the Diamond Jubilee of Queen Victoria. Hay dreaded it: The town was growing intolerable, he wrote, with six miles of lumber deforming the streets. But everything passed off without incident and Hay admitted to Henry Adams that the Jubilee had been "an explosion of loyalty that amazed John Bull himself." It was a curious thing, he went on, that there had been no monarch in England of special distinction since Elizabeth. Most of them were far worse than mediocre; only William III, a foreigner, had any merit, "and yet the monarchial religion has grown day by day till the queen is worshipped as more than mortal." London was packed with prominent Americans, some of them politicians who had helped pass the recent Tariff Bill. Hay was amused to see them "resting from the slaughter of grouse, and marking down their pyjamas to get them under the $100 limit." That winter Hay, accompanied by Adams and other friends, went up the Nile, but the blowing up of the *Maine* in Havana Harbor and the threat of war with Spain brought him back to London quickly. He assured Senator Lodge on 5 April 1898 that the friendship and sympathy of Great Britain towards the United States was beyond question. "I find it wherever I go—not only in the press but in private conversation. If we wanted it—which, of course, we do not—we could have the practical assistance of the British Navy." By the end of the battle of Santiago, 3 July 1898, the United States had acquired the beginnings of an empire (Puerto Rico and the Philippines), all within ten weeks. The British, old hands at acquiring empires, were impressed. In August 1898, Hay accepted the post of secretary of state and sailed home a month later.

Castle Street (no longer exists, now part of Charing Cross Rd)

Benjamin West moved to a house on this street in April 1764, close to the National Gallery and fashionable Leicester Square. His neighbors included Joshua Reynolds and the aged William Hogarth. West married Betsy Shewell on 2 September in the local parish church of St. Martin's-in-the-Fields. Her cousin, Matthew Pratt, lived with them for the next two years while studying under West and working as his assistant. Here Pratt painted his most famous piece, *The American School* (now in the Metropolitan Museum, New York), depicting five young artists in West's painting room (the Italian term *studio* had not yet been introduced). The title was, perhaps, more apt than Pratt realized, since he was the first of three generations of young American artists who were to work under West, the future president of the Royal Society.

Little by little West began to feel at ease as a London artist. He painted the portraits of Dr. Oliver Goldsmith, who had just published *The Vicar of Wakefield,* and Governor James Hamilton of Philadelphia. Benjamin Franklin called on the young couple twice in February 1765 and the two men discussed the British mistreatment of Americans. West, however, could not and did not complain, for in the Society of Artists' Exhibition of 1766 his two entries, *The Continence of Scipio* and *Pylades and Orestes Brought as Victims Before Iphigenia* (now in the Tate Gallery), were highly successful. "The great crowd of the year," it was said, "is about Mr. West's pictures." West's use of history, mythology, the bible, classical tragedy and allegory resulted in moralizing, story-telling pictures, which were easy for the general public to understand and, more important, soon led him to the most powerful patron of all, King George III.

On 13 February 1767, a well-dressed stranger knocked at West's door on Castle Street. His name was Charles Willson Peale. He had just arrived from Maryland and, like other Americans, fearful of being considered provincial he had spent the morning buying correct attire for London: a light blue half-dress suit, gloves, shoes, black stockings and a beaver hat. West found lodgings for the 26-year-old newcomer in Silver Street, at Golden Square. For the next two years Peale was West's close associate in the painting room, preparing canvases, painting drapery, posing for figures and doing odd repairs. One evening, when West was a dinner guest at the table of the Archbishop of York, his host spoke of an episode in Roman history which, he felt, would make a majestic picture: the pathetic story told by Tacitus of Agrippina returning to Brindisi with the ashes of her husband. The result was West's painting, *The Landing of Agrippina at Brundisium with the Ashes of Germanicus*. The bishop was so pleased with the painting that he spoke about it to the king, who promptly sent for the young American.

Charles Peale well remembered the excitement and preparations for the private audience. Attired in court dress, the American chose his sword carefully because, as he told Peale, it was important that he seem "to belong to the higher orders of society." With *Agrippina* safely wrapped and held securely under his arm, Benjamin West set off for BUCKINGHAM PALACE.

Catherine Street Map D

Theatre Royal, Drury Lane. The first theater was built in 1663. Beginning with Nell Gwynne, who made her debut in Dryden's *Indian Queen* two years later, "Drury Lane" as it is called, provided many a royal mistress and many a noble wife. David Garrick, the great Shakespearian actor, played here from 1742 until 1776, when he brought in Sarah Siddons, whose warm, rich voice and majestic presence held audiences in awe. She was unequalled as Lady Macbeth, a role she first played in 1785 and continued in for twenty-seven years.

One of the first Americans to see her in the role was Abigail Adams, who told her sister, Mrs. Shaw, "I saw Mrs. Siddons a few evenings ago in *Macbeth*, a play, you recollect, full of horror. She supported her part with great propriety; but she is too great to be put in so detestable a character." When Mrs. Siddons played, Abigail continued, it was as hard to get a box as to get a place at court:

> The first piece I saw her in was Shakespeare's *Othello*. She was interesting beyond any actress I have ever seen; but I lost much of the pleasure of the play, from the sooty appearance of the Moor. Perhaps it may be early prejudice; but I could not separate the African color from the man, nor prevent that disgust and horror which filled my mind every time I saw him touch the gentle Desdemona.

*The London Hippodrome
in 1902.
(See page 71.)*

Egyptian Hall on Piccadilly,
1800s.
(See page 201.)

UNPARALLELED EXHIBITION!
The 14 Ioway Indians!
AND THEIR INTERPRETER,
IN
CATLIN'S INDIAN GALLERY,
EGYPTIAN HALL,

Just arrived from the Upper Missouri, near the Rocky Mountains, North America.

"WHITE CLOUD,"

The Head Chief of the Tribe, is with this interesting party, giving them that peculiar interest, which no other party of American Indians have had in a Foreign Country; and they are under the immediate charge of G. H. C. MELODY, *who accompanied them from their country, with their favourite Interpreter,* JEFFREY DORAWE.

Mr CATLIN, who is the writer of this, and who was acquainted with most of the men of this party, while sharing the genuine hospitality of this tribe in their own country, and who is to present them and their native modes to the English people, vouches for the fact that this party is chiefly composed of the most influential men in the tribe, and that they are by far the most pleasing and just representation of the North American Indians ever seen in England.

The vouchers which these people bring from the Indian Agents, and also from the President of the United States, whose written permission they possess, as the reward for instances of the most extraordinary individual merit, entitle them to much respect; and their personal appearance and purely native modes, to the attention of the curious.

THE DELEGATION CONSISTS OF:
CHIEFS

MEW-HU-SHE-KAW—(White Cloud) first Chief of the Nation.
NEU-MON-YA—(Walking Rain) third Chief.
SE-NON-TY-YAH—(Blister Feet) great Medicine Man.

WARRIORS AND BRAVES

WASH-KA-MON-YA—(Fast Dancer.)
NO-HO-MUN-YA—(One who gives no attention.)
SHON-TA-YI-GA—(Little Wolf.)
WA-TAN-YE—(One always foremost.)
WA-TA-WE-BU-KA-NA—(Commanding General.) The Son of Walking Rain, 10 years old.
JEFFREY—(The Interpreter.)

SQUAWS,

RUTON-YE-WE-MA—(Strutting Pigeon) White Cloud's wife.
RUTON-WE-ME—(Pigeon on the Wing.)
OKE-WE-ME—(Female Bear that Walks on the back of another.)
KOON-ZA-YA-ME—(Female War Eagle sailing.)
TA-PA-TA-ME—(Sophia) Wisdom; White Cloud's daughter.
CORSAIR—(A Papoose.)

This exceedingly picturesque group, with their "SHORN and CRESTED HEADS," will give their WAR and other DANCES, SONGS, GAMES, &c., all of which will be fully explained by Mr CATLIN, in his ROOMS in the EGYPTIAN HALL, each day and evening of this week, as follows :—

~~From Half-past 2 to 5 in the Day,~~ *and from Half-past 8 to 10 Evening.*
Doors Open half-an-hour previous.

ADMITTANCE, ONE SHILLING.

Printed by T. BRETTELL, 40 Rupert street,

Ioway Indians.
Poster, 1840.
(See page 201.)

Barnum and Bailey.
Poster, 1844.
(See p. 201.)

Mrs. Siddons was lucky, Abigail explained, in having her brother, John Kemble, frequently play opposite her, "so that both her husband and the virtuous part of the audience can see them in the tenderest scenes without once fearing for their reputations."

Such was not the case four years later, on Tuesday evening, 11 May 1790, when Gouverneur Morris, accompanied by Mrs. John Penn (the wife of William Penn's grandson), watched *The Marriage of Figaro*. The diplomat recorded in his journal: "The intended Wife of Figaro is very well done by the intended Wife of Lord Derby, Miss Farren. She is said to be perfectly chaste and his Lordship is I suppose well satisfied on that Subject, but the Caresses of the Stage are not exactly what one would wish to be exhibited on one's intended Bride." Eliza Farren married Lord Derby in 1797. On another evening, Morris saw Mrs. Jordan, future mistress of George IV, play in *Twelfth Night*. After the performance, on leaving the theater alone, Morris was surrounded by a number of prostitutes, but got safely home "in Spite of their kind Invitations."

John Howard Payne, 21, arrived in London in March 1813 and took a room in the Tavistock Coffee House, Covent Garden, described as "a good house much frequented by theatrical and other gentlemen." He promptly wrote to the manager of Drury Lane, "I am an American, recently arrived in this country. My pursuit is theatrical. It is my wish to appear at Drury Lane Theatre as soon as it may be convenient. Lest my playing might prove unworthy of a refined British audience, I should wish to make my earliest efforts without being publicly known." Two months later he made his bow on the stage at Drury Lane as Norval in *Douglas*, a romantic tragedy. The bills announced that the part of Norval would be "enacted by a young gentleman, his first appearance in London." Such a generous reception by the manager created immediate jealousy in the rest of the cast and, on the evening of Payne's debut, his leading lady feigned illness and had to be replaced. The *Weekly Dispatch* declared it "remarkable that a youth from a remote country—a country nearly 200 years behind us in the improvement of every art—should have the courage to come before a London audience under every possible disadvantage." His acting was satisfactory, but his accent was considered provincial. In July the theaters closed for the summer season and Payne joined his friend Washington Irving in Paris.

It was not as an actor but as a playwright that Payne was to know fame in London. On 3 December 1818 his tragedy *Brutus* opened with Edmund Kean and was performed over fifty times that winter, a record in those years. Payne received £183 for his five-act drama which went toward paying off his debts. The following year he took over the management of Sadler's Wells on ROSEBERY AVENUE.

Edwin Forrest opened at Drury Lane on 17 October 1836. He played Spartacus in *The Gladiator,* written by Robert M. Bird, American playwright and novelist. Forrest, 30, had gained experience supporting Edmund Kean in Shakespearian roles when the English actor toured America. His playing of Othello in New York had established him as the leading American actor of the day. Not all of his friends approved his assault on London. James K. Paulding, the well-known author of *John Bull in America,* argued that Forrest's reputation was secure without British endorsement. "Washington never went to Europe to gain immortality," he wrote, "Why should you?" The answer, of course, was that Washington had beaten the British on American soil, and so Forrest would go to London to take on the British in their own stronghold. It was a big risk—to be a real success, he would have to excel in Shakespearian roles. The competition was stiff—over at fashionable Covent Garden, three leading English actors, William Macready, John Vandenhoff and Charles Kemble, were performing in *Othello.* Furthermore, the top price there was only four shillings, whereas at Drury Lane it was seven. Nevertheless, Forrest's opening night went well; Drury Lane was packed and at the final curtain the audience bombarded him with bravos. One voice in the gallery shouted out, "Welcome to England!" a refrain immediately taken up by the rest of the audience. When Forrest thanked them and asked for applause for his countryman, Bird, the playwright, there was polite clapping. Clearly they wanted Forrest. The following morning the reviews spoke of his herculean build, his "thew and sinew," his "Jericho-trumpet voice," and his avalanche of physical energy. There were reservations about his delivery, "a provincial flavor," but his naturalness on stage more than overcame this minor shortcoming.

One of Forrest's first callers was William Macready, leader of the opposition at Covent Garden and London's foremost actor, who felt obliged to welcome his colleague from America. To his surprise, Macready found that he liked him. In his diary he noted Forrest's "noble appearance, his manly, mild, and interesting demeanor." He invited Forrest to dinner on 30 October, but during the intervening week things started to irritate the Englishman—at Drury Lane, Forrest was a triumph in Othello and was being proclaimed "the most extraordinary actor of the day." The first guest to arrive for dinner was the young Robert Browning. Imagining that it would please his host, the poet proceeded to sing the praises of Edwin Forrest, quoting review after review to the 43-year-old Macready who, unknown to Browning, wore his ego on his sleeve. But the dinner went well, Forrest not sensing Macready's increasing antagonism. The American played to full houses at Drury Lane for two months, including nine performances of *Othello*, eight of *King Lear* and seven of *Macbeth*. On the final night he was presented with a gold snuffbox. Macready, who by this time had begun to loathe him, noted in his diary that a clown at Drury Lane had been similarly honored for "throwing 31 somersaults successively." A triumphant Forrest confided to his mother, "I never have been more successful, even in my own dear land." Forrest had had competition from another American performer in London that fall. The minstrel-man T.D.("Daddy") Rice was performing his famous "Jim Crow" song and dance routine and playing Gumbo Chuff in *Oh! Hush! or, Life in New York* at the Royal Surrey Theatre.

After going on tour in the English provinces, Forrest returned to Drury Lane where, on 27 February 1837, he opened in *Richard III*. According to the *Times,* "his figure never appeared more erect and noble, nor his action more graceful and unrestrained." Over at Covent Garden, Macready suddenly announced his own production of *Richard III*. It had the effect he had hoped for: it scared the manager of Drury Lane who told Forrest that he could perform *Richard III* only one night a week. The battle between Macready and Forrest, unique in the history of theater, had begun, to culminate thirteen years later with several deaths in the Astor Place riot when the Englishman performed in New York. Happily, Forrest's anger with the Drury Lane manager and with Macready was diffused by his meeting Catherine Sinclair, whom he soon married at St. Paul's Church, COVENT GARDEN.

Paul Robeson opened here in Jerome Kern's *Show Boat* in 1929, when his singing of "Ol' Man River" made him a celebrity overnight. He gave a concert at the Royal Albert Hall and sang at private receptions, including one given by the press magnate Lord Beaverbrook. He met writers such as Rebecca West and H.G. Wells, and lunched at the Houses of Parliament. After the United States, he found England relatively free from racial prejudice. However, when he was invited by Lady Sybil Colefax to a party in his honor at the Savoy Hotel, he was refused entrance to the Grill Room. In the ensuing furor, the Savoy management professed astonishment that such a mistake could have been made. The matter even reached the floor of the House of Commons, where Labour Prime Minister Ramsay Macdonald said that he did not see how anything could be done officially by the government about such discriminatory practices.

Robeson lived with his wife Essie and their one-year-old son in a house overlooking Hampstead Heath. Aged 31, a graduate of Columbia Law School, the tall and dramatic-looking black singer had an immense appeal for a number of society women in London; within a year, the Robesons separated. His next major role was as Othello at the Savoy Theatre on the STRAND.

Cavendish Square Map C

17   President Ulysses S. Grant, his wife and son Jesse, stayed here from 31 May to 5 July 1877. The first American president to visit England, he received a triumphant welcome. The *Times* in a long tribute announced that "after Washington, General Grant is the president who will occupy the largest place in the history of the United States"; no mention was made of the shameless corruption of his recent administration. Grant, who had the stamina of a horse, thrived on the constant welcomes and speeches. Each day calmly smoking cigars, he went from a luncheon with endless toasts to an afternoon reception followed by a heavy dinner and then a late evening reception. On 26 June, the Grants took a private train down to Windsor to spend the night at the castle and have supper with Queen Victoria. In good old American style, they brought along their "pet," as they called their 19-year-old son Jesse, only to discover that he had not been invited to the supper. A minor diplomatic crisis arose, Jesse acted as if he were 10, duchesses mediated, and an invitation was finally, if grudgingly, granted. During the supper the queen spoke to each guest and later pronounced Jesse "a very ill-mannered young Yankee." The following morning, the Grants returned to London without seeing the queen again. That evening they were honored at a banquet given by the Duke of Devonshire, where fifty peers sat at the table.

What was exceptional about Grant's visit to England was his immense popularity. Raised in modest circumstances in Georgetown, Ohio, he had become president of the United States. The English middle classes cheered him. When he visited Newcastle, poor people poured into the city by wagon and by foot to champion him. Coalminers representing sixteen collieries paraded through the city with their bands and banners proclaiming, "The Workman is the Pride and Stay of the Country." The Newcastle dockers carried a new banner of blue silk with a crimson border, bearing the motto:

A golden era bursts upon the world
The principle of right shall soon prevail
Meek truth and justice soon shall lift their heads
And wrong shall sink to everlasting night.

If Grant had wished, he could have been elected to Parliament overnight. Instead he left for Paris to continue on his two-year trip around the world, perhaps the grandest tour an American president ever made.

(20) "I will not come back to go to the American army or starve in Boston," wrote the 19-year-old Mather Brown to his family. Grandson of Mather Byles, the famous Bostonian minister, a descendant of generations of Puritan clergymen, Brown had decided to become a painter and arrived in London in 1781. He had already learned to draw from Gilbert Stuart and was taken on as a student by Benjamin West. Talented, industrious, shrewd and with an unbounded confidence in himself, within two years Brown had become the new star in the American colony. He worked at Windsor Castle, painted a full-length likeness of the Prince of Wales (the future George IV)—a portrait as flashily vulgar as its subject—and promptly styled himself "Historical Painter to His Majesty and the Duke of York." An English correspondent noted: "Mr. West paints for the Court and Mr. Copley for the City. Thus the artists of America are fostered in England, and to complete the wonder, a third American, Mr. Brown of the humblest pretenses, is chosen portrait painter to the Duke of York. So much for the thirteen stripes—so much for the Duke of York's taste." Brown, barely 24 and now far from humble, took a fine house here in fashionable Cavendish Square, a few doors down from George Romney:

> I have just moved into a very elegant house, where I have genteel apartments for my pictures, and cut a respectable appearance which is of great consequence for one of my profession. My rent is 25 guineas per annum and I have laid out this week as much more for furniture. My name is elegantly engraved on a brass plate on the door, and I board myself with the help of a lodger in the house as cheap as I can. I am just entering the world...

Brown did portraits of Thomas Jefferson and John Adams, and became one of the favorite painters of John and Abigail Adams. It may seem surprising today that patriots such as John Adams would consort with fellow Americans who refused to serve their country, but such men were seen as artists rather than citizens, a class apart, living off the vanity of the wealthy. Nothing useful was expected from them and few found it amiss in America that painters who took no interest in the war should go and paint in England. Mather Brown exhibited frequently at the Royal Academy between 1782 and 1790 and lived the rest of his life in England.

Chalcot Square

7   Sylvia Plath and her husband rented an unfurnished flat, the fourth floor of this five-story house, in January 1960. The rent was six guineas a week, and from the open window they could hear the lions and seals in the zoo in Regent's Park. It was an exciting year. Plath's first volume of poetry, *The Colossus,* appeared, revealing a disciplined, well-crafted and intensely personal style, followed by the birth of her daughter Frieda. Her fifty-line poem, "Words for a Nursery," was accepted for publication by *Atlantic.* She was interviewed with her husband, Ted Hughes, also a poet, on BBC

radio, for a program called "Two of a Kind." She said that her dream was to have a place big enough so that they could yell from one end to the other without hearing each other, and in the mail that followed came an offer of the use of just such a big house and garden. She spent nine days in the St. Pancras Hospital having her appendix taken out, but she was cheered up while recuperating by a visit from her husband, "an absolute angel," who brought her a letter containing a contract from the *New Yorker*. It offered her $100 for the right of first refusal of her poems during one year. She was delighted to accept, particularly since she sent all her poems first to the *New Yorker* anyway. She was interviewed in the prestigious *Observer* by a critic who considered her the most serious woman poet since Emily Dickinson. But in the summer of 1962 her husband left her and, after a few months in Devon, she returned with her children to face London alone in FITZROY ROAD.

Chandos Street, Cavendish Square Map A

3   Washington Irving took rooms here in mid-September 1829 after being made secretary to the American Legation in London. He had been living in Granada, Spain, when news of his appointment, arranged without his consent by his brothers, reached him. He accepted in the belief that it would counter comments back home that he had permanently deserted his native land. He had been abroad for fourteen years. One of his first jobs as secretary was to replenish the wine cellar. Since "the table enters largely into Diplomacy," wrote Irving, a cask of old sherry "should carry sound argument in every glass—some such liquor as that with which Lady Macbeth undertook to convince the pages of King Duncan." If nothing else, the diplomatic correspondence, even the most mundane, took on a certain flair thanks to the author of *Rip Van Winkle*. Recognized in England as the leading American writer of the day (Oxford University conferred an honorary degree on him), Irving was besieged with requests from writers for aid. He helped the radical William Godwin, husband of Mary Wollstonecraft, find an American publisher for his novel *Cloudsley*. He sent the manuscript of Thomas Moore's *Life of Byron* to Ebenezer Irving in New York urging publication. He placed and saw through the press in London the poetry of William Cullen Bryant. On his own account he finished *The Voyages of the*

Companions of Columbus for publication in London by John Murray.

While diplomatic chores delayed work on *The Alhambra,* they afforded Irving an intimate view of London society. William IV was crowned on 26 June 1830, and the festivities included a brilliant dress ball at the Duke of Wellington's. "The king was there in great spirits," Irving told his brother. "He spoke to everyone right and left in the most affable manner, and I observe that he has an easy and natural way of wiping his nose with the back of his forefinger, which I fancy is a relic of his old middy habits." (Irving was referring to the king's having gone to sea as a midshipman when he was 14.) During the summer of 1831, Washington Irving found himself at the head of the American Legation at 8 Argyll Street fulfilling the role of chargé d'affaires, while continuing to receive only his secretary's salary of $2,000 a year. He told his brother Peter, "I attended the queen's drawing room, a dinner at the Duke of Somerset's, and a full dress ball at the Duke of Devonshire's; so that I had to change my dress four times in the course of the day, to racket about from post to pillar and did not get to bed until two o'clock." It could not be done, he said, on his salary.

When the new American minister, Martin Van Buren, arrived in London on 13 September 1831 to take up his post, Irving resigned and spent the winter in London completing *The Alhambra,* selling the English rights for 1,000 guineas. The following April he sailed for home and set foot in New York on 21 May 1832 after a seventeen-year absence. Here, to his happy surprise, he was the guest of honor at a welcome-home dinner of three hundred leading citizens at City Hall on 30 May. In his speech he announced his intention of remaining in America for the rest of his days, which drew loud applause. But he returned to England in 1842 and again in 1846.

Charing Cross Road Map D

10   Phoenix Theatre. Paul Muni opened here in Arthur Miller's *Death of a Salesman* on 28 July 1949. The part of Willy Loman, said Muni, seemed to be the one he had been looking for all his life. Preferring to build the character himself, he had avoided watching Lee J. Cobb play it on Broadway. During the crossing in June on the *Queen Mary,* he worked with Elia Kazan every day. It was a difficult and exhausting role. Rehearsals began on 2 July and when not on stage Muni holed up in his dressing room with his dictaphone. He was always cold in England, and would arrive at the empty theater bundled in multiple sweaters. Since the play was so American, half the cast had been brought over from America under a special dispensation from the British actors' union, Equity. Kevin McCarthy and Frank Maxwell played the two sons, Katherine Alexander was Linda, and Finlay Currie played Charley. Jo Mielziner came to London and duplicated the New York set. Muni and his wife Bella had been provided with Sandford Manor House, a 17th-century house near King's Road, Fulham, by the British management. Bella disliked it from the first day, complaining that "it smelled of cabbage." On the Fourth of July, Muni was invited to the traditional party given by the American ambassador. He did not go, saying—apparently seriously—that he was not Paul Muni but Willy Loman, and he did not think Willy would have been invited. After twenty-six days of exhausting rehearsals, Muni was still pleading for more time. (He always pleaded for more time.) The opening night for him was a nightmare. Preview performances are not allowed in England and there had been no out-of-town practice runs—everything seemed to depend on that one evening. Muni fluffed several times, falling back on an over-detailed performance; at the final curtain he was convinced that he had destroyed the play. But the audience called him back for fifteen curtain calls. The *Times* found the play "beautifully produced" and "meticulously well acted." Kevin McCarthy as the son tormented by his own insufficiency gave a performance of "remarkable intensity and integrity." Paul Muni rendered the salesman "helplessly and hopelessly amiable and pitifully, if exasperatingly, immature." He had more than met the test by "carrying at least half the weight of the play."

Charlotte Street, Fitzroy Square Map B

16 Fitzroy Tavern. Built in 1893, this pub became a favorite haunt of the painter Augustus John and his circle, and later of writers including Evelyn Waugh, John Lehmann, George Orwell and Dylan Thomas. Thornton Wilder began to ˙requent the Fitzroy on his first visit to England in July 1928. The success of

The Bridge of San Luis Rey (Pulitzer Prize, 1927) had brought him fame in England, but it was his proposed four-week walking tour of Europe in the company of Gene Tunney which caught the imagination of the British press. Wilder, the 31-year-old mild and bespectacled teacher of English, "a little like a curate," had become the preceptor of the 30-year-old world heavyweight boxing champion Tunney, who had just retired from the ring after twice defeating Jack Dempsey. The *Daily Mail* announced that "not since Sinclair Lewis has an American author captured English attention as Thornton Wilder." The writer had hoped to rent Henry James's former home in Rye, but ended up with a house in Surrey where he spent July with his mother and his sisters. Tunney arrived early in August and the two men lunched with George Bernard Shaw and his wife. Wilder and Shaw took an instant dislike to one another. Shaw had not liked *The Bridge,* and the American found him "smug and affected in his patriarchal role," a judgment shared by Leon Edel a few years later. At the end of August, the odd couple, writer and fighter, left England for Paris. They began their walking tour in the French Alps in mid-September.

(84)   William Dunlap arrived in June 1784 and took rooms here in the home of Robert Davey, artist. For one guinea a week, the 19-year-old Dunlap enjoyed a painting room, a bedchamber, board, fire and candles. He called on Benjamin West in Newman Street, with whom he had come to study, but it was soon apparent that he lacked discipline, preferring the Vauxhall Gardens and, especially, the theater to the easel. When his father learned of his evening pursuits, he was summoned back to New York. There he became a successful dramatist, translated and adapted French and German plays, managed the Park Theater and became the first historian of the American theater. Later in life, he reflected on his three years in London as a time "of mirth and midnight revelry...I look back with astonishment at the activity of my idleness." Yet it was precisely those "idle" evenings spent at Drury Lane and the Haymarket theaters that eventually led to his rich and creative career.

Robert Fulton, 22, took over Dunlap's rooms here in the summer of 1787. Possessed of many talents and mechanical genius, he had studied painting in Philadelphia for four years. He arrived in London with forty guineas in his pocket and a letter of introduction to Benjamin West. Invited to the master's home, Fulton began working under his direction and was soon accepted as a student at the Royal Academy.

Like all Americans in the 18th century, Fulton suffered from the prohibitive cost of postage. When letters were to be sent home, Americans often dropped by a London coffee shop in the hope of meeting a fellow countryman returning home who would carry them. Recipients paid for the postage. In a letter dated 31 July 1789, Fulton asks his mother,

> to write small and close that you may say a great deal in small cumpas for the ships often put the letters ashore at the first port they make. They then come post to London and I have often paid half a guinea for a small package of letters. The better to accomplish this you buy letter paper as it is thin for we pay according to the weight and not the size so if you can send me a pound of news upon an ounce of paper I shall save almost a guinea by it.

This explains why so many Americans wrote general news letters which could be read aloud to friends and neighbors and handed on to relatives.

Like any struggling young painter, Fulton went from one financial crisis to another. When he told his mother, "I am frequently Changing my Lodgings to suit my Convenience," it was to reassure her; it was most inconvenient for a young artist to be obliged to keep moving all his possessions and the truth was that he could not pay the rent. In 1791, after four years in London, Fulton obtained his first important commission for a portrait which enabled him to move to a more elegant address, MARGARET STREET, just off Cavendish Square.

Chelsea Manor Street Map F

52 Chesil Court. John O'Hara, in May 1938, took a three-month lease on a flat here found for him by his English publisher, Faber and Faber. Six months earlier, he had borrowed $900 from his brother and had married Belle Wylie. They had decided to spend a year in England, but the lack of central heating and the failure of the English to enjoy O'Hara's drinking habits cut short their stay to the summer. Only three short stories can be credited to this period: *Richard Wagner: Public Domain?, A Day Like Today,* and *No Mistakes.* Thirty years later, at a Foyle's luncheon in London marking the paperback publication of *The Lockwood Concern,* a more subdued O'Hara recalled, "On my earlier visits, while I was still a young man, I gave what might be called a series of private lectures in such cultural institutions as the Ivy restaurant, the Savoy Grill, the 400 Club, Quaglino's, the Savage Club and various locals [pubs] in S.W.3."

Cheltenham Terrace, Chelsea Map F

Whitelands House. William Saroyan rented a flat on the eighth floor for the summer of 1966 in this large block on the corner of Cheltenham Terrace and King's Road. He was joined by his 23-year-old son and 20-year-old daughter, and told them that this was perhaps their last chance to talk and that he was available at all hours. "Starting sometimes about nine at night, we talked until almost daybreak. Both of them astonished me by their strange lack of common sense, world awareness, or insight into human meaning." They talked for eight full weeks, except during those evenings which Saroyan spent gambling at Crockford's and at the Colony Club, where he estimated his losses at $20,000 for the summer.

Cheyne Walk Map F

2 John Barrymore, his wife Michael Strange and their children took this house in November 1924. Barrymore had just finished playing Hamlet in New York city and decided on the supreme challenge—to play the role in London. No English producer was interested in backing an American actor, so Barrymore financed his own production. He leased the Haymarket Theatre and engaged an all-English supporting cast headed by Fay Compton as Ophelia. The opening night audience, on 19 February 1925, glittered with celebrities from Mayfair, while letters were represented by John Masefield, Somerset Maugham, Arnold Bennett, George Moore and George Bernard Shaw. James Agate of the *Sunday Times* found Barrymore's performance "magnificent...we know ourselves to be in the presence of a fine and powerful mind." Other critics also found him excellent, but not of the class of a David Garrick, an Edmund Kean or a Henry Irving. One afternoon Barrymore appeared before a women's organization dedicated to the advancement of the arts. At the end of his talk, a studious Englishwoman asked, "In your opinion, Mr. Barrymore, did Hamlet ever have sexual relations with Ophelia?" "Only in the Chicago production, madam," he replied. The original six-week run was extended by an additional nine weeks and when the play closed on 18 April 1925 Barrymore had not only recouped his $25,000 investment but had made a $10,000 profit which he was soon to need. Involved in an affair with Mary Astor, he left Cheyne Walk and moved to the Ritz Hotel. Shortly afterwards his wife took their children back to New York where she obtained a separation agreement and an order for $18,000 a year support.

(74) James McNeill Whistler moved here in September 1902, returning to his favorite site in London, overlooking the Thames. He was dying and he knew it. Afraid that flawed or unfinished canvases might find their way into the market, he sorted through his work. One day a visitor found his fireplace full of obvious ashes; he said nothing, but Whistler quickly remarked, "to destroy is to exist, you know." His friend the art collector Charles Freer bought nine lithographs, nine watercolors, two pastels, one oil and some sketches for £1,363—Whistler's work was fetching high prices now and there would be no more. American collectors, including the gambler Richard Canfield, began to hurry to Cheyne Walk; by Christmas, Whistler was too tired even to walk over to see Edwin Abbey on Tite Street. His old friend the French art critic Theodore Duret came over from Paris; Whistler showed him his recent etchings, but had difficulty speaking. He died on 17 July 1903.

96-100 Lindsey House. Whistler moved next door to this faded but once splendid house in January 1863. Three years later, he leased part of Lindsey House itself where he lived and worked until 1878. He had already discovered Japanese woodcuts and his house soon contained simple matting on portions of the bare floors, Japanese fans, an Ukiyo-e print and an occasional etching of his own adorning the otherwise bare walls. The furniture in his studio consisted of a chair, a bench, a screen, an easel and a small table for the palette. The walls were done in pale yellow to pick up the light. Compared to the comfortable clutter of Victorian England, his rooms reflected the stark severity of the Orient. His mistress of five years, Jo, was a great contrast: her voluptuous figure and coppery-red hair were already known thanks to paintings such as *The White Girl* (now in The National Gallery of Art, Washington, D.C.). Their neighbors, Rossetti, Swinburne and Meredith, frequently dropped by—and Whistler enjoyed the bohemian atmosphere of Tudor House, where Rossetti's collection of exotic animals, including peacocks, roamed inside and out at will. But more important for Whistler than Jo or the neighbors was the view; it was his favorite. Lindsey House overlooked the Thames. Whistler required his models to sit for four, six, sometimes eight hours, day after day, as he rubbed out constantly and began again. Models wept from fatigue and clients who sat for their portraits complained bitterly. The Thames, on the other hand, did not complain; it was always there waiting. To sketch it Whistler had only to sit on the balcony.

Whistler's mother arrived in December 1863. Jo discreetly moved out, but nevertheless remained nearby, a loyal model and mistress who gave far more than she got. Whistler, who had not seen his mother in ten years, was content—he was being looked after by two women, both of whom posed for free. He began the portrait of his mother in 1867, with Mrs. Whistler, dressed in black, sitting silently on a straight-backed chair. The painting progressed painstakingly slowly, as always. Rossetti, who had been close to his own mother, understood the sensitivity of the portrait. Swinburne, who enjoyed both Whistler and his mother, spoke of the picture's "intense pathos...and tender depth of expression." It was shown at the Royal Academy Exhibition of 1872. The critic for the *Times* wrote: "A dim, cold light fills the room, where the flat, grey wall is only broken by a solitary picture in black and white....And here in this solemn chamber sits the lady in mournful garb. The picture has found few admirers..." for which, concluded the critic, the artist had only himself to blame. The influential *Examiner* explained that it was "not a picture," nor was it art; English critics and academicians agreed. Whistler never sent another picture to the Royal Academy.

The following year, a neighbor came by to have his portrait done. Sitting down for the first time, Thomas Carlyle exclaimed, "An' now, mon, fire away!" Whistler began, but only on a long series of preliminary studies. At first, Carlyle enjoyed Whistler's stream of anecdotes but, as the sittings dragged on and Whistler had still not even started the portrait, Carlyle grew increasingly impatient. Eventually, when Whistler had completed the face, another model sat in Carlyle's long black coat for the rest. Over the next twenty years before it was sold, Whistler was forced to pawn the painting frequently. He was saved financially by the shipping magnate, Francis Leyland, who sat for his portrait here in Chelsea. Whistler also painted Leyland's wife and their daughters, and at Leyland's handsome London house in PRINCES GATE he created the famous Peacock Room. In 1878, just when he had made sufficient money to build his own house and studio a few blocks away on TITE STREET, disaster struck. The leading art critic John Ruskin pilloried him in a review; Whistler countered by suing for libel. It was the most celebrated art trial of the 19th century and was held at the Court of Exchequer in WESTMINSTER.

Clerkenwell Close

Aaron Burr returned to London on 16 October 1811 after a two and a half year absence. He had spent a year in France and early in October had set sail for America from Amsterdam. But the *Vigilant,* an American ship, was barely out of sight of land when a British warship pulled alongside and ordered her to Yarmouth. The former vice-president decided to call on friends during his enforced stay, received permission to visit London and hurried to the capital. He did not return to his old lodgings at CRAVEN STREET for he was desperately short of funds. Instead he took "furnished lodgings at eight shillings a week" in Clerkenwell Close; he was too proud to admit to his friends in London, even to Jeremy Bentham, that he had no money. He subsisted by selling the trinkets he had purchased for his beloved daughter Theodosia; he even tried to sell the samples of false teeth consigned to him by his Parisian dentist, M. Fonzi. After four years of exile and wandering in Europe, he was desperate to see his family again. He was joyous when the news came that the *Vigilant* was finally ready to sail. A few days later, he learned that U.S. consular officials had warned the captain against taking Burr back to America. Refusing even to refund his fare, the captain sailed without him. By the time he found an American captain, Potter of the *Aurora,* who did not care what American consuls advised, he no longer had £25 for the passage. Receiving his passport from John Reeves, the director of the Aliens Office in London who had befriended him three years before, he offered him his set of Pierre Bayle's *Dictionnaire Historique et Critique* for £10. Reeves gave him the £10, telling him to keep the dictionary and return the money when he could. Unable to raise the rest of the fare, Burr was forced to return to Reeves who loaned him an additional £20.

The *Aurora* weighed anchor on 28 March 1812 and sailed down the Thames, Burr traveling under the name of Mr. Arnot. On 4 May he landed in Boston, concealing his identity from all but a few friends. On 7 June he was back in New York, where he learned of the death of his grandson Aaron Burr Alston. His daughter Theodosia, his epistolary companion during his four years of exile, decided to rejoin her father in New York. She sailed from Charleston on 30 December 1812 on the schooner *Patriot*. The ship disappeared at sea, and no survivors were ever found.

Cleveland Street Map A

(2)   Thomas Sully, 26, a Philadelphian painter, arrived in England in July 1809. Like others before him, his trip to London had been financed by merchants from Philadelphia (seven gifts of $200 each), on condition that he study under the noted American painter Benjamin West and bring back seven copies of old masters for his benefactors. But unlike the others, Sully, who was married, left $1,000 behind him to support his wife. When he arrived in London, he moved in with another young artist, Charles Bird King, 24, from Newport, Rhode Island, who had been studying under West for four years. King immediately asked his new fellow lodger how long he intended to stay in England. "Three years, if I can," answered Sully. "And how much money have you brought with you?" "Four hundred dollars." "Why, my good sir," answered King, "that is not enough for three months." Undaunted, Sully decided to buy a stock of potatoes, bread and milk on which he managed to survive for eight months before returning to Philadelphia. He was not without admiration for King whom he described as "the most industrious person" he had ever met, limiting himself to four hours' sleep every night and at meals always reading "some instructive book." Sully became a student of

Benjamin West and studied at the Royal Academy, but he learned most from Thomas Lawrence, the famous English portrait painter. Unfortunately, most of his short time was taken up fulfilling his obligation to his seven benefactors, and he finished his seventh copy a week before sailing home.

In America, where portraiture continued to be the primary artistic activity during the first half of the 19th century, Sully soon became a leading painter; in his long career he produced almost 2,600 paintings, mainly portraits. Twenty years later, he returned to England and was commissioned to paint the young Queen Victoria. His works include *Washington's Passage of the Delaware* (now in the Museum of Fine Arts, Boston) and *Mother and Son* (in the Metropolitan Museum, New York). The portraits of Charles Bird King, who returned to America in 1812, include John C. Calhoun and Henry Clay (in the Corcoran Gallery, Washington, D.C.).

141 Samuel Morse took rooms here in 1813 with fellow art student Charles Robert Leslie. The two young men studied under Benjamin West and Washington Allston and were both accepted in the Royal Academy. Leslie wrote to his sister, "I have lately been made a student in the Academy.... I now have access to the library every Monday, beside the privilege of wearing my hat in the Academy, and coming in with a greater swagger than before." They were frequently joined in the evenings by the 25-year-old painter and writer Benjamin Haydon, actor John Howard Payne, the 26-year-old portrait painter Charles Bird King from Rhode Island, the essayist Charles Lamb and Samuel Coleridge. The author of *The Rime of the Ancient Mariner* had separated from his wife, was addicted to laudanum, and suffered from loneliness. "Coleridge," wrote Morse, "was a frequent, almost daily visitor to our studio." To rescue the poet from his fits of despondency, Morse and Leslie would improvise arguments upon aesthetics and appeal to the poet for his opinions. "On one occasion," wrote Morse, "I heard him improvise for half an hour in blank verse what he stated to be a strange dream, which was full of those wonderful creations that glitter like diamonds." Morse recognized in *The Ancient Mariner* "some of the thoughts of that evening." When they could afford it, they all dined at the York Chop House in Wardour Street. One evening in 1813, Allston, King, Leslie, Lamb, Morse and Coleridge shared a box at the Drury Lane Theatre to see *Remorse,* a tragedy by Coleridge. At the end of the play, the public called for the author, who simply bowed but did not speak. "His emotions," wrote Morse, "would have precluded the idea of his speaking on such an occasion."

Morse's letters to his family leave a fine picture of the London of 1811-15, as he prowled about the city taking mental notes: "There is a singular custom with respect to knocking at the doors of houses which is strictly adhered to. A servant belonging to the house rings the bell only; a strange servant knocks once; a market man or woman knocks once and rings; the penny post knocks twice; and a gentleman or a lady half a dozen quick knocks. A nobleman generally knocks eight or ten times very loud." Early American visitors to London were all bothered by the hurly-burly of the city. As Morse explained to his parents:

> The cries of London, of which you have doubtless heard, are very annoying to me.... The noise of them is constantly in one's ears from morning till midnight, and, with the exception of one or two, they all appear to be the cries of distress. I don't know how many times I have run to the window expecting to see some poor creature in the agonies of death, but found, to my surprise, that it was only an old woman crying 'fardin apples' or something of the kind. Hogarth's picture of the enraged musician will give you an excellent idea of the noise I hear every day.

The woman was actually crying "farthing apples" (1/4 of one penny). What Morse does not mention are the cries of the harlots, which European visitors described in detail but to which Americans, including Morse, rarely allude.

Morse returned to America in 1815 and achieved a considerable reputation as a portrait painter. He returned to Europe in 1829 and continued painting but was to become fascinated by electricity and Ampère's idea for an electric telegraph, which eventually led to the code which bears his name.

Cork Street

Hall's Hotel. Gertrude Atherton, novelist from San Francisco, stayed here in 1889 and on subsequent visits to London. While writing in Paris, she had received a letter from the English critic and poet, William Sharp, telling her that he was about to publish a review of her novel *Hermia Suydam* in the *Spectator*. He told her that he thought that she was the "coming American woman," one who understood the meaning of true realism and had the courage to depict it, and invited the 32-year-old novelist to visit him in London. Atherton recalled, in her autobiography *Adventures of a Novelist* written many years later, that she was so excited that she could not sleep for two nights after receiving the invitation. It was recognition in England that counted and she hurried to London. Two of her early novels dealing with California were brought out in paperback at two shillings each by the major English publisher John Murray, who purchased all rights in advance for £40. During one of her first dinners in London at the house of Walter Sickert, the painter, she met Whistler: "He monopolized the conversation at table, delivering himself freely of his opinions of his fellow artists." None incurred his favor. Edwin Abbey was a mere historian on canvas, John Singer Sargent was a landscape painter who had been seduced into portraiture by titled women. Whistler was always the hero of his own anecdotes, Atherton noted, but added, "they were the more interesting for that." Atherton returned to London in the summer of 1895 with her manuscript of *Patience Sparhawk and Her Times* which was accepted for publication by John Lane of the noted Bodley Head Press in Vigo Street. The sensation that summer was the trial of Oscar Wilde. Three of his plays, *A Woman of No Importance, An Ideal Husband* and *The Importance of Being Earnest,* were on the boards, their titles sprawled across every omnibus and billboard. Suddenly, Atherton recalled, they disappeared overnight. The trial began with full reports in every newspaper, followed by blank silence. Atherton sent copies of the first issues to a friend in New York. They never arrived, and she concluded that they had been suppressed by the London Post Office.

After the success of Atherton's next book, *American Wives and English Husbands,* she was asked to write reviews. An Englishman, Frederick S. Oliver, had written a book on Alexander Hamilton and in her review (for the *North American Review*) she commented on the book's atmosphere of scholarly leisure. One could visualize the author, she wrote, in the seclusion of his library, doubtless in the depths of the countryside, dwelling lovingly upon each polished sentence and apt turn of phrase. Atherton, like other American authors in England, wrote in drab, chilly hotel rooms, swaddled in pullovers, and carried romantic notions of her English counterparts seated near a warm fire, gazing out over the rolling downs as they casually perfected a sentence. A year later Atherton received a letter from the author explaining that he was the manager of Debenham and Freebody, one of the largest department stores in England. He had written the book in snatches on holidays, weekends and, most of all, while traveling to and from work on the London underground.

(30)   Peggy Guggenheim opened her first art gallery, Guggenheim Jeune, here in January 1930. Marcel Duchamp was her adviser, "he taught me the difference between Surrealism, Cubism and abstract art." The first catalog contained a preface by Jean Cocteau translated into English by Samuel Beckett. In February, she introduced Kandinsky's watercolor drawings and gouaches to England. The catalog contained statements by André Breton and Diego di Rivera. "I know of no painting more real, authentic and beautiful than his," wrote di Rivera, "none more rich in material both for dream and sensuous enjoyment." None sold. In May, Peggy Guggenheim planned an exhibition of contemporary sculpture with works by Brancusi, Laurens, Hans Arp, Pevsner, Henry Moore, Duchamp-Villon and Calder. Most of them had to be shipped from France. When the works arrived they were denied access into England on the argument that all imported manufactured goods were subject to a substantial *ad valorem* duty, unless certified as art by the director of the Tate Gallery. The director, James B. Manson, denied such certification. In the flurry of protests, St. John Hutchinson, K.C., wrote to *The Daily Telegraph:* "That on the word of Mr. J.B. Manson works of art can be forbidden entry into this country is of the greatest importance.... It may be difficult to tell the difference between works of art and commercial masonry, but it would be fatal if a censorship of this kind were set up. The issue, of course, is not affected by the mere fact that Brancusi is acknowledged throughout Europe to be a serious artist. Let us avoid dictators even if the dictator is the Director of the Tate Gallery." Other letters were more explicit in their references to Hitler's banning of "degenerate art," which was at its height in March 1938. Manson's decision was reversed and the exhibit took place, but as best Peggy Guggenheim would recall later, none of the pieces sold. In June 1939, she decided to close the gallery and to open a museum of modern art in London. She persuaded Herbert Read to resign his editorship of the *Burlington Magazine* and to assume the directorship of the museum. The *London Times* welcomed the project: "London has lagged behind New York in providing a permanent exhibition centre for modern art. At a time when New York's well-known Museum of Modern Art is opening in a bigger and better building come news that a similar museum is to be established in London." To house the collection Peggy Guggenheim made arrangements to rent the Portland Place residence of Kenneth Clark. By August, with the approach of World War II, she abandoned the project, but not before paying Read half of his promised five-year salary.

Covent Garden Map D

Richard H. Dana, author and lawyer from Cambridge, Massachusetts, spent Wednesday evening, 16 July 1856, listening to a debate at the House of Lords and afterwards, profiting from the fine weather, walked to Covent Garden, famous for its food and entertainment:

> It being about midnight, I stroll through the purlieus of Covent Garden, all alive with Gin Shops, gas lights, flaunting women, and rattling carriages, and into Evans' famous Cyder Cellar. Here is a hall, as large as the largest concert rooms in America, open to all, with good music, vocal and instrumental, and supported solely by what the people who enter it buy to eat or drink. It was crowded, almost to suffocation. Only men are admitted, and the conduct of all was decent and orderly, and the constant passing in and out, showed the great number of people who visit it in the course of the night. The walls are lined with portraits, copies, chiefly of actors and poets, and each guest has given him a pamphlet of the ballads and songs sung here, among which, arranged in order of time, are many of the rarest old English ballads, and among the modern I found some of Longfellow's. After midnight, as it was, little ragged boys were running along on the sidewalks about Covent Garden, turning somersets and standing on their heads, begging pennies from 'kind gentlemen' for 'poor boy and poor parents at home.'

St. Paul's Church. Edwin Forrest married Catherine Sinclair here on Friday, 23 June 1837. The famous tragic actor, whom his young bride described as "the handsomest man on whom my eyes have ever fallen," had just completed his first season at Drury Lane. His future father-in-law had not exactly been enthralled at the prospect of his daughter leaving for America, least of all with an actor. During their courtship, Mr. Sinclair had called on the 31-year-old Forrest at his rooms in 5 Tavistock Row and had asked him what settlement he intended to make on his daughter. Forrest bristled at his "damned impertinence" and told him that he was not buying a female slave and that he would not settle a single dollar on Miss Sinclair. If she could not trust him for her money, she had better not trust him for her happiness. It was a short meeting. Mr. Sinclair trudged home to 28 Alfred Place, just off Bedford Place, to announce that the wedding was off. It was then that he discovered that his beautiful and beloved 19-year-old daughter was no longer the docile child he had imagined. She told her father that Forrest was the handsomest, kindest man in the entire world, the only man she could ever love or marry—and that if she were forced to accept him without paternal blessing, then she would do so. Mr. Sinclair knew when he was beaten, and attended the wedding. English journalists announced that Forrest had abandoned tragedy for comedy and was about to appear in an afterpiece entitled "Matrimony," honeymooning in Paris before returning to America. The wedding was attended by the United States minister to Great Britain, Andrew Stevens, and the American banker, Joshua Bates and their wives. One journalist reported that "Forrest led his young and lovely bride to a new and splendid carriage expressly manufactured for the occasion, and with the aid of four beautiful gray horses, richly caparisoned, the young couple started for Windsor where they were to pass the first portion of their honeymoon." From Windsor, they went to Paris, returned to London, and sailed to America on 8 August on the *United States*. In New York, the beauty and vivacity of the new Mrs. Forrest were immediately appreciated. It seems almost a shame to add that a decade later they were divorced after a sensational trial during which each accused the other of flagrant infidelities.

Coventry Street Map C

39   Formerly the Mapleton Hotel. In the late 1950s Jack Kerouac set foot in England at Newhaven with a total of fifteen shillings in his pocket. Unshaven, carrying a backpack, this older member of the beat generation immediately caught the eye of the

British immigration officials. His passport revealed that he had recently been in Morocco, a land identified with drugs in the minds of officialdom. "My dear fellow," the immigration official is supposed to have said, "you can't come into England with fifteen ‹ bob." (Kerouac's version of his arrival at Newhaven in *Lonesome Traveler* (1960) does not ring true. No British immigration official would ever address a traveler as "my dear fellow," and it is most unlikely that an official would use the slang term "fifteen bob," particularly to a foreigner.) Asked how he intended to live in London, Kerouac explained that he was going there to pick up a royalty check from his publisher before returning to New York from Southampton on the *Ile de France*. He had no book with his name on it proving that he was author, but he found a magazine in his backpack with an article discussing him and Henry Miller. According to Kerouac, the official beamed and said, "Henry Miller? That's most unusual. We stopped *him* several years ago. He wrote quite a bit about Newhaven." (Miller had indeed been refused entry into England in 1932. He was detained overnight at Newhaven and sent back to France the next morning.) When Kerouac got to London, he borrowed enough money from his agent to spend a week in a modest top-floor room. In Piccadilly he was accosted by a group of teddy boys who asked him if he knew Gerry Mulligan. On Good Friday, he listened to the *St. Matthew Passion* at St. Paul's Cathedral, during which he cried most of the time, and saw "a vision of an angel" in his mother's kitchen. While buying a ticket for his boat train for Southampton, he discovered the Old Vic and went to see *Anthony and Cleopatra*. "It was a marvellously smooth and beautiful performance, Cleopatra's words and sobbings more beautiful than music.... knew that I had seen Shakespeare as it should be played."

Cranbourn Street Map D

The Talk of the Town. Formerly the London Hippodrome. It was opened in 1900 as a music hall, and the first American to perform here was Irving Berlin in June 1913. During his Atlantic crossing, the 25-year-old composer jotted down some notes for a new song. When he played it for the first time on the stage of the Hippodrome, "Alexander's Ragtime Band" took the audience, and then all of London, by storm. The *London Daily Express* wrote:

"Go where you will, you cannot escape from the mazes of music he has spun. In every London restaurant, park and theatre you hear his strains. Ragtime has swept like a whirlwind over the earth and set civilization humming."

Craven Street Map D

(25)   Herman Melville took rooms at Mrs. Morgan's lodging house upon his arrival in London on 6 November 1849. Aged 30, his first book *Typee* had been a success in England and now he had come to place his latest manuscript, *White Jacket*. He began by calling on Richard Bentley on New Burlington Street who had just published his *Redburn,* and outlined the story of *White Jacket,* which was based on his service on board the man-of-war *United States.* Bentley offered £200 for the privilege of publishing the first 1,000 copies, but would make no advance. Although Melville termed it a "liberal offer," he decided to try other publishers. He called at Longmans, 37 Paternoster Row, where he met Mr. Longman himself; "very polite," but his offer was no better than Bentley's. After two other fruitless calls, he "stopped at the American Bowling Saloon in the Strand," on his way back to Craven Street.

Melville enjoyed wandering through the city and simply talking with Londoners. His *Journal* for Saturday, 10 November, reads:

> I lounged away the day—sauntering through the Temple courts and gardens, Lincoln's Inn, The New Hall, Gray's Inn, down Holborn Hill through Cock Lane (Dr. Johnson's Ghost) to Smithfield (West). And so on to the Charter House, where I had a sociable chat with an old age pensioner who guided me through some fine old cloisters, kitchens, chapels. From the Charter House through the Goswell Street Road to Barbican towards London Wall. Asked an officer of the Fire Department where lay St. Swithin's. He was very civil and polite and offered to show me the way in person. "Perhaps you would like to see the house where Whittington was born? Many Londoners never saw it." "Lead on," said I—and on we went—through squalid lanes, alleys, and closes, till we got to a dirty blind lane; and there it was with a slab inserted in the wall. Thence, through the influence of the Fire Officer, I pushed my way through cellars and ante-lanes into the rear of Guildhall, with a crowd of beggars

who were going to receive the broken meats and pies from yesterday's grand banquet (Lord Mayor's Day). Within the hall, the scene was comical. Under the flaming banners and devices, were old broken tables set out with heaps of fowls, hams, etc., pastry in profusion—cut in all directions—I could tell who had cut into this duck, or that goose. Some of the legs were gone— some of the wings, etc. (A good thing might be made of this.) Read the account of the banquet—the foreign ministers and many of the nobility were present. From the Guildhall, strolled through the Poultry to the Bank and New Exchange—thence, down King William Street to Fish Street Hill, and through Eastcheap to Tower Hill.

The Fire Officer was better intentioned than he was informed. The "dirty blind lane" to which he led Melville was College Hill, where at number 20 there is a plaque indicating the site of the mansion where Richard Whittington once lived. He was actually born in Gloucestershire, and came to London where he made his fortune. He was elected lord mayor four times, beginning in 1397.

After three weeks in London, Melville spent a month on the continent and then came back to his fourth-floor rooms here on Craven Street. Upon his return he was delighted to receive Bentley's note for £200 at six months' notice for *White Jacket*. He went to Baring Brothers, the American bankers in Bishopsgate, where he got a letter of credit on America for £180 or $900 in exchange. Among the rest of his mail was an invitation from the Duke of Rutland to stay at Belvoir Castle in Leicestershire, but the date proposed was a month away and Melville was missing his young wife and their baby. "I ought to be home," he wrote, yet "I should very much like to know what the highest English aristocracy really and practically is. And the Duke of Rutland's cordial invitation to visit him at his Castle furnishes me with just the thing I want." But homesickness prevailed, and he decided to take the next ship back. He enjoyed a final dinner at Morley's Hotel with his new friend Henry Stevens and Horatio Somerby, the American genealogist who also lived at Morley's, and who joined him on board the SS *Independence* for the voyage home.

30   "I should not, Sir, be surprised at his embarking shortly for England, and his making some Proposals to HM's Government....His Fortunes are desperate and whatever He suggests should be treated with great Caution." It was in February 1808 that

George Canning, the British foreign secretary, learned of the impending arrival in London of one of America's most famous exiles. In this letter marked "most confidential," Phineas Bond, the British consul in Philadelphia, continued, "He has said frequently of late that He required but a Station Point and that with a moderate supply of money He could soon collect such a force as would be competent to subdue the Floridas conquer Cuba and very probably revolutionize South America and that he could suggest such plans to Great Britain." The consul warned his superior that "any protection afforded to him would be construed into a Violation of all our Assurances of a Disposition to cultivate good will in the United States." Such a description only fitted one man in American history—Aaron Burr, former vice-president of the United States. While Canning took careful note of this message it is unlikely that he worried; many an able adventurer had come to London with secret proposals and confidential information. The British Foreign Office stood to learn something from President Jefferson's most hated enemy—and at no expense. Burr had recently been found innocent of treason before Chief Justice John Marshall, but he still risked mob violence, especially in his home state of New York. His entry into England would be proof of Britain's firm belief in freedom for the individual; and, as soon as he was of no further use, he would be asked to leave, thus also proving Britain's steadfast desire to maintain friendly relations with its former colonies.

A few months later, on the evening of 9 June 1808, a mysterious "G.H. Edwards" bade farewell to his daughter in New York to keep a rendezvous with a pilot boat in the Narrows that was to carry him to the packet *Clarissa Ann*. As he was rowed out on the Hudson, he must have recalled the morning where, four years earlier on the opposite bank, he had fought and killed Alexander Hamilton. When the ship made a brief stop in Halifax, Aaron Burr strode ashore and introduced himself to Nova Scotia's commander-in-chief, Sir George Prevost. He obliged Burr with letters of introduction to friends in London, and instructions for officials in Falmouth to allow "G.H. Edwards" to proceed "without delay" to London. The packet dropped anchor in Falmouth on 13 July and three days later Aaron Burr set foot in the British capital. On his first day in London, Burr hurried to the War Office where he delivered dispatches from Sir George in Halifax to Viscount Castlereagh, secretary for war. By the end of the week, he had met

Baron Mulgrave, first lord of the admiralty, and George Hammond, the former British minister to the United States who smoothed the way for his introduction to George Canning.

Foreigners in England had to register with the Aliens Office where Burr made the following declaration:

Declaration of Aaron Burr, an alien, taken before John Reeves, Esq., the 10th day of August, 1808.

—Declare, 1st, your name, age, place of birth, rank, occupation or profession.

Aaron Burr, United States, rank of citizen, forty and upward.

—Your last and principal residence before your arrival in this Kingdom.

New York.

—For what reason or purpose are you come?

I am known personally to Lord Mulgrave and Mr. Canning.

—When and where did you land in this Kingdom?

July, Falmouth.

—Where do you now reside and have you resided since your arrival?

London. Craven street, No. 30.

—Sign your name.

The undersigned was born within the king's allegiance and his parents British subjects.

A.Burr.

Burr's insertion of being "born within the king's allegiance" of British parents was to lay the ground for his claim to British citizenship which he would make the following year. His claim was to be refused, with no reasons given.

The day after his declaration, he received an invitation from Jeremy Bentham to spend some days at his country home, Barrow Green, near Godstone, Surrey, twenty miles south of London. Bentham, whose *Introduction to the Principles of Morals and Legislation* (1789) held that the greatest happiness of the greatest number is the fundamental principle of morality, was the foremost philosopher in England at the time. Burr took the stage to Godstone on the morning of 18 August and reached Barrow Green at 4 p.m. Bentham gave him an "affectionate reception" and showed him over his workshop, giving him "license over his papers." During the three-day visit, a keen friendship developed between the two men; both were interested in Latin American colonies escaping Spanish domination. Before Burr left, he had accepted his host's invitation to move to his London residence on

Queen's Square Place. After his departure, Bentham told his brother of Burr's past: "Military matters and management of parties, of one of which he is the head ... are his forte: but, besides that, he is better qualified to pursue all my ideas, as well as better disposed for it than any man I have ever met with, or ever expect to meet with." On a more personal side, he confided, "Eating and drinking he cares next to nothing about: any thing you may happen to have for dinner will serve for him. Fruit is what he is fondest of. With the sugar dish on the table, he will keep eating little bits of it like a Turk."

Burr returned to London and moved from Craven Street into Bentham's house, The Bird Cage on Queen's Square Place. He informed his host, "I called last evening at the Bird Cage (a most beautiful Cage and from which one would never wish to escape);" he had found the housekeeper already expecting him. He spent September trying to convince British officials to back his plan to help liberate certain Spanish American colonies. His schemes had coincided with British interests the previous February, but seven months later this was no longer the case. In the interim, Napoleon had invaded Spain and placed his brother Joseph on the Spanish throne. The British temporarily dropped their plan to help liberate Venezuela, and decided to aid the Spanish in their struggle against French occupation. In October, Burr confessed to Bentham, "I have no longer the slightest hope.... I am an object of suspicion and alarm." He spent Christmas in Scotland where he met the young Walter Scott and Lord Francis Jeffrey, editor of the *Edinburgh Review*.

In February 1809, he was back in London and met twice with Lord Melville, the first lord of the admiralty. Melville confirmed Burr's fears about the British government: "the same equivocal and temporizing conduct towards the United States," wrote Burr, "the same tardiness and indecision regarding the Spanish colonies." There was no reason for Burr to stay longer in England, but he required a passport to leave. Jeremy Bentham had returned to London, and Burr found sharing The Bird Cage too confining; he moved to rooms at 35 James Street where, on 4 April 1809, "four coarse-looking men" came with a warrant for his arrest and took him to prison. No reason was given. Burr protested and was released within a few days with a letter of apology from Lord Liverpool. However, the letter also stated that Burr's presence in Great Britain "was embarrassing to His Majesty's government."

Edwin Booth and his daughter Edwina
in 1880.
(See page 16.)

1788

THEATRE ROYAL, HAYMARKET.

Lessee and Manager - - FREDERICK HARRISON

Every Evening at 8 o'clock.
Matinées: Every Thursday and Saturday at 2 o'clock.

SHAKESPEARE'S

HAMLET

Claudius, *King of Denmark*	MALCOLM KEEN
Hamlet, *Son to the late, Nephew to the present King*	JOHN BARRYMORE
Polonius, *Lord Chamberlain*	HERBERT WARING
Horatio, *friend to Hamlet*	GEORGE RELPH
Laertes, *Son to Polonius*	NIGEL CLARKE
Rosencrantz ⎱ *Courtiers*	⎰ JEVAN BRANDON-THOMAS
Guildenstern ⎰	⎱ MICHAEL HOGAN
Osric	FREDERICK COOPER
A Priest	HARDING STEERMAN
A Messenger	STANLEY ROBERTS
A Gentleman	HERBERT WHITMAN
Bernardo	ROY TRAVERS
Marcellus	JOHN MICHAEL
Francisco	A. G. POULTON
Player King	E. HARCOURT WILLIAMS *William A*
Player Queen	ARNOLD BOWEN
Player King ⎱ *In the Play*	⎰ BURNEL LUNDBEC
Player Queen ⎰	BYAM SHAW
The Poisoner ⎰	VADIM URANEFF
First Grave Digger	BEN FIELD
Second Grave Digger	MICHAEL MARTIN-HARVEY
Fortinbras, *Prince of Norway* ...	SHAYLE GARDNER
Ghost of Hamlet's Father	COURTENAY THORPE
Gertrude, *Queen of Denmark, Mother to Hamlet*	CONSTANCE COLLIER
Ophelia	FAY COMPTON
Gentlewoman	PEGGY WEBSTER

Court Ladies—ALLISON LEGGATT, GRACE O'CONNOR, JOAN BYFORD, MAUD LESTOCQ, VERA BOGGETTI.
Courtiers—H. HUMBLESTONE WRIGHT, CLAUDE BASFORD, RUSSELL SEDGWICK, RICHARD TURNER, FRANK EDGAR, ERIC LESTER.

The Play produced by JOHN BARRYMORE.

The Hamlet *program
with John Barrymore.
(See page 60.)*

*Above: John Barrymore as Hamlet
and Fay Compton as Ophelia. (See page 60.)
Below: The Girl From Up There with Edna May. (See page 234.)*

The Ritz Hotel circa 1907. (See page 204.)
Insert: Douglas Fairbanks and Mary Pickford in England, 1920.
(See page 204.)

Fred Astaire and Adele Astaire
on the roof of the Savoy Hotel, 1923.
(See page 239.)

Lawrence of Arabia
photographed by Lowell Thomas, 1918.
(See page 23.)

On 25 April he received a passport for Goteborg in Sweden, and two days later he sailed from Harwich. His only consolation was that his passage was paid for by the British government.

36   Benjamin Franklin and his son William arrived in London on 26 July 1757 and spent the first night at Peter Collison's house on Mill Hill. The next day they moved to the Bear Inn on Basinghall Street where they spent a few days before finding lodgings here on Craven Street with Margaret Stevenson, a widow living with her daughter Mary. Franklin, 51, little suspected that he was to live on this street for some thirteen years. He took four rooms and his accounts show that he lived well. He began by purchasing wigs, morning swords, a sword knot, two pairs of silver shoes and knee buckles and copies of the *Gentleman's Magazine.* Two servants had accompanied him from Philadelphia. His son William was entered in the Middle Temple to study for the bar. Franklin had come to England to represent the Pennsylvania Assembly, which sought to tax the estates of the descendants of William Penn. In mid-August he made his first call at Thomas Penn's house on Spring Garden. The atmosphere was polite but hostile and, thanks to the procrastination of the lawyers representing the Penns, a year went by with nothing accomplished.

After suffering from "a violent cold and something of a fever" which began in September and lasted two months, Franklin hired a coach of his own for twelve guineas a month. Feeling obliged to justify the expenditure to his wife in Philadelphia, Franklin explained, "I found that every time I walked out I got fresh cold; and the hackney coaches at this end of the town, where most people keep their own, are the worst in the whole city, miserable, dirty, broken, shabby things, unfit to go into when dressed clean, and such as one would be ashamed to get out of at any gentleman's door." He dined out frequently, attended the Royal Society, and played chess at the Pensilvania Coffee House in Birchin Lane; by Christmas, he felt as much at home in London as anywhere. He made the gesture of inviting his wife to join him in London, confident that she would never venture across the ocean.

The atmosphere in Craven Street was joyful, casual and comfortable; Margaret Stevenson had become almost a sister to him, Mary almost a daughter. His son William studied law by day and London by night. Franklin's ability had been recognized by those who mattered: writers, scientists and philosophers. He journeyed to Oxford University where he received the degree of Doctor of Civil Law *honoris causa*. He discussed prose style with the historian David Hume: "I hope, with you, that we shall always in America make the best English of this island our standard." He spent hours with the famous botanist Peter Collinson who had introduced the hydrangea to England. He whiled away many a delightful hour in Printing House Square with men such as William Strahan, the printer of Johnson's dictionary. He preferred to spend his evenings discussing politics in coffee houses to attending performances of Handel.

Franklin had come to England originally for one year and five had slipped by. He did succeed in winning the right for Pennsylvania to tax the Penn estates, but he advised moderation in its application. By the time he left England in 1762 he had become the unofficial representative of America. "In two years at the farthest," Franklin wrote upon his return to his friend and fellow printer William Strahan, "I hope to settle all my affairs in such a manner as that I may then conveniently move to England." Back home he missed the learning, wit and elegance of London. The chance to return came with the new British program for taxing the colonies—the Grenville Acts, which included the Stamp Act. The Pennsylvania Assembly decided to appeal directly to George III and Franklin accepted their offer to represent them. On 7 November 1765 he set out to board ship at Chester, sixteen miles downstream on the Delaware, accompanied by three hundred friends and admirers on horseback. He expected to be away for one year. Five weeks later, he arrived at Craven Street—and lived there for the next ten years. (Mrs. Stevenson, accompanied by her faithful lodger, moved in 1772 from number 36 to another house on Craven Street, which is no longer standing.)

During the winter of 1765 bitterness over the Stamp Act continued to grow. Franklin discussed responses and tactics with other American agents in London, such as the Lee brothers of Virginia, Ralph Izard and Henry Laurens of South Carolina, and John Boylston from Boston. The Thatched House Tavern on ST. JAMES'S STREET became their headquarters. The final drama was played out in the Houses of Parliament where Franklin spoke before a crowded house on 13 February 1766. The act was repealed the following month. But Franklin still remained uneasy.

The house on Craven Street was run to suit Franklin. He got

up early and took his "tonic bath,"—that is, he sat in his bedroom "without any clothes on whatever, half an hour or an hour according to the season, either reading or writing." Sometimes, before dressing, he would return to bed and "make a supplement to my night's rest of one or two hours of the most pleasing sleep that can be imagined." Since Franklin failed to share the English belief that cold and discomfort in the winter were necessary and somehow virtuous, he reduced the opening in his fireplace to three feet by two, invented an iron frame with a sliding plate that acted as a draught, and got more heat from less fuel. The idea was promptly copied by several of his English friends. He shaved himself every morning, breakfasted lightly before his coach called for him, then sallied forth in his old-fashioned full-bottomed wig and his suit of figured Manchester velvet. Dinner was usually between three and four o'clock. In the evenings he might attend the Royal Society in Crane Court, almost a club for him, or join the Honest Whigs every other Thursday at the St. Paul's Coffee House or simply stay home, playing cards and talking.

Franklin was soon representing Georgia, New Jersey and Massachusetts as well as Pennsylvania. His emoluments by 1770 came to £1,500, enough for him to live like a gentleman. If he suffered from spells of gout and recurrent colds, he did not suffer from the absence of his wife. In his correspondence with her, little phrases such as "just home from a venison feast where I drank more than a philosopher ought" reveal a contented life. When Mrs. Stevenson and his niece Sally Franklin went to Rochester for a month leaving young Mary Stevenson in charge, Franklin wrote *The Craven Street Gazette,* a daily parody of newspaper gossip about the court, to amuse the travelers and to tease Mary.

This morning Queen Margaret, accompanied by her first maid of honour, Miss Franklin, set out for Rochester.... It is whispered that the new family administration promises, like all other new administrations, to govern much better than the old one.

We hear that a certain great Person (so called from his enormous size) of a certain family in a certain street is grievously affected by the new changes, and could hardly be comforted this morning, though the new ministry promised him a roasted shoulder of mutton and potatoes for his dinner.

We have good authority to assure our readers that a cabinet council was held this afternoon at tea; the subject of which was a proposal for the reformation of manners and a more strict observance of the Lord's day. All pious people applaud this measure, and it is thought the new ministry will soon become popular.

It is now found by sad experience that good resolutions are easier made than executed. Notwithstanding yesterday's solemn order of council nobody went to church today. It seems that the Great Person's broad-built bulk lay so long abed that the breakfast was not over till it was too late to dress. At least that is the excuse. In fine, it seems a vain thing to hope reformation from the example of our great folks.

We hear that from the time of her Majesty's leaving Craven Court Street House to this day, no care is taken to file the newspapers; but they lie about in every room in every window and on every chair, just where the Great Person lays them when he reads them. It is impossible government can long go on in such hands.

The American newspapers brought news of new resolutions and new violence: the Boston "Massacre," the Boston Tea Party, and later Lexington and Concord. In London Franklin saw the reactions—the Coercive or Intolerable Acts, the Boston Port Act, the Quebec Act, each of them one more step on the road to war. Franklin's position of moderation (he had urged that Boston pay for the "Tea") was becoming more and more untenable. He was in constant touch with the English supporters of America. William Pitt, earl of Chatham, had already argued for repeal of the Stamp Act and was now speaking against the government coercive policy; he had a few supporters—Shelburne, Camden, Edmund Burke and the 26-year-old Charles James Fox. On 19 January 1775, Franklin was a special guest in the House of Lords, where his host Pitt read a motion urging the king to withdraw the troops from Boston. He told his fellow lords that the Americans were doing what the English must not forget how to do: defending English liberty. The motion was defeated by 68 to 18 with 24 bishops voting against. Ten days later on Sunday morning, 29 January, Pitt called on Franklin here at Craven Street, bringing with him a plan transcribed in the form of an Act of Parliament which he asked Franklin to read. Pitt held that only Americans should tax Americans, and that their charters were inviolable. He proposed that the Continental Congress be made official and permanent.

Pitt's coach and livery waiting for two hours at the door caused a stir among Franklin's modest neighbors on their way home from church. As Franklin admitted later, "such a visit from so great a man, on so important a business, flattered not a little my vanity." Pitt left the proposed text with Franklin and they agreed to meet again four days later. But the bill, when finally proposed by Pitt, was roundly defeated. Until the end, Franklin hoped that the ministry of Lord North would be defeated and that America might stay within the empire. On 13 March he wrote to Charles Thomson that even the ministers were not "cordially united," that they were supported by "accounts from America that all was fluctuating there. Our only safety is in the firmest union and keeping strict faith with one another." On 19 March Franklin spent several hours with Edmund Burke who, three days later, made his great speech on conciliation, but to no avail. Franklin had no alternative— he made plans to sail.

His last day in Craven Street was spent with fellow scientist and philosopher, Joseph Priestley. The Englishman noted later that people often thought Franklin cold and reserved, but on that final day he recalled that Franklin was deeply stirred by the prospect of civil war. While his things were being packed, he read from American newspapers, telling Priestley what to extract from them for use in the English newspapers. Suddenly he could not go on, for his eyes were filled with tears. If there should be a war, he told Priestley, America would win but it would take ten years, and he would never live to see the end. He sailed from Portsmouth on 21 March with his grandson Temple, the fruit of his own son's philandering in London. He arrived in Philadelphia on 5 May. His wife had died the previous winter, alone. The day after his return, he was appointed by the Philadelphia Assembly a delegate to the Second Continental Congress. (Franklin's lodging at 36 Craven Street is being converted into the Franklin Museum.)

Crawford Street Map A

18 Crawford Mansions. T.S. Eliot and his bride Vivienne Haigh-Wood moved into this modest flat just off the Edgware Road in the summer of 1915. It was a rough area of London; their charwoman, who talked crudely of abortions, went down into literary history as Lou in *The Waste Land*. Eliot had just finished a year at Oxford University on a fellowship, where his readings in Oriental philosophy had left him, he wrote later, in "a state of enlightened mystification." Instead of returning to Harvard to complete his Ph.D., he got married. This was not what his businessman father had had in mind, and he promptly stopped his allowance. Eliot, 26, spent a year teaching in an English grammar school before joining the staff of a bank. His wife Vivienne had attracted him by her odd combination of melancholy, disillusionment, fragility and sensitivity. She was good-looking, seductive and vivacious, her moods changing like the English weather. She enjoyed his mind and appreciated his poetry. Their new friend, the older and experienced Bertrand Russell, instantly divined in her what the young and innocent Eliot could not possibly have seen, her mental illness.

Eliot had already sought out Ezra Pound in HOLLAND PARK CHAMBERS who, after reading the first verses of *The Love Song of J. Alfred Prufrock,* had recognized his genius. But for a young American poet to make his way into London literary circles was never easy. Pound had tried to gain notoriety by infuriating people, only to find himself surrounded by ever-spreading antagonism. When Aldous Huxley first met Eliot, he wrote him off as "just a Europeanized American, overwhelmingly cultured." Eliot's punctiliousness became a family joke with Virginia and Leonard Woolf. They found his desperate efforts to be English deliciously comic. "Come to dinner," Virginia wrote to her brother-in-law, "Eliot will be there in a four-piece suit." What she did not understand was that Bostonians were far more conscious of class than anyone in London society, and Eliot was intensely aware of being an outsider. The turning point came one afternoon when Katherine Mansfield read *Prufrock* aloud to Lytton Strachey, Clive Bell, Aldous Huxley and other members of the Bloomsbury group. When she finished there was nothing but applause. By December 1917 Eliot was reading his poetry to fashionable society in the Mayfair drawing room of Lady Colefax in order to raise money for the Red Cross.

Over the next three years Eliot prepared himself for a long poem, but the demands of working at the bank during the day and those imposed on him by his wife in the evening had begun to exhaust him. Her illness, crisis, convalescence and relapse, like the seasons, kept recurring. In October 1921 Eliot himself went to see a nerve specialist and was given a three-month leave of absence from the bank. British doctors, he said, did not understand his "psychological troubles," and he left for treatment in a clinic in Switzerland. But his breakdown was also the moment of creation. Before returning to London, he stopped in Paris and asked Ezra Pound what he thought of the thousand or so lines of poetry he had just finished. Pound found them sprawling and chaotic, settled to work at once and whittled them down to less than five hundred. He suggested deleting a long passage of heroic couplets. "Pope has done this so well," advised Pound, "that you cannot do it better; and if you mean this as a burlesque, you had better suppress it, for you cannot parody Pope unless you can write better poetry than Pope—and you can't." The advice was sound and Eliot, although he thought the couplets excellent, deleted them. At the time, 1921, Eliot was a recognized poet in England and enjoyed access to all the literary talent there, yet he had chosen to submit his poem to a fellow American. Today, the importance of Pound's contribution is known and Eliot's decision fully justified. *The Waste Land,* the most important poem in English of this century, appeared in 1922. Five years later, Eliot became a British citizen. A year after that, he moved with his wife to a larger and more comfortable flat at 68 Clarence Gate Gardens. He was awarded the Nobel Prize for Literature in 1948.

Cromwell Road, South Kensington Map G

144 Henry Harland and his wife took a flat here in November 1890. Harland, a graduate of City College of New York, had written novels about Jewish life in the United States under the pseudonym of Sidney Luska. After a year in Paris, the young couple moved to London where their Saturday evenings soon became popular. Guests included Whistler, Edmund Gosse, Henry James, Aubrey Beardsley and, toward the end of 1893, Verlaine. Harland's desperate yearning to be a successful writer had been detected by James who told Gosse that unfortunately his literary longings were "unaccompanied by the *faculty.*" Harland picked another route to fame, the establishment of a periodical. In an interview with the New York *Herald* given a few years later, he described how on a foggy New Year's Day, 1894, the idea for the *Yellow Book* was born:

> Aubrey Beardsley and I sat the whole afternoon before a glowing open coal fire. We declared to each other that we thought it quite

a pity and a shame that London publishers should feel themselves no longer under obligation to refuse any more of our good manuscripts.

" 'Tis monstrous, Aubrey," I said.

" 'Tis a public scandal," said he, and then and there we decided to have a magazine of our own.

Harland, literary editor, and Beardsley, his 21-year-old art editor, called on John Lane at 6B Vigo Street where it was agreed that the celebrated Bodley Head Press would print the magazine. The next question was that of contributors. Harland and Beardsley first called on their neighbor at 34 De Vere Gardens. Henry James later recalled, "I was invited, and all urgently, to contribute to the first number, and was regaled with the golden truth that my composition might absolutely assume, might shamelessly parade in, its own organic form." Put in non-Jamesian language, the editors would not presume to edit. James was secretly flattered that he had been the first to be approached and that he was being offered as much space as he liked. He contributed "The Death of the Lion." Other participants included the literary historian George Saintsbury, Edmund Gosse, Max Beerbohm, the poet William Watson, the novelist George Moore and Mrs. Craigie, novelist and playwright, publishing under the name of John Oliver Hobbes. Lavish illustrations were provided by Beardsley who courted respectability by procuring two studies by Sir Frederick Leighton, president of the Royal Academy.

The day of publication arrived, 16 April 1894, and the bookstores on Charing Cross Road took on a distinctly yellow hue. As for the bow window of the Bodley Head, the display there created "such a mighty glow of yellow at the far end of Vigo Street that one might have been forgiven for imagining that some awful potent had happened, and that the sun had risen in the West." That evening the *Yellow Book* dinner was celebrated at the Hotel d'Italie on Old Compton Street. During the first weeks, the public demand for the books was overwhelming, with every copy sold at five shillings each. Oscar Wilde, indignant that he had not been asked to contribute, promptly labelled the book "loathsome," "dull," and "not yellow at all." The next three issues appeared with less fanfare and fewer sales. Then, as the fifth volume was about to be released in April 1895, Oscar Wilde was arrested and taken to Bow Street police station. The angry crowd outside noticed that he was carrying a large book bound in yellow. Actually it was a French novel—Wilde would never have been seen in public with the *Yellow Book*. But crowds mistook it and soon bricks were being hurled through the windows of the Bodley Head publishing house. John Lane mourned that the affair "killed the *Yellow Book*" and very nearly him as well. A delegation of Lane's authors asked him to have Wilde's books withdrawn from the Bodley list and Beardsley sacked as art editor, since he had illustrated Wilde's *Salome* and, in the public mind, was connected with the homosexual scandal. Beardsley was duly released and with him went the artistic talent that had set the *Yellow Book* apart from its competitors. Volume thirteen was the last. Nevertheless, Harland and Beardsley had gained the notoriety they had sought. In 1900, Harland's novel *The Cardinal's Snuff-Box* was a great success and he and his wife could afford to move to the fashionable Kensington Place Mansions in De Vere Gardens.

Cumberland Terrace, Regent's Park Map A

16   Mrs. Wallis Simpson rented a four-story furnished house here in September 1936. Her friendship with the Prince of Wales, by this time King Edward VIII, had begun three years earlier on GEORGE STREET. All of British high society knew about it, all of America and Europe had read about it in their newspapers; only the British public was still unaware. The king had a "gentlemen's agreement" with the magnates of the British press that they were not to write about it. Prime Minister Stanley Baldwin had personally obtained the silence of the *Times*. Subscribers to foreign periodicals were surprised to discover that various articles and news items had been blocked out. In the House of Commons, Miss Ellen Wilkinson, M.P., asked why in two recently imported issues of American magazines each had three pages missing. Of course, she received no meaningful answer. In October, Mrs. Simpson's divorce case was heard in Ipswich, a sleepy county town in east Suffolk where Cardinal Wolsey had been born. Her solicitor chose the town, guessing correctly that her presence would pass unnoticed by the locals. Some twenty journalists were, nevertheless, present and foreign newspapers carried the story. One American paper announced: "King's Moll Reno'd in Wolsey's Home Town"—a simple line which said it all.

One evening in early November, the king came to dinner here

in Cumberland Terrace. He told Mrs. Simpson that the prime minister had asked him to persuade her to drop her petition for divorce, but that he had replied that the divorce was her concern and not his. The prime minister disagreed, and made it clear that any thought of marriage between the king and a divorcee was out of the question. The couple went down to Windsor for a quiet weekend, but they had barely reached Fort Belvedere when a messenger arrived from London bearing a letter from Major Alexander Hardinge, the king's private secretary. It made two points: the British press could no longer be expected to remain silent, and the government would probably resign, forcing a general election in which the king's conduct would be the principal issue. Major Hardinge concluded with his own advice: Mrs. Simpson should go abroad "without further delay." It was a sensible suggestion, but the king was furious and found the letter and writer impertinent. Mrs. Simpson returned to London to discover her name in every newspaper. The *Times* observed that "there are many daughters of America whom the king might have married with the approval and rejoicing of his people," but that such daughters did not include a lady who "had already two former husbands living from whom in succession she had obtained a divorce." Not one newspaper had a kind word to say about her. Hostile crowds gathered outside her house, every mail brought sacks of abusive letters and daily threats, and a brick was hurled through her window. Early in December, escorted by Lord Brownlow and a detective, she was driven down to Newhaven by the king's chauffeur and took the night ferry for France.

The king gave up the throne on the morning of 10 December 1936. That evening he gave a farewell speech to the British people. It was settled that he should receive the title of Duke of Windsor: as a royal duke he could never sit in the House of Lords and meddle in domestic affairs. It was also decreed that he could never set foot again in Britain without the permission of his brother, the new king. He was granted an allowance of £25,000 a year. By 11 p.m. that night, he had boarded HMS *Fury* at Southampton on his way to a lifetime in exile.

Curzon Street Map C

Crewe House, built in 1730 and since altered, is a private mansion of a type once more frequent in the West End of London than we can now imagine. The two-and-a-half-storied stuccoed front with bow-fronted wings rises above a portico of four attached Ionic columns. Lying a good way back from the street, Crewe House was once home to two American ambassadors: Frank B. Kellogg (1924-25) of Kellogg Pact fame, and Alanson B. Houghton (1925-29).

De Vere Gardens, Kensington Map G

34   Henry James signed a 21-year lease in December 1885 for a fourth-floor flat, number 13, in De Vere Mansions West. In a substantial Victorian building with a lift, the flat contained a sitting room and a study with an enormous window overlooking London where James put his desk. There was a "grand salon" which also served as a library, a comfortable bedroom, a guest room and servants' quarters. From his windows James could see Palace Gate leading into Kensington Gardens where he would walk after a long day at his desk. For the first time in his life he enjoyed looking for old pieces of furniture and decorating the rooms to his own taste. He wanted large fat sofas, solid tables and chairs, nothing original, "expectedness everywhere." For his salon he chose the "richest crimson." He engaged a husband and wife as live-in servants at £10 per month. He got a dog, a dachshund, upon whom he lavished affection. Robert Browning was a neighbor. As he told his brother William, the place was "perfection." Among James's first writing here was an essay on London, the city of his adoption, in which he expressed his affection for "dirty Bloomsbury on one side and dirtier Soho on the other." As an observer and recorder of Victorian society in the 1880s, James was provided with some fascinating unmasking of sexual mores. Sir Charles Dilke, a gentleman of eminent respectability and a possible successor to Gladstone, was accused of having committed adultery with Mrs. Donald Crawford, an infantile society belle. In court, she pointed to him as "the man who ruined me." Oscar Wilde had gone to Reading gaol for homosexual offences. The Irish nationalist leader Parnell had been involved with Katherine, wife of Captain O'Shea. James attended his trial in 1889 and described it as "thrilling." Victorian ladies were not all virtuous, and some English gentlemen behaved like cads. These goings-on were important for James since they would permit him a greater freedom in the actions of his characters. His first major novel from his new home, *The Tragic Muse,* was a cheerful mural of English life and art, complete with a picture of the London stage. In December 1888, he received a letter from an English actor who had his own troupe asking him if he would consider adapting *The American* for the stage. James was intrigued. He loved the theater and was aware that a successful play paid much more than a successful novel. With a £250 advance, he went to work. By June 1890, the play was ready, or so he thought. But when *The American* went into rehearsal, he found himself rewriting scenes which did not sound right—speeches had to be more colloquial, actors objected to certain lines. Most important of all was teaching the tall and good-looking Edward Compton how to talk "American." James suggested that he speak "a little from the nose." The play opened near Liverpool to warm applause. James enjoyed being dragged up onto the stage and giving himself up to "a series of simpering bows." During the strenuous rehearsals in London in the old Opera Comique Theatre in the Strand, sandwiches and other delicacies were brought to rehearsals from De Vere Mansions by James's two servants. "No other playwright, in my tolerably long experience," wrote the American actress Elizabeth Robins, who played Claire de Cintre, "ever thought of feeding his company." The opening night, 26 September 1891, was a social success. Robert Lincoln, the American minister, was there and newspapers wrote of the various "millionaires" present from across the Atlantic. But the play was more melodramatic than the novel warranted; it was obscure at points and the London critics were at best lukewarm. It was only the presence of the Prince of Wales one evening which kept the play alive. James felt it was "humiliating" to be beholden to royalty for part of the run, but seventy nights was far from poor. He devoted the next four years to writing plays, but stopped after a mortifying fiasco at St. James's Theatre in KING STREET. He had begun to spend his summers at Lamb House in Rye, Sussex, and at the turn of the century, he moved there permanently.

Devonshire Place

(54)   James M. Mason arrived in London on 29 January 1862 as Confederate commissioner to England. He took rooms at the Fenton Hotel at 63 St. James's Street before establishing his residence here close to Regent's Park. His voyage over had made of him an unexpected celebrity. His ship, the British packet *Trent,* was stopped by the USS *Jacinto* sailing under a Union flag, and Mason and his fellow commissioner to France, John Slidell, were made prisoners and taken to Boston. There was an uproar in England: this was a national insult and an act of piracy against a neutral country. The British fleet readied for action, additional troops were dispatched to Canada, and an official note was sent to Washington asking for the immediate release of the two Confederate commissioners. The Confederacy was delighted, since a break between England and the Union seemed possible. Lincoln had apparently only two choices: to lose face by backing down or to make war. But the British Foreign Office was more sophisticated. The American captain had surely acted upon his own initiative, they suggested, and they could not believe that his action represented the official policy of the United States. A relieved Lincoln agreed, and both commissioners were quietly released and permitted to continue on to Europe.

Mason had come to England to seek official recognition for the Confederacy, and was seen by the secretary for foreign affairs, Lord Russell, two weeks after his arrival. He began by presenting the South's contention that their nation was not the result of a rebellion. It comprised thirteen sovereign states, embraced an area of 800,000 square miles and had a population of twelve million. It was entitled to be recognized as a separate and independent power. Russell listened in silence and, when Mason finished, told him that England could do nothing. He gave no indication that he personally favored recognition of the Confederacy, and Mason never realized that he was speaking to a sympathetic ear.

Over the following months, the English Confederate lobby, which included some Members of Parliament, made concerted moves to get a debate in the Commons. The Confederacy, they argued, was not fighting for the support of slavery but for independence. An independent South would buy manufactured goods from England rather than from the North. They would pay with cotton which England needed. Finally, the South was far from being beaten on the battlefield. Outside of Parliament, the British land-owning aristocracy favored the South. It was true that the working classes favored the North, but their opinion hardly counted. Mason, 63, was a gregarious soul, typically Southern in his love of social gatherings where talk flowed easily. He told his wife that he found the English elite to be "the type of our best Virginia circles...yesterday, for instance, the Marquis of———called, (I can't give name for fear of Yankee interception) to congratulate me upon the success at Richmond. I visited this really *noble-man* at his estate and remained four days; nothing could be more cordial and genuine than the hospitality I received." While Mason was busy socializing, Russell was quietly working in the Cabinet for Confederate recognition and Gladstone was working in Parliament. In early October, Gladstone made his famous speech, "Jefferson Davis has created a nation," but a week later news of the Antietam campaign reached London. Lee's invasion of the North had been stopped. Lincoln issued the Emancipation Proclamation; it was a superb diplomatic victory. Suddenly, the war was one of freedom and democracy versus slavery; the British government could not consider recognizing the Confederacy for the time being. Mason waited another year for news of a Confederate victory but instead came the news of the fall of Vicksburg. He notified Russell of the termination of his mission to London and in September 1863 he left for Paris.

Devonshire Street

(35)   Robert Frost came to the opening of the Poetry Bookshop on the evening of 8 January 1913. The place was so crowded that to listen to the readings he had to perch on the staircase leading to the balcony. The conversation with the man next to him went as follows:

"You're an American, aren't you?"
"Yes. How did you know?"
"Shoes. Writing?"
"Yes."
"Poetry?"
"Yes."
"Do you know your fellow countryman, Ezra Pound?"
"Never heard of him."
"Well, if you ever meet him, you won't be foolish enough to say that to his face."
"No."

Robert Frost, his wife and their four children had arrived in England the previous September and were living in a small house outside Beaconsfield in Buckinghamshire, 21 miles north of

London. Frost, 38, had just had his first book of poetry, *A Boy's Will*, accepted for publication in London. The stranger at the poetry shop introduced himself as Frank S. Flint, poet and critic, and soon persuaded Frost to meet Pound. A few days later Frost received a calling card from Pound on which was written, "At home—sometimes." He was hurt by the arrogance of the wording but since he knew no one in London except Flint he could not afford to be proud. Nevertheless, he let a month go by before calling at 10 KENSINGTON CHURCH WALK where he was promptly scolded by Pound for having taken so long to answer his invitation. Pound was in a dressing gown and invited Frost into his minute living room and climbed back into his bath. Fairly shallow, when not in use it was kept under the bed. When needed, Pound pulled it out and filled it with cans of hot water from the boiler. It was like an affair, Pound noted in a poem, it cooled off quickly. When Frost spoke of his new book and admitted that he had not yet received a copy of *A Boy's Will*, Pound dressed hurriedly and led him over to the publisher where he saw the first bound copy with its attractive pebble-grained and copper-colored cloth binding. The thin volume was carried back to Church Walk, where Frost was given a magazine to look at while Pound read the poems. He particularly liked "In Neglect." In a gush of sudden appreciation, Frost poured out a dramatic and not very accurate story of the origin of the poem, of how his grandfather and uncle had drafted wills which had deprived him of monies which should rightfully have been his. He described how he had tried everywhere in vain to find a publisher for his poetry in America. This impressed Pound who suggested that he leave so that he could get to work on a review of the book for *Poetry*. But he did want Frost to come with him to meet Yeats at WOBURN WALK. Later, when Frost saw the review, he was appalled to discover that Pound had revealed the story about the disinheritance, and had painted a grim picture of Frost, another poor American poet being scorned by "great American editors." It was one of Pound's favorite themes that American poets had to come to London to find publishers. Only when their success was assured did American publishers, sure to make a profit, accept them. Frost never forgave Pound for publishing his indiscretions.

After a year in Beaconsfield, Frost decided to move to a cottage in Gloucestershire. The Frost family stayed for a week above the Poetry shop in April 1914. With the help of Harold

Monro, owner of the shop, they enjoyed exploring London before joining the poets John Drinkwater, Wilfred Gibson, Lascelles Abercrombie and Rupert Brooke in the village of Dymock.

Dover Street Map C

21   Brown's Hotel. Theodore Roosevelt took rooms at this fashionable hotel on 14 November 1886 in preparation for his marriage to Edith Carow on 2 December at St. George's Church, Hanover Square. They began their honeymoon here. Roosevelt, 28, profited fully from his final fortnight of freedom by accepting as many invitations as he could, hunting with the Essex and Norfolk hounds and accepting honorary memberships at the Athenaeum and St. James's clubs. He became friends with historian James Bryce, author of *The American Commonwealth* (1888), who took him to the House of Commons. Thanks in part to this friendship, Bryce later served as British ambassador to the United States from 1907-13 where he was very popular. Roosevelt also became friendly with the historian George Trevelyan, a valued correspondent in future years. On their way back from their honeymoon trip, the Roosevelts stayed briefly in London again. Deciding that his wife should see "a really first-class English country home," Roosevelt accepted an invitation to do some hunting in Warwickshire, telling Henry Cabot Lodge, "Isn't it funny to think of a rabid American like me having such a courtesy extended him by Lord North?"

Franklin and Eleanor Roosevelt were "ushered into the royal suite, one flight up, front" on 16 June 1905. The young couple were on their honeymoon and, since they were identified with Theodore Roosevelt (Franklin was a distant cousin), president of the United States, they found themselves with a sitting room that measured 30 feet by 40 feet, two double bedrooms, each with a bath, and an impressive bill to match. The following day they visited Allenswood School at Southfields, near Wimbledon, where Eleanor had gone to school from 1899 until 1902. They dined with the American ambassador Whitelaw Reid and his wife at the palatial Dorchester House on Park Lane (it was torn down in 1929 to make way for the Dorchester Hotel). Roosevelt did what most affluent American men do in London—he spent time with his tailors in Savile Row. After three days in London the Roosevelts left for Paris.

Mark Twain returned to London on 18 June 1907. That day newspaper placards carried two headlines: "Mark Twain arrives" and "Ascot Cup stolen." This provided him with excellent opening material for after-dinner speeches.

He had come to England to receive an honorary degree from Oxford University. Aged 72, wearing a derby, spectacles and carrying a cotton umbrella ("the only kind the English won't steal"), he held an American style press conference in the hotel lobby, telling reporters that he was going to show Oxford "what a real American college boy looks like." A week later, wearing his Oxonian scarlet gown, Mark Twain marched to All Souls' College with Rodin, Saint-Saens and Kipling. The undergraduates singled him out as their hero and newpapers referred to "Mark Twain's Pageant." He was genuinely touched by this distinction, perhaps because he had had such a different life from that of the well-groomed students surrounding him—his father had died when he was twelve and he had had to go to work. Back in London, he lunched with Bernard Shaw, Max Beerbohm and Arthur Conan Doyle and dined with the staff of *Punch* at their offices on 10 Bouverie Street. Twain had spent many happy times in London and kept putting off his return to America, since he knew he would never see England again; indeed, he died three years later. But before finally leaving on 13 July, he wrote a short description of a "Family Hotel," actually the terribly respectable Brown's Hotel:

> They are a London specialty, God has not permitted them to exist elsewhere. The once spacious rooms are split into coops which afford as much discomfort as can be had anywhere out of jail for any money. All the modern inconveniences are furnished, and some that have been obsolete for a century. The prices are astonishingly high for what you get. The bedrooms are hospitals for incurable furniture. I find it so in this one. They exist upon a tradition; they represent the vanishing home-like inn of fifty years ago, and are mistaken by foreigners for it. Some quite respectable Englishmen still frequent them through inherited habit and arrested development; many Americans also, through ignorance and superstition. The rooms are as interesting as the Tower of London, but older I think. Older and dearer. The lift

was a gift from William the Conqueror, some of the beds are prehistoric. They represent geologic periods. Mine is the oldest.

Charles Lindbergh and his wife Anne Morrow frequently stayed at Brown's Hotel when they came to London. Lindbergh had moved his family to England in the winter of 1935; they lived in a 14th-century house named Long Barn in Sevenoaks Weald, Kent, some 26 miles from London. During the next four years Lindbergh returned to America only once, but traveled constantly. He enjoyed access to ambassadors and military attachés in most European countries, and visited Germany in the summer of 1938 where he was impressed by the strength of the German airforce. He felt that the English had an island mentality, trusting blindly in a large navy and not understanding the implications of modern air warfare. Lindbergh thought that France would collapse quickly if the Germans attacked and that London would then be destroyed by German air bombers and England forced to surrender. There were two solutions: either England should start mass producing aircraft, or she should seek accommodation with Hitler. Lindbergh's inspection of the Vickers and Hawker aircraft factories had shown him that while the English worked lovingly on each aircraft they had little understanding of or interest in mass production. Chamberlain's policy of appeasement at all costs, which led to the Munich Pact in the summer of 1938, was the only course left to England. During that critical summer, Lindbergh was frequently closeted with American Ambassador Kennedy at the embassy in GROSVENOR SQUARE. It was Lindbergh who provided Kennedy with the facts, figures and understanding of air warfare— arguments which Kennedy used almost verbatim in his reports to the State Department. Both Americans thought that England was asleep, refusing to spend the money needed for rearming and yet expecting that in the war that was obviously coming America would come to her aid. Since England was clearly going to lose, Lindbergh and Kennedy argued, there was every reason for America not to become involved.

One sunny afternoon in September 1938, a week after the Czechoslovakian borders were closed, Lindbergh walked to Piccadilly Circus and saw Londoners lined up outside a gas mask station. In his *Wartime Journal* he commented, "Makes one think, to see gas masks being fitted in the center of London." He promptly telephoned the Army and Navy Store and was told that they sold gas masks but that there was a six-week waiting period. Ambassador Kennedy provided him with two American masks instead. One evening after dinner here at Brown's Hotel, the Lindberghs took the lift up to their rooms and got off by mistake on the floor above. They walked down the richly carpeted stairs and turned left: "There, standing facing us in the center of the narrow hallway, directly in front of our door, was Haile Selassie! Black beard, tunic, and all, just as his pictures show him to be." As the Lindberghs approached, the Ethiopian emperor quickly withdrew into his room and closed his door. Faced by an empty hallway, Lindbergh had the impression of having seen an apparition or "some wild animal visible for a moment in a clearing, then gone like a flash."

Downing Street Map D

10　This plain brick terraced house on a modest and unassuming street was built in 1680 and acquired by the Crown in 1732. It has since served as the official residence of the prime minister, although many early prime ministers preferred to remain in their own grander town houses and rented number 10 out to junior ministers. It was here that Prime Minister William Pitt, aged 26, received John Adams on 24 August 1785. The two men discussed the evacuation of British forts on the frontier; the reimbursement to Americans for slaves set free by the British forces; a treaty of commerce, and the repayment of American debts to British merchants contracted before the war. Pitt argued that it was traditional that interest on loans run in spite of war; Adams replied that American lawyers contended that the late war represented "a total dissolution of all laws and government, and, consequently, of all contracts made under those laws." Moreover, he doubted that any American jury would award interest to a creditor. "This observation appeared to strike him," commented Adams. Pitt felt that France was profiting more than England from its commerce with America. "Upon this," continued Adams, "he asked me a question which I did not expect. 'What do you really think, Sir, that Britain ought to do?'" England should import more from America, of course, replied Adams. "As this was a sprightly dialogue, and in very good humor," Adams felt that he could "push him a little." He went on to praise the virtues of spermaceti oil, which America could furnish, over vegetable oil, which was then being used in England for night illumination:

> The fat of the spermaceti whale gives the clearest and most beautiful flame of any substance known in nature," continued Adams, "and we are all surprised that you prefer darkness, and consequent robberies, burglaries, and murders in your streets, to the receiving, as a remittance, our spermaceti oil. The lamps around Grosvenor Square, I know, and in Downing Street, too I suppose, are dim by midnight, and extinguished by two o'clock; whereas our oil would burn bright until nine o'clock in the morning, and chase away, before the watchmen, all the villains, and save you the trouble and danger of introducing a new police, into the city.

The young minister listened attentively, but showed no sign of adopting this American solution to all the ills and dangers of London by night.

By December 1785, John Adams felt ready to satisfy John Jay's curiosity concerning the talents of Pitt, who had entered Parliament at the age of 21 and had become prime minister only two years later.

> Mr. Pitt is very young. He has discovered abilities and firmness upon some occasions; but I have never seen in him any evidence of greater talents than I have seen in members of Congress, and in other scenes of life in America, at his age.... In American affairs he has oscillated like a pendulum, and no one can yet guess when he will be fixed. His attention appears to have been chiefly given to two objects,—preserving tranquility and raising the stocks.

Winston Churchill became prime minister in May 1940 and lived and worked here until his political defeat in 1945. Almost every American of importance who visited or stayed in England during the war years was invited here. Churchill used to sleep late in the morning, take a lengthy nap after lunch, work until dinner at 8 p.m. and then hold working sessions with ministers and generals until 2 or 3 a.m. He plied his evening guests with brandy and whisky, his favorite drinks. His advantage was simple; by 1 a.m. bleary-eyed Americans gave up arguing and "the P.M.," as he was called, generally got his own way. One of his favorite

Americans was Ed Murrow, the CBS newscaster. Churchill knew that Murrow broadcast nightly at 12:45 a.m. and again at 3:45 a.m. He would call Murrow at 2 a.m. and invite him over for a nightcap. One afternoon Murrow dropped by to pick up his wife who had lunched there with Mrs. Churchill. Upon recognizing Murrow's voice, Churchill ambled out of his study and said, "Good to see you, Mr. Murrow. Have you time for several whiskies?"

James B. Conant, president of Harvard, came to England in February 1941 to organize close cooperation between American and British scientists. He was accompanied on the train from the airport to London by Brendan Bracken, Churchill's personal assistant. Toward the end of the journey, Bracken casually mentioned that Churchill would expect him to lunch. Conant was more than flattered by such an unexpected invitation, suspecting, and rightly so, that it was Bracken who had taken the decision after sizing him up during the journey. When Churchill learned that he was to have lunch with a famous university president, he was appalled. Never having attended a university, he asked Bracken, "What shall I talk to him about?" As Bracken later told the story, Churchill was expecting an old man with a snowy white beard exuding learning and academic formality. Instead, the 47-year-old Conant arrived in a tweed suit. The luncheon went so well that Conant was invited to return.

Earl's Court Exhibition Hall

Entertainment began on this site in 1887 when imaginative use was made of these twelve acres of derelict land between railway lines. The first big exhibition was Buffalo Bill's Wild West Show which unloaded at the POOL OF LONDON. The show played daily from 9 May until 31 October 1887 grossing well over £350,000, making, as Colonel William Cody put it, a "barrel of money." William Gladstone came to watch a rehearsal; afterwards the colonel introduced the former prime minister to Red Shirt, the chief of the Sioux warriors, explaining that he was "one of the great white chiefs of England." The two chiefs chatted amiably. This is the Wild West show as described by a leading English journalist:

As we took our places in one of the boxes which edge the arena where Buffalo Bill's Wild West Show is given, we could not help being struck with the effectiveness of the scene before us ... At the edge of the ash-covered circle in the center were drawn up on parade the whole strength of the Wild West company. There were the various tribes of Indians in their war-paint and feathers, the Mexicans, the ladies, and the cowboys, and a fine array they made, with the chiefs of each tribe, the renowned Sergeant Bates, the equally celebrated Buffalo Bill, the stalwart Buck Taylor, and others who were introduced by Mr. Frank Richmond who, from the top of an elevated platform, described the show as it proceeded ... Few, perhaps, of the audience would have remembered, without the lecturer, the history of the pony express, or have enjoyed fully the exposition by one of the leading cowboys of the way in which the mails were carried! The emigrant train, which next wended its way across the arena with its teams of oxen and mules, its ancient wagons, and their burden of families and household goods, to be attacked by a tribe of redskins, who were soon repulsed by the ever ready cowboys, was an equally interesting resurrection of a method of peopling the soil practised even now in the remoter regions of the West. The next sensation was created by Miss Lilian Smith, "the California girl," whose forte is shooting at a swinging target. She complicates her feats by adding all kinds of difficulties to her aim, and her crowning achievements of smashing glass balls made to revolve horizontally at great speed and clearing off ball after ball on the target just mentioned to the number of twenty were really marvellous. The part of the entertainment most novel to Londoners was undoubtedly the riding of the "bucking" horses. As Mr. Richmond explained, no cruelty is used to make these animals "buck." It is simply "a way they've got." The horses are saddled *coram publico,* and the ingenious manoeuvres by means of which this is accomplished were extremely interesting. Some escaped from their masters, and had to be pursued and lassoed; others had to be thrown down in order that they might be mounted. When the cowboys were in the saddle came the tug of war.... The attack on the Deadwood stage coach, was very effective and, as in an attack on a settler's homestead, there was a great amount of powder burnt. Mustang Jack performed the startling feat of clearing a horse sixteen hands high, having previously covered thirteen feet with a standing leap. Buffalo Bill's speciality is shooting whilst riding a full gallop, and he does this to wonderful perfection. He is accompanied by an Indian, bearing a basketfull of glass balls, which he throws high into the air, and Mr. Cody smashes each with unerring aim whilst both horses are going at a hard gallop. The buffalo hunt was immensely realistic. There was also some interesting feats, riding by two ladies and several short races between them, and also between Indian boys mounted on mustang ponies. Summing up the Wild West show from an English and theatrical point of view, we should say that it is certain to draw thousands from its remarkably novel nature.

Queen Victoria requested a performance at Windsor Castle but when she learned that it was too big a show to move, she came to Earl's Court. The show opened as usual with the American flag carried by "a graceful well-mounted horseman" with the statement that it was "an emblem of peace and friendship." As the standard-bearer rode by, the queen rose from her seat and bowed impressively toward the banner, while her military escort saluted and gentlemen took off their hats. Quite unexpectedly, William Cody insisted, "there arose a genuine heart-stirring American yell from our company as seemed to shake the sky." After the performance, the queen, interested in fire-arms, talked with Lilian Smith and Annie Oakley about the mechanism of their Winchester repeaters. She so enjoyed the show that she asked for a special performance on 20 June so that she could bring her many royal guests who would be in England for her Jubilee. That morning, during the simulated attack by the Indians, the Deadwood coach carried four kings, those of Denmark, Greece, Belgium and Saxony, along with the Prince of Wales, with Buffalo Bill as driver. The Prince of Wales, who had learned poker from the American ambassador, leaned toward Cody and said, "Colonel, you never held four kings like these before." "I've held four kings," replied Cody, "but four kings and the Prince of Wales makes a royal flush, such as no man ever held." This is the way Cody first told it, but later versions had the storyteller reply, "four kings and the Royal Joker." Seen for the first time ever was the square dance on horseback ridden to a Virginia reel. One of the girls induced her horse to jump to music and to stand on his hind legs and bow. "Dead-shot Annie" Oakley was accompanied by pistol-packing Georgie Duffy, rough rider from Wyoming and Dell Ferrel from Colorado. Buffalo Bill and his show corresponded perfectly to the British notion of the Far West, a land rich with cowboys and Indians, sharpshooters, rough riders, bronchos, buffaloes and stage coaches. Londoners loved it.

To repay some of the immense hospitality he had received in London, Cody gave a rib-roast breakfast. The one hundred American guests included Joseph Pulitzer, Chauncey Depew, president of the New York Railroad, Simon Cameron, the political boss of Pennsylvania, Senator James Blaine and many prominent Englishmen. In front of a tent a hole was dug and filled with red-hot coals. Ribs of beef were suspended from tripods above, while Indian cooks slowly turned them. The English were particularly interested in the Indian cooking. The menu consisted of ribs of beef, Indian style, grilled salmon, stewed chicken, lobster salad, American hominy, corn, potatoes, coconut pie, apple pie, Wild West pudding, all washed down by milk, coffee and swigs of bourbon. It was a wondrous breakfast interrupted only by the afternoon performance which all the guests watched, some not being quite up to saddling their horses for the long trail home. When the final show was given, the conservative *Times* wrote simply, "The Wild West was irresistible."

Eaton Square Map F

80   George Peabody came to London in 1837 and negotiated a large British loan which helped save the finances of the state of Maryland. He also purchased, for his own account, other American state securities while their price was low, thereby laying the basis for his personal fortune. Born in Massachusetts in 1795, he was described in his passport, signed by Henry Clay, as 6 feet 1 inch tall, with a rather large nose, small mouth, pointed chin, low forehead, light blue eyes and dark brown hair. He settled in London at 11 Devonshire Street and, within ten years, George Peabody and Company became known as a dependable American banking house. He tried, he said, to give his bank "an American atmosphere; to furnish it with American journals; to make it a center for American news, and an agreeable place for my friends visiting London." Peabody, a bachelor, worked ten hours a day, six days a week, and frequently on Sundays. "I consider you," a friend wrote from Baltimore, "like a horse in a mill condemned to your perpetual round, though if that gives you more pleasure than any other life would give, hold on to it." As the years passed and his fortune grew, Peabody admitted to his sister, "I am almost tired of making money." At the age of 59, he took on an American partner

Paul Robeson in Trafalgar Square
in 1958.
(See page 248.)

Helen Hayes in The Glass Menagerie
at the Haymarket, 1948.
(See page 137.)

*Irving Berlin on British television
in 1946.
(See page 7.)*

The Theatre Royal, Haymarket,
1905.
(See page 137.)

Actress Ruth Draper in a sketch
in London.
(See page 103.)

Tallaluh Bankhead pays a nostalgic visit to her former home on Farm Street off Berkeley Square.
(See page 105.)

Junius Spencer Morgan, whose son John Pierpont, a student at the University of Göttingen in Germany, spent the summers working in the bank at 22 Old Broad Street in the heart of the City of London. In a letter to his cousin, the 19-year-old John Pierpont Morgan described his employer as "a very agreeable gentleman and very full of wit, but a regular old bachelor. If you could have seen the quantity of nic-nacs which he carried with him to America, you would have thought he was going to some unexplored region."

Now relieved from the daily pressures of investment banking, Peabody had time to think about what to do with his fortune. After talking in London with his friend, Senator Reverdy Johnson from Maryland, one result was the Peabody Institute in Baltimore. But the banker was aware that he had made his fortune in England, and it was here that he wished to do something for the lasting benefit of the poor of London. His first idea was the installation of drinking fountains. Water would be centrally purified, then pumped to a network of fountains to be erected throughout the poor areas of the city. Up till then water had been supplied and sold by private companies, forcing many of the poor to drink from open sewers. There had been serious outbreaks of cholera in London in the 19th century but, as the problem was slowly being tackled by the authorities, Peabody dropped the idea. It was the great social reformer, Lord Shaftesbury, whose account of the slums in London gave Peabody his idea. "The dwelling," Shaftesbury said, "of all ages and both sexes, crowded in the same room, brothers and sisters in the same beds, the crimes, the fevers, the dreadful air, the prostration of all energy, the impossibility of doing the people any good until they can *dwell* better." Peabody decided that he would set up a fund to provide housing for the poor of London. In the founding letter published in the *Times* of 26 March 1862, he explained: "It is now 25 years since I commenced my residence and business in London as a stranger but I did not feel myself a 'stranger' or in a 'strange land,' for in all my commercial and social intercourse with my British friends I have constantly received courtesy, kindness and confidence." The purpose of the fund was, he explained, "to ameliorate the condition of the poor and needy of this great metropolis and to promote their comfort and happiness." He gave £150,000 which he soon increased to £500,000 ($2,500,000), an unheard-of sum at the time. He put in four conditions. Beneficiaries had to be

Londoners by birth or residence. They had to be poor and have good moral character. No applicant could be excluded on the grounds of religious belief or political bias. Finally the administration of the fund was not to be influenced by sectarian religion or party politics. One problem was "Which poor?" The trustees decided that housing would be provided for working men and their families who had very low incomes, rather than for charity cases such as the disabled. The first block of Peabody Buildings opened in 1864 in Commercial Street, Spitalfields, an area of desperate slums made even more notorious by Jack the Ripper. By 1882, the fund owned 3,500 dwellings housing 14,600 people, and today has almost 12,000 houses and flats with more than 40,000 tenants.

George Peabody was invited to the Guildhall where, on 10 July 1862, with regal pageantry, the Lord Mayor of London made him a Freeman of the City of London, the first American ever to receive this honor. Upon his death in 1869, his body lay in state at Westminister Abbey and was then borne back to America in a British warship.

90   George Bancroft, Massachusetts statesman and historian, established his household here on 1 November 1846. Appointed minister to the court of St. James, he spent much of his three years in England gathering material for his landmark ten-volume *History of the United States* (1834-74). "People here have heaped me full of documents, Lord North's daughter gave me all she had, and all reminiscences to boot. The Duke of Grafton sent to my house a big box holding the most private papers of the old Duke with the key and unbounded license to use the contents at my discretion." His gratitude for such treasures did not prevent his *History* from being violently anti-British.

"The condition of this country is sad beyond measure in all that relates to the labouring classes," commented Bancroft who was one of the few well-to-do Americans to remark on what he saw as the increasing gap between the poor and the rich in Victorian England. To William Cullen Bryant in Massachusetts he wrote, "The general poverty here is appalling.... There is *no hope* for the poor. Their youth is dreamy and doleful; their prospect of age horrible." Is the purpose of the London police to prevent crime, as the English claim? asked Bancroft. Not at all; their first job is to keep the poor and the thousands of barefoot and starving children out of the sight of the respectable people of London. In 1848, as Britain anxiously watched the overthrow of the French king Louis-Philippe and riots were put down in Liverpool, Manchester and London, Bancroft observed that there was no real danger of upheaval in England for the "habits of subserviency to the aristocracy are so branded into the national character." Such truths, however, did not prevent his "constant enjoyment of the most refined and cultured society" during three years in comfortable Eaton Square. His dinner guests included historians Macaulay and Carlyle, Dickens, Tennyson and Ralph Waldo Emerson. As he told a friend, "In the way of social entertainment, nothing can exceed what this island offers." Before Bancroft left England in late August 1849, he received the degree of Doctor of Civil Law from Oxford University. He felt honored, but saw no reason to modify his comment made to President Polk two years earlier on how the British felt about Americans: "They do not love us, but they are compelled to respect us."

Ebury Street Map F.

120   Ruth Draper took a "lovely big double room in front" on the top floor on 1 June 1920 for two months. She described herself as a "character actress," presenting a series of sketches entirely created by herself, without stage or props. On the eve of World War I, she had already performed before private groups in England, she was now making the move from gifted amateur to professional actress. For her London opening she had booked the Aeolian Hall at 135 New Bond Street for a matinee on 29 January 1920. The following day the *Times* critic wrote: "For two hours yesterday afternoon Miss Ruth Draper kept a large audience smiling and laughing, now and then feeling a little lump in the throat.... Her observation is wickedly keen, her expression of it is pointed till it is as clear and bright as a diamond." The *Observer* concluded: "Miss Draper sees intensely, understands piercingly, and can express cleanly ... at the bottom of it all lies sympathy. She can jest because she understands."

With her name up in lights she opened at the Coliseum Theatre, St. Martin's Lane, at £100 a week, a salary which was rapidly increased when she pointed out that she received 40 guineas for a private engagement. She found the acoustics of the

Coliseum marvellous, much better than in some of the large drawing rooms in London. She enjoyed the British public, saying "they are *childlike* in its best sense, completely concentrated, attentive, warm hearted, generous and sincere, almost in their absorbed delight." Her repertoire numbered about thirty-five sketches; she had no written text for she never liked what she wrote. Every performance was different; the fluidity of her changing, inspired monologue and gestures was part of her genius. In an age when women of her class (her father was a successful doctor) did not work and certainly did not go on the stage, she enjoyed "the contentment that comes from carrying out a definite job, the feel of the envelope of crisp notes on Saturday night."

Edward Street, Portland Place

(21)   Washington Irving returned to England in 1815 to try to save the family importing business in Liverpool. During these dreary years on Merseyside he met and stayed with Walter Scott, who described his 35-year-old guest as "one of the best and pleasantest acquaintances I have made this many a day." When the business finally went bankrupt, Irving moved to London and, encouraged by Scott, turned to writing.

By August 1818 Irving was installed on Edward Street, five minutes' walk from Regent's Park, working on sketches of "Westminster Abbey," "The Christmas Dinner," "Stratford-on-Avon," "John Bull" and "The Stagecoach." To these *English Scenes Seen by an American Visitor* he added six American scenes including "Rip Van Winkle" and "The Legend of Sleepy Hollow." In March of the following year, he sent them off to New York and over the summer was delighted to learn of their success.

On the morning of 20 November 1819 Washington Irving received a very unpleasant shock: the offer of a job. Walter Scott proposed that he edit a weekly magazine in Edinburgh for £500 a year, an excellent salary at the time. Irving needed the money, and the offer was a major compliment which made a refusal all the more embarrassing. "I am unfitted for any periodically recurring task, or any stipulated labour of body or mind," he replied. "I have no command over my talents such as they are; am apt to be deserted by them when I most need their assistance and have to watch the veerings of my mind as I would those of a weather cock."

He took this opportunity to tell Scott that his essays had succeeded in America beyond his "most sanguine anticipations," and when Scott came down to London two months later to receive his baronetcy, he persuaded John Murray, the "Prince of Booksellers," to publish *The Sketches*. By summer 1820, Washington Irving was known throughout London. He told his friend Henry Brevoort, "you know Murray's drawing room is a complete rendezvous of men of talent; where you meet with the first characters of the day; and it has been for some time past an almost daily resort of mine." In September, with the book safely behind him and selling well, Washington Irving was joined by his brother Peter and the two of them left for Paris.

Egerton Gardens, Brompton Map F

44   Garden House. William Burroughs lived here for three weeks in May 1956. He had come from Tangiers in the hope that medical treatment under Dr. John Dent in London would rid him of his addiction to drugs. After two weeks, he boasted to Allen Ginsberg, "I am completely recovered now, very active, able to drink." It was then that he discovered the restrictive British licensing hours. After making a long trip to the East End of London to find a pub with a jukebox, he finally located it only ten minutes before closing time. "I have tried to like England," he told Ginsberg, "but it's not possible. I'd sooner live in hell."

Farm Street, Mayfair

(1)   Tallulah Bankhead bought in 1927, a small two-story house over the mews, close to the Jesuit Church of the Immaculate Conception. She had come to London four years earlier at the age of 20 and opened in *The Dancer*. A second-rate melodrama, it nevertheless ran for forty-three weeks. During her eight years in London, which she later described as "the happiest and most exciting of my life," she appeared in sixteen plays, with her salary rising from a modest £30 a week to £500. Finally she could afford a Bentley—dark green and cream, with hood, fenders and body sheathed in leather, it cost £2,400 (a mere $12,000). Her love for elegant cars was well known. In October 1930 the *Daily Mail* announced: "Probate has been granted of the will of Sir Guy

Francis Laking, third baronet, who died in St. George's Hospital, Hyde Park Corner, on August 4, at the age of 26. By his will he left 'to my friend Tallulah Bankhead all my motor-cars.'" Everyone knew that they had been close friends, but few knew that Sir Guy was a prankster. This was his last prank. He didn't own a motor-car.

Tallulah Bankhead developed an enormous following among young women so that, although she never appeared in a great play, she always drew an audience. Arnold Bennett devoted a long article to her mystique:

> It begins on the previous afternoon. At 2 p.m., you see girls, girls, girls in seated queues at the pit and gallery door of the Tallulah theatre. They are a mysterious lot, these stalwarts of the cult. . . . Then the end of the show. The loudest roar and shriek of all. Storms. Thunder and lightning. Gusts. And Tallulah, still virginal, withstanding everything with a difficult smile.

Tallulah was frequently the toast of London, with admirers ranging from England's most eligible young guard officers to Winston Churchill. One day she met the prime minister, Ramsay MacDonald, who invited her to lunch at the Houses of Parliament. After lunch he drove her back to her theater. All the police recognized him and saluted as he drove by. Tallulah recalled getting a great kick out of "tooling down Piccadilly, the prime minister by my side."

Fitzroy Road, Primrose Hill

23   Sylvia Plath moved into this house with her two children in December 1962, excited by the idea that Yeats had lived here for six years. She wrote home that one day she hoped to buy the house. She was recognized as a poet in London, reading at the Royal Court Theatre, participating in programs at the BBC, and her novel *The Bell Jar* was about to be published in London. But there was a darker side to her life. Her husband had left her the preceding summer; she was seeing a psychiatrist and talked in her letters of hoping to be able to "get off sleeping pills." She told her mother that she was going to "face all the people we know and tell them happily and squarely I am divorcing Ted." It was a brave statement, but the winter of 1962 in London was the darkest, coldest and most foggy in almost a hundred years. Her poems began to show a growing detachment from life and an increasing fascination with death, as she searched her own passions with impeccable and ruthless art. She took her life on 12 February 1963. Five years later, these final poems which are considered her finest were published in *Ariel*.

Fleet Street

(135)   Silas Deane arrived in London on 28 March 1783. He told a friend: "I have suffered a compleat shipwreck of fortune and am trying to pick up some of the scattered and broken parts to begin anew."

Born in Groton, Connecticut, he graduated from Yale in 1758. A delegate to the Continental Congress, he was chosen to go to France in April 1776 to obtain arms to fight the British. In Paris, at the suggestion of the French government, he signed a contract with Caron de Beaumarchais and within eighteen months seven shiploads of military supplies reached the American front. In September 1776, Congress sent Benjamin Franklin and Arthur Lee to join him. Two years later, Deane was recalled by Congress to answer accusations of profiteering made by Lee. After numerous appearances and delays lasting a year, with no formal charges brought, Deane was dismissed, a ruined man.

He came back to France, bitter and almost penniless. Thoroughly depressed, in May 1781, he wrote to a friend in America that even if independence were won, one question remained, namely, "whether the revolution must ultimately be considered as a blessing or a curse." Recommending accommodation with Britain, he gave the sealed letter to his longtime American friend, Dr. Edward Bancroft, for mailing home. But Bancroft, unbeknownst to Deane, was a spy in the pay of the British, and sent a copy to London. The British published the letter in New York as part of their propaganda to convince reasonable Americans to abandon the war; Deane's enemies were quick to characterize his recommendation as tantamount to treason.

Meanwhile Deane's presence in Paris had become an embarrassment to both Benjamin Franklin and to the French. With a small gift from the French government, he moved first to the Flemish city of Ghent and then in 1783 to England. In London the charge of treason levied in America was somehow confirmed by a most unexpected incident. One afternoon during his first week in Fleet Street, as he was discussing the possibility of land sales in upper New York State with some Americans, there was a knock at the door. Unable to afford a servant, Deane bade the person enter. Benedict Arnold walked in. The two men had not met since 1775. After a five minute chat, Deane escorted Arnold out and asked him not to return. But the damage was done. Two months later news of their meeting appeared in American gazettes and the names Deane and Arnold became linked as traitors. In an effort to exculpate himself Deane called on his longtime friend the diplomat John Jay at 30 Harley Street. He was not invited in. Later he wrote two letters. Finally, Jay replied: "You are either exceedingly injured or you are no friend to America; and while doubt remains on that point, all connexion between us must be suspended. I was told by more than one that you received visits and were on terms of familiarity with Gen. Arnold. Every American who gives his hand to that man, in my opinion, pollutes it."

In August 1788, he fell ill and spent four months confined to his chambers. "In this state advantage was taken," Deane told his brother, "and I was plundered of almost all my cloathes, and many papers of importance." Later that month in Paris, a man called on Thomas Jefferson with Deane's account book and letter book offering to sell them. Complaining that Deane had taken him for 120 guineas, and unable to obtain other satisfaction, he had laid his hands (he did not say how!) on these important papers. Jefferson confided to John Jay: "On the perusal of many of them, I thought it desirable that they should not come to the hands of the British Minister." He felt that he could obtain the damaging material for 50 or 60 guineas and added: "Indeed, I would have given that sum to have cut out a single sentence which contained evidence of a fact not proper to be committed to the hands of enemies." Jay approved of the purchase and advised Jefferson to buy the remaining six or eight volumes. Jefferson replied that as he knew that this contact would make them pay dear, he would write to a friend in London "to endeavor to purchase them from Deane himself, whose distresses and crapulous habits will probably render him more easy to deal with." The friend in London was none other than the spy Dr. Bancroft. By September, Deane was up and about and feeling better and Bancroft replied that there existed no other books. This was totally untrue, but it satisfied Jefferson.

On 22 September 1789, Deane, aged 52, boarded the packet *Boston* off Deal, Kent, on his way to Canada. On the following day, he was mysteriously taken ill and died. The *Gentleman's Magazine* wrote at length of him and concluded: "The epicedium of Mr. Deane may be this: He was second to very few politicians in knowledge, plans, designs and execution; deficient only in placing confidence in his compatriots, and doing them service before he got his compensation, of which no well-bred politician was before him ever guilty." In 1842, Congress voted his heirs $37,000 as a partial restitution of his expenses and his reputation.

Garden Court, Middle Temple

(2) Arthur Lee moved into chambers here in 1770. A member of the famous Lee family of Westmoreland County, Virginia, he had been educated at Eton, and then took a medical degree at Edinburgh and returned home. He soon tired of practicing medicine in Williamsburg, and returned to London to become a lawyer. Here with his brother William, he represented the Mississippi Company in land speculation, became a partisan of John Wilkes, and started writing political pamphlets explaining to the British the causes of American unrest and warning them of the consequences. He soon became the spokesman for the radicals of Massachusetts with the approval of Samuel Adams. When his request to the British government for a royal grant for his family of 2.5 million acres at the confluence of the Ohio and Mississippi rivers was turned down, he construed this answer as being "truly antiamerican." Apparently unconscious of his persistent ambitions for himself and his family, he nourished the self-image of an austere practitioner of self-denial, a sort of ideal New Englander. But his correspondence reveals his need for office, position and power. Seeking to replace Benjamin Franklin as agent of Massachusetts in London, he complained of the old man's "cunning," lamenting to Samuel Adams: "Dr. Franklin frequently assures me that he shall sail for Philadelphia in a few weeks; but I believe that he will not quit us until he is gathered to his fathers."

In 1774, Lee published *An Appeal to the Justice and Interests of Great Britain*. After a solid argument which concluded that "taxation and representation are constitutionally inseparable," Lee maintained that if the British coercive policy were maintained,

America would revolt within five years and France would intervene. Four editions of *An Appeal* appeared in England within six months and one in New York.

In 1775, Franklin finally left England and Lee took over the agency for Massachusetts. He also passed the bar examinations. That December, the Committee of Secret Correspondence chose Lee as one of their two European agents. They asked for knowledge of "the disposition of foreign powers to us" and reminded the 35-year-old Lee that his task required "great circumspection and impenetrable secrecy." A week later, while dining with London's new lord mayor, John Wilkes, he was introduced by his host to the French playwright, Caron de Beaumarchais, whose comedy *The Barber of Seville* had just opened in London. Having gathered from Beaumarchais that he sympathized with the American cause and that he had important connections at Versailles, Lee discreetly invited him to his lodgings. In February 1776, Lee made American needs clear to Beaumarchais: munitions, arms, cannon, picks, shovels, tents, blankets, material for uniforms, and perhaps the aid of two artillery experts. In exchange, Lee, going far beyond his instructions, promised a secret treaty of commerce which would enable France to reap all the benefits which had enriched England. Beaumarchais hurried back to Versailles where he outlined Lee's request and his offer to come in person to France.

The French had no desire to have someone as compromising as Lee in France. Beaumarchais was chosen as the intermediary and over the next three months, he called on Lee four times here in Garden Court. (These meetings were carefully noted by British authorities.) He explained to Lee that France was prepared to help the American rebels, but could not do so openly for it would lead to war with England. In a meeting on 26 May, Beaumarchais outlined his plan. He was forming a private trading company, with the tacit approval of the French authorities, to ship military supplies to America, which Congress would pay for with tobacco. Secrecy was essential. Lee agreed and Beaumarchais returned to Paris. But in July, Silas Deane arrived in Paris from Philadelphia, fully empowered by Congress to obtain supplies to equip an army of 25,000 men. Deane was sent by French Foreign Minister Vergennes to see Beaumarchais and the two men soon signed a contract. Over the next eighteen months, seven shiploads of French military supplies reached American shores. Lee was furious when he discovered that he had been bypassed. He wrote to Congress that the arms were in reality a secret gift from the French court and that Deane and Beaumarchais were billing Congress falsely. In October 1776, Congress appointed Lee as a commissioner to France to join Benjamin Franklin and Silas Deane. He left London two months later for Paris.

George Street Map A

5 Bryanston Court One. Mrs. Wallis Simpson and her husband Ernest took a flat here directly above the main entrance on the second floor in 1930. It comprised three bedrooms, a drawing room, a dining room, a modern kitchen, and four servants' rooms elsewhere in the same building. Mrs. Simpson decorated the flat aided by Syrie Maugham, the wife of the novelist. Once a week she sat and listened to her husband go over the household accounts. He made meticulous notes in his tiny handwriting in a ledger, recording the purchase of every pound of sugar and each bottle of vinegar. There was little of the skylark in Ernest Simpson. One of her more exciting acquaintances was the young American beauty, Lady Thelma Furness, wife of the British shipping magnate, twin sister of Gloria Vanderbilt, and close friend of the Prince of Wales. It was through Lady Furness that Mrs. Simpson met the future king of England. From 1933 onwards, the prince began to drop in here at Bryanston Court about 5 p.m. for a drink after a long day at the palace. Mr. Simpson got back from the city about 7 p.m. and sometimes their guest would stay on for dinner. The Simpsons were invited occasionally for weekends at the prince's hideaway, Fort Belvedere, a pseudo-Gothic hodge-podge in Windsor Great Park. Within a year, although the British public knew nothing, all of Mayfair was aware that Wallis Simpson had replaced Lady Furness in the affections of the prince. Mr. Simpson was a model of discretion, appearing less and less at Fort Belvedere and traveling further and further abroad on business. Finally the Simpsons separated. Mrs. Simpson was invited to Balmoral, the royal castle in Scotland where, as she wrote in her book, *The Heart Has Its Reasons,* she introduced "the three-decker toasted sandwich as a late supper item." But a little incident took place on the day of her arrival. The prince had been due to open the new Aberdeen Infirmary, but had asked to be excused as he was still in mourning for his late father. That same day, however, he was seen meeting Mrs. Simpson at the Ballater train station. Local gossips went quickly to work, and by the time she returned to London there were already references to the Balmoral "episode." Mrs. Simpson spent a week at Claridge's Hotel, before moving to CUMBERLAND TERRACE.

Gloucester Place

(18)   Benedict Arnold and his wife Peggy spent their last years here. They had first arrived in England in January 1782 from New York. Peggy, an exceedingly beautiful young woman and the daughter of Edward Shippen, the chief justice of Pennsylvania, had been most apprehensive. Away from home for the first time, the wife of a traitor to a cause which had many friends in England, she faced presentation at court. Her part in helping her husband escape from West Point by feigning madness was well known. Arnold, protected by his arrogance, had been much less concerned. His attempts to deliver West Point and its garrison to the British had not failed for lack of trying. If he had not achieved the kind of glory under British colors that he had once achieved while an American, it was due to jealousy and suspicion on the part of senior British officers who had prevented him from obtaining a command where he might again have shone. What was important to Arnold was that the people who mattered in London should accept him—and most of them did. Lord Germain, who had directed British strategy during the war, treated him with respect. Sir Guy Carleton, governor of Canada, gave him his arm on his introduction to the court, a small gesture but a significant one. The Prince of Wales, heir apparent to the throne and the future George IV, made a point of strolling arm-in-arm with the hawk-nosed American hero in Vauxhall Gardens. George III was kind and considerate and wanted his views. When the news of the surrender of the British army at Yorktown reached London, most Englishmen considered the war lost, but the king wished to continue the conflict, fearing that if he did not get the colonies back into the empire his political and personal prestige would diminish. At the request of the king, Arnold drew up his *Thoughts on the American War*. His plan, to bring the colonies back into allegiance, was an odd compound of common sense and total nonsense. Most Americans, he contended, could not express their dissatisfaction with the United States because they were excluded from elections. The farmer groaned under his taxes, Congress was bankrupt, American currency was worthless, the Continental army was rife with desertion and with the French army going home, a new opportunity was about to arise. Much of this was true, but the point that Arnold, and the king as well, failed or refused to see was that Americans in 1782 would never consent to a reunion with England. History had moved ahead of both George III and Benedict Arnold.

Arnold was paid £6,000 for his defection. (He claimed that he had been promised £10,000 by Major André.) He was issued a permanent commission as a colonel in the British army with a salary of £450 a year until the end of the war and then half pay for the rest of his life. Both George III and the queen were taken with his wife Peggy, who received a pension of £500 for the rest of her life, plus a pension for each of their five surviving children. Arnold's three sons by his first marriage all received commissions in the British army. It was a handsome settlement but Arnold's love of extravagant living soon forced him into commerce. Enterprising by nature, he bought a brig, the *Lord Middleton* and, leaving his family in London, sailed to the new loyalist settlement of St. John, New Brunswick, where he landed in November 1785. He set up as a merchant but soon found that his reputation had preceded him. Although he made money, he was distrusted and frequently hated, and within two years he was back in England.

Like most former Americans in London, the Arnolds had no English friends. They frequented a number of loyalists, drawn together by common tragedy, living saddened and increasingly embittered lives. They were friends with Samuel Fitch, who had been advocate general to the admiralty court in Boston and had fled with his family to London. There was William Vassal, former high sheriff of Middlesex County in Massachusetts, and Daniel Coxe, a member of the governor's council in New Jersey—all were painfully aware of their poverty, their exile and their colonial origins.

One day Arnold and his wife were spied in Westminster Abbey reading the following inscription: "Sacred to the memory of Major John André, who, raised by his merit, at an early period of life, to the rank of Adjutant-General of the British forces in America, and, employed in an important but hazardous enterprise, fell a sacrifice to his zeal for his King and Country, on the 2nd of October, 1780, aged twenty-nine, universally beloved and esteemed by the army in which he served, and lamented even by his foes. His gracious Sovereign, King George III, has caused this monument to be erected." Arnold must have wondered what inscription, if any, would be found on his own tomb. The answer was none.

Benedict Arnold died on Sunday morning, 12 June 1801, at the age of 60, and was buried at St. Mary's in Battersea. The *Gentleman's Magazine* recorded that "seven mourning coaches and four state carriages formed the cavalcade." Peggy Arnold moved to nearby Bryanston Street where she died in 1804.

Golden Square

(14)   Thomas Jefferson took rooms here on 11 March 1786. The square was still very fashionable; half a century later, when Dickens placed Ralph Nickleby's gloomy house here, the square had deteriorated. Jefferson had come to London from Paris at the urging of John Adams who welcomed him to his home in GROSVENOR SQUARE. The two American statesmen hoped to profit from the presence of the ambassador of Tripolitania to settle the question of the seizure of American ships by Barbary Coast pirates. On 18 March, Jefferson and Adams were received at a levee by George III and the queen. Jefferson thought it "impossible for anything to have been more ungracious than their notice of Mr. Adams and myself." This rude reception confirmed Jefferson's opinion of the British that "of all nations on earth, they require to be treated with the most hauteur. They require to be kicked into common good manners." A few days later Jefferson was received by the Marquis of Carmarthen, the minister for foreign affairs, and having proposed a possible treaty of commerce between the two countries, noted the "vagueness and evasions of his answers to us." It was obvious, he told Richard Henry Lee, that the English "feel we shall be glad of their commerce on their terms." Jefferson was a frequent visitor to the theater, at Drury Lane and Covent Garden. He attended dinner parties, patronized a London tailor and sat for his first portrait, done by fellow American Mather Brown for £10. He consulted Copley, West and Trumbull regarding the statue of George Washington which was being designed for the state of Virginia. They all concurred that it should be done in modern dress rather than classical garb, thus going against English tradition at the time. Nevertheless Jefferson was delighted by the ingenuity of English artisans. "The mechanical arts in London are carried to a wonderful perfection," he observed. He felt particularly that the use of steam was "likely to have extensive consequences." As for the booksellers, "the splendor of their shops," he told a friend, "is all that is worth looking at in London." The English garden charmed him, "it excels all the earth." Accompanied by John Adams, Jefferson took a postchaise and visited Hampton Court, Birmingham, Worcester, Blenheim and Oxford. At Stratford-on-Avon, they visited the bard's house. "They showed us an old wooden chair in the chimney corner where he sat," recorded Adams. "We cut off a chip according to custom." On 26 April Jefferson was happy to leave England for, as he told a friend, "this nation hates us, their Ministers hate us, and their King more than any other man." (For an idea of Golden Square as it was in Jefferson's day, look at the building, numbered 23 and 24, which houses the Portuguese embassy.)

Gower Street, Bloomsbury

(104)   John Gunther and his wife Frances lived here from April 1935 until September 1936. Correspondent for the Chicago *Daily News* in Vienna for five years, he was suddenly tranferred to London. He began writing *Inside Europe,* the first in the famous series, here on Gower Street and in his office in Bush House on Aldwych. He took seven months to finish the writing, revising until the last moment as new political events occurred. One morning a startled secretary found him still at his typewriter in Bush House at 9 a.m. *Inside Europe* was published in England by Hamish Hamilton in February 1936, where its sales were greater than any other work of non-fiction by an American since Mark Twain. In the *Daily Telegraph* Harold Nicolson wrote: "Fair, intelligent, balanced, well informed... it will provide the intelligent reader with exactly that sort of information on current affairs which he desires to possess." In September 1936 Gunther resigned from the Chicago *Daily News*, returned to America and began work on *Inside Asia.*

Gracechurch Street

(30)   An impecunious 21-year-old, Gilbert Stuart moved here in the fall of 1776. He lodged with the female cousins of his good friend Benjamin Waterhouse, a medical student who was to become the first American physician to establish inoculation as a general practice. Stuart had already proved his potential as a portrait painter by a series of brilliant first sketches, but he never completed them. This fact had escaped his friend Waterhouse who, anxious to help, "devised another plan to benefit him":

> Dr. George Fordyce, a very learned Scotch physician, whose medical and chemical lectures, I every morning attended in Essex Street, during between two and three years, was a philosophical physician much admired by his pupils, I proposed to my fellow-students to procure a fine engraving of our favorite teacher. The proposal took at once, and I was authorized to have the portrait taken by my friend and companion, Gilbert Charles Stuart, and they each one paid me their half-guinea subscription, and I was unwise enough to let my needy friend have the greater part of it before he commenced the painting, which I never could induce him even to begin. This was a source of inexpressible unhappiness and mortification, which at length brought on me a fever, the only dangerous disease I ever encountered. After my recovery I had to refund the money, when I had not a farthing of my own, but what came from the thoughtful bounty of my most excellent kinsman, Dr. Fothergill, who would never afterwards see Gilbert Charles Stuart.

Stuart finally called upon Benjamin West in NEWMAN STREET where he began his career as a serious painter.

Great Marlborough Street

(46)   Washington Irving took rooms here on 16 July 1821. He had spent the winter in Paris writing plays with his friend John Howard Payne and had returned to London to prepare *Bracebridge Hall*, a series of romantic sketches, and a sequel to *The Sketch Book*. Three days after his arrival he witnessed the coronation of 60-year-old George IV at Westminster Abbey:

> There was a magnificent procession of all the nobility in their robes and jewels and coronets; and the judges in their gowns and

wigs; and all the other functionaries in their proper costumes. All the world was there; holyday was given in all the Schools; the Servants were permitted to look out of the garret windows in the streets where the procession did not pass; in those where it did, every window was hired out for several golden guineas; you have no idea what sums of money were expended by the nobility and the gentry; even my Landlady had an old silk gown made quite new for the occasion, and her two daughters had red morocco shoes and coronation ribbands on their hats. The King looked amazingly grand; dressed in a huge robe of ermine and velvet, with a splendid crown, and long ringlets hanging down his back. I was quite surprized to see the old gentleman with such a fine head of hair, until I was told that it was false; but that it was the rule for the King to have long flowing ringlets on his coronation day; because the kings wore them in old times. He had so much clothes on that he had to employ six lads to help him carry it.

A few days later, Washington Irving unexpectedly received a letter from the Trustees of Columbia College in New York City conferring on him the diploma of Master of Arts. In his acceptance letter he wrote that "nothing is nearer to my heart than the desire of meriting the good opinion of my countrymen; and, above all of my Townsmen." That sentence was intended to silence the critics who were already suggesting that America's most popular writer preferred to live in Europe. Irving came to Europe in 1815 and stayed seventeen years, in spite of all his protestations of missing home. One thing was certain that summer: for all his new found popularity, the 38-year-old bachelor missed his friends in Paris. "Sitting here in smoky London, scribbling to the tolling of church bells, on a rainy Sunday, I have no home here in London to dine at on Sundays, with a family circle to make me feel as if I were among my own."

By scribbling, Irving was referring to his professional writing, which advanced steadily. The manuscript of *Bracebridge Hall* was ready by December and he sent a copy to New York to secure the copyright. In London, John Murray brought the book out in May 1822 paying the author the handsome sum of 1,000 guineas. But the anxiety of seeing the book through the press brought on a recurrence of Irving's lameness and swelling in the ankles. Before leaving England to take the waters in Wiesbaden, he accepted an invitation from the very wealthy Thomas Hope, who had furnished his house, Deepdene, "in a style of taste and magnificence of which I can give you no idea," wrote Irving, "yet with all this they are delightfully frank, simple and unpretending." Like many Americans who had been guests in large English country homes, Irving added that this was "the true place to see English people to advantage."

> We breakfast at ten, excepting such as choose to breakfast in their own rooms; which is at every one's option. The breakfast is tea, coffee, eggs, hot rolls, bread etc. After breakfast the company lounge about either in their room, the library, the drawing room, grounds or garden. At one o'clock, the bell rings again for *Lunch* (i.e. the Luncheon) this is a meal of some importance. There are several hot dishes; such as poultry, light dishes of cutlets, etc., with cold meats, tarts, fruits, wines etc. After Lunch there are several hours to get rid of it by reading, lounging about the apartments, retiring to your room to read, write, etc. strolling about the grounds, driving or riding about the neighborhood. At half past six the bell rings to give warning that dinner is at hand; when the company retire to their rooms to dress for dinner—as dinner is a meal at which the fashionable world in England always appear in full dress. At seven o'clock the second dinner bell rings, when the company assemble in the drawing room and in a little while the dinner is announced as served, when all repair to the dining room. After the ladies retire from table and the gentlemen have sat some time over their wine (which they do not sit by any means so long at as formerly) coffee is announced, when the gentlemen join the ladies in the drawing room, or library which are adjoining, and take coffee. This is generally between nine and ten. Tea is served up shortly after, at which one of the ladies presides, and the evening is passed in conversation; music; and lively little games which the English have learnt from the French, and which task the ingenuity and call out the invention and agreeable talents of the company. Some cool beverage such as lemonade etc. is brought in towards the latter part of the evening and about twelve o'clock, the company breaks up for the night.

Irving thus describes a way of life where from fifteen to fifty guests would spend up to a week together. This was not the hunting season, when the men and a few of the women would be gone much of the day. Such a style of hospitality, at its height in the 19th century, was largely abandoned with the coming of World War I and totally given up after 1939.

*Street urchins in the East End of London
in 1893.
(See page 69.)*

Queen Victoria's Jubilee procession in Trafalgar Square.
June 1887.
(See page 216.)

*Insert: Harriet Beecher Stowe's model for Uncle Tom,
Josiah Henson, being received by Queen Victoria.
(See page 245.)*

Above: Morley's Hotel in Trafalgar Square. (See page 265.)
Below: Homes for poor Londoners built by George Peabody.
(See page 197.)

Great Ormond Street

(37)   Conrad Aiken took rooms here in June 1920 and stayed three months. After graduating from Harvard in 1911 as Class Poet, he had come to Europe where he had begun what he termed his own education in poetry and in sex. One had led him to his friend from Harvard T.S. Eliot in Paris, and the other to "Irene," a prostitute in Leicester Square. He had returned to Cambridge the following year and married a senior at Radcliffe, Jessie McDonald. They had spent a chilly autumn in London where Aiken wrote a narrative poem of 460 lines about a street walker, "a girl who falls in love with one of her customers, lives with him for a time, then is drawn by circumstances and her conscience to give him up." The poem, called "Leicester Square" was published in the *Little Review*.

In 1920, Aiken came alone to Great Ormond Street with the idea of setting up a home for his wife and two children. He used to lunch with T.S. Eliot, who worked at Lloyd's Bank, and discuss the advantages and disadvantages of living in England. "Eliot is here for life," he told his wife. Later, when the author of *The Love Song of J. Alfred Prufrock* had a nervous breakdown, Aiken told a friend that Eliot's problem was due, he suspected, "to the strain of being an Englishman." By the end of the summer, Aiken had decided to return to America and join his family in South Yarmouth on Cape Cod. As he explained to Eliot, "I cannot work here. I find your adopted people unexpectedly stifling and sterile. It is a nation of 'shut-in personalities.'" Aiken had fallen into the dilemna of so many Americans who live in England. They begin to miss America, return home—and then begin to miss England. After a year in South Yarmouth, Aiken returned to London with his family, telling a friend, "Now that I've weathered the first front, I like England hugely. They're a damned intelligent family." He could think of worse things, he added, "than spending one's life here." They took a flat in Notting Hill before moving to Rye, Sussex, where, a stone's throw from Henry James's Lamb House, they bought Jeake's House built in 1689. Aiken settled down to writing and earned money by editing a very popular anthology of American verse for Secker's, in London. In 1924 he also edited Emily Dickinson's *Selected Poems* which established her literary reputation.

Great Queen Street

(59)　　　Freemasons' Hall. The first World Anti-Slavery Convention opened on 12 June 1840 with over five hundred delegates present. Two American delegations, Massachusetts and Pennsylvania, were headed by William Garrison, Elizabeth Cady Stanton and Lucretia Mott. A royal ruckus broke out on the first morning when the British Executive Committee unanimously determined that "ladies were inadmissible as delegates," but it graciously accorded them permission to sit in the balcony on condition they not speak. The greatest opposition to women came from the British clergy who argued that woman's subjection had been divinely decreed when Eve was created. The Reverend A. Harvey rose, bible in hand, and professed great respect for women—within their sphere. He believed that if he gave his vote for women to vote and speak in such an assembly, he would be acting in opposition to the word of God. An American delegate, George Bradburn, speaking with a voice like thunder, declared that if the clergy could prove to him "that the Bible taught the entire subjection of one-half of the human race to the other" the best thing he could do for humanity would be to bring together all the bibles of the universe and make a bonfire of them. But no one can beat the British on rules of procedure and in a second vote women were again excluded. Thus many remarkable women come from throughout the world, wrote Elizabeth Cady Stanton, were condemned "to listen in silence to the masculine platitudes on woman's sphere." William Garrison and a number of the American male delegates withdrew from the assembly floor and spent the twelve days in the gallery in silence. All the American delegates shared rooms at 6 Queen Street Place, but since some of the men accepted the exclusion of women, there were "discussions at every meal...heated and at times so bitter" that some sought more peaceful quarters. During the weeks which followed, Elizabeth Stanton became close friends with Lucretia Mott, a broad, liberal thinker who opened "a new world of thought" for her. After their return home the two women organized the first woman's rights convention in the United States held in 1848 in Seneca Falls, New York.

Great Russell Street Map B

(55)　　　John James Audubon took lodgings here on 21 May

1827. He had brought over his drawings of American birds and was looking for an engraver for the series which he hoped to sell by subscription in England. He received an invitation to dinner from the naturalist John Children, secretary of the Royal Society, and at the insistence of his friend, Bentley, he bought a new black suit and sallied forth "attired like a mournful raven." The following morning he learned with joy that the Earl of Derby had put his name down as a subscriber. An hour later, Bentley dropped in with the news that three men had just been hanged at Newgate for stealing a sheep. "My God!" Audubon wrote, "how awful are the laws of this land, to take a human life for the theft of a miserable sheep." He was to dislike England more and more, partly because the contrast between the rich and the poor was a "torment" to him; furthermore, the only birds in Great Russell Street were sparrows. But London possessed more skilled engravers in one alley than in all of Philadelphia, and the 42-year-old Audubon had to get his life's work published and sold. At ten guineas for each set of five engravings, only the wealthy could afford them and the wealthy lived in London. By July, he had selected an engraver, Robert Havell, and for the next two years, every day and "often several times a day" he would walk the quarter mile to 79 Newman Street where he went over Havell's work. In the evenings he spoke before groups in clubs and public halls and displayed his portfolio. He was invited to almost every important house in London, "the Marquis of Lansdowne, Lord Grey, Stuart, Auckland etc. My work was praised sky-high, and yet I only had one copy ordered, I mean a Subscriber for the whole." As he told his beloved Lucy in Bayou Sarah, Louisiana, "I do anything for money now a days—I positively last week made 22 Pounds 10 shillings by drawing trifles in a Scotch Lady's Album. That enabled me to purchase six Gilt frames to forward six Pictures to the Liverpool Exhibition." These oil paintings included a duck, a rabbit, common fowl, pigeons, a partridge and an otter. Each measured 42 by 28 inches and were priced at twenty to thirty guineas apiece. By the end of the first year, he had one hundred subscribers and a profit of over £500. His plan was to bring over his wife and their two sons and to stay five years. Toward the end of 1827 he moved to 95 Great Russell Street, "about 500 yards from the British Museum," where the light in the studio was better. But something unexpected slowly began to happen to him. As he worked on his paintings of black cocks, grouse and white-headed eagles, and finished his drawings of branches of hickory and black walnut, he grew homesick. "I see the very spot where my gun felled such or such a Bird and I almost enjoy my life in the woods a second time." So he decided to go home, leaving the edition in the very capable hands of engraver Robert Havell and John Children of the British Museum. After drawing up a contract with the two men who had become his good friends, Audubon sailed from Portsmouth on 1 April 1829. Audubon's *Birds of America,* color engravings of some five hundred species, was issued serially in an elephant folio edition between 1827 and 1838 in London where it enjoyed a major success. It enabled Havell to move to a more prestigious address on Oxford Street.

British Museum. To Ernest Hemingway:

> Dear Pappy:
>
> I can't think of any more appropriate place to write you from than the reading room of the British Museum with Englishmen as thick as Englishmen & a draft on the back of my neck which I can feel in my balls. (I think it is my balls.) I'm writing about the King of England. You remember him.

The writer was Archibald MacLeish who had come to England for *Fortune* to cover the 25th anniversary of King George V's accession to the throne on 6 May 1935. He told Hemingway that he had just seen forty horses lined up on the royal parade ground with a man in front of each horse blowing a trombone and another waving a flag. The object was to get the horses used to fanfare. The sight had made him fall over with laughter.

Great Titchfield Street, Marylebone

(132)   Washington Allston, a handsome 21-year-old artist from Charleston, South Carolina, arrived in London in June 1801, with his Harvard classmate and traveling companion, Edward Greene Malbone. The two men shared rooms here until November.

Allston made a drawing of the Royal Academy's plaster *Gladiator,* showed it to Benjamin West and was admitted in October as a student in the Royal Academy of Arts. The 24-year-old Malbone, a self-taught painter of miniatures, was honored when West "condescended to walk a mile to pay me a visit and told me that I must not look forward to anything short of the highest excellence." After looking at a miniature portrait of Allston done by Malbone in water colors on ivory, West declared that he had seldom seen a miniature that pleased him more. Yet, after working at the academy for a few months, Malbone astonished Allston by declaring that he had nothing more to learn in England and returned to Charleston. In America, his miniatures, noted for their grace and delicacy in tone, brought him great success, but his career was cut short by tuberculosis in 1807.

Allston, who became known as America's first fully-fledged Romantic artist, felt at home in England, although he harbored few illusions about London and its citizens. To a friend he wrote:

> Figure to yourself the extremes of misery and splendor, and you will have a better idea of it than I can give you. Scarcely a luxury but you may command here; and scarcely a scene of wretchedness but you may witness at the corner of every street. Indeed, the whole city appears to be composed of princes and beggars. I had no idea before of pride unaccompanied by some kind of merit. But here no one has pride without fortune. Indeed, the most respectable among the middle ranks appear to have no consequence excepting in boasting of the acquaintance of some one in rank; and among the greater part, so shameful is their venality, they will condescend to flatter the most infamous for a penny.

Allston left the Royal Academy in 1803 and, with another American painter, John Vanderlyn, set off for Paris and then Rome.

Grosvenor Square   Map C

Since Abigail and John Adams took a house here in 1785, an American presence in Grosvenor Square has been almost uninterrupted. Indeed, so many buildings were occupied by the American military high command during World War II that the square was nicknamed "Eisenhowerplatz." Today the American embassy occupies the west side while in the center stands the British memorial to President Franklin D. Roosevelt. The maximum contribution permitted in 1945 for this memorial was five shillings; the cost was raised in one day by 200,000 donations. The bronze was unveiled by Mrs. Roosevelt in 1948.

9   The choice of John Adams as first minister plenipotentiary to Britain could hardly have been bettered. One of the first to protest against the Stamp Act, he had helped in framing the Declaration of Independence and in drafting the Peace Treaty in Paris. The 50-year-old great-grandson of a Devon yeoman was plump, and rosy-cheeked, with masterful blue eyes and a strong firm mouth. It was frequently said that he looked like a typical John Bull, a description which rankled and moved him to declare vehemently: "I am an American." It was Abigail Adams who found the house, as she told her sister, thanks to her "good genius." It is one of the two original houses in the square to have survived. Adams signed a 21-month lease in June 1785 for £160 per annum. The house was not as large as their mansion in Paris, but with four stories and a kitchen in the basement it was ample for a small family. The following month, Adams's 19-year-old daughter Nabby described the house to her younger brother John Quincy. The dining room of state, "which will hold 15 persons with ease," was on the ground floor while another ground-floor room served as the family dining room. Off this was a "long room" which their father had turned into "an office for doing Publick business." The main drawing room was on the first floor next to a small " ommon sitting parlour" and another "very small one which serves to breakfast and sit in." Another "long room," presumably over that downstairs, was where "Pappa has put his Library—and in which he usually writes himself." Nabby's own bedroom was on the third floor from which she could see "the tops of all the Houses which surround us—and I can count a hundred Chimneys."

Abigail was delighted with Grosvenor Square, telling her sister: "It is one of the finest squares in London. The air is as pure as it can be so near a great city. It is but a small distance from Hyde Park, round which I sometimes walk but oftener ride. It resembles Boston Common, much larger, and more beautiful with trees." Across the square lived Lord North, the British prime minister during the War of Independence. The thought of having their former enemies as neighbors amused Abigail, who remarked, "We have not taken a *side* with Lord North but are still *opposite* to him."

Life in London was expensive. Eight servants were necessary; they lived on the top floor. Entertainment was part of diplomatic life. On 1 October 1785, Abigail told her sister, "yesterday the whole diplomatic corps dined here; that is, his Lordship the

Marquis of Carmarthen, and all the foreign ministers, fifteen in all." It was usual, continued Abigail, "at a large entertainment, to bring the solid food in the first course. The second consists of lighter diet, kickshaws, trifles, whip syllabub etc.; the third is the dessert, consisting of the fruits of the season, and sometimes foreign sweetmeats. As good luck would have it, Captain Hay returned from the West Indies, and presented us with a noble turtle, weighing a hundred and fourteen pounds, which was dressed upon this occasion." At this first large dinner no women were present, and Abigail arranged to sup with friends.

The presence of fifteen foreign ministers signified a diplomatic success—namely the increasing recognition of the United States—but the real objects of Adams's stay in London were never achieved during his tenure. He had come to resolve three issues: the British evacuation of the western outposts at Ogdensburg, Erie, Niagara, Oswego, Sandusky and Mackinac; the settlement of American debts to British creditors, and a treaty of commerce between the two nations. But Adams quickly discovered that the British saw no advantage in a commercial treaty since, as he told John Jay, "in all events this country is sure of American commerce." Equally disturbing was the British belief "that the American States are not, and cannot be, united," a belief constantly reaffirmed by American loyalists in England. As long as individual states retained individual rights in foreign commerce, Adams felt that he was wasting his time in London. On the issue of prewar debts owed by the new American citizens to British subjects, Britain had reason to complain. Abigail explained to her sister: "the immense debt, due from the mercantile part of America to this country, sours this people beyond measure.... Indeed I pity their situation ... at the same time I think our countrymen greatly to blame." But faults lay on both sides: the British navy continued to impress American seamen, even in the Port of London, and many an American sea captain arrived in bitter mood at the door of 9 Grosvenor Square. In a letter of 22 September 1787 to the Marquis of Carmarthen, the British foreign secretary, Adams described such a visit:

> His name is John Douglass, commander of the ship Four Friends, American built, and the property of Andrew Van Tuyl, merchant, of New York. He informs me that, as two of his people were going on shore for provisions for the day, they were seized by the press-gang and forced on board his Majesty's brig,

Dispatch, then lying at execution dock; that the gang then came on board his vessel and attempted to open his hatches, when his chief mate opposed them, and informed the officers that they were American citizens.

The gang left, but the captain feared their return before the following morning. This, continued Adams, "will distress him exceedingly, as his ship is completed for sea and bound for New York. The names of the two men pressed are Joseph Cowley, a native of the City of New York; the other is a negro man, called Primus."

Before leaving England, Adams sat for John Trumbull. In 1786 in Paris, Trumbull had begun his most famous painting *The Declaration of Independence* (now in Yale University Art Gallery), probably at the suggestion of his host, Thomas Jefferson. The following summer Trumbull brought the canvas to London where "Mr. Adams was taking leave of the Court of St. James, and preparatory to the voyage to America, had the powder combed out of his hair. Its color and natural curl were beautiful, and I took that opportunity to paint his portrait in the small Declaration of Independence." The Adams family left London on 30 March 1788 and arrived home on 17 June, to a hearty welcome from Governor John Hancock and the people of Boston.

American Embassy. Joseph Kennedy arrived here in a cold steady drizzle on the evening of 1 March 1938; it was, he later decided, symptomatic of his sojourn in London. This was his first appointment as an ambassador and he soon discovered that it did not include the number of prerogatives that he had imagined. A British official had unhesitatingly refused to waive the six-month animal quarantine for the French poodle and Airedale terrier that Mrs. Kennedy wanted to bring over. The law was to prevent the introduction of rabies to England, the official had explained, and the rank of the dog's owner had nothing to do with it. Kennedy was more successful with the British press. A few days after his arrival, when he played golf and shot a hole in one, he quipped to admiring reporters, "I am much happier being the father of nine children and making a hole in one than I would be as the father of one and making a hole in nine." When he received the press in his office here in the embassy, he chewed gum, sat with his feet on the desk and called the queen of England "a cute trick." American reporters were embarrassed; but their English counterparts found him "wonderfully American": wealthy, vulgar, crude, friendly, energetic, accessible and obviously on the make. To Francis Williams, Kennedy seemed to be the tycoon who combined all the disagreeable traits of all the very rich men he had ever met, "with hardly any of their virtues." The British Foreign Office considered him unlearned in history and politics, untrained in diplomacy, a great publicity seeker with an evident desire to become the first Roman Catholic president of the United States. (It was probably his yearnings for the 1940 presidency which had prompted Roosevelt to offer him the post in London.)

Not all impressions of Kennedy were negative, for he knew how to charm. He set out to win the friendship and confidence of Prime Minister Neville Chamberlain and succeeded admirably. When the British foreign secretary, Lord Halifax, toasted him as being "so representative of modern America," Kennedy was delighted. Moreover, Kennedy caused a sensation when he decided to end the practice of the American ambassador presenting American debutantes to the queen, thus sparing himself and his staff from an entire month of confrontation with all the American mothers in England, each maneuvering to get her daughter presented at court. The headline of the Hearst-like *Daily Mirror* read: "Ambassador Stops U.S. Debs Pestering." The *Daily Herald* announced: "Social Climbers Take Tumble." From Washington James Roosevelt cabled: "President greatly pleased. Congratulations!"

There was less praise for his political acumen. Kennedy had worked hard on his first speech, to be delivered before the American-oriented Pilgrims' Club, before submitting a draft to the State Department for clearance. Secretary of State Cordell Hull was upset by its tenor. Just when Germany had absorbed Austria and Hitler was already threatening Czechoslovakia, Kennedy's speech included such statements as: "Our people do not see how we could usefully participate in the adjustments of international relations," and: "I think it is not too much to say that the great bulk of the people is not convinced that any common interest exists between them and any other country." This isolationist tone reflected his own belief and coincided with the desire of Chamberlain and the British cabinet to avoid war at any price. But Hull, himself about to make a speech with an "internationalist" thrust, had Kennedy's draft toned down. To their astonishment, Kennedy then telephoned the State Department and requested that Hull postpone *his* speech so as not to conflict with his own. On 17 March 1938, Hull, with the close support of Roosevelt, said publicly that the failure of America to accept international responsibilities would result, in the long run, in danger to the nation. The next day in London, Kennedy told his British audience—in a speech broadcast to American listeners—that the United States neither intended to attack anyone, nor expected to be attacked, and would act only when and if her own citizens were threatened. It was apparent that Kennedy was already wooing the American electorate all the way from Grosvenor Square.

On 22 September 1938, Kennedy had a long conversation with Charles Lindbergh, who had just returned from a visit to Germany as guest of Hermann Goering, head of the German air force. Lindbergh was convinced that the German air force was stronger than the rest of Europe's combined. Kennedy sent these estimates to Washington, and arranged a meeting between Lindbergh and the British secretary for air, which helped reinforce Chamberlain's opinion that Britain was not sufficiently prepared for war. (Today, however, it is known that German aircraft production was nowhere near as high as Lindbergh had been led to believe.) In his first speech after the Munich Pact, in which England and France acquiesced in the German seizure of much of Czechoslovakia, Kennedy advanced what he termed a pet theory of his own—that "the democracies and dictators should cooperate for the common good, rather than emphasize self-apparent differences." In London, the pro-Chamberlain *Times* found the speech excellent and felt it would contribute to "the final re-establishment of some better system of collective security for peace." In America, however, almost all editorial comment was opposed to Kennedy's stand. The New York *Post* wrote that Kennedy's proposal to make a friend of Hitler was beyond understanding, although, in all fairness, Kennedy had proposed not friendship but appeasement. Now closely associated with the Chamberlain government, he had done what no professional diplomat would ever have done: he had become involved in local politics. Roosevelt decided that, rather than withdraw Kennedy so close to the presidential election in 1940, he would circumvent him. Distrusting Kennedy's analysis of Britain's ability to defend herself, he sent over a series of American observers. Kennedy complained bitterly to Washington and, when Roosevelt began to talk to Churchill directly without informing him, the ambassador resigned. He left England on 22 October 1940.

20   General Eisenhower had his headquarters here in the summer of 1942. Despite his immense popularity with the British press, as the new American commander he had yet to prove himself. He soon established a personal friendship with Vice-Admiral Lord Louis Mountbatten who frequently accompanied him on field exercises. Both men believed in the earliest possible attack against the French coast, a move vigorously opposed by the rest of the British high command. The result was Operation Torch, a compromise, the Anglo-American invasion of North Africa. Eisenhower lived at Claridge's on BROOK STREET. He left for Gibraltar on 2 November 1942.

47   General Eisenhower was named Supreme Commander of the Allied Expeditionary Forces in January 1944 and established his offices here. The planning for the Normandy landings in June, Operation Overlord, took place here. So many Americans were present in London that springtime that Eisenhower preferred to live in Telegraph Cottage on Coombe Hill, Kingston-on-Thames.

Guilford Street, Russell Square Map B

62   Mark Van Doren and Joseph Krutch took "the coldest room in London" in September 1920. Armed with John Gay's *Trivia, or The Art of Walking the Streets of London,* they tramped through the city until settling down to finish their dissertations for Columbia University at the nearby British Museum. In order to meet the English, they persuaded the *Times* to insert in its "agony column" a notice: "Two young Americans, literary, but interested in everything, desire London friends." From the thirty replies, they answered twelve, including those from "several pairs of girls with whom we went for tea and dancing." Both young men returned to New York city where they were to enjoy distinguished careers as writers and faculty members of Columbia University.

Alvin Langdon Coburn from Boston, accompanied by his mother, took rooms in a house on this street in 1899. The following year in the exhibition of the Royal Photographic Society held in nearby Russell Square, the 18-year-old photographer had nine photos among the 375 on display, which included twenty-one by Edward Steichen. Within a few years he had become friends with photographers such as Frederick H. Evans. It was here on Guilford Street that he photographed the well-known English socialist Edward Carpenter, author of *Towards Democracy* (1902). In 1906 Coburn was invited to give a one-man show at the Royal Photographic Society. George Bernard Shaw wrote in the preface to the catalogue: "Mr. Alvin Langdon Coburn is one of the most accomplished and sensitive artist-photographers now living.... Mr. Coburn can handle you as Bellini handled everybody; as Hals handled everybody; as Gainsborough handled everybody." Shaw knew what he was talking about, having been photographed in the nude by Coburn in the pose of Rodin's *The Thinker,* revealing a very muscular and athletic-looking torso. One afternoon Coburn went with Henry James to St. John's Wood to photograph the little gateway and house which served as the illustration for the second volume of *The Tragic Muse.* He did a series of photographs for display in James's novels. He attended the London County Council School of Photo-Engraving in Bolt Court off Fleet Street. In 1904 he wrote to Steiglitz: "After all, there is no place like London." Coburn lived on and off for many years in this city, moving in 1909 to LOWER MALL in Hammersmith.

Half Moon Street, Piccadilly Map C

7   Flemings Hotel—the building dates from 1730. Henry James moved here on 4 March 1869. His dark rooms on the ground floor, decorated with wax flowers, seemed during his first week like "an impersonal black hole in the huge general blackness." He could hear the din of Piccadilly at the end of the street. Homesick and aged 26, he wished he were back in Quincy Street "with my head on my mother's lap and my feet in Alice's!" But a note of hospitality was immediately struck when he was invited to the floor above for breakfast. Here he shared fried sole, toast and marmalade with two young bewhiskered and well-dressed Englishmen who questioned him closely about President Grant's new cabinet. Later, James was delighted to meet fellow Bostonian Charles Eliot Norton, his wife and his sisters. Thanks to Norton, doors opened into "light, and warmth and cheer"; he dined with John Ruskin and visited Rossetti in "the most delicious melancholy

old house at Chelsea." After a month of London life, he told his mother that he was in "the best of health and spirits." During eleven weeks in England, he told his father, he had spent £120 which included a large amount of cab-hire. Such an expenditure drew the inevitable advice from Boston.

Green Park Hotel. Edmund Wilson spent July 1945 here. He was in uniform as an accredited journalist for the *New Yorker* and had arrived in time for the British elections. He accompanied Harold Laski who told him that 1 per cent of the population owned 55 per cent of the total wealth of England and that only 1 per cent of army officers came from working-class parents. On 26 July the new socialist government came to power, led by Clement Atlee; Labour had won 388 seats out of 640, defeating the Conservatives led by Winston Churchill. Wilson was in sympathy with the socialist victory, but again felt enveloped by the fearful drabness of daily life which he had experienced two months earlier in KNIGHTSBRIDGE. Then it had been the theater which provided him with his only joy in London; this time it was the opera. Somewhat against his will, he was taken to see Benjamin Britten's new opera *Peter Grimes* at Sadler's Wells, and suddenly found himself not watching an experiment but living a work of art. The opera possessed him, kept him riveted to his seat during the action and keyed up during the intermission, dropping him at the end "purged and exhausted." Britten had succeeded in harmonizing "the harsh, helpless emotions of wartime." The opera, Wilson felt, could have been written in no other age—it had captured the blind anguish, the hateful rancors and the will to destroy of those years.

His walk home late at night through the newly lit streets was different. He ran the gauntlet of the prostitutes that lined Piccadilly and Green Park. They would brush him with their "Come 'ere sweetie," or a simple "Hullo" in their quiet English voices which, with their pale dim forms, made them seem part of the night, like moths.

Hallam Street, Portland Place Map A

84 Weymouth House. Edward R. Murrow and his wife Janet spent most of World War II in this five-room flat on the second floor, "five hundred paces" (carefully measured in the blackout) from his office in the BBC studios on PORTLAND PLACE. Murrow was on the air live to America six evenings a week at 12:45 a.m. and 3:45 a.m., London time; afterwards, he frequently came home with friends such as Ernie Pyle, Elmer Davis, Vincent Sheean and Quentin Reynolds. They would be joined by other newspaper correspondents from Fleet Street who had finished filing their dispatches for the morning newspapers back home. With a fire burning, coffee on the stove, sandwiches in the kitchen and a bottle of scotch, as London awakened to another gray morning, a poker game would usually be ending. Sometimes with close friends such as Jan Masaryk, foreign minister of the Czech government in exile, John Winant, American ambassador to England, and newspaper man Eric Sevareid, they simply talked through the night.

As Murrow told the story of London in his famed CBS series "This is London," covering the fifty-seven consecutive Luftwaffe night attacks from 7 September to 3 November 1940, chronic fatigue began to tell on him. He became a chain smoker, lost weight, and ground his teeth so badly when he slept on the floor in the BBC shelters that his fellow correspondents and newscasters would awaken him to complain. During the evening before going on the air Murrow would roam London chatting equally with the poor in the East End and the wealthy in Mayfair, searching for stories. In a Mayfair hotel, Murrow found a group of "old dowagers and retired colonels" settled on overstuffed settees in the hotel lobby. It wasn't very safe but, as one colonel put it, "You would at least be bombed with the right sort of people." By 1941 Murrow had become recognized as the most important American newsperson in England. The Blitz was over and during these bleak years he had time for quiet dinners, establishing friendships with British socialist leaders Harold Laski and Ernest Bevin, and with Eleanor Roosevelt and Clark Gable, who were all guests here in Hallam Street.

Hamilton Place, Park Lane Map C

Inn on the Park. Howard Hughes slipped into the Inn at 2:30 a.m. on Christmas morning 1972. The previous forty-eight hours had been hectic for the 67-year-old billionaire recluse. He had been living in Managua, Nicaragua, when it was hit by a major earthquake on 23 December. That evening he flew in a private jet to Fort Lauderdale, Florida, landing at midnight to discover IRS agents waiting to serve him a subpoena. He refused to get off the plane and refused to allow them on. Both sides spent the night making frantic phone calls to Washington, D.C. The IRS was finally called off, for Hughes had recently contributed $100,000 to the 1972 presidential reelection fund at the request of Richard Nixon. He was allowed to leave for London.

Two weeks later in his penthouse suite overlooking Buckingham Palace, Hughes received the sweet news that the U.S. Supreme Court had just reversed all lower court decisions in the case of TWA *vs.* Hughes. He found himself $180 million richer after twelve years of litigation, and British reporters who gathered in the Inn were told by a Hughes aide that he was "absolutely ecstatic." He felt so good that he decided to celebrate and relive his past glory—to fly again. He had not piloted a plane in twelve years. Indeed, he had rarely been out of bed during that time, was poorly coordinated and could not read without a magnifying glass. His pilot's license had expired in the 1950s. He sent out aides to scour London to buy a leather flight jacket and a snap-brim Stetson like the one he had worn back in the 1930s. Five months later on Sunday 10 June, he was driven to Hatfield Airport, just north of London. With his aides resolutely declining his invitation to go aloft, Hughes flew a Hawker Siddeley 748 with an English copilot who hoped to sell him the plane. Fortunately no one was killed. Late on Wednesday night, 19 December 1973, Hughes was smuggled out of the Inn on the Park and whisked to a private airport where, with six of his aides and two doctors, he boarded a private DC-9 and left for the Bahamas.

Hanover Square Map C

(10)   Brunswick House Hotel. Daniel Webster, his wife and his daughter Julia took rooms on 5 June 1839, and were soon "as comfortable as we should have been at our own fireside." On their first morning, Webster left for a "literary breakfast" where he met Wordsworth, Richard Milnes the poet, and Henry Hillam the historian. Carlyle's description sent to Emerson remains famous:

> Not many days ago I saw at breakfast the notablest of all your Notabilities, Daniel Webster. He is a magnificent specimen; you might say to all the world, This is your Yankee Englishman;

limbs such as we make in Yankee land! As a logic-fencer, Advocate, or Parliamentary Hercules, one would incline to back him at first sight against all the extant world. The tanned complexion, that amorphous craglike face; the dull black eyes under their precipice of brows, like dull anthracite furnaces, needing only to be *blown;* the mastiff-mouth, accurately closed: I have not traced as much of silent Bersirkir-rage, that I remember of, in any other man.

At 58, the senator from Massachusetts was well known in England and was seen, indeed saw himself, as a future American president. He was courted in political circles, where he was careful not to appear as spokesman for America. Convivial by nature, he thoroughly enjoyed London society and the unending parties, returning one morning at sunrise from a ball at Buckingham Palace. Mrs. Webster noted, "it is impossible to describe the confusion and excitement we endure daily." Webster, easily recognized in Boston or Philadelphia, enjoyed the anonymity of London. "That is a queer feeling...a stranger in London is in the most perfect solitude in the world. I like these strolls by myself." He frequented the Houses of Parliament where he found the speakers to show excellent temper, politeness and mutual respect. Most of all he was impressed by the amount of work accomplished by members of Parliament:

> They are universally men of business; they have not *six-and-twenty* other legislative bodies to take part of the law making off their hands; and where there is so much to be *done,* it is indispensable that less should be *said.* Their debates, therefore, are often little more than conversations across the table, and they usually abide by the good rule of carrying the measure under consideration *one step,* whenever it is taken up, without adjourning the debate.

After two months in London the Websters toured England and were entertained lavishly on the Earl of Derby's 20,000-acre estate. They stayed at Lowther Castle which, with its quarter-mile-long terrace and forty-six servants, Webster found "a comfortable shelter against the wind." As a Yankee he deplored the idleness of the rich, yet he was drawn to these men of power and enjoyed riding to hounds with his well-bred hosts. The travelers returned to London in time for the wedding on 24 September of Julia to Bostonian Samuel A. Appleton at the historic St. George's Church,

Hanover Square. The following month they visited Paris before returning home.

25 Thomas Wolfe took a service flat here on 26 March 1935 and stayed for two months. *Of Time and the River* had just been published and Wolfe had been drinking in Paris while waiting for the New York reviews. Maxwell Perkins, his editor at Scribner's, cabled him: "Magnificent reviews, somewhat critical in ways expected, full of greatest praise." Even this was not sufficiently reassuring for the 35-year-old writer who cabled back and asked Perkins for the "straight plain truth." His patient editor assured him that his book, a sequel to *Look Homeward, Angel,* was being talked of everywhere as a truly great book: "All comparisons with greatest writers. Enjoy yourself with light heart." If there was one thing that Wolfe was unable to do it was to enjoy himself with a light heart. At least he stopped drinking and came to London where for £25 a week he had a bedroom and a well-furnished living room with a coal fire and excellent maid service. A valet like *Ruggles of Red Gap* brought up breakfast every day and set a morning table with the *Times,* and Wolfe would begin the day with bacon and eggs, kippers, toast, marmalade and tea. During his stay, he got to know the popular English novelist Hugh Walpole. He told Perkins that he had heard that Walpole was unhappy with his American publisher Doubleday, and that he would do all he could to bring him to Scribner's if Perkins was interested. He described Walpole as a "very amiable, genial, robust appearing kind of man," with generous feeling in him toward young writers. He lived in "a magnificent apartment overlooking Green Park, with three flunkies to wait on him." He had "sold out" to success and comfort. During these months in London Wolfe was living off an advance of $2,000 from Scribner's and was torn between scorn and envy of Walpole's lifestyle. Toward the end of April, Wolfe accepted an offer from his German publisher for his latest book, and an invitation to Berlin.

Harley Street Map A

62 William Bingham and his wife arrived in London in July 1783, their first stop in a grand tour of Europe. Bingham had just made his fortune trading in military supplies in the West Indies during the revolution. Anne Bingham, a young American beauty, was described by Abigail Adams as "the finest woman I ever saw." On board ship she began by being seasick, then homesick, and finally morning-sick being three months pregnant, but she survived and soon loved London.

The Binghams first took a house in Bloomsbury Square where the countryside was so close, Bingham wrote, "a carriage could be off the pavements in five minutes." They spent August in Richmond at the country seat of John Penn, grandson of William Penn, and in the fall they moved to this smart residential street leading into Cavendish Square. One of their first American guests was John Jay. Tired from the peace negotiations in Paris, he suffered from acute insomnia and a pain in the chest. His doctor sent him to relax and take the waters at Bath, but Jay preferred living here on Harley Street. He visited the Royal Society at Somerset House where Bingham introduced him to Dr. Richard Price, philosopher and famed defender of American rights. He joined the Binghams at Drury Lane Theatre to see the celebrated Mrs. Siddons in Thomas Otway's *Venice Preserved.* Both Americans also enjoyed the bustle and company at the New York Coffee House near the ROYAL EXCHANGE.

As a merchant and representative of other American merchants, Bingham hoped for a commercial treaty with Britain now that war was over. An independent America had quickly discovered that trade was far more profitable with England than with their ally France. Lord Shelburne, the prime minister, supported such a treaty, but his ministry fell and his successors were reluctant to grant any concessions. The Binghams dined at fashionable Shelburne House in Berkeley Square. (Designed by the famous architect Robert Adam, its typical Adam white-on-gray dining room with its Joseph Rose plaster ceiling was taken to New York and has been reassembled intact in the Metropolitan Museum.) Here they met men such as young William Pitt and Francis Baring, the merchant banker; conversation included the need for an official American representative in England. On 6 November, Bingham asked Dr. Benjamin Rush to "tell Congress of the need to immediately appoint a minister, or a resident to this Court." In another letter to his friend and Congressman Thomas Fitzsimmons, he modestly proposed himself for the post, adding, "It would look too much like parade to have it known that I have made such offers.... I therefore trust to your discretion and delicacy." The post, however, did not go to Bingham but to one of his guests here on Harley Street, John Adams.

In December Anne Bingham was safely delivered "of a fine girl." The following spring, the Binghams were guests in Lord Shelburne's magnificent country house, in Bowood Park, where the librarian Joseph Priestley had been succeeded by Jeremy Bentham. The Binghams continued on to Bath, Blenheim and Oxford. Before leaving for Paris in June 1784, they armed themselves with introductions to the royal courts of Europe.

Haymarket Map C

6 Haymarket Theatre. Charlotte Cushman opened here in *Romeo and Juliet* on 30 December 1845, playing Romeo to her sister Susan's Juliet. They took London by storm, the play having a run of eighty nights, almost unheard of at the time. The *Times* critic wrote: "It is enough to say that the Romeo of Miss Cushman is far superior to any Romeo we have ever had. The distinction is not one of degree, it is one of kind. For a long time Romeo has been a convention. Miss Cushman's Romeo is a creation; a living, breathing, animated, ardent human being."

Tennessee Williams's *Glass Menagerie,* directed by John Gielgud, opened here on 28 July 1948. The critics were lukewarm, but liked the acting of Helen Hayes: one headline read "Bad Play Well Acted." Actually, for Americans who had already seen the play, Hayes's portrayal of Amanda was professional but uninspiring. She lacked the inner fire, emotion and quiet desperation of Laurette Taylor who had played the role in New York. In London there had been major publicity, Tennessee Williams had just won the New York Drama Critic's Circle Award and the Pulitzer Prize. The opening night audience glittered with diamonds and top names headed by Princess Margaret. A huge opening-night party was given by Lady Sybil Colefax, London's most famous hostess, and her guests included the princess. But there was no sign of the playwright. His mother, who had come to London to share the success of her famous son, received a telegram on the afternoon of the opening: "Am in Paris. Will be at Haymarket in time for opening." Later that afternoon she received a second telegram: "Departure delayed because of Laundry foulup. May not make it in time for curtain." The third telegram read: "Missed plane. Go to Sybil's party without me. I will be there before it is over." A specially ordered horse-drawn carriage awaited him outside the theater, but Williams was still in Paris. His absence was not altogether an accident. While watching the rehearsals in England two weeks earlier, he had heard John Gielgud discussing curtain calls and suggesting that the author should not take a bow on the opening night. This might have been acceptable, but the story reached Tennessee Williams that Gielgud had also said, "I don't want the beautiful effect of the play diminished by a perspiring little author with a wrinkled shirt and a messy dinner jacket coming up on stage." The play did not enjoy a long run in London, but it was revived at the Haymarket in 1965 and played for forty-three performances. His other plays, *Cat on a Hot Tin Roof*, *The Night of the Iguana* and *A Streetcar Named Desire*, were all extremely successful in London.

Carlton Hotel. Fred Astaire and his sister Adele moved here in 1924 while performing in *Stop Flirting* at the Shaftesbury Theatre, SHAFTESBURY AVENUE. They returned to the hotel one evening to find it surrounded by barricades and bobbies—Douglas Fairbanks and Mary Pickford had come to stay. The hotel was destroyed in World War II.

Henrietta Place, Cavendish Square

(21)   Dysart Hotel. Booth Tarkington from Indiana spent October 1903 here with his father, his mother and his wife. At 34, he was pleased to be recognized in London where his novel *The Gentleman from Indiana* was selling well and his play *Monsieur Beaucaire* was in its third season.

Henrietta Street, Covent Garden Map D

5   Charles Frohman, theatrical manager and producer, took a modest office here in 1894. Aged 34, he was already well known in New York for successes such as *Shenandoah*. He had come to England because he believed that in order to produce the best English-speaking plays in the United States, and to produce

American plays in London, he had to know English playwrights, actors and actresses on their own ground. He spent the first two seasons watching the London stage and meeting dramatists. He began with one of his New York successes, *The Lost Paradise,* at the Adelphi Theatre. It failed. In 1897, he backed the American actor-playwright William Gillette in his own play, *Secret Service,* also at the Adelphi, and scored his first major success in London. Gillette, who became enthralled by *The Memoirs of Sherlock Holmes* (1894), created a play *Sherlock Holmes* and a character with which he became permanently associated when he returned to New York. Frohman then introduced his first female American star, Annie Russell, in Bret Harte's story, *Sue.* This was also a success and at the end of the year he took a 19-year lease on the prestigious Duke of York's Theatre on ST. MARTIN'S LANE.

15   Formerly St. Martin's Register Office. It was here that Sinclair Lewis—in his Savile Row pin-striped suit, wing collar, pearl-gray hat, carrying a cane and wearing a yellow flower in his lapel—married journalist Dorothy Thompson on 14 May 1928. The ceremony was witnessed by Lewis's publisher Jonathan Cape and his wife. Dorothy Thompson, 34, had met the 43-year-old divorced Lewis in Berlin. In her book, *I Saw Hitler,* published in 1932, she contended that Hitler would never achieve national power—and she was equally wrong in marrying Lewis, as she very soon discovered. The civil ceremony was followed by a church one at the Savoy Chapel, where the minister gave, not so much a sermon, as a plea to the novelist to write books that men will "go to for strength when they are in despair." Lewis, who was staying at the Savoy Hotel working on *Dodsworth,* had met the playwright Noel Coward in the Grill Room and was delighted to hear his opinion that *Elmer Gantry* was "the greatest book of the century." After the wedding, the two writers left on a three-month caravan trip around the British Isles.

Hertford Street, Hyde Park Corner   Map C

41   Formerly the American Women's Club. Edna St. Vincent Millay stayed here when she came up to London from Shillingstone, Devon, during the last six months of 1922. Each morning in the village she would walk from the thatched cottage which she shared with her mother to a "little white-washed and straw-carpeted hut" where she worked on *The Harp-Weaver and Other Poems*. (The book won a Pulitzer Prize the following year.) Her only companions were "two horses, seven cows and a large flock of sheep," gracing her dooryard and the hills beyond. "I have a table and chair in it and a rope hammock, and that's all," she told her friend Edmund Wilson. "I love it. You would probably hate it." When in London she made no attempt to meet other poets, but one day in Cambridge she spied the classical scholar A.E. Housman, author of *A Shropshire Lad*, and chased his retreating tall, thin gray figure and cotton umbrella for half a mile until he turned in at Trinity College. She was too afraid to speak to him, which was a pity, for some ten years later he wrote to the director of the Fitzwilliam Museum at Cambridge: "Some things of Edna St. Vincent Millay which I have seen make me think her the best living American poet."

High Holborn

(270)   Inns of Court Hotel. John Burroughs spent a week here in October 1871. Naturalist and author of *Wake Robin*, Burroughs made the nature essay widely popular. At the end of his first day in London, he wrote to his friend Walt Whitman, "I have just come from St. Paul's and feel very strange. I don't know what is the matter with me but I seem in a dream. St. Paul's was too much for me and my brain actually reels. I have never seen architecture before. I have seen a building with a living soul. I saw for the first time what power and imagination could be put in form and design—I felt for a moment what great genius was in this field." Burroughs recovered from his ecstasy, and called on Carlyle who delighted him with reminiscences about Walter Scott, Scotland and birds. He left for France from Newhaven where he spent a day on the South Downs watching for larks. Although late in the season, he heard dozens. He did not find their song as melodious as the American lark, "but the wonder is its length and continuity and strength. There the bird is spread out against the sky two or three hundred feet above the earth, pouring out its song in perfect ecstasy for eight or ten minutes." A delicate essay in *Winter Sunshine* developed from that day on the downs.

Above: Whistler in court. Sketch by Max Beerbohm. (See page 277.)
Below: Patrons outside John Singer Sargent's studio
at 31 Tite Street. Sketch by Max Beerbohm. (See page 256.)

Mark Twain photographed in London.
March 1900.
(See page 253)

*Pictured from left to right are Victor Plarr, Sturge Moore,
W.B. Yeats, Wilfred Blunt, Ezra Pound, Richard Aldington, and Frank Flint.
Photo taken on 18 January 1914. (See page 148.)*

Sinclair Lewis and Dorothy Thompson after their wedding at Savoy Chapel, London, 14 May 1928.
(See page 139.)

Holland Park Map G

Holland House. This Jacobean mansion was built in 1606 and passed by marriage to the Earl of Holland. The widow of the 3rd Earl of Holland married Joseph Addison, who composed many of his *Spectator* articles here. From the 1780s onwards, the house was a social center for Whig politicians, and writers such as George Canning, Richard Sheridan, Byron, Talleyrand, Wordsworth, Scott, Palmerston and Dickens. Thomas Moore, the Irish poet, said, "Poets inclined to a plethora of vanity would find a dose of Lady Holland now and then very good for their complaint."

James Fenimore Cooper was a dinner guest here in April 1828. He arrived by hackney coach and spent the first half hour with Sir James Mackintosh, writer and member of Parliament, visiting the house and gardens.

> We went into the library, which is a fine room, on the second floor, including the whole depth of the house. There were recesses for reading and writing. My companion showed me tables at different ends of the room, and stated that there was a tradition that Addison when composing, was in the habit of walking between the two, and of aiding his inspiration by using the bottles placed on them for that purpose. I beg you not mention this, however, lest it excite a sensation among the 'ripe scholars' of New York.

The dining room had a ceiling "in the style of Elizabeth's reign, being much carved and gilded." The dinner table was square and therefore there was no system of precedence—Lord Holland sat at one corner. "During dinner, as the stranger, I had the honour of a seat next to Lady Holland," Cooper continued, "She offered me a plate of herrings between the courses. Being in conversation at the moment, I declined it, as I should not have done, according to strict etiquette, especially as it was offered by the mistress of the house...besides, I never suspected the interest involved in the affair. 'You do not know what you say,' she goodhumouredly added—'they are *Dutch*.' 'Dutch!' I involuntarily repeated, though I believe I looked at the same time as if it was a herring after all. 'Certainly; we can only get them *through an ambassador*.'" Cooper concluded: "What a luxury would a potato become, if we could contrive to make it contraband! I shall hold a Dutch herring in greater respect, as long as I live."

Today, only the ground story, the arcades of the central

portion, the east wing and the gateway have been preserved. In summer, open-air plays, ballets and concerts are performed on the front terrace which is known as the Court Theatre. The garden ballroom has become a public restaurant.

Holland Place Chambers, Kensington Map G

5   Ezra Pound, 28, took a small dark flat at the end of this short alley in March 1914. After five years in London, he had become a recognized poet and critic in intellectual circles in both America and England. The following month he married Dorothy Shakespear in the nearby St. Mary Abbots church. One afternoon in September, they served tea and talked with a rather prim and quiet young American, Thomas Eliot. That evening, Pound wrote to Harriet Monroe, the editor of *Poetry,* telling her that he had just read "the best poem I have yet had or seen from an American. Pray God it not be a single and unique success." *The Love Song of J. Alfred Prufrock* amazed him because Eliot had "modernized himself *on his own.*" He urged publication but Monroe did not like the poem. An infuriated Pound sent her back two letters in one day and the poem was published the following year.

Pound first learned of an unknown Irish author, James Joyce, from the poet W.B. Yeats. The two men entered into correspondence, and a year later Pound helped Joyce obtain a £75 grant from the Royal Literary Fund. In 1917 he received the first chapters of *Ulysses* and told the author, "Wall, Mr. Joice, I recon' your a damn fine writer, that's what I recon'. An' I recon' this here work o' yourn is some concarn'd litterchure. You can take it from me, an' I'm a jedge." He arranged for serialization in the *Little Review,* which lasted until the U.S. Post Office seized copies in 1920 on the basis of obscenity. In September 1918, the *Times Literary Supplement* wrote of Pound's *Pavannes and Divisions:* "We could annotate nearly every page of the book with eager agreement or dissent. This means that it is worth reading. You may wish that you had Mr. Pound before you in the flesh, to tell him what you think of him; but that, no doubt, is exactly the effect he wishes to produce on you." Today, Pound's literary fame rests on his *Cantos* of which the first three were composed here. In spite of living in London for twelve years, he understood little of England and the eccentricities of those who made up, for instance, the Bloomsbury group. Sir Herbert Read witnessed his awkward meetings with the Sitwells with whom he shared common goals: "It was very difficult for anyone to take him seriously in person (and it was his *persona* that he used to project)...apart from his exotic appearance, he rattled off his elliptic sentences with a harsh nasal twang, twitched incessantly, and prowled round the room like a caged panther. He was not made for compromise or cooperation, two qualities essential for any literary or artistic 'movement'."

During these last years in England Pound became interested in politics. In 1919 Clifford H. Douglas published *Economic Democracy,* in which he claimed that he knew the cause of economic depressions and how they could be avoided. Understanding little of economics, Pound still felt that Douglas provided sound answers to the glaring inequality evident in England. Eight years later, living in Italy, he wrote, "I personally think extremely well of Mussolini," and claimed that it would be impossible to compare the last three American presidents to him without insulting him. His subsequent support of fascism is well known. In 1920, thanks to John Quinn, New York lawyer and patron of the arts, he was appointed a correspondent for the American magazine the *Dial,* at a salary of $750 a year. He settled in Paris in December 1920. He was glad to be rid of England. The feeling was perhaps mutual.

Hornton Street, Kensington

The Red House. Herbert Hoover and his family moved to this modest eight-room home in 1907 from HYDE PARK GATE. The lease stipulated, among other things, that the tenants should not permit their cows to wander in Kensington High Street. Hoover, 33, was already wealthy; having sold his partnership in a British mining company for $169,000 he established his own consulting firm at 1 London Wall in the City. Within a few years, he had offices in Paris, Petrograd, New York City and San Francisco. Engineer, metallurgist, geologist, financier and promoter, he was already being described as "young Hoover, the great engineer." Engineers with a knowledge of international corporate financing were virtually unknown in England at the time and Hoover was moving fast. He listed his occupation as "mining engineer"—it had a reassuring ring to it, he wrote—rather than a promoter of oil drilling which was in fact what he was doing. He financed a friend's publication, *Mining Magazine* (1909), which soon became authoritative throughout Europe. An anonymous article on mining shares, accompanied by the editor's testimony to the "good faith and unusual knowledge" of the author, included on the "best buy" list a number of companies quietly controlled by Hoover. By 1910 he admitted to a friend that he was worth $3 million. When he sold oil wells in Peru to Jersey Standard, one of the accountants cracked, "It's a wonder they aren't all in jail." Not that Hoover was dishonest, but these were rough-and-tumble times and British financiers with Oxford accents in the City had little to teach the California engineer.

The Hoover family spent summer evenings in the large rose garden behind the Red House entertaining American friends, or in their country home at Stratford-on-Avon where Hoover became the honorary treasurer of the Shakespeare International Alliance. Hoover took to writing on mining, game conservation and in 1912, with his wife, he translated Agricola's *De Re Metallica*. Hoover likened the outbreak of World War I in August 1914 to an earthquake with everyone in a total state of shock. But it was war that brought Hoover his first experience of public service: he headed a relief committee at the Savoy Hotel in the STRAND.

Hyde Park, the Serpentine Map F

During the exceptionally cold winter of 1763-64 London's lakes froze over, and among the American skaters was the 26-year-old Benjamin West, who performed the Philadelphia Salute to the applause of the crowd. The *Morning Herald* for 4 February 1764 reported: "There never was a more brilliant exhibition than Hyde Park afforded on Sunday—Ministers, Lords, Commons, all on the ice. Of the Commons Mr. West the celebrated painter, and Dr. Hewitt were the best. They danced a minuet on their skates, to the admiration of the spectators."

Hyde Park Corner

Formerly St. George's Hospital. Built in 1733 looking north on to Hyde Park, the hospital provided patients with the benefit of country air "which in the opinion of the physicians would be more effectual than physick in the cure of many distempers, especially such as mainly affect the poor who live in close and confined spaces." In 1768, John Hunter joined the staff. A pioneer in comparative anatomy and morphology, he introduced many surgical techniques, including a method of ligating aneurisms that is still in use. Thomas Young, professor of natural history and Henry Gray, whose *Anatomy* (1868) went into over thirty editions, worked here. The hospital and medical school were moved to Tooting in South London in 1980.

Philip Physick studied medicine at the University of Pennsylvania, and in 1789 became a pupil of John Hunter as house-surgeon here at St. George's. He worked under the great surgeons of the day, Astley Cooper and Abernethy, and was elected a member of the Royal College of Surgeons in 1792. He returned to Philadelphia where he became professor of surgery at his old university. Physick was the first in America to employ gastric lavage with the stomach tube. He invented a guillotine for the amputation of the uvula which became the antecedent of modern tonsil guillotines. Thomas C. James, a friend of Physick, also worked at St. George's under John Hunter. He devoted much of his time in London to obstetrics in the Story Street Lying-in Hospital, and in 1793 returned to Philadelphia and was later appointed professor of midwifery at Pennsylvania. Most of the American medical students who studied here at St. George's also worked across the river at Guy's Hospital on ST. THOMAS'S STREET.

Hyde Park Gate, Kensington Map G

39 Herbert Hoover and his wife kept a flat here in this discreet Victorian lane from 1901 until 1907. Hoover first came to London in December 1897 when he was 23, at the request of the British international mining company, Bewick, Moreing and Company; it was the first time he had ever been east of the Mississippi. After two months in London he went to work as an engineer in the gold mines of Australia for $600 a month, three times his previous salary in California. Five years later, he was named a partner. During these years, Hoover and his family traveled constantly in Australia, New Zealand, Burma and Ceylon, returning to London every year, especially for the birth of their two sons, Herbert, Jr. in 1903 and Allan four years later, who were both born here at Hyde Park Gate. Hoover was highly critical of British industry, its low productivity and untrained management. He suggested to Lloyd George that machinery be put into coal mines and worked to death, instead of the British system of working the coal miners to death. In a debate at Oxford University as to whether engineering should be included in its instruction, Hoover argued that until Oxford and Cambridge recognized engineering as a profession, instead of a trade, the best British brains would never enter the field. While technical colleges had existed for a long time in England, their graduates were looked down upon; at the beginning of the 20th century, American mining engineers held the top jobs throughout the British empire. Later in life, Hoover liked to tell the story of how he crossed the Indian Ocean in a first-class cabin and a British lady passenger, on learning his profession, exclaimed, "Oh! I thought you were a gentleman!" In December 1907, Hoover and his family moved to HORNTON STREET in Camden Hill.

Jermyn Street

(76)   St. James's Hotel. Cornelius Vanderbilt and his party of thirty-five guests took suites here on 2 June 1853 after a ten-day crossing to Southampton on his new yacht *North Star*. Nothing quite like it had been seen before in England. The *Illustrated News* in New York gloated: "What will the wealthy noblemen of England—the proprietors of sailing yachts of fifty and one hundred tons—say to a citizen of the United States appearing in their waters with a steamship yacht of twenty-five hundred tons...a noble specimen of American mechanical skill." The noblemen, of course, said nothing, and Vanderbilt had the good taste not to follow the suggestion of some of his guests that the *North Star* sail up the Thames into the heart of London. One of the first visitors to call upon Vanderbilt was the American banker in London, George Peabody. His offer of his boxes at Covent Garden was accepted, and that evening the party heard Meyerbeer's opera *Les Huguenots* with soprano Giulia Grisi. The Americans were surprised at the discretion of the audience, who pretended not to notice the arrival of Queen Victoria in "a rich, white dress, exceedingly *décolletée*," and Prince Albert, "tall, stout and partially bald...anything but aristocratic."

Vanderbilt and his family were guests of honor at a dinner given at the Mansion House by the lord mayor, but the two most memorable visits of the group during their week in London were Madame Tussaud's waxworks and the Thames Tunnel. The first underwater tunnel in the world, 1,200 feet long, opened in 1843 for foot passengers; it became a railway tunnel in the 1860s and still carries underground trains. Both visits reflected the interests of Vanderbilt and his friends in innovation and technology. While the English aristocracy made a point of sailing clear of the commodore while he was in London, the popular English newspapers were fascinated by the concept of the self-made millionnaire epitomized by Vanderbilt and his yacht. The great difference between the two countries, one reporter wrote, is that in England a man is ashamed of having made his own fortune, unless he has done so "in one of the few roads the aristocracy condescend to travel by—the bar, the church or the army." And the *Daily News* of 4 June 1853 noted that Mr. Vanderbilt was the legitimate product of his country, and cited him as an example for their own:

> We want the Vanderbilts of England to feel what they are, and to show it. We don't ask each of them to build a monster yacht. We do ask that they assert the greatness of their position. We do require that they shall do everything, by providing amply for education, to elevate the class to which they belong, and put it upon a level to which it is entitled. The middle classes of England are the creators of its wealth and the source of its power. Let them take example from America and not shrink from acting.

(81)   Cavendish Hotel. There has been a hotel on this site since the 18th century. Mrs. Rosa Lewis, "the duchess of Jermyn Street," bought the Cavendish Hotel in 1904 and remained until her death in 1952.

Edith Wharton spent ten days here in July 1913. Finally free after lengthy divorce proceedings, she enjoyed the atmosphere of the hotel. Rosa Lewis, an excellent judge of people, found Edith Wharton to be of "the very best Americans." In a particularly perceptive insight, she wrote, "She struck me as having a very fine mind, but a very shy and retiring disposition, very difficult to get at....I think she's never been really unlocked, and that most of her emotions have gone into her books." Over the years, Edith

Wharton returned every summer to London for at least a fortnight. While she enjoyed the company of Lytton Strachey, she was never cordial to the Bloomsbury group. She was on her guard against Virginia Woolf, who had implied that American writers (i.e. Wharton and Henry James) should cultivate their native idiom and avoid striving after the king's English.

Thomas Wolfe dropped by the Cavendish on 18 April 1935. "Saw old Rosie—very red of face and drunk, propped up on sofa— also two whores fixing stockings—asked for Mr. Jackson Gregory knowing that he had been here once, so did she, I think—'Yes, he often stops here but is not here at present—Drop in again, dear.'"

Kensington Church Walk, Holland Street Map G

10   Ezra Pound moved here in November 1909. He took a first-floor room with two windows looking south onto a secluded courtyard of three-storied houses reached by an intriguing alley. The landlord, Sam Langley, was "positively the best England can produce at *any* level," wrote his eight-shilling-a-week lodger. Mr. Langley was the manager of a nearby grocery and Pound obliged him occasionally by delivering groceries. That winter, the English publisher J.M. Dent and Sons accepted *Spirit of Romance;* Pound, 24, told his parents, "I seem to fit better here in London than anywhere else, if I can only guess what's the answer to the problem of sustenance." A temporary answer lay in teaching at the Polytechnic on REGENT STREET.

One of Pound's first guests was William Carlos Williams on his way back from France to Rutherford, New Jersey, to begin practising medicine. Williams recalls going with Pound and his future wife Dorothy Shakespear to WOBURN WALK to see William Butler Yeats:

> It was a studio atmosphere, very hushed. We tiptoed in. Yeats, in a darkened room, was reading by candlelight to a small, a very small gathering of his protégés, maybe five or six young men and women, members of the Abbey Theatre group. He paid no attention whatever to us and went on reading: reading, of all things, Ernest Dowson's *Cynara* in a beautiful voice, I must say, but it was not my dish.

A few nights later, the trio attended a benefit lecture given by Yeats at the Adelphi Club on the work of some of the younger Irish poets. It was a fashionable affair, presided over by Sir Edmund Gosse, librarian of the House of Lords. When Yeats claimed that these young poets were consistently denied an audience in England and therefore were obliged to resort to drink, Gosse banged down on the bell and stopped his distinguished speaker. Yeats began to repeat the argument and Gosse banged the bell again. The lecture broke up in confusion. When Williams left a week later, Pound wrote to his mother, "I feel that Bill's mind has duly benefited from his brief sojourn." His guest saw things in a slightly different vein. While he had had no objection to sleeping on "a sort of armchair convertible to cot," he had found the intense literary atmosphere fatiguing. In his autobiography he recalled, "I don't know how Ezra stood it, it would have killed me in a month. I was glad to get away."

Pound met D.H. Lawrence early in 1910. Both writers were aged 25 and Lawrence, already fascinated by the United States where he would live for three years, was intrigued by everything about Pound. His fine, chiseled features were set off by a mass of fiery, curly red hair, completed by a red moustache and a red beard trimmed to a point. His gray-blue eyes were shielded by a pince-nez. His voice was high-pitched and shrill—almost feminine, in contrast to his general virility. He never sat still but jumped and twisted in his chair as he quoted from poet after poet. Outside on Kensington High Street his tall figure—in a pearl-buttoned velvet coat, pearl-gray trousers, a loose-flowing dark cape, a Malacca cane with a silver top and, occasionally, a sombrero—cut a distinct and increasingly familiar figure. Such display, however, merely concealed his poverty. Occasionally an overnight guest at Church Walk, Lawrence summed up the difference between their attitudes: Pound's god was beauty, his own was life. Theirs was an awkward relationship. Both felt the originality of the other, and each was ill at ease. Three years later, when Pound began actively to promote the work of Lawrence, he described him to Harriet Monroe as a "detestable person but needs watching." In his review of Lawrence's *Love Poems and Others* in the July 1913 issue of *Poetry,* Pound wrote, "When Mr. Lawrence ceases to discuss his own disagreeable sensations, when he writes low-life narrative, as he does in 'Whether or Not' and in 'Violets,' there is no English poet under forty who can come within shot of him." Here Pound was ten years ahead of English critics.

Robert Frost called and introduced himself, and the two men then walked together to Frost's publisher to pick up a copy of his first book of poetry, *A Boy's Will*. While Pound came to admire Frost's writing, and would read "The Death of the Hired Man" to anyone who cared to listen, the two men never became friends. Another visitor was the poet John Gould Fletcher. Born and raised in Arkansas, a wealthy Harvard graduate, he had begun by financing the printing of his own poetry. Pound read his work carefully, made suggestions and treated him as a disciple. Within the next two years Fletcher would win a Pulitzer Prize for his poetry. Pound was by this time being noticed by English critics. *Punch* punned about "Ezekiel Ton," but made amends by declaring his verse to be "the most remarkable thing in poetry since Robert Browning." Yeats told a friend that Pound was "full of the middle ages... to talk over a poem with him is like getting you to put a sentence into dialect. All becomes clear and natural." Early in 1912, Pound signed a contract with the English publisher Stephen Swift, by which he agreed to give him all his future books in return for £100 a year in advance royalties for a period of ten years. He gave a magnificent party to celebrate his firm financial future. Barely a year went by, however, before Swift's manager ran off to Tangiers with the funds and Swift went out of business—a misfortune which was somehow symptomatic of the financial problems that always plagued the American poet. Nevertheless, he began to hold "Tuesday evenings" where anyone on business or wanting to introduce a new poet was sure to find him in.

He found rooms opposite his own on Church Walk for the poet Hilda Doolittle, his friend from Pennsylvania, and an English poet, Richard Aldington. With Pound as leader, they founded a new "movement" in poetry called "Les Imagistes." Influenced by classicism, Chinese and Japanese poetry, and the French symbolists, they condemned the exuberant imagery and sentimentality of Victorian poetry. They declared that poetic ideas were best expressed by actually rendering concrete objects rather than simply commenting upon them: poets had to produce a hard, clear, concentrated poetry, free of artificial vocabulary, meter and image. Pound edited their first anthology, *Des Imagistes,* before abandoning the leadership of the movement to Amy Lowell. Here on Church Walk, in October 1913, he was photographed by his fellow American Alvin Langdon Coburn. The following February, he published his first article on art, "The New Sculpture," devoted to the Frenchman Henri Gaudier-Brzeska and to his fellow American Jacob Epstein. His friendship with Dorothy Shakespear had blossomed. Pound somehow managed to convince her father that he could support a wife—and to prove it he produced a fistful of pound notes which he had just received for an article. Happily, she had a small private income. In spring 1914 Pound moved to chambers in nearby HOLLAND PLACE.

Kew Gardens

Officially known as the Royal Botanic Gardens, Kew Gardens cover 300 acres. They were first mentioned in 1678 by the diarist Sir John Evelyn, who paid a visit to Sir Henry Capel in Kew "whose orangerie and myretetum are most beautiful and perfectly well kept." The gardens were laid out by "Capability" Brown in the 18th century and opened to the public. Ralph Waldo Emerson visited them on 5 April 1848 and wrote to his wife:

> the day was the finest of the year, the garden is the richest on the face of the earth. Adam would find all his acquaintances of Eden here; here are cactuses 1000 years old, here baobab, lotus, papaw, upas, chocolate, clove, cinnamon, caoutchouc, banian, gutta-percha, green tea, bohea tea, and all the rest, growing peacefully together, to the comfort of botanists.

King Street, Covent Garden

(43)　　Low's Family Hotel, known later as Froome's, opened here in 1774. Around 1830, Evans, a comedian from the Covent Garden Theatre, opened supper rooms with singing, which became Evans's Music Hall.

Abigail Adams and her daughter Nabby arrived in London on the evening of 19 July 1784. Even the last lap of their journey had been eventful. After docking at Chatham, on the way to London, the coach immediately ahead on Blackheath Common was held up. The robber was captured. "The poor wretch, ghastly and horrible," wrote Abigail, "a youth of twenty, attempted to lift his hat, and looked despair." By 8 p.m. they were safely settled in Low's Hotel where John Adams stayed when in London. Abigail had been expecting to join her husband after a five-year separation and was bitterly disappointed to discover that he was in the Hague and that her son "Master John" had recently left London. The following morning, Abigail, having decided that the hotel was too expensive, settled her bill of one and a half guineas for tea the previous evening, lodging and breakfast. Accompanied by an American friend, Charles Storer, the two ladies moved to the Adelphi Family Hotel on ADAM STREET.

Gouverneur Morris left Harwich at six o'clock on Saturday morning, 27 March 1790, and arrived at "five o'clock at Froome's Hotel, Covent Garden." He continued in his journal: "Thus in eleven hours we have come about seventy five miles" at a cost, he calculated, of one shilling and sixpence per mile. That evening he dined at the hotel on oysters and the following morning went for a stroll in Hyde Park, where he found "the Numbers both of Persons and Carriages far beyond my Expectation." He called on Lady Tancred, who received him alone in her library. "A very good-looking Woman," he noted, "as she desires very politely to see me I think I shall become a Visitant, for if I am to stay here any Time some Resource or other will certainly be wanting." Morris, aged 38, was a man of immense charm and in spite of his wooden leg, enjoyed great success with the ladies in Paris and now in London. He ended his first full day by dining at the house of the French ambassador, the Marquis de La Luzerne, whom he had known in Philadelphia. When he got back to his hotel, he found an invitation to meet the British foreign secretary, the Duke of Leeds, the following afternoon.

Morris had come to London as an informal emissary for George Washington. He was to sound out the British government on its willingness to evacuate the northwest forts (Oswego, Erie and Detroit) in compliance with the provisions of the Peace Treaty of 1783, and pay for slaves carried away by the British armies when they had left America. He was also to explore the possibility of negotiating a treaty of commerce. Morris was far from optimistic, and that evening the French ambassador told him that the British would never surrender the forts because they protected their fur traders against the Indians. Morris was received at Whitehall with exquisite politeness, the Duke of Leeds saying that Great Britain deeply desired "a friendly and commercial intercourse between the two countries." But he showed little disposition to open negotiations. It was not an auspicious beginning. During the following months, Morris learned that the British were awaiting developments in Europe, particularly the revolution in France, before negotiating with America, who did most of her trade with Britain anyway.

Morris was far too sophisticated to feel humiliated by titled British officials (not the case with many of his successors), and was determined to enjoy life in London. One of the first aspects of British life that he detected was that Englishmen were far more at ease with one another than with women. Horse riding, hunting, reading newspapers in the library and drinking port in the club were all preferable to having to face women. In English drawing-rooms "the arrangement of the company was stiff and formal, the ladies all arranged in battalia on one side of the room." After one such evening, Morris confided to his journal, "Mrs. Kennedy, in good spirits, invites my Attentions. I of course bestow some small Share. Mrs. Mallet seems not unwilling to extend her Dominion but this will not do for me. Converse with Mrs. Phyn. Beauty, Sense and Softness joined, but I have vowed Fidelity upon another Altar." Comforting neglected English wives filled many an evening that summer and occasionally an afternoon here in Covent Garden.

Morris, who had lost his left leg ten years earlier in a fall from a carriage in Philadelphia, hoped to profit from British mechanical skills to get a replacement for his wooden leg. On 17 April 1790 he recorded: "A Mechanic arrives who is to make me a Leg. Upon Examination of the Stump he says that I shall be able to take the Benefit of the Knee Joint. If this be so it will certainly be an Improvement but he acknowledges that the Machinery will be less solid than the simple Stick which I now use." Though he had his "right Leg taken in Plaister of Paris as a Model by which to make a left Leg of Copper," Morris found the workmen awkward and, after two more visits, he abandoned the idea.

Morris constantly received callers in his hotel suite here in Covent Garden. John Penn, the spendthrift descendant of William Penn, worried about the management of his estates in Pennsylvania, and dropped by almost daily; Morris's compensation lay in the beauty of Mrs. Penn. Another visitor was the author of *Common Sense*, Thomas Paine, who was working on an iron suspension bridge: "Payne calls to ask if I will visit the Scaffold of his Bridge, which he says may be converted into a useful Roof for a Barn." Finally, Morris went in his carriage to Lisson Grove (Lissom Green in his journal) to see a large model of the suspension bridge, but did not find it "so handsome as he [Paine] thinks it is." He also wondered how strong it was and concluded "it has a very light Appearance."

An affable and competent lawyer, what he found most aggravating were requests by Americans that he act as an informal judge to settle their disputes: "[John Paul] Jones and [Dr. Edward] Bancroft call before I am drest, the former takes Breakfast with me and they enter upon the Discussion of their business which goes into unnecessary length. I therefore express my Opinons in clear and pointed terms and then set about my Business." Lunch in the nearby Piazza Coffee House was shared with James Boswell, and at 11 p.m. Mrs. Phyn ("beauty, sense and softness") called in her carriage to take Morris to the pleasure gardens at Ranelagh. Late the following morning, the indefatigable diarist recorded: "I get Home about four o'Clock, which is long after daylight." There were compensations for a hardworking American diplomat in London. Morris returned to Paris at the end of September 1790.

King Street, St. James's

(26)   Willis's Rooms. On Friday evening, 4 July 1851, eight hundred guests headed by the Lord Mayor of London sat down at a banquet surrounded by walls decorated with American flags and the Union Jack, and the portraits of a young Queen Victoria and George Washington draped in their national colors. At 11 p.m. the band struck up "See the Conquering Hero Comes" and the guests rose as their host George Peabody from Massachusetts welcomed the 84-year-old Duke of Wellington. The duke was introduced to the American minister Abbot Lawrence, to Governor Neil S. Brown of Tennessee and to other prominent Americans, then dancing began in the ballroom lit by five hundred wax candles in cut-glass chandeliers. "Peabody's Independence Day dinner" as it became known, for it would be held annually, was not given without considerable anxiety upon the part of the host. Tactful Americans in London had always avoided celebrating the Fourth of July. But the Great Exhibition at the Crystal Palace in Hyde Park that summer had drawn many Americans and American exhibits: Alfred C. Hobb's unpickable lock, Samuel Colt's revolvers, Hiram Power's statue of a Greek slave, Cyrus McCormick's reaper and Richard Hoe's printing press. When Peabody asked Lawrence if he thought he should give a Fourth of July dinner, the American diplomat had replied: "I am quite satisfied that the fashionables and aristocracy do not wish to attend this ball." The idea of English ladies and gentlemen sitting through an entire dinner with a group of midwestern manufacturers was too much to visualize. To English society, these self-made men appeared boastful, frequently vulgar and without exception, brash. But the 56-year-old banker Peabody, who had started work at the age of 11 as an apprentice to a grocer, trusted his own judgment, and went ahead with the dinner. It was an outstanding success. The Americans were correctly attired and outdid one another in telling stories—the English hadn't enjoyed an evening so much in years. London newspapers were unanimous in acknowledging how much this "eminent American merchant" had done for Anglo-American relations. Peabody, a bachelor, "retiring in manner, rather reticent of speech," was emboldened by the success, and the following July he gave another dinner. It became Peabody's practice to toast first the queen and then the president of the United States which, for an American, was as daring as to celebrate American Independence in the capital of the British empire. Only once, in 1854, did an unfavorable reaction occur. Dan Sickles, secretary of the American legation, walked out, while James Buchanan, U.S. minister, refused to stand during the toast to the queen.

St. James's Theatre. Henry James spent the month of December 1894 here attending rehearsals of his new play, *Guy Domville*. Euphoric one day, he was in despair the next. He told a friend, "I may have been made for the Drama—God knows!—but I certainly wasn't meant for the Theatre." He felt that he had staked everything on this production. A mere dramatist with a play might or might not succeed. But he was Henry James, a celebrated novelist, risking his entire reputation before all of London. It was true that there had been a large advance sale of seats. When the night of the opening came, Saturday, 5 January 1895, James's nervousness was unbearable. He went for a long walk alone through the cold of the London parks. This was a time, he noted "when a man needs a religion." He had long decided not to watch the play and planned to spend the evening in a nearby pub where Edmund Gosse would bring him the news, act by act. Instead he went to a nearby theater, the Haymarket, where he thought Oscar Wilde's latest play, *The Ideal Husband*, might soothe him. Instead it did just the opposite. Meanwhile among the critics watching *Guy Domville* was George Bernard Shaw for the *Satur'ay Review*, others included H.G. Wells and Arnold Bennett. Many of James's friends were there, some had even come from America. The first act had gone well. Its literary quality had pleased Shaw. The second act with a long drinking scene had gone badly. When the third and final act opened, a note of pending tragedy was supposed to be struck by Guy's line: "I'm the *last*, my lord, of the Domvilles!" Suddenly a voice was heard from the gallery, "It's a bloody good thing y'are." Tragedy collapsed into farce accompanied by jeers from the gallery. It turned into a disaster. James entered the theater by the back stage door unaware of the incidents in the third act. When the final curtain came down, the well-known actor George Alexander, who had played Guy Domville, received the ovations to which he was accustomed. Then James's many supporters in the stalls began to call for the author. Alexander, who had been unnerved by the events of the evening, decided that perhaps the author's presence might placate the rowdy element. He led on the author by the hand. James had assumed that the applause for Alexander had been for the play, and before he had a chance to bow, the gallery exploded with jeers, hisses and catcalls. The artistic elite answered with polite clapping which only infuriated those in the gallery who fought back with howls of derision. James stood paralyzed. It was worse than any nightmare. "The hoots and jeers and catcalls," he later told his brother, "were like those of a cage of beasts at some infernal zoo." Weary, bruised, disgusted and sickened, James escaped into the night alone and walked back alone to his home in DE VERE Gardens, his theatrical career over.

Knightsbridge Map F

66   Hyde Park Hotel. Edmund Wilson spent April 1945 here. Of all the American observers in England at the end of the war, he was the most perspicacious. He found that London had a certain flavor of Moscow about it: the regimentation and tension required by the war effort had produced an atmosphere which reminded him of the 1930s in the Soviet Union. There were constant queues of shabbily dressed people forever getting registered and having to have passes to do things. There was the quietness of everybody, the submissiveness, the patience, the acceptance. "The parks," Wilson recalled, "seemed muted like Russian parks." Everything was rationed, everything was drab. Graham Greene told him that life

during the war had been dramatic because there had been danger—
every simple act had a special awareness, any minute could be the
last. Now that life was suddenly safe, it was also blank. The new
socialist government was about to offer security "from the cradle
to the grave." Risk had been eliminated. The former working class
had evolved into a new lower middle class which provided an eager
and growing market for the worst in movies, radio and journalism
that the United States had to send them. "Our Hollywood stars,"
wrote Wilson, "are already their stars, our best-sellers, their best-
sellers... the British feed themselves on our banality without
catching our excitement and gusto." But there was one exception,
the theater. There were three Shakespeare plays running in
London, as well as the film of *Henry V,* John Webster's *The
Duchess of Malfi,* and a dramatization of Jane Austen's *Emma.*
There were plays by Ibsen, Shaw, Chekhov, Strindberg and Noel
Coward performed with a competence "obsolete on Broadway."
Each evening Wilson watched performers such as Ralph
Richardson, Laurence Olivier, John Gielgud, Sybil Thorndike and
Peggy Ashcroft. These were the only stars in the gray dawn of
post-war England.

Ruth Draper returned to England early in March 1946 and
went first to Hornchurch, Essex, where she put flowers on the
grave of her nephew, Flight-Lieutenant Draper, killed in the war.
She arrived in her beloved London a few days later, where her suite
overlooked the park, Kensington Gardens, the Serpentine, "the
duck pond and lovely old trees and the Row with riders and
children going by every morning." She had first performed in
London in 1913 and returned to England some six or seven times
between the wars. She felt at home in London and hurried to see
St. Paul's, still standing surrounded by devastation but "with the
rubble all neatly cleared away." She told her sister, "The churches
are tragic evidence of the horror, yet strangely enough the lovely
steeples stand." The character actress who had turned so many
London audiences to brief tears was herself, she wrote, "near to
tears those first days." London, she continued, "is like a beloved
person, with a soul—and one feels exactly as one would toward a
friend who has been tortured and scarred, but remains undaunted,
valiant and calm." As her English friends reappeared, she began to
feel better. She opened to packed houses, and among her fans was
Queen Mary, accompanied by the 20-year-old Princess Elizabeth.

"She and the Queen roared," Draper told a friend, as she performed "Doctors," "Vive la France," and the "Immigrant."

At 6:45 p.m. on 16 March 1946 Ruth Draper addressed the entire British nation on a direct BBC broadcast. Recalling her many happy memories of Britain over thirty years, she made reference to the recent war and the role shared by both America and England. She closed saying, "Please think of me more than ever before, as an American—understanding and fraternal." Five years later, on 23 November 1951, she was named Commander of the British Empire and received the award from King George VI at Buckingham Palace.

Knightsbridge Hotel. Gertrude Stein and Alice B. Toklas stayed here in January 1913. They had come to see John Lane, publisher of Beardsley and the *Yellow Book* and a man with a reputation for interest in "advanced" literary works. Presumably Gertrude's style was too advanced even for Lane for, although she found him to be "an awfully funny man," he refused to publish her. She enlisted the help of the English art critic Roger Fry, telling her friend Mabel Dodge, "Roger Fry is being awfully good about my work. It seems that he read *Three Lives* long ago and was much impressed with it." The efforts of her new Bloomsbury friends were to no avail and her first publication in England, *Composition as Explanation,* was not until 1926.

Lancaster Gate Map G

109   Marlborough Court. Bret Harte lived here from July 1895 until his death in 1902. His popularity as author of *The Outcasts of Poker Flat* and *Plain Language From Truthful James* had declined quickly in America, but in England interest in tales of gold mining in California continued. Harte churned out imitations of the stories which had won him fame for magazines such as the *Strand* and the *Idler.* He lived at Lancaster Gate as a guest in the home of Monsieur Van de Velde, chancellor of the Belgian delegation in London. On the chancellor's death, he stayed on with his wealthy widow who performed several roles for him, including that of secretary. Constantly threatened by the arrival of his wife, he warded her off with all forms of excuses, "to come to London to a hotel, or even to lodgings—living as you ought to live as my wife— even in the plainest way, would cost more than my income would permit, and much more than for me to come to New York. I have been able to live in London solely because I lived with the Van de Veldes, half as a guest, under circumstances that enabled me to send you three thousand dollars per year." Anna Harte came anyway, to visit their married son living in Caversham in Berkshire. When they met for the first time in more than fifteen years, Harte and his wife were total strangers, and he did not invite her to come to London. By 1901 Harte was suffering from cancer and he died on 5 May 1902. At his funeral in Frimley churchyard in Surrey, his wife and Marguerite Van de Velde faced one another for the first time. (Harte kept a room at 74 Lancaster Gate.)

Leicester Square Map D

Leicester Square was laid out in 1670 and was soon surrounded by handsome buildings. It was very fashionable until the end of the 18th century, when some of the houses were converted into hotels patronized mainly by foreigners—the Cavour and the Sablonière on the south corner of the east side of the square were the best known. Exhibition halls, Turkish baths, oyster rooms and theaters followed. The garden in the square was described in 1850 as "very ruinous and dilapidated." Recently it has been improved.

(17)   Sablonière Hotel. Benjamin West and John Trumbull called on General Tadeusz Kosciuszko, Polish hero of the American Revolution, in June 1797. Kosciuszko, who had led the unsuccessful 1791-94 fight for Polish independence, had just been released from prison in Russia. He was staying in London on his way back to the United States, still limping badly from wounds received in Poland. When the two Americans entered his room, they found him sketching London from his window. Embarrassed by his bandages and his crutches, he declined to pose for West. But no sooner had West returned to his studio in NEWMAN STREET than he began a portrait from memory, placing the general on a couch with St. Paul's and the Thames seen through the window. His crutches against the wall, his sketching paper and portfolio at hand, books on the floor, Kosciuszko is depicted in a Byronic pose, his face and eyes pensive, witnessing the defeat of his army and his own exile. West gave a copy of this extraordinary picture—already announcing the romanticism of the 1820s—to the general, who later presented it to Thomas Jefferson.

(28)   John Singleton Copley and his family moved here early in 1776. Copley, 37, was on the threshold of a new career. With a well-lit studio and a fashionable address (at the time known as Leicester Fields) to reassure wealthy patrons, he became, over the next seven years, a leading portrait painter, excelling in history painting of a startling sort. Rejecting mythology and ancient warriors, Copley chose instead the personal dramas of his time. He showed an Englishman still living, in the throes of a terrifying experience he had had as a youth. Brook Watson, a prosperous London merchant and future lord mayor of the city, had asked Copley to recreate the scene when, at the age of 14, Watson had been swimming off Havana, Cuba, when a shark attacked him and bit off his leg. His wooden leg bore out the story. The catalog of the 1778 Royal Academy exhibition described the picture as "a boy attacked by a shark, and rescued by some seamen in a boat: founded on a fact which happened in the harbour of Havannah." The drama in *Watson and the Shark* (now in the Museum of Fine Arts, Boston) captivated both critics and the public. Copley followed this with his massive *Death of the Earl of Chatham* which he exhibited alone in a hall in SPRING GARDENS.

On 5 December 1782, while Copley was working on a portrait of Elkanah Watson, painter and subject suspended the sitting to hurry over to the House of Lords to hear George III announce the end of the War of American Independence. Upon their return, according to Watson, Copley "with a bold hand, a master's touch, and I believe an American heart" painted the stars and stripes on the flag flying from a ship in the background. "This, I imagine," Watson wrote later, "was the first American flag hoisted in England." Copley, however, American heart or no, did not return to Boston. In 1783 he moved to the fashionable ST. GEORGE STREET.

The Alhambra Palace opened as a music hall in 1860. Houdini, 26, arrived in London in 1900 in the hope of getting an engagement. British managers were wary of brash young Americans with portfolios full of American newspaper clippings praising their acts, but Houdini caught the interest of the manager of the Alhambra when he said that he would challenge members of the audience to bring manacles onto the stage from which he couldn't escape. Not wanting to be taken for a fool, the manager decided to test the young man's claim by taking him to Scotland Yard. There, Superintendent Melville obligingly had Houdini's arms wrapped around a pillar and handcuffs snapped over his wrists. The superintendent and the manager promised to return in an hour. They had not even left the room before Houdini was at their side. "Here, I'll come with you," he said. (Handcuffs, Houdini knew, opened when rapped in a particular way against a hard surface. By first putting his arms around a pillar, the police had in fact facilitated his escape.) Houdini was given a tryout with a week's contract. He was soon the talk of London, and played at the Alhambra for six months at £60 a week before continuing in Germany. (The Alhambra Palace was pulled down in 1936.)

Empire Theatre and Cinema. The Royal London Panorama opened in 1881 with scenes from the Charge of the Light Brigade, but even the patriotism of Victorian England did not prevent its bankruptcy. The building was converted into the Empire Theatre, which was replaced by the Empire Cinema in 1928.

George Gershwin wrote the score for the musical *The Rainbow* which opened here on 3 April 1923. Thanks to Al Jolson's recording of "Swanee," Gershwin's name was known throughout England. To entice him to London, English producers had offered him a round-trip ship passage plus $1,500 and a percentage of the takings. These were far better conditions than he had ever received in New York. When he was going through immigration control at Southampton, the inspector looked at his passport and said, "Oh, you wrote *Swanee*, what are you writing now?" Gershwin was thrilled—he had been recognized by the first Englishman he had met. This had to be a good omen.

The cast was part American and part British, and during rehearsals Gershwin thought that the American jokes didn't sound right from the English comedian—he suggested that they be given to an American actor. On the opening night, the play got a poor reception until the last-act finale when the British comedian, bitter because his part had been drastically cut, stepped out of character, went to the footlights and angrily shouted that American actors were being favored over English ones. He had to be dragged off the stage and the comedy ended in disaster. The following day this incident received far more coverage in the newspapers than the musical, which closed after a few days. At least Gershwin already had a return ticket to New York. From that day on he was wary of "good omens." Three years later he was back at this theater, where *Lady Be Good* was a tremendous success.

Lincoln's Inn Fields Map D

This spacious and tranquil square, delightful to visit, was laid out in 1618 by Inigo Jones. Lincoln's Inn is a group of buildings belonging to the four legal societies that have the exclusive right to admit people to practice at the English bar. Many great lawyers have lived and worked here, including Sir William Blackstone, whose *Commentaries on the Laws of England* (1765) exerted a major influence on the legal profession both in England and the United States.

58 Ralph Waldo Emerson attended a dinner here on 25 April 1848. His host, John Forster, had swapped the bar for literature and had written the biography of Charles Dickens, one of his dinner guests that evening. When Emerson's friend, Thomas Carlyle, appeared at the door, Forster greeted him with a loud, "My prophet!" Since there were only gentlemen present, Emerson noted that "the conversation turned on the shameful lewdness of the London streets at night." Carlyle and Dickens said that chastity in the male sex was as good as gone and that in England it was so rare "that they could name all the exceptions." Emerson felt that it betrayed a fatal rottenness in the country and wondered how any boy could grow up safe. Carlyle replied that he believed that the same things were true in America. "I assured them that it was not so with us," Emerson countered, "for the most part, young men of good standing and good education with us, go virgins to their nuptial bed, as truly as their brides." Dickens said that if his own son were particularly chaste, "he would be alarmed on his account, as if he could not be in good health." Emerson later described the evening to his wife: "I met Dickens at Mr. Forster's, and liked him very well, did not observe the dandy of which everyone speaks, in him. He was cordial and sensible."

It was this house, number 58, which Charles Dickens chose as the residence of Sir Leicester Dedlock's lawyer, Mr. Tulkinghorn, in *Bleak House:* "a large house, formerly a house of state ... let off in sets of chambers now; and in those shrunken fragments of greatness lawyers lie like maggots in nuts."

Auctioning a ticket to America.
Savoy Hotel, 17 August 1914.
(See page 245.)

*For the first time in history
American troops marching through London,
August 1917.*

After parading down Piccadilly,
they rested in Green Park,
and then marched to Waterloo where they left for France.

*A Guardsman speaking to a Beefeater
at the Tower of London.
(See page 264.)*

Litchfield Street

(18)   Joel Barlow and his wife Ruth lived in a flat on the first floor of this house during 1792-93. Barlow, a Yale graduate, had come to France representing the Scioto Land Company which held options to buy three million acres of land in Ohio at one dollar an acre. In 1792, its promoter went to prison in America for fraud and Barlow, pursued by furious French investors, hid first in Paris and then in London. During his four years in Paris, Barlow had become enamoured of the French Revolution and all its principles, and turned to political writing. The timing was appropriate: when the Barlows arrived in London the revolution was a topic of intense interest. Edmund Burke had published his famous *Reflections on the Revolution in France,* to which Thomas Paine replied from Paris with *The Rights of Man.* Barlow was soon associating with the English friends of the French Revolution, scientist Joseph Priestley, philosopher Richard Price, actor and author Thomas Holcroft, William Godwin and his future wife, Mary Wollstonecraft. She and Ruth Barlow became close friends.

Early in 1792 appeared Barlow's *Advice to the Privileged Orders in the Several States of Europe Resulting from the Necessity and Propriety of a General Revolution in the Principle of Government*—a typically catchy 18th-century title. Selling for one shilling and sixpence, the book soon went through three editions. Next to his friend Thomas Paine's *Rights of Man,* Barlow's *Advice* was the work considered most seditious by the British government. When Thomas Hardy (no relation to the novelist), secretary of the influential Society for Constitutional Information, was later tried for sedition, the crown prosecutor declared as he brandished a copy in court: "Barlow's book you will find is in the plainest and most unequivocal language, as I understand it, an exhortation to all people to get rid of kingly government." The prosecutor was right, but was unable to show that Hardy did more than approve of Barlow's *Advice,* and the case was dismissed.

Barlow next wrote a satire, *The Conspiracy of Kings,* in which he warned kings to be aware, "for the hour is come." He sent a copy to his friend, Thomas Jefferson, adding, "though one of my kings died while the poem was in the press, it was not my fault." The king was Leopold of Austria, brother of Marie-Antoinette. When the French Convention proclaimed itself ready to bring freedom to all of Europe, an ecstatic Barlow wrote *A Letter to the National Convention* and sent it to Thomas Paine to deliver in Paris. In it he made a series of specific proposals for the new French constitution, derived from the American experience. He was against large salaries for officials, imprisonment for debt, capital punishment, colonization and standing armies. Representation should be based on population and not on property. Barlow was made a French citizen and slipped away to Paris where he addressed the Convention. His correspondence with his English friends was used by the British government in their sedition trials of 1794. Ironically enough, Barlow—who dreamed of writing the great American epic, *The Vision of Columbus* (1787), revised as *The Columbiad* in 1807—is remembered today for a charming little poem written in France, called "The Hasty Pudding."

Lord North Street Map D

13   Bernard Berenson arrived in London on 10 January 1888 where he was greeted by a pea-soup fog which hung in the air and made his eyes "smart horribly." Aged 23 and on his way to spend a semester at Oxford, his first concern was his wardrobe. A suitable dress suit, made-to-order as was the custom, cost £8; a "day" suit £5; a well-furled umbrella 22 shillings; a top hat 50 shillings. He confessed to a friend that it actually frightened him to be "so happy away from Boston." After Oxford he went to Italy. When he came back to London two years later, he frequented the home of the Costelloes at 40 Grosvenor Road, thick with Fabian socialists and intellectual aesthetes including George Bernard Shaw and Oscar Wilde. The author of the newly-published *Picture of Dorian Gray* immediately recognized a fellow genius, called on Berenson here on Lord North Street and gave him a copy of his book. Berenson visited the London galleries with his new student, the young and beautiful Mrs. Mary Costelloe, sister of Logan Pearsall Smith and mother of two children. Together they admired canvas after canvas celebrating sacred and profane love—a singular union of interests misunderstood by so many, Mr. Costelloe, for instance. Mrs. Costello left her husband and, after his death in 1899, married Bernard Berenson with whom she had been living for eight years.

During the summer of 1894 in London, Berenson gave ten lectures on Italian masters to those who cared to spend two guineas. More important, his slender volume *The Venetian*

Painters of the Renaissance was published by G.P. Putnam and appeared simultaneously in New York and in London. His constant shortage of money was soon to end. From London he wrote to Mrs. Isabella Gardner, a wealthy Boston socialite, about a Botticelli which he felt he could get for about £3,000. She sent a check and the picture went to 150 Beacon Street and finally to the Fenway Court Collection in Boston.

Lots Road

Charles Tyson Yerkes, Chicago financier, established the headquarters of his Underground Electric Railways Co. of London (U.E.R.L.) late in 1901. Over the next four years, Yerkes more than any other man was responsible for the modernization and the enormous expansion of the London underground. His formula for success was, in his own words, to "buy up old junk, fix it up a little and unload it upon other fellows." His amalgamated transport undertaking in Chicago had gone bankrupt, but not before he had succeeded in unloading his own shares for $20 million. In London, Yerkes settled in the fashionable Hotel Cecil on the Strand and invited British investors to join him in a united underground network which, he claimed, "cannot but be profitable." (The catch was, profitable for whom?) He carefully avoided the term "shares" and permitted Londoners the privilege of subscribing to "trust securities." Within three years he had raised £15,000,000, more than half of it in America. But his costs were massive. He electrified the District Line and built three new tube railways: the Baker Street & Waterloo; the Charing Cross Euston and Hampstead, and the Great Northern Piccadilly & Brompton. Yerkes brought over a number of American electrical engineers, headed by James R. Chapman and seconded by S.B. Fortenbaugh from General Electric, Schenectady. To supply the electricity, he built the largest traction generating station in the world, 453 feet long and 275 feet wide at Chelsea on the bank of the Thames. The District Line was the first to be electrified: 1,000 men worked from 1 a.m until 5 a.m., reconstructing the track while the trains were at rest. The Otis Elevator Co. supplied 170 lifts. The first rolling stock order for 258 carriages was placed with the American Car & Foundry Co. of Berwick, Pennsylvania. The carriages were shipped to Liverpool, assembled at Trafford Park, Manchester, hauled on their own wheels down the London & North Western Railway to the Camden goods yard and then, in the small hours of Sunday mornings, pulled on flat trucks by teams of fourteen horses across London to the tube's depot at London Road, Southwark.

Part of the secret of Yerkes's success was simple. While his British competitors waited for permission to build from the myriad and conflicting authorities, few of whom understood the process of electrification, Yerkes simply went ahead and built. He asked for permission only as the work neared completion, gambling that because so much British capital was at stake the authorities would not dare refuse him. As in Chicago, aided by outright bribery, he turned out to be right. He had publicly estimated 60 million passengers a year for the Piccadilly line, 50 million for Hampstead and 35 million for Bakerloo. His predictions and their resulting profits had made wonderful reading but, alas, only half that number of passengers actually traveled in 1905, the first year, for a motor bus boom had begun. In October 1905 Yerkes faced a grim meeting with U.E.R.L. shareholders. The trains were running well, but Yerkes's miscalculations and misleading financial information—he had already served two years in prison in Philadelphia—had become apparent. There were not only no profits but the prospect of staggering losses. By now ill, Yerkes retreated to the Waldorf Astoria Hotel in New York, where he died on 29 December 1905. Two monuments to him remain—the Lots Road power station at Chelsea with its two 275-foot chimneys and the Yerkes Observatory in Williams Bay, Wisconsin.

Lower Mall, Hammersmith

Thameside. Alvin Langdon Coburn, 27, moved in 1909 into this charming old house overlooking the Thames. He set up two printing presses as well as a studio and darkroom. "Like Whistler, Mr. Coburn has the advantage of looking at London much more imaginatively than any born Londoner could," wrote George Bernard Shaw. He might have added that both Americans were also fascinated by life on the Thames and lived close to the river. Later that year, Coburn's book *London* appeared with twenty photographs of the city. From his presses at Thameside he produced the photogravure illustrations for his books, *London* and *New York,* and for H.G. Wells's *The Door in the Wall.* Coburn began photographing rehearsals of plays, such as John

Galsworthy's *Justice,* George Meredith's *The Sentimentalists* and Maeterlinck's allegory *The Blue Bird.* Among those who sat for him were Thomas Hardy, Frank Harris, editor of *Vanity Fair,* John Masefield, Maurice Maeterlinck, Sir Henry Wood, Henry James, Feodor Chaliapin and Ezra Pound. When Coburn was invited to hold a one-man show at the Camera Club in London, Pound wrote the preface to the catalog. Unfortunately, much of his work was destroyed in 1928 when an exceptionally high tide breached the wall protecting the river bank and filled his basement with mud.

Lowndes Street Map F

37 Carlton House. James Russell Lowell and his wife took a house here in the spring of 1880 and stayed for five years. After serving as American minister in Madrid for three years, Lowell had happily accepted the transfer to England. His first year was marked by the continuing trouble between England and Ireland where among the most violent Irish rebels were Irishmen who had been naturalized in the United States and had returned to Ireland to fight for the cause. His duty as minister was to discriminate between men who were American citizens and innocent of any infraction of British law, and those who were using the cover of American citizenship to hide their illegal actions. This was easier said than done.

Lowell had taught European literature at Harvard and gave several lectures in England. The University of St. Andrew's even proposed him as their rector, which drew strong opposition as he was an alien. A veritable storm in a teacup ensued. The press was divided, but *Punch* sided with Lowell in a lengthy poem, part of which read:

> Whig, Tory, and Rad should count votes, did he need 'em
> To honor the writer who gave *Bird o' Freedom*
> To all English readers. A few miles of sea
> Make Lowell an alien? Fiddle-de-dee!

What had begun as a sort of joke became less and less humorous and to save embarrassment Lowell withdrew his candidacy, which he had never offered in the first place. His only regret was that he would never be able to place "Univ. Sanct. Andr. Scot. Dom. Rect." after his name in the Harvard catalog. "Couldn't they count me as they do Louis XVII, though I never reigned?" he asked a friend wistfully.

James Lowell had first arrived in England more than thirty years earlier, as if, like many New Englanders, he had a score to settle with the old country. But he had mellowed, and told Charles Norton back at Harvard that he liked London and that he had learned to see the advantage of a great capital. "It establishes one set of weights and measures, moral and intellectual, for the whole country. It is, I think, a great drawback for us that we have as many as we have States." In his fifth year, as he was enjoying his vast popularity as a recognized writer in London, his wife suddenly died. "I am more than ever at a loss what to do with myself." Three months later he returned to Southborough, Massachusetts.

Ludgate Hill

Fleet Prison. First mentioned in 1170, the old Fleet Prison stood near the east bank of the Fleet river on Ludgate Hill. Destroyed in 1780 in the Gordon riots, it was "rebuilt in a commodious manner," with a "felons' side" and a "masters' side," a rectangle four stories high with 109 rooms, "nearly all with fireplaces," and a courtyard for exercise. The larger the sum paid to the keeper, the better the accommodation given to the prisoner. By the 18th century, it mainly held debtors. It was torn down in 1846.

John Howard Payne was escorted to Fleet Prison on 31 December 1820. Although in debt after having run the Sadler's Wells Theatre for the season, Payne still managed to afford a room with windows and was permitted visitors. His New Year's resolutions, he wrote, included paying attention to religion, reading the bible and exercising "more prudence, economy and punctuality." He also noted in his diary "never to owe money to one's landlord. Little debts are always worse than big ones." Happily, the making of these virtuous decisions was interrupted by a visit from Mrs. Glover, a good-looking actress who had appeared in Payne's *Brutus*. Over the next two months she provided that companionship not generally associated with British prisons. Nevertheless, winter days were dreary. His diary for 7 January read: "A deep reddish fog all day." 9 January: "The fog was such all day as to exclude the light; the air was red and murky and I burned candles without intermission." The following day Payne was gripped by a "death-like melancholy." But on 17 January he received "a parcel from France without name or letter." It contained a play *Thérèse; or the Orphan of Geneva*, by the French playwright Victor Ducange. Payne read it and decided to translate it and adapt it for Drury Lane. 18 January: "Sent shirt to pawnbrokers and got enough money to buy a day's provisions and begin work on Thérèse." In three days he had done three acts. 21 January: "Wrote Thérèse till late at night. Passed a miserably sleepless night, counting the clocks, and when I slept the characters rushed through my brain, all conversing and speaking the emphatic passages." Mrs. Glover, who was playing in *A School for Scandal* at Drury Lane, took the play and gave it to Elliston, the manager. Elliston wasted no time. He called on Payne in prison two days later, and the play opened on 2 February 1821. It was a triumph. The *London Magazine* hailed it as "the best and most successful melodrama ever produced at Drury Lane." Two weeks later *Thérèse* was published; the first edition of a thousand copies sold out immediately. Elliston brought Payne £140 and on 1 March 1821 he was able to write in his diary: "Liberty! delicious liberty!" His success, however, spurred other creditors to press their claims and, having reclaimed his trunks from his landlady at 4 Southampton Street, he hurried to Paris where he composed "Home, Sweet Home."

Manchester Square Map A

Hertford House. Built in 1776 as the town residence of the Duke of Manchester, it was later acquired by the Marquess of Hertford. Sir Richard Wallace, the natural son of the fourth Marquess of Hertford, died in 1890 leaving his paintings, furniture and objets d'art to the nation. (Hertford House, containing the Wallace Collection, is open to the public.)

William Bingham and his wife were frequent guests here in 1783 while living on HARLEY STREET. After a three-year grand tour of Europe, the self-made millionnaire decided to build a house suitable for lavish entertaining on his return to Philadelphia. Having been a guest in many stately homes in Europe, he decided on copying this one. This mansion, he wrote, exhibits "a remarkable show of simplicity united with elegance." He had a plan sketched of it with the precise dimensions of every room. He then set about buying stonework and furnishings for shipment home. At the Coade manufactory at Lambeth he bought marble jambs, headpieces for chimneys, marble slabs and stone ornaments such as *fascia,* medallions, moldings and keystones. Other purchases included 18 large mirrors; 20 rush-bottomed chairs; 24 mahogany chairs with morocco bottoms; 12 mahogany armchairs; 6 large armchairs and a matching sofa covered with Gobelin tapestry; a set of 12 rosewood chairs with backs in the form of lyres, festooned with pink and yellow silk; a harpsichord; a pianoforte; dove cages; 7 urn mahogany knife cases; 14 patent brass lamps; one 350-piece set of blue china with gilt edges, and 2,000 ounces of silver in tureens, vases, bowls, dishes, trays, candlesticks, ladles, knives, spoons—and the first silver-pronged forks ever seen in America. For Anne Bingham's bedroom he bought a mahogany bedstead seven feet square with canopy and curtains. A full-length portrait of the famed actress Mrs. Siddons in "The Grecian Daughter" was stowed away with marble busts of Voltaire, Rousseau and Franklin. Cases of paintings, busts and mantel ornaments from Italy were stacked next to those from France containing dinner and tea sets of Sèvres porcelain.

When the time came for them to depart, Miss Abigail Adams, who had accompanied the Binghams upon their presentation at St. James's Palace two weeks earlier, told her brother John Quincy: "Mr. Bingham called this morning—their baggage is all on board and they are only waiting for a fair wind." She revealed no sadness at their leaving. On the second Monday of March 1786, with their eight servants safely on board, the ship bearing the Binghams and the finest workmanship that Europe had to offer (including two magnificent carriages made specially in London that had to be strapped on to the deck) cast off from the Pool below Tower Bridge and set sail for home. Bingham built his mansion on Third Street in Philadelphia.

Mansfield Street Map A

5   Charles Francis Adams and his family moved into the American embassy here in May 1861. Appointed minister to England by Lincoln, he was unprepared for the hostility toward the Northern states which emanated from the British governing classes. If it was true that the great body of the English people and the newspapers favored the free states, it was because their sympathy was largely rooted in antislavery sentiment. But this feeling soon deteriorated in the face of mounting assertions by Northern leaders that the main object of the war was not abolition of slavery, but reunion. Without a declared goal of abolition, most of the English felt that the war was pointless: indeed why didn't the Southern states have the right to secede if they wished? Adams's son, Henry, aged 23, who had come to serve as secretary, recalled that upon their arrival his family felt like "early Christian martyrs about to be flung into the arena of lions, under the glad eyes of Tiberius Palmerston." (Palmerston was prime minister.) As Adams prepared to present his credentials to Queen Victoria at Buckingham Palace, he learned that his predecessors, George M. Dallas and James Buchanan, had obeyed a directive of the secretary of state and had appeared in plain black suits. Their republican devotion to the homely virtues had not been appreciated in court circles in London. Not only was it seen as lacking in respect for Queen Victoria, but its silent assumption of moral superiority was judged far more ostentatious than all the traditional panoply of silk stockings and gold lace. As Adams pondered on what to wear, a British diplomat gently pointed out that plain black suits were worn by butlers in stately English homes. That decided Adams immediately. Silk and gold it would be. The interview lasted but a few moments and Adams found the queen gracious and dignified.

The Confederate victories of Lee and Jackson during the first year convinced the English that the Union could never win. Little by little, the pessimism among the Adams family and their few supporters in London became wearying. But happily, the two hours Adams spent each day seeing visitors passed quickly. A great many Englishmen wished to join the Northern army, and many suggestions to save America were presented. A Mr. Alison saw the problem as being quite simple: the United States had only to establish a national church, inaugurate a monarchy and do away with the division of the country into states, and America's troubles would dissolve. Mr. Alison wrote out these recommendations and asked that they be conveyed to Mr. Lincoln at once. Other suggestions for ending the war were less practical. In April 1862, the Adams family moved to PORTLAND PLACE.

Mansion House Street Map E

Mansion House, built in 1752, is the official residence of the lord mayor of London for his year of office. Nathaniel Hawthorne accepted an invitation to the lord mayor's banquet here in 1855. His only condition was that he should not be asked to speak. The mayor acquiesced. "In the entrance hall I was received by a body of footmen dressed in a livery of blue coats and buff breeches, in which they looked wonderfully like American Revolutionary generals." Hawthorne shook hands with the lord mayor in a reception room and then proceeded with some three hundred guests into the banqueting room, known as Egyptian Hall, to the strains of a powerful band. Here glass gleamed and silver glistened over an acre or two of snowy damask, over which were set out all the accompaniments of a stately feast. "We found our places without much difficulty, and the chaplain implored a blessing on the food—a ceremony which the English never omit, yet consider, I fear, not so much a religious rite as a sort of preliminary relish before the soup." When the after dinner wine was placed on the table, the lord mayor rose and drank to everyone from the loving cup. Then with both hands he presented the covered cup to the guest next to him who lifted the lid, drank, replaced the lid and passed the cup to his neighbor, until the entire company found themselves "entangled in one complicated chain of love." When the richly ornamented silver goblet reached Hawthorne, he noticed that almost all the wine was still in it. Being curious and with a view perhaps to recommending it to his countrymen, he took "an honest sip" to discover that it was a poor claret mingled with water, sugar and spices. As speech followed speech and toast followed toast, Hawthorne sipped contentedly glass after glass of champagne, until he had never felt cosier or safer. Suddenly into this tranquility came a thunderbolt. The lord mayor began to introduce him. *The Scarlet Letter* had been published five years earlier followed by *The House of Seven Gables;* he was serving as American consul in Liverpool.... Hawthorne's mind was blank— indeed, it was not terribly clear. In desperation he turned to his three English dining companions who suggested that he begin his speech with a compliment to the mayor, expressive of the hereditary reverence in which his office was held by the Puritan forefathers (whether quite the fact or not). Then, flexible with the oil of his own eloquence, he could slide into the endless topic of Anglo-American relations to which his Lordship had just made a weighty allusion. Let Hawthorne himself finish the drama:

> Seizing this handful of straw with a death-grip, and bidding my three friends bury me honorably, I got upon my legs to save both countries, or perish in the attempt. The tables roared and thundered at me, and suddenly were silent again. But, as I have never happened to stand in a position of greater dignity and

peril, I deem it a strategem of sage policy here to close these Sketches, leaving myself still erect in so heroic an attitude.

Maple Street

(49)   Washington Allston returned to England in August 1811 after an eleven year absence, accompanied by his wife and a 20-year-old Yale graduate, Samuel F.B. Morse. The Allstons took an apartment here on Maple Street (then known as London Street) and one of their first callers was the painter Benjamin West. His former teacher, now a septuagenarian, was astonished at the progress that Allston had made since his first stay in England. West immediately recognized a certain Renaissance flavor in Allston's biblical subject *The Dead Man Revived by Touching the Bones of the Prophet Elisha* (now in the Pennsylvania Academy of Fine Arts, Philadelphia), which won the gold medal and 200 guineas two years later at the British Institution show. This prize brought Allston commissions and encouraged him to pursue biblical and mythological themes, such as *Elijah in the Desert Fed by the Ravens* (now in the Museum of Fine Arts, Boston).

Margaret Street

(67)   Robert Fulton, 26, had already painted in London for four years under the guidance of Benjamin West when he moved here, close to fashionable Cavendish Square. The year was 1791 and Fulton had two "portraits of young gentlemen" accepted in the exhibition of the Royal Academy, four pictures in the exhibition of the Royal Society of British Artists, and his first important commission. Viscount Courtenay, future Earl of Devon, invited Fulton to his country seat, Powderham Castle, near Exeter, to do his portrait. The young viscount was so delighted with the painting that he presented Fulton to his friends, and the future inventor spent the summer earning sufficient money both to pay off debts and save—a feat for any young artist. In a letter to his mother, he recalled the long and lean four years during which "many, many a silent solitary hour have I spent in the most unnerved Study anxiously pondering how to make funds to support me... happily beloved by all who knew me or I had long ere now been Crushed by Poverties Cold Wind—and Freezing Rain." Now secure from the elements, Fulton did a series of historical paintings and exhibited in the Royal Academy

Exhibition of 1793. He was still facing competition from several remarkable American painters—John Singleton Copley, Gilbert Stuart and John Trumbull, not to mention Benjamin West. A good, but not outstanding painter, Fulton decided at about this time to turn to engineering, a decision that must have been regarded by his friends as sheer folly. Oddly enough, he celebrated this turning point in his life by moving to a house only two doors from Benjamin West, 18 NEWMAN STREET.

Mortimer Road, Kilburn

Harlestone Villa. Gutzon Borglum, sculptor and painter, arrived in London in 1896 from his native California. He had already studied in Paris, worked in Spain and had discovered upon returning home that it was not the Eldorado he had imagined. After finishing three paintings for Leland Stanford, the millionnaire suddenly died and his wife refused to pay for the paintings on the grounds that there was no written contract. In London, Borglum took a studio apartment in West Kensington before moving to Harlestone Villa where he had a rose garden and a room in which to work. He did a statuette of John Ruskin (a copy is in the Metropolitan Museum, New York). Paid commissions came slowly. A year after his arrival, he noted in his diary: "Six years ago I said to myself, 'I'll be great at thirty, or never.' I am thirty. I have had the disturbing pleasure of being called 'master' by the French critics and some Americans, yet at the moment I cannot spend sixpence without wondering where the next one will come from." In 1898, he painted a series of panels for the new Queen's Hotel in Leeds built by the Midland Railway Company. They represented the four seasons, with lithe, slender maidens dancing with garlands of flowers. The critics praised them, while the stout directors of the railway company were reassured because they understood them. In London he painted murals for private homes. One day in 1901, the young daughter of a Californian friend came to stay; her name was Isadora Duncan. As she danced on the lawn here in St. John's Wood scattering rose petals that she had been gathering, Gutzon felt "the fresh western breeze that came with her," filling him with nostalgia. Isadora left for Paris and Gutzon for New York. He had scarcely arrived back in America when he received an incredible commission from England. The Midland Railway Company was building a massive and ornate 296-bedroom hotel in Manchester, the Midland Hotel, and wanted twelve enormous panels. They offered five thousand guineas ($25,000)—the largest order for art work ever placed by the English in America. There was, however, one problem—it was payment on delivery. Borrowing funds from friends, Borglum returned to England in 1903 to oversee the instalment of the panels. The central figure in a 27-foot high panel showed Sir Lancelot escorting Guinevere to King Arthur's court. The other eleven paintings were scenes from *A Midsummer Night's Dream*. While Borglum was happy with his success, it was nevertheless ironic. He was first and foremost a sculptor and would win fame with his gigantic Mount Rushmore National Memorial in South Dakota, yet in England he was known only as a painter.

New Bond Street Map C

92 Charlotte Cushman, a 28-year-old actress from Boston, arrived in London on 6 December 1844 and put up at the Maurice Hotel in Covent Garden. When the producer J.M. Maddox first met the tall, strong, large-boned actress, he found the idea of her appealing to a British audience almost ludicrous. Still, she had come to London on the recommendation of the famous English actor William Macready, so Maddox took a chance. He offered her the role of Bianca in Milman's *Fazio* for one performance, followed by a limited run with the American actor Edwin Forrest at £7 a night. The single night without Forrest would give her a chance to display her own talent without the risk of being overshadowed by another actor. Maddox invited the London critics for her debut. As the evening approached, her nerves tightened and suddenly she became quite hoarse. She had a doctor "burn" her throat with a solution of nitric acid to relieve the pain. That night at the Princess Theatre, the first act of *Fazio* passed uneventfully. But in the second act, as Bianca's jealousy became apparent Cushman's acting took on an almost religious intensity, creating a tension in the audience that was finally released in storms of applause. When an exhausted Cushman reached her room, her dresser told her "You've got 'em, mum, you've got 'em." The following morning the London *Herald* cried: "Miss Cushman is tall and commanding, having a fine stage figure...her career in this country will be a most brilliant one." The *Times* stressed "the great characteristics of Miss Cushman are her earnestness, her intensity." For impetuous, irresistible passion, "she has not at present her superior." The *Sun* expressed the opinion that soon swept the capital: "America has long owed us a heavy dramatic debt for enticing away so many of our best actors. She has now more than repaid it by giving us the greatest of actresses, Miss Cushman." When she went on to play Lady Macbeth opposite Edwin Forrest, the London *Illustrated News* commented simply: "Miss Cushman is the chief attraction of the evening." Forrest was livid.

Before the season was over, Cushman also played Emilia, Beatrice and Portia. Her new salary permitted her to move here to New Bond Street where on the second and third floor for £3 a week, she had a drawing room, a bedchamber, rooms for her companion Sally and for her brother, a storeroom and a watercloset. She hired a grand piano. Her highest salary in America had been $50 a week; here she was earning $450 a week and estimated, almost exactly, that in two to three years she would be able to save $40,000. She spent the summer on tour and on returning to London took an elegant house on BAKER STREET. (Above Cecil Guy's, the building and its light interior has little changed since the 18th century.)

149   Thomas Hutchinson, the last royal governor of Massachusetts, arrived in England in August 1774. He had scarcely settled on New Bond Street with his son and daughter when Lord Dartmouth called to present him to the king. Hutchinson, still in his sober New England dress, was embarrassed to appear at court in such attire, but his reservations were swept away by Lord Dartmouth who told him that George III was most impatient to hear the latest news from Boston. The audience lasted two hours during which the governor was amazed by the king's knowledge of America (much greater than that of most of his ministers, he thought), and his numerous detailed questions concerning the rebel leaders. The former governor was forced to admit the personal integrity of his enemies, and likened Samuel Adams to a New England John Wilkes. In 1765, Hutchinson had been chief justice during the passage of the Stamp Act. Although he had done all in his power to prevent its enforcement, he had been seen by the populace as supporting it, with the result that his house in Boston had been sacked and gutted by the mob. His own devotion went wholeheartedly to Massachusetts and to New England, but like all Tories he was convinced that the prosperity of his countrymen was bound up with their continuing to remain within the British empire. Indeed, in this last sentiment he was probably joined in 1774 by half of America. It was his sincere belief that conditions in America were not yet ripe for independence. He never felt himself to be an Englishman, but always and solely an American who believed that his policy would be the most beneficial one for his own country. But the task he had set himself was impossible. Aged 53, he failed to understand the changes which had come about in popular feeling in America. Like other loyalists in London, he firmly believed that the revolt would be quickly crushed, the family quarrel patched up, and he and his children would be able to return to their home in Milton in their beloved Massachusetts. In retrospect, his mistake was to accept the governorship in 1769. He failed to reveal to the king the real conditions, the bitter hostility and determination of much of Massachusetts. He minimized the danger of the revolt and did not point out what many Englishmen foresaw—that armed insurrection would be the inevitable consequence of the king's policy. His audience ended with the king assuring him of the entire satisfaction he felt with his administration of Massachusetts. His governor's salary was continued while he was in London, and the king even offered him a baronetcy, the highest honor conferable on colonials.

Hutchinson's household on fashionable New Bond Street was run by his pretty 20-year-old daughter Peggy. She helped preside over dinners attended by fellow loyalists and New Englanders such as Judge Jonathan Sewell, Samuel Curwen, Joseph Taylor, Daniel Silsbee and the Reverend Isaac Smith, future librarian at Harvard College. Although she did not share her father's Tory beliefs, Peggy Hutchinson was loyal and hoped for his success in bringing about reconciliation between the two countries. To help celebrate Thanksgiving, she sent home for cranberries and cheese; the novelty of living in London had worn off—the weather in August, she complained, was as cold as November in Massachusetts. As for the young, handsome, English nobleman whom her sister-in-law in Milton pictured her marrying, Peggy replied frankly, "New England was the only place for pretty fellows." She did not reveal in her letters home that she had contracted consumption. By the summer of 1777 her gaiety had disappeared. She died that fall aged 23. In his diary, her father noted with classical New England restraint: "A distressing day for me."

Peggy had barely been buried when the news reached London of the surrender of General Burgoyne's army of 5,000 men at Saratoga. Hutchinson was further than ever from returning home. When he had arrived in London, he had been regarded as being, after Franklin, the most eminent American of his time, but within two or three years his usefulness and knowledge had worn thin. Frequently a guest, he was rarely consulted. When the revolution broke out, Governor Hutchinson had probably been the wealthiest man in New England. But in 1779 an Act was passed "to confiscate the estates of certain notorious conspirators against the Government and liberties of the late Province." He learned of his own impoverishment one evening in a London coffee house, where he chanced upon a Boston paper and read of the advertisement for sale of his home and all the property he possessed in America. When his son Billy also died of consumption, he barely recorded this new tragedy in his diary. Everything he had striven for was wrecked. A man of unquestioned integrity, he had attempted to serve both king and country, and knew that he had failed in both. He filled in the long days by finishing the third volume of his *History of Massachusetts*. Alone, fearful of dying in exile, in 1779 he moved to modest dwellings on Sackville Street. He passed away the following year.

(169-174)   Clarendon Hotel. John Charles Fremont, former senator from California, took an extensive suite for his family upon their arrival in London in late March 1852. The Clarendon was "perhaps the best hotel in London" where you could get "a genuine French dinner, and for which, you seldom paid less than three or four pounds." It suited Fremont, who had achieved wide fame exploring the Rocky Mountains ten years earlier with his guide, Kit Carson. Together with his wife Jessie, daughter of Senator Benton from Missouri, the two entered the social whirl of London. Mrs. Fremont was presented to Queen Victoria, who made an "impression of womanly goodness combined with a look of power." Fremont was guest of honor at a dinner given by the Royal Geographical Society, and the family took tea with the aged Duke of Wellington. But one evening in early April, as Fremont was about to climb into a carriage to go to dinner, he was arrested for debt by four Bow Street officers. His political past in California had unexpectedly caught up with him. Five years earlier, appointed civil governor of California, he had drawn a draft for $15,000 against James Buchanan, secretary of state, to pay for supplies for U.S. troops in northern California. Congress had made no appropriations and the draft was refused. Since the government could not be sued, the note-holder sued Fremont and a lengthy civil suit began. In England debtors were still taken to prison, and Fremont spent the night in the famous King's Bench Prison across the river in Southwark. He was bailed out the next morning by the American banker George Peabody, and promptly left for Paris. One of the most controversial figures in western history, chosen in 1856 as Republican presidential candidate, he died in 1890, bankrupt.

New Burlington Street Map C

3 In 1785, Gilbert Stuart signed a lease here for £105 a year, a mere bagatelle for a leading painter earning thirty guineas for a bust, sixty for a half-length and a hundred for a full-length portrait. He gave a dinner for forty-two people, with musicians from the Drury Lane Theatre. On ordinary evenings, he put up seven cloak-pins in his hallway, issuing a standing invitation for any male friend to join him who called and found an empty pin. After a day of portraiture, "I flung down my palette and pencils," wrote Stuart, "took my hat and ran about the park for an hour, then home, got ready for dinner, and approached my dining room with the certainty of meeting as clever men as could be found in society." What he lacked, he decided, was a wife. Given his earnings, there was no obstacle—and on 10 May 1786, he married Charlotte Coates, the 18-year-old daughter of a physician. Modestly attractive, she brought no dowry. Free of Benjamin West's discipline and Mrs. West's motherly supervision, Stuart began to revert to his earlier instability and was soon dangerously in debt. Collapse came within one year. The house, its contents and all his canvases were seized by the sheriff. In October 1787, Stuart surfaced in Dublin, Ireland, where he spent five years before returning to America and finally settling in Boston. Aged 50, still addicted to storytelling, fine food and wine, Stuart became the patriarch of American painting. His influence dominated American portraiture well into the 19th century.

Newman Street

An early English guide to London noted that "artists cluster around Newman Street." Indeed the list of residents here reads like a roll call of artists and sculptors.

(7)   A self-confident, well-dressed, 27-year-old Gilbert Stuart took a house here in 1782 just across from his mentor Benjamin West. With the immense success of his *Portrait of a Gentleman Skating,* Stuart had achieved overnight a place among the leading portrait painters of the day, just behind Reynolds, Gainsborough and Romney. Now he was beginning to earn £1,000 a year and was soon spending considerably more. Interested in music and the theater, he drew friends from the orchestra of the Drury Lane Theatre and actresses from behind the curtain. A footman was needed to open the door and serve dinner which was prepared by a French cook, while Stuart conducted his many guests through his gallery of portraits. Flushed by his own success, increasingly vain, he adopted what he believed to be the code of a gentleman, and the result was a grotesque caricature. With an open table and a fine cellar, actor friends and hungry musicians were never lacking. As for his portraits, "I tasked myself to six sitters a day," he wrote. Since he enjoyed painting faces, he engaged his sitters in conversation in order to catch their glance and person lity. He preferred, he said, to "pin the sitter's head to the canvas," and used an assistant to fill in the rest. After three years, he decided that he needed more impressive quarters and moved to NEW BURLINGTON STREET where disaster awaited him.

(14)   Benjamin West moved into a handsome new house here in 1774 and stayed until his death in 1820, at the age of 82. Over the years he made extensive additions. The gallery, with two other rooms, made three sides of a garden. A visitor described the garden as "very small but elegant, with a grass plot in the middle and busts upon stands under an arcade." From his window in his painting room, West could see the garden walls of the Middlesex Hospital. William Dunlap, who arrived in London in 1784 to study here under West, recalled half a century later:

> The impression made upon an American youth of eighteen by the long gallery leading from the dwelling house to the lofty suite of painting rooms—a gallery filled with sketches and designs for large paintings—the spacious room through which I passed to the more retired atelier—the works of his pencil surrounding me on every side—his own figure seated at his easel and the beautiful composition at which he was employed [*Lear*

and Cordelia commissioned by Catherine II, Empress of Russia]
as if in sport, not labour—are all recalled to my mind's eye at this
distance of half a century.

John Trumbull first called on West in July 1780. He was
immediately accepted as a student and began working along side
Gilbert Stuart who became a close friend. Trumbull, obliged to
leave England the following summer, returned to London in
January 1784 and resumed work in West's studio. He followed a
strict regimen, waking at 5 a.m. to study anatomy and painting all
day, with a lunch break at 2 p.m. In the evenings, he attended
classes at the Royal Academy or accompanied Benjamin West
among his large circle of artists, diplomats and aristocrats. Upon
completing his first portrait, Trumbull had "the vanity," as he
recalled later, to show it to Sir Joshua Reynolds, the most
celebrated portrait painter in London. Reynolds took one glance
and said in a quick, sharp tone, "That coat is bad, Sir, very bad. It is
not cloth—it is tin, bent tin." The criticism was true, but the 28-
year-old Trumbull's pride was wounded. In the autumn of 1785, he
began work on subjects of the Revolutionary War including the
death of General Warren at the battle of Bunker's Hill. Half a
century later, writing his autobiography in New Haven, he recalled
an evening spent in West's house:

> When the Bunker's Hill was pretty far advanced, he [Mr.
> West] said to me one day, "Trumbull, will you dine with me
> tomorrow? I have invited some of my brother artists, and wish
> you to be one of the party."
>
> He received his friends in his painting-room, where by
> direction my picture was standing in an advantageous light.
> Among the guests was Sir Joshua Reynolds, and when he
> entered the room he immediately ran up to my picture— "Why,
> West, what have you got here—this is better colored than your
> works are generally." "Sir Joshua," was the reply, "you mistake—
> that is not mine—it is the work of this young gentleman,
> Mr. Trumbull. Permit me to introduce him to you." Sir Joshua
> was at least as disconcerted as I had been by his "bent tin;" the
> account between us was fairly balanced.

One afternoon in September 1785, West was glancing over
canvases at John Greenwood's Auction House when he spied a 4-
foot by 6-foot dirt-and-wax encrusted landscape painting lying in a
corner. He secured it for twenty guineas amidst the snickers of
English buyers. Back in Newman Street, he cleaned the painting

carefully and found, as he had suspected, that it was a Titian. Refusing an immediate offer of 1,500 guineas, he rearranged his gallery to give *The Death of Acteon* a place of honor. The *Morning Post* described it as an "indisputable and pre-eminent" Titian from the collection of Charles I of England; they went on to suggest that the auctioneer change his name from Greenwood to Greenhorn.

Early in March 1786, Abigail Adams paid a visit to West's gallery here on Newman Street. In a letter to her sister, she spoke only of one painting, *The Death of General Warren at the Battle of Bunker's Hill* (now in Yale University, New Haven) which Trumbull had just completed: "To speak of its merit, I can only say that in looking at it my whole frame contracted, my blood shivered, and I felt a faintness in my heart. He is the first painter who has undertaken to immortalize by his pencil those great actions which gave birth to our nation." Benjamin West called it the "best picture" of a modern battle ever painted. In July, Trumbull accepted Jefferson's invitation to join him in Paris.

As history painter to the king, West was able to afford the £1,600 annual upkeep of this house, including five servants. During the half century that he lived and worked here, West was a generous friend and adviser to younger artists, particularly American painters studying and working in England. Men such as John Singleton Copley, Gilbert Stuart, Mather Brown, Washington Allston and Samuel Morse were all students here, worked here or were guests here.

(18)   Robert Fulton moved here in the fall of 1793, having decided to give up painting and become an engineer. While doing portraits in Devon and Cornwall the previous summer, his attention had been drawn by the canal at Habbacot Down, near Bude. He devoted the next three years to what he termed his "system of creative canals," which he drew together in *A Treatise on the Improvement of Canal Navigation,* published at the Architectural Library, High Holborn in 1796. Also about this time, Fulton became interested in Robert Barker's panorama, which had just opened in Leicester Square. Convinced that the French would enjoy such a show and that there was money to be made, Fulton left for Paris where he opened his own panorama in 1800. It was a tremendous success and he devoted the profits to the development of his two newest dreams, the submarine and the torpedo. After three years of experiments financed in part by Napoleon, he returned to London in 1804 to demonstrate his new naval weapons.

(70)   James McNeill Whistler, aged 25, rented a first-floor back-room studio here in 1859 for ten shillings a week. He tied a piece of string from wall to wall across the middle of the one long room over which he hung a piece of silk drapery. "This was supposed to separate the parlour from the bedroom," noted a friend. This was the first of his several studios in London, where he lived most of his life until his death in 1903. Whistler had become fascinated by the grimy docks, decaying wharves and soot-laden barges which lined the Thames. One of his first etchings, *Black Lion Wharf,* revealed this ramshackle and mysterious background in stark, realistic terms. In the Royal Academy Exhibition of 1860, five of his etchings and one painting, *At the Piano,* were accepted for display. The director of the National Gallery, Sir Charles Eastlake, escorted the Duchess of Sutherland to get a closer look at *At the Piano,* saying "There, Ma'am, that's the finest piece of painting in the Royal Academy." It sold for thirty guineas. Even better, his etchings had been reproduced and were selling at £2 a proof. Meanwhile, one of Whistler's models, Joanna Hiffernan, an Irish girl with coppery-red hair and a temperament to match, had become his official mistress. As intelligent as she was beautiful, she took over his tangled business affairs and became his agent. Her father, an Irish laborer, made no objection, referring to Whistler as "me son-in-law." In September, 1861, Whistler and Jo moved to Paris.

Norfolk Street (no longer exists)

(35)   Washington Irving moved to a private hotel here late in October 1805. "I have a parlour-bedroom and cabinet on the ground floor. I am not too far removed from the Coffee houses, exchange, while the Theatres are close at hand." Aged 22, he had been sent to France the previous year on the Grand Tour.

On leaving New York Irving had promised his family that he would send them a full account of his observations and experiences. While fulfilling this promise with a series of sketches, he realized that he was a writer. Like most London visitors, he wrote home about the fog.

> Two or three nights ago the fog was so dense that altho the City was lighted with its usual number of lamps and all the Strand

was illuminated by innumerable shop windows yet it was impossible to discern any object at a distance of ten feet and in crossing the streets the risk of being run over by carriages was imminent. It was a complete scene of confusion & bawling—I have not yet learnt how many were killed in the streets... for my part I swallowed so much of it that my throat has been sore ever since and I am troubled with continual coughing and sneezing.

But Irving did not experience a real London fog—they lasted for several days, with visibility of only three to four feet and all traffic at a standstill. London had been troubled by an atmosphere overladen with particles of soot at least since the 16th century when Shakespeare referred to "Drooping fogge as blacke as Acheron." As Londoners burned more and more coal the pall of soot grew worse, particularly toward the end of the 19th century. James Fenimore Cooper recorded keeping three fires burning seven days a week in a modest house in London in winter. The fog which began on 27 December 1813 blanketed London for seven days; that of November 1879 lingered until the following March. The last major London fog, December 1952, caused 4,000 deaths and resulted in stringent air controls.

During Irving's stay, on 21 October 1805, Lord Nelson was killed at Trafalgar in his naval battle against the French. On the evening of 6 November London was illuminated to celebrate his victory but, as Irving noted, with the national hero dead the song of triumph was repressed even "among the lowest of the mob." He spent December visiting Oxford, Bath and Bristol before sailing for home on 23 January 1806.

North Road, Haringey

17   Byron Cottage. Willa Cather, Dorothy Canfield and Isabelle McClung called on A.E. Housman in July 1902. Willa Cather had been an intense admirer of his collection of poems *A Shropshire Lad* and had written in her Nebraska column: "I wonder who and what this man Housman may be." Before making the pilgrimage to Haringey, she had toured Shropshire and had even called at the Shrewsbury Public Library where no one seemed to know anything about the author. This was not surprising for Housman lived here in Byron Cottage from 1886 until 1905 during which he composed *A Shropshire Land*. Cather had created a poet in her mind—a robust retired army officer or a brawny blacksmith singing immortal lyrics about his native countryside. The three young American women writers arrived uninvited and the 43-year-old Housman, professor of Latin at the University of London, expecting his three Canadian nieces whom he had never met welcomed them in warmly. It was only when they were seated in his shabbily furnished living room on the first floor complete with secondhand Latin and Greek dictionaries on the shelves that he realized his error. Cather began by explaining to their reluctant host what his poems meant to her. It was soon apparent that the shy and shabbily dressed bachelor abhorred talking about anything so personal as his poetry and an awkward silence enveloped the group. Groping for a subject Dorothy Canfield mentioned her work on French poetry at the British Museum. Housman, delighted to find a subject which protected him against his admiring guests, talked for ten minutes on the relationship between Latin and early French poetry. It was obvious that he was happy when the three women suggested that they take their leave. In the bus going back to their hotel in Bloomsbury, Dorothy Canfield apologized for monopolizing the conversation. Magnanimously Willa Cather replied: "But Dorothy you saved the day." She then burst into tears of rage, exasperation and disillusionment. In London she wrote on the grinding poverty of the East End, of the Albert Embankment "night and day thronged with drunken, homeless men and women who alternately claw each other with their nails and give each other a chew of tobacco." She told her readers that Kipling's description of the poor "who are perpetually drunk, and howl in the streets like jackals, men and women together," was no exaggeration. It was many years before she could bring herself to talk of the man whom she had come to meet who had written "When I was One-and-twenty."

Northumberland Avenue

Metropole Hotel. William Cody, better known as Buffalo Bill, stayed here from 16 April 1887 until early November while his Wild West Show took place at EARL'S COURT.

꙾

Oakes Ames, professor of botany at Harvard, took rooms here on 19 October 1905. He specialized in orchids and during three weeks in London studied the collections in the British Museum and Kew Gardens, but spent most of his time in the Natural History

Museum at South Kensington. The grandeur of Victorian architecture in museums was designed to impart a vast sense of dignity to the achievements of man and thereby Britain. None was more impressive than the Natural History Museum, nor was anyone more impressed than Professor Ames. Ensconced at a magnificent desk, reserved for the happy few, he proclaimed to his wife:

> Here they seem to realize that institutions given over to the higher studies should be dignified and impressive. Here you do not feel the sense of opinion for renumeration in cash. You at once grow proud of your distinction from the moneyed occupations and feel that your presence among the workers in the arts and sciences is respected and approved. Here they give proper attention to the man who endeavors to prove himself worthy of scientific recognition.

Thornton Wilder accompanied by three students took rooms at the Metropole in July 1928. The three young men soon discovered that their 31-year-old English teacher had some odd practices which they had not noticed at their Lawrenceville school. Wilder rose at dawn and read for three hours. If the weather was fine, he left the hotel before breakfast for long solitary walks through a still sleepy city. In their daily tours of London, they found his enthusiasm tiring: "Boys, there's history in every speck of dirt. The Romans were right here—centuries ago. Think of that! Come on now, don't go to sleep. You've only got seventy years. Everybody buy a notebook and write down your impressions." One of the students recalled that it was a great relief when they separated after three weeks. One of Wilder's favorite haunts in London became the Fitzroy Tavern in CHARLOTTE STREET.

Old Bond Street Map C

14 Colnaghi's Art Gallery. Many American art collections have been enriched by purchases made or arranged by Bernard Berenson. From his home outside Florence he frequently sent instructions to Colnaghi who bought pictures at his behest, made payments to vendors, and took care of crating and shipping. In 1895, Berenson, barely 30 years old, made a bold offer to Boston socialite, Mrs. Gardner: if she would permit him to advise her in art matters, it would not be many years before she would possess "a collection almost unrivalled—of masterpieces, and masterpieces only." Mrs. Gardner accepted. Over the next thirty years Berenson selected many of the paintings which eventually made up the Fenway Court Collection in Boston. Of the sixteen which were purchased at Colnaghi's, one of the earliest was Rembrandt's *Self-Portrait* done in 1629, purchased for £3,000, followed by the Holbein twin portraits of *Sir William and Lady Butts,* bought for £17,000. Berenson received a five per cent commission on all such transactions. During most of Berenson's dealings with Colnaghi, the gallery was located at 13 Pall Mall.

Old Compton Street, Soho Map D

Soho's main shopping street has drawn foreigners since 1700. The ground floors were turned into exotic food shops, restaurants and pubs. After the the Paris Commune in 1871, the street became popular with French exiles.

16 Van Wyck Brooks took a room here above a restaurant in 1907. Brooks, 23, a Harvard graduate, was one of the many young Americans who came to London at the beginning of the 20th century determined to succeed as a writer. He began by working for the Curtis Brown newspaper agency at Ludgate Circus where his task consisted of clipping stories from English newspapers and rewriting them in the "breezy style" the management insisted on for American readers. Among his assignments was one on trained dogs at railway stations collecting contributions for widows of railway employees, and another on an earl who fell into a lake and drowned, the theory being that any news about British earls interested American readers. Viewed from Cambridge, Massachusetts, his job on Fleet Street had a romantic ring to it but in the steady rain of London with a salary barely sufficient to pay for his unheated room, the romance soon wore off. In his spare time Brooks worked in the reading room of the British Museum where he met "half of Harvard," including his former professor of French, Irving Babbitt, who took him out and walked him "four times around Russell Square." Like other Americans Brooks enjoyed the social life in London, listening at dinner to George Bernard Shaw proving that the world and women could get on very well if men were abolished altogether. In February 1908 he moved to a village in Sussex where four months later he completed *The Wine of the Puritans,* which was published in London that fall and in America a year later. In it he argued that American culture had been so pervaded by puritanism that the artistic side of the nation's life had been seriously neglected. It was a thesis that did not excite all of England, but his manuscript at least found a publisher. It was a beginning. He returned to America in the fall of 1908 where he later became a respected critic. He won the Pulitzer Prize in history for *The Flowering of New England* (1936).

Old Mitre Court

(5)   The White Friars Club, made up of writers, humorists and journalists, gave a dinner here in the winter of 1873 to honor three Americans—Mark Twain, Joaquin Miller and Ambrose Bierce. During the 1870s, the American western writer Miller became the fad in London society, who simply doted on these eccentric fellows hailing from San Francisco (or so they claimed). Miller, born in Indiana, went to the Oregon frontier where he worked as a gold-miner, became an express rider, wrote for a newspaper and published two volumes of poetry. Moderately popular in America, in London he soon became the "frontier poet of Mayfair," publishing *Songs of the Sierras,* followed by *Songs of the Sun Lands.* A born showman, dressed in Western regalia, he told more wild tales about the old West than any other American in town. Staid Victorians loved him. He was the very embodiment of what a western journalist was supposed to be. Fleet Street proclaimed him the "Byron of Oregon"; whether Miller recognized the sarcasm is not known.

Ambrose Bierce, raised in Ohio, had worked as a journalist in San Francisco, where his daily page, "The Town Crier," was popular. During three years in London, he published a *Dictionary of Slang* and *Nuggets and Dust,* and wrote sketches for the well-known weekly, *Fun.* One of his favorite readers was William Gladstone. At the White Friars Club dinner Miller showed up with hair flowing to the shoulder, buckskin jacket, red sash and a huge knife in his belt as though he might have to hack his way to the table of honor. When the fish course was served, Miller picked up the fish by its tail and ate it whole, leaving his two fellow Americans aghast. The speaker of the evening was Bierce, whose studied indifference and cold sarcastic turn of mind was something new among after-dinner speakers. The following story told by Bierce illustrates the popular American humor of the time much appreciated by his English audience. A farm boy has just brought in his father's severed head after an accident with a mowing machine:

"Where did you get it?" asks the mother.

"Why, Ma, that's pap's."

"John, when your mother asks you a question you should answer that particular question. Where did you get this?"

"Out in the medder, then, if yer so derned pertikeller... the mowing machine lopped it off."

"My son, the gentleman whom you hold in your hand... has punished you a hundred times for meddling with things lying about the farm. Now take that head back and put it down where you found it, or you will make your mother very angry."

Oxford Street Map C

400   Selfridge's. Gordon Selfridge, a young executive at Marshall Field's department store in Chicago, visited London in 1906. Deciding that England knew how to make things but did not know how to sell them, he returned two years later to open his own store. With a personal investment of £300,000 and a similar sum put up by a British investor, Selfridge's was designed and built by Daniel Burnham of Chicago. With a facade of Portland stone and forty-foot Ionic columns, the "department store" was built in the record time, particularly for England, of ten months. It had eight floors covering six acres. The best buyers and a sales staff of 1,200 were recruited. A window dresser was brought in from Chicago. Strolling through the 130 departments in answer to the slogan, "Why not spend a day at Selfridge's?" the British public was delighted to find goods displayed with taste as if in an exhibition. Instead of keeping merchandise out of customers' reach on high shelves, Gordon Selfridge presented it at eyelevel, on counters where it could be handled. To the *Times,* "the interior presented the appearance rather of a fair than a mere shop." In the first week more than one million customers and sightseers swept through the doors; they lingered at the soda fountain and dined in the spacious restaurant where women alone or in pairs were made particularly welcome. The cosmetics department was put just inside the main entrance to entice female passersby. Selfridge brought such ideas to London as the "Bargain Basement," and the slogan, "There are only so-many shopping days to Christmas." He kept attractive window displays floodlit after closing hours, an idea soon copied by his competitors.

Gordon Selfridge, born and raised in Ripon, Wisconsin, entertained members of the royal family at his West End mansion, Lansdowne House in Berkeley Square, and gave a general election night party at his store for 3,600 guests. He kept a pied-à-terre at 8 Farm Street just off Berkeley Square, where among his neighbors was Tallulah Bankhead. In his seventies, lonely after his wife's death, he began to shower gifts upon young actresses. He spent more than his substantial income, owed more than £250,000 to the Inland Revenue and £120,000 to the store. In 1939, his fellow directors voted him off the board and gave him an annual pension of £2,000. He died in England in 1947 at the age of ninety.

Pall Mall Map C

80   Schomberg House. The British government became owner of this house in 1859. The house was reconstructed behind its original facade in 1956 and is now occupied by the War Department. Toward the end of the 18th century, Dr. James Graham opened his Temple of Health and Hymen here with its famous "Grand Celestial State Bed." Below a dome lined with mirrors, the bed had colored sheets and mattresses "filled with the strongest, most springy hair, produced at vast expense from the tails of English stallions." From his "celestial throne," Graham delivered his "very celebrated lecture on Generation," before his patients enjoyed the pleasures of the bed complete with music for £50 a night. They supposedly conceived perfect babies as "even the barren must do when so powerfully agitated in the delights of love." Alas, it is not known how many Americans, if any, owed their existence to this bed. For one thing it was probably too expensive. Dr. Graham ended his days in a lunatic asylum.

In her diary for Friday, 16 May 1913, Queen Mary noted: "We went to tea at Schomberg House and heard a little American lady Miss Draper recite too delightfully." Ruth Draper, 29, began what was to be a long career in London and throughout England by appearing before private groups at the houses of great hostesses. She performed before King George V and a group of royal relatives, including the Connaught and Battenberg families. While in London, her guide and friend was Henry James.

107   Athenaeum Club, intellectually the most elite of all the clubs of London, opened in 1830. Ralph Waldo Emerson wrote to his wife in March 1848 that he was honored to have been elected during his temporary residence in England. It is "a privilege one must prize, not because only ten foreigners are eligible at any one time, but because it gives all the rights of a member in a magnificent library, reading-room, a home to sit in and see the best company, and a coffee room, if you like it, where you eat at cost."

Henry James was to be found frequently at the Athenaeum. At the end of a long day's writing, he would dine here socially and could enjoy the use of a fine library. The club extended his sense of home and became a luxurious annex to his own more modest lodgings. On 2 March 1877 he wrote to his sister Alice:

> It is very late at night and I am in the delightful great drawing room of the Athenaeum Club where I have been reading the magazines all the evening, since dinner, in a great deep armchair with such a comfortable place to repose my book and such a charming machine to sustain my legs! I don't want to excite your animosity—but I might, were I to depict the scene that one may usually view here—in this same drawing room, at 5 o'clock in the afternoon:—all the great chairs and lounges and sofas filled with men having afternoon tea—lolling back with their laps filled with magazines, journals, and fresh Mudie books, while amiable flunkies in knee-breeches present them the divinest salvers of tea and buttered toast!

(118)   The first annual exhibition of the Royal Academy of Arts opened here on Wednesday, 26 April 1769, with 136 works of art. Among the public was Horace Walpole who noted that it was viewed by "a very crowded and brilliant rout of persons of the first position." America was represented by Benjamin West with two paintings, *Venus Lamenting the Death of Adonis* and *Regulus*. King George III paid 400 guineas for *Regulus* and ordered two companion pieces for Buckingham House, an honor which did not go unnoticed by West's fellow painters. Public recognition of the American artist came two years later with his most famous painting *The Death of General Wolfe* (now in the Grosvenor Gallery, London). First, the subject was modern. James Wolfe, the British commander, had led his troops in a surprise attack against the French garrison at Quebec and, at the moment of victory, had died on the battlefield in the arms of his officers. Secondly, all the characters were in modern dress rather than in the traditional costumes of antiquity. When West was working on this battle scene and word leaked out that Wolfe was represented in his actual uniform, there was general condemnation. The king let it be known that he thought it ridiculous that heroes should appear in bloodstained coats, breeches and in cocked hats. It was generally felt that modern dress would not only degrade the work, but would introduce a vulgarizing innovation to the Royal Academy. One day while West was working in his studio on PANTON SQUARE, the Archbishop of York and Sir Joshua Reynolds, president of the Royal Academy, called to emphasize the danger "which every attempt at innovation necessarily incurred of repulse and ridicule." They urged West to "adopt the classic costume of antiquity" as much more becoming, given the inherent greatness of the subject, rather than "the modern garb of war." Faced by two of the most influential men in England, the 31-year-old West replied carefully:

> I began by remarking that the event intended to be commemorated took place on the 13th of September 1759, in a region of the world unknown to the Greeks and Romans, and at a period of time when no such nations, nor heroes in their costumes, any longer existed. The subject I have to represent is the conquest of a great province of America by the British troops. It is a topic that history will proudly record, and the same truth that guides the pen of the historian should govern the pencil of the artist. I consider myself as undertaking to tell this great event to the eye of the world; but if, instead of the facts of the transaction, I represent classical fictions, how shall I be understood by posterity!
>
> I want to mark the date, the place, and the parties engaged in the event; and if I am not able to dispose of the circumstances in a picturesque manner, no academical distribution of Greek or Roman costume will enable me to do justice to the subject.

It was agreed that the two visitors would return when the painting was completed. If they did not approve, the painting would be consigned to a closet, regardless of West's own view. Upon the appointed day, the two men arrived and Sir Joshua "without speaking," recorded West, "after his first cursory glance, seated himself before the picture, and examined it with deep and minute attention for about half an hour." Reynolds then rose and said to the archbishop, "Mr. West has conquered."

Above: The entrance to the Metropole Hotel.
The coach is bound for Hampton Court.
Below: The lounge of the Metropole Hotel 1914. (See page 185.)

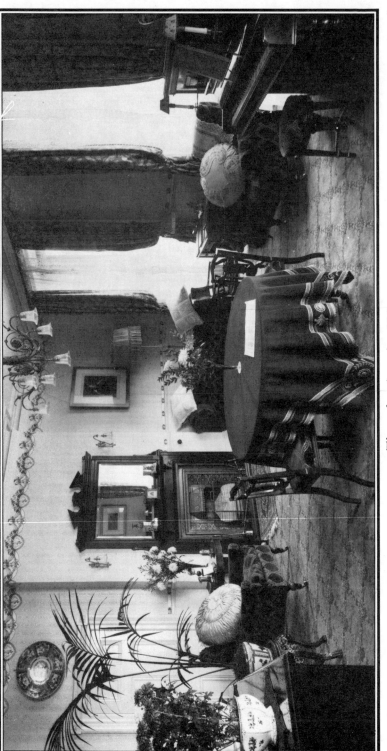

The salon in suite 310
in full Victorian splendor.
(See page 185.)

Bedroom 203.
(See page 185.)

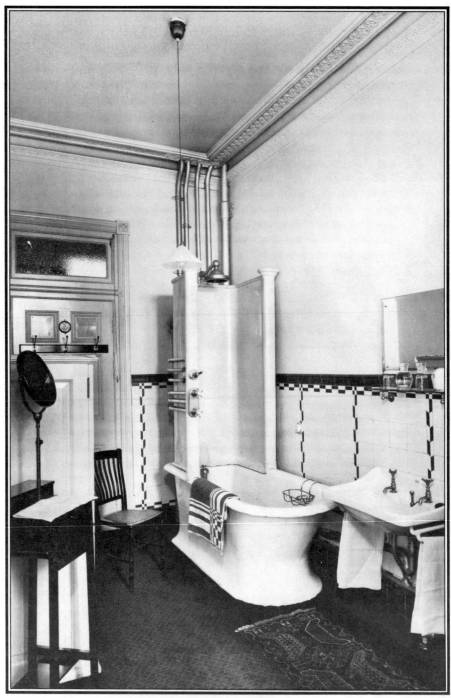

The deluxe bathroom
in suite 307A.
(See page 185.)

The entrance to the Savoy Hotel.
The Savoy Theatre is on the right, 1924.
(See page 245.)

The Winter Garden of the Savoy Hotel,
1911.

(See page 245.)

From the opening day of the 1771 exhibition, *The Death of General Wolfe* was a sensational success. William Pitt, who had put Wolfe in command at Quebec, stood in line to see it. The English public had witnessed no other modern painting like it. They felt that they were present and sharing in this tragic but inspiring moment. The scene of the massed soldiers, a spire of Quebec City, the masts of British ships standing in the St. Lawrence, swirling smoke, threatening black clouds, and a tiny patch of sunlight in the sky as a background to the dying soldier aroused not only admiration but emotion. It came at the very time when Englishmen were ready for a work glorifying English heroism, sacrifice and victory. Lord Grosvenor purchased the painting for £400. The king regretted his earlier prejudices, and ordered a copy.

In 1802, Rubens Peale, 20, and his brother Rembrandt, 23, arrived in London with the skeleton of a mammoth. They had helped their father, the painter Charles Peale, unearth the remains near Newburgh, New York. Sure of making their fortune, they rented the former Royal Academy, redecorated the inside in green baize, and mounted the bones on a pedestal. It was the first time that Londoners had laid eyes on that animal of the Pleistocene epoch and the show caused a sensation. Rembrandt lectured to audiences on the mammoth and printed a leaflet entitled *An Historical Disquisition on the Mammoth or Great American Incognitum, an Extinct, Immense, Carnivorous Animal Whose Remains Have Been Found in North America.* But like so many other adventurous young Americans, Rubens and Rembrandt discovered that a sensation in London was like a snowstorm—it did not last. After lugging the enormous skeleton to the provinces, tempers rose, debts mounted and with their failure to sell their "unique discovery," they sailed home broke.

(125)   James Christie began his business in 1767 and moved here three years later, auctioning everything from chamber pots to sedan chairs. With the French Revolution, objets d'art began to dominate the sales and in 1797 two American painters, Benjamin West and John Trumbull, hoped to make a fortune here.

While in Paris the previous summer, Trumbull had met the famous French art dealer, Jean Baptiste LeBrun. The French art market had collapsed with so many aristocrats selling their collections before fleeing. With funds put up by West and himself, and with LeBrun's advice, Trumbull returned to Paris and purchased over a hundred masterpieces which he had shipped to England. The London broker had given the order to get the precious crates to the custom house as soon as possible. But the ship arrived on the eve of 12 August, the birthday of the Prince of Wales, which was a holiday in all public offices. The London docks had not yet been built and merchandise was landed with lighters. Let Trumbull continue the story:

> The lighter-men brought my cases safely to the custom house quay, when finding no one to receive them, the custom house closed, no business doing, and all the porters and watermen making merry, they thought they might as well join. It was near low water, so they made the lighter fast with a chain to one of the posts, for perfect security, and then went their way for a frolic. In the evening when the tide came in, the bow of the boat being held down by the chain, she gradually filled with water, and my cases being light, floated out.

Fortunately for Trumbull, his future fortune was spied floating on the Thames by a watchman who gave the alarm. The cases were finally retrieved and Trumbull brought the sodden canvases to West's studio where he spent a somber four months becoming an art restorer. Benjamin West, who by then bitterly regretted his participation with Trumbull, decided that they should auction the dried-out masterpieces. This turned out to be yet another error. Christie advertised the sale in *A Catalogue of the Most Superb and Distinguished Collection of Italian, French, Flemish, and Dutch Pictures, a Selection Formed With Peculiar Taste and Judgment by JOHN TRUMBULL, Esq., during his late Residence in Paris, from some of the most CELEBRATED CABINETS in FRANCE... which will be sold at Auction by Mr. CHRISTIE, at his Great Room in Pall Mall, on Friday, February 17th, 1797.* Ninety-one paintings, including masterpieces such as *Virgin, Christ and St. John* by Raphael fetched the very modest sum of £8,217. Since no minimums were permitted, West was even forced to purchase some himself when the bids were ridiculously low. Trumbull and West still had some of the pictures fifteen years later. In 1823 Christie's moved to their present address in King Street.

Panton Square (formerly on New Conventry Street)

Benjamin West moved here from CASTLE STREET in 1769,

realizing that his future lay in England. He bought a country house on the Thames at Hammersmith and a smaller house with a painting room here on the corner of Coventry Street. As he explained to his former patron, Dr. Jonathon Morris:

> I have endeavoured to accommodate and settle myself in a domestic life with my little family which consists of my Dear Betsy, her little boy, a servant or two—one house in the country four miles distance from town where Betsy and her little boy stay eight months in the year, and another in London where I carry on my painting. And by that I get exercise of coming into town and going out to them every day.

Here he did his most famous painting, *The Death of Wolfe,* exhibited in the Royal Academy exhibition in PALL MALL in 1771. When Thomas Penn asked him to paint a scene commemorating his father's settlement in Pennsylvania, his *William Penn's Treaty with the Indians when He Founded the Province of Pennsylvania in North America* (now in the Pennsylvania Academy of the Fine Arts) was immediately acclaimed in the 1772 academy exhibition. Drawing on his childhood memories, he had painted the brick houses and the shadbelly clothes worn, or so he thought, by the elderly Quakers of the day, seated with the Indian braves under the great elm at Shackamaxon. Both the subject and the figures were new to European art. The picture told a story with gestures and facial expressions which everyone could understand. Over the next two centuries, an engraving of the picture appeared in every imaginable place: on china platters, gravy boats, tin trays, bed quilts, tavern signs and Christmas cards. These were happy and productive times for West. In August 1772, he had a second son, Benjamin, godchild of Benjamin Franklin. He was appointed historical painter to George III with an annual stipend of £1,000 and was soon able to afford a new house on NEWMAN STREET.

Over the years, West had been in correspondence with John Singleton Copley who was working in Boston. In the 1766 exhibition in London, Copley's painting, *Boy with a Squirrel,* had been considered a triumph. West suggested that he come to study in Europe and begin, as West himself had done, in Italy. Copley, who was the same age as West, married with children, hesitated over such a separation and such expenses. By 1774, however, the Boston Tea Party and local fighting convinced Copley that he should leave. After a swift 29-day crossing, he arrived in London on 10 July. He traveled up from Deal, Kent, in a post chaise "as genteel as any Chariot that roals through your Streets," he wrote to his family back in Boston, "with a Postillion well Dress'd as any you have seen in the service of the first gentlemen of fortune among you." He put up for the first few nights at the New England Coffee House and, having "procured some things to be Decent in," called on his compatriot and correspondent. With characteristic warmth, West invited him to stay but Copley preferred to live nearby. "I am within a few doors from Mr. West's....I have the first floor, very Genteel, for which I pay a Guinea per week. It consists of two Chambers, with a small room to powder in."

West introduced Copley to Sir Joshua Reynolds, who showed him his own collection of portraits and took him to the Royal Academy where Copley saw for the first time students drawing from a nude model. He also saw West's *Death of General Wolfe* which, he found, "sufficient of itself to Immortalize the Author." It was here in London that the 36-year-old Copley, already with 350 portraits behind him, finally saw paintings which he had only been able to visualize before from prints or books. He had been led, he discovered, to expect more than he found and yet this was reassuring. "The works of the great Masters are but Pictures," he told Henry Pelham, "and when a man can go but a very little beyond his contemporarys, he becomes a great Man, the difference between Raphael, Titiano, Angelo and the common run of moderately good Artists, is not as great as one would imagine."

Copley dined with a relative, Thomas Hutchinson, the former governor of Massachusetts, and a party of twelve Bostonians, on "Choice Salt Fish." The conversation included the Boston Tea Party, in which Copley had played an unsuccessful role as mediator. After six weeks of "seeing and absorbing" in London, on 26 August 1774, a light-hearted Copley set off for Rome.

Park Lane Map C

97   Helen Hayes lived here in Beatrice Lillie's flat in 1948 while rehearsing *The Glass Menagerie* under John Gielgud. Each day she walked a different way to the Haymarket Theatre until after a fortnight she had exhausted all the possibilities. She then walked each day down Grosvenor Street where she would stop and mourn before a stately old house that had been badly damaged in the Blitz:

> Its entire front had been blown away, leaving it with the appearance of a great doll's house, with all its rooms exposed to the prying sun and rain. On the second floor was an exquisitely paneled room with carved garlands that might have been Grinling Gibbons'. A community of pigeons lived there—such filthy tenants. Ten years later, on a return trip to London, I made straight for Grosvenor Street, and there was my house, its facade restored, mellowed, distinguished.

Dorchester Hotel. John Steinbeck stayed at the Dorchester in June 1958. As he walked through the lounge one day, he came across John Galbraith seated at a table reading a review of *The Affluent Society* in *Time* magazine. It called his book a "vague essay with the air of worried dinner-table conversation." "That's all right, Ken," Steinbeck reassured the Harvard economist, "I've always said that unless the bastards have the courage to give you unqualified praise, ignore them." Galbraith was on his way back to Boston from lecturing in Warsaw and was full of stories told by the party faithfuls. Steinbeck's favorite was: "Under Capitalism man exploits man, whereas under Communism it is just the reverse." He had breakfast here with Adlai Stevenson who was on his way to the Soviet Union. One of Stevenson's several missions was to try to get the publishing officials there to join the Universal Copyright Convention, a cause that Steinbeck also pressed himself the following year in the USSR. As they sat and sipped dreadful English coffee, both agreed that the greatest danger to the Republic was not the Soviets but Richard Nixon.

Peabody Avenue Map F

A fine example of George Peabody Buildings can be seen on this Peabody Estate, situated east of Chelsea Bridge, adjoining Grosvenor Road, just off the Embankment. The four-story 19th century buildings, each with two stairways and containing eight flats per floor, are clearly identified alphabetically with a large A, B, C or M engraved in the arch over the entrance to the stairways. Today, the buildings give somewhat the impression of a military installation, but they reflect the Victorian standards of economy, utility and discipline, values which helped George Peabody make his fortune. The outbuilding containing the original bathrooms—

one bath per week per tenant—can still be seen on the west side next to the bicycle sheds which could be rented for two pence per week. There was one laundry room on each floor in each building. Tenants had the right to a half day per week in the laundry and one long weekend every two months. Since most of the working class in Victorian England had no source of income after they stopped working at 65 years of age and faced spending old age in the poorhouse, the Peabody Trust permitted them to finish their days in their homes even if they could no longer pay rent. Rules required that all children under sixteen be off the street by 8 p.m. Today every flat has its own bathroom and the curfew for the children has long been abolished. New Peabody buildings reflect the latest standards of architecture and comfort but remain modest.

Piccadilly Map C

116 Athenaeum Court. John Steinbeck arrived in London in June 1943 as a correspondent for the *Herald Tribune.* He went first to the Savoy Hotel, but soon found it far too noisy, so he then took this apartment which overlooked St. James's Park. He told his wife, Gwyn, that when he looked out of his windows, "all of London I have ever read about is there." He could see St. Paul's, Whitehall, St. James's Palace, and "a little farther right is Big Ben, so close that I can set my watch by it." To his surprise he found himself famous in England and his columns were carried in the mass-circulation *Daily Express.* He had never really written for newspapers before and, unhappy with some of his writing, he consulted William Shirer. The two men became friends; Shirer, soft-spoken and thoughtful, "wore well," wrote Steinbeck, "rather like an old Harris Tweed jacket."

One evening Steinbeck was invited to the Embassy Club where he found himself facing a hostile group of young American correspondents. After a few drinks, they told him that his war reporting "stunk." Steinbeck was upset by this experience. He was far more at ease with top journalists like Quentin Reynolds, Ernie Pyle and Ed Murrow, who were far too good to be worried by a 41-year-old writer from Salinas, California. One morning as he left his flat he walked into Burgess Meredith, who had played in the film *Of Mice and Men* and who was busy making a film for the US army; Steinbeck later helped him with the dialogue. London was overrun with American correspondents but, apart from an occasional air raid, the real war at this time was going on in North Africa. Suddenly, in the second week of August, Steinbeck was told that if he wished to go to North Africa, he would have to be ready by 3:30 that afternoon. That evening he was on a transport plane to Algiers.

(137) Gloucester House, formerly at the west corner of Old Park Lane. Lord Elgin, British minister to the Ottoman Empire, brought the marble sculptures of the Parthenon back to England in 1804. The first fifty cases weighing 120 tons were laid out in a large shed rented by Elgin. Controversy surrounded the marbles from the first day. The figures were different from the accepted models of Greek perfection—they were vigorous and masculine, possessing muscles and veins, revealing emotion and strain. If they were what Benjamin West called them, "the perfection of art, where nature dominated everywhere," then it followed that the "classical" pieces in private collections and in dealers' shops were worth far less. Amidst the uproar, Elgin offered the collection to the British government for £62,440, to cover his costs. Keats wrote his ode "On a Grecian Urn" while Byron in *Minerva* blasted the "hireling artists" who wished to make "the state receiver of his pilfered prey." Lord Elgin permitted a few artists, including Benjamin West and his students, to come and copy the statues. In 1811, Samuel Morse wrote home to his family that with his fellow painter, Charles Robert Leslie, he would "rise at 5 o'clock in the morning and walk about a mile and a half to Burlington, where are the famous Elgin Marbles, the works of Phidias and Praxiteles, brought by Lord Elgin from Athens. From these we draw three hours every morning, wet or dry, before breakfast, and return home just as the bustle begins in London." In 1815, Elgin, his life ruined, received £36,000 from the British government for the collection. The money went to his creditors.

(139) Lord Byron moved here in 1815 shortly after his marriage. One of his rare American visitors was 24-year-old George Ticknor from Boston, who was on his way to study at Göttingen in Germany before taking up the post of Smith Professor of the French and Spanish languages at Harvard.

20 June 1815 I called on Lord Byron today. Here again my anticipations were mistaken. Instead of being deformed, as I had

heard, he is remarkably well built, with the exception of his feet. Instead of having a thin and rather sharp and anxious face, as he has in his pictures, it is round, open, and smiling; his eyes are light and not black; his air easy and careless, not forward and striking; and I found his manners affable and gentle, the tones of his voice low and conciliating, his conversation gay, pleasant, and interesting. He talked, of course, a great deal about America; wanted to know what was the state of our literature, how many universities we had, whether we had any poets whom we much valued, and whether we looked upon [Joel] Barlow as our Homer. He certainly feels a considerable interest in America, and says he intends to visit the United States.

Byron had just read the account of the expedition of Lewis and Clarke who ten years earlier had followed the Missouri to its source, crossed the Rockies and descended the Columbia River to the Pacific. He said that he had never envied any men more in his life. Their conversation was suddenly interrupted by the news of the battle of Waterloo which had taken place two days earlier. Bonaparte, the messenger reported, was thought to be in full retreat towards Paris. Byron regretted Wellington's victory and explained, "I didn't know but I might live to see Lord Castlereagh's head on a pole. But I suppose I sha'n't, now." (Castlereagh was the British foreign secretary who had organized the coalition against Napoleon.) A few minutes later, Lady Byron came in. Ticknor found her pretty rather than beautiful and noted in his *Journal*:

> She is a baroness in her own right, has a large fortune, is rich in intellectual endowments, is a mathematician, possesses common accomplishments in an uncommon degree, and adds to all this a sweet temper. She was dressed to go and drive and, after stopping a few moments, went to her carriage. Lord Byron's manner to her was affectionate; he followed her to the door, and shook hands with her, as if he were not to see her for a month.

A week later Ticknor was invited to share their private box at Drury Lane to watch London's newest attraction, Edmund Kean, who had just triumphed as Shylock. But that evening Ticknor's attention was drawn to Lady Byron rather than to Kean. Two days later as he prepared to leave, Ticknor dropped by to say goodbye to the young couple, who had shown him more hospitality than anyone in London. The author of *Childe Harold* gave Ticknor a copy of his poem and said that he hoped they would meet in America. The following year Byron, separated from his wife, left England never to return.

(156)   Bath Hotel. John and Abigail Adams, accompanied by their daughter Nabby, took "two rooms and two chambers" here on 28 May 1785, and stayed for two months. Adams had been appointed minister to the Court of St. James and upon the advice of the British ambassador in Paris had hurried to London to be in time to pay his respects to King George III on his birthday, the 4th of June. London was packed. Parliament was in session, there was a celebration of Handel's music in Westminister Abbey and there were preparations for the king's birthday. All this drew "a vast concourse of carriages" which made their hotel in Piccadilly "too public and noisy for pleasure." While John Adams spent the week preparing his introductory address for the king, a delicate task given the recent American victory, Abigail Adams searched London for a suitable house where, as she told her sister, "my good genius carried me to one in GROSVENOR SQUARE.""

(170-73)   Egyptian Hall. In this large exhibition hall built in 1812, the showman William Bullock put Napoleon's luxurious bullet-proof carriage on display in 1815 and made £35,000 profit in one year. Exhibits included a family of Laplanders "complete with house and reindeer," 18-year-old Siamese twins, and a moving panorama of the Mississippi painted on three miles of canvas.

George Catlin's Indian Gallery opened on 1 February 1840. In the center of the large hall stood a Crow tepee made of buffalo skins, while six hundred paintings depicting North American Indians hung from the walls. Catlin's two grizzly bears were not allowed in Piccadilly and lodged at the London Zoo. The British press enjoyed the show and the *Art Union* declared Mr. Catlin's collection to be "a work of deep and permanent interest." The first twelve months drew 32,500 visitors and brought in £1,880. Expenses were considerable. Rent for three rooms was £550 a year and Catlin barely broke even. Nevertheless on 29 October 1840, his wife Clara wrote home: "He has leased his rooms for another year and they have taken £50 off the rent. He is now trying the experiment of lighting by gas. He was obliged to put the fixtures up at considerable expense, but there are many who cannot go in the day who would like to go at night...there is a rumor that the British Museum is interested." Catlin believed that his entire collection of paintings would be bought either in London or by Congress and remained optimistic. His illustrated books—*Letters and Notes of the Manners, Customs, and Condition of the North*

American Indians...in Two Volumes with Four Hundred Illustrations...Published by the Author, At Egyptian Hall, Piccadilly—sold well. Fourteen Ioway Indians led by White Cloud chanted war cries and performed songs and dances in the hall. These "real live American Indians" attracted simple sightseers and the most popular journalist of the day, Charles Dickens. He described Catlin as "an energetic, earnest man" and his Indians "squatting and spitting on the table before him," as "mere animals and wretched creatures; and their dances no better than the chorus of an Italian Opera in England." The third year a group of nine Ojibway Indians turned up in London and Catlin hired them. When one Indian, Cadotte (*Strong Wind*), got involved with an English woman and had to marry her, English newspapers stopped speaking of the "noble savage." Ironically it was Catlin who suffered the most from the press. After three years in Piccadilly he broke camp and moved to Paris and bankruptcy.

General Tom Thumb appeared here from 20 March until 20 July 1844. Thanks to the showmanship of P.T. Barnum, his three daily performances were sold out, bringing in $500 a day and frequently more. "At the fashionable hour, sixty carriages of the nobility" were counted outside the hall blocking all passageway on Piccadilly. Barnum and his ward lived in a mansion in fashionable Grafton Street in the former residence of Lord Talbot. Beginning with the Duke of Wellington, the Duke and Duchess of Buckingham, Sir Robert and Lady Peel and Lord Chesterfield, the English nobility competed for the honor of speaking to Tom Thumb in private. Baroness Rothschild sent her carriage to bring him to her mansion. After a two-hour visit, a "well-filled purse" was pressed discreetly into Barnum's ready hand. He attended three or four private parties a week each for a ten-guinea fee. Portraits of the general were published in all the pictorial papers, polkas and quadrilles were named after him, songs were sung about him while a play called "Hop o'my Thumb" was performed successfully at the Lyceum Theatre. But the greatest fan of Tom Thumb was Queen Victoria, who invited him on three occasions to BUCKINGHAM PALACE. Each time Barnum had a large placard over the entrance to Egyptian Hall which read: "Closed this evening, General Tom Thumb being at Buckingham Palace by command of her Majesty."

Exhibitions at Egyptian Hall frequently included scenes from America, a country of cowboys, Indians, buffalo, vast plains, massive Rocky Mountains and the Niagara Falls. Not all these extraordinary scenes mounted by British showmen necessarily pleased the passing American visitor. John Sherburne, correspondent for the *Saturday Courier* of Philadelphia, came to London in 1846 and was much upset by a large painting on display (entrance fee sixpence), which depicted the buying and selling of slaves.

> In one group slaves were seen naked, held down by men, while a young lady branded them with a hot iron; in another group, naked slaves were seen lashed to posts with iron masks, while suffering under the lash, and a young lady standing by holding a candle and counting the stripes. Around this painting were hung divers instruments of torture, some of which I had in my hand, viz: the iron mask, thumb screw, ladies' parlour whip, overseer's whip, ladies' branding iron, iron bracelets, chains etc.

The indignant journalist told his readers that he found the show to be a gross imposition and libel on the Southern states without a shadow of foundation. He challenged the audience present, including the artist and the owner, to contradict his assertion. He did not mention if anyone accepted the challenge, and concluded that exhibitions such as these were the cause of much prejudice existing in England against the slave-holding states.

The humorist Artemus Ward opened here on Tuesday evening, 13 November 1866, with his successful "Artemus Ward among the Mormons." The audience saw a vast panorama of changing scenes beginning in San Francisco, the land of gold, moving to Virginia City, the land of silver, to the home of the Mormons, land of salt. As the scenes progressed, Ward told stories under the guise of explanations. Program notes reveal the humour of the day:

> A Bird's Eye View of Salt Lake City.
>
> Brigham Young's Harem. Mr. Young is an indulgent father, and a numerous husband. For further particulars call on Mr. Ward at Egyptian Hall, any evening.
>
> The Endowment House. The Mormon is initiated into his faith here. The Mormon's religion is singular and his wives plural.

The Desert, again. A more cheerful view. The Plains of Colorado. The Colorado Mountains "might have been seen" in the distance, if the artist had painted 'em. But he is prejudiced against mountains, because his uncle once got lost on one.

Brigham Young and His wives. The pretty girls of Utah mostly marry Young.

Ward had begun as a reporter for the *Cleveland Plain Dealer* in 1858 with a series of letters supposedly written by a carnival manager who commented on current events in a New England dialect. He joined *Vanity Fair* the following year and was soon known in England. During the six months Ward spent in London, he contributed eight articles to *Punch* for fifteen guineas each, all under the heading, "Artemus Ward in London." But Ward, 32, was dying of tuberculosis and on the evening of 23 January 1867 he appeared for the last time in Egyptian Hall.

Ritz Hotel. Douglas Fairbanks and Mary Pickford took a suite here on Monday 22 June 1920. Thanks to the 5,000 cinemas in England which were totally dependent upon American films at the time, the 37-year-old actor and his bride were already heroes. The next day, they set out in an open car to attend a Theatrical Garden Party on the grounds of the Chelsea Hospital. As they drove up to the gates, women in the crowd put out their hands to Mary, who reached out to them instinctively. But the women didn't let go, and she found herself being pulled out of the car in spite of her husband's attempts to hold her in. The women got the car door open and the young star was dragged to the ground. The *Times* described the scene as "appalling." Badly frightened, scratched and with her clothes torn, she was finally rescued by a cordon of British police. The couple was driven back to the Ritz in a closed car only to discover the hotel under virtual siege. They did not leave their suite and, that evening, having heard a rumor that the honeymooners were to come down for dinner, hundreds of people burst into the hotel and swept through the dining room looking for them. After a sleepless night, they arranged to take refuge with the Duke and Duchess of Sutherland at their country estate, Sutton Court, near Guildford, Surrey. The following morning constables lined the Arlington Street door to the hotel as the two Americans prepared to leave. Several women nevertheless broke through the police ranks and leaped onto the moving car, "still clinging like limpets as it drove off," the *Times* concluded indignantly.

Pool of London

This reach of the Thames has two parts, the Lower and the Upper Pool, divided by Tower Bridge. The Pool below the bridge was London's main port from Roman times up to the building of the enclosed London docks in the 19th century.

By the time the steamship *State of Nebraska* dropped anchor here in the Upper Pool on 22 April 1887, its passengers, animals and cargo had already caught the imagination of London. First down the gangplank onto the town pier, within a hundred yards of Traitor's Gate leading into the Tower of London, came Buffalo Bill. He was followed by Annie Oakley and 9 women (including 5 squaws) and 92 Indians headed by Red Shirt, with braves drawn from the Sioux, Cheyenne, Kiowa, Pawnee and Ogalallas tribes, many of whom had never been off their reservations before. Last off were over a hundred cowboys including Sweeney's Cowboy Band of 36 musicians wearing gray shirts, slouch hats and moccasins. The cowboys helped to unload from the ship 180 horses, 18 buffalo, 10 mules, 10 elk, 5 wild Texas steers, 4 donkeys and 2 deer. Actually, many of the men had already come into London by train from Gravesend a few days earlier and had set up camp at Earl's Court. But William Cody, the eternal showman, decided that they should return to Gravesend, sail up the Thames and arrive in London as a single company. Watched by half the schoolboys of London, three special trains took the show to the station at EARL'S COURT.

Portland Place Map A

Broadcasting House. Designed in 1929, the building was already too small by the time it was completed three years later, for the BBC had expanded their overseas services. In 1940 they opened offices in the former Langham Hotel.

At 11:15 a.m. on Sunday 3 September 1939, British Prime Minister Neville Chamberlain spoke to England from Downing Street to announce the declaration of war against Germany. At noon, Ed Murrow, the CBS newscaster, did the first of his many wartime broadcasts from a studio in the basement of Broadcasting House which he used for the duration of the war. He had not had time to write a script and sat opposite a new and nervous censor with a finger on the cut-off switch in case any military secrets were violated. Murrow began:

Forty-five minutes ago the prime minister stated that a state of war existed between Britain and Germany. Air-raid instructions were immediately broadcast, and almost directly following that broadcast the air-raid sirens screamed through the quiet calm of this Sabbath morning. There were planes in the sky, whose, we couldn't be sure. Now we're sitting quite comfortably underground. We're told that the all-clear signal has been sounded in the streets but it's not yet been heard in this building.

No wonder, for the news service was heavily protected. The doors and windows of Broadcasting House had already been sandbagged, which muffled outside noise. Furthermore, Murrow had to descend three flights, through a gas-tight door on each floor, to the sub-basement in order to broadcast. That first "attack" was caused by a private French plane which flew unannounced into British airspace; subsequent air-raids would be genuine. During the Blitz in September 1940, Ed Murrow and Fred Bate from NBC sought to make live broadcasts from the rooftop of Broadcasting House while an air raid was in progress. But such spontaneous eyewitness accounts could not be censored and British officials, afraid that they might give something away, refused to allow it. Murrow then put on his tin hat, went up onto the roof with a BBC technician, and made a recorded broadcast during an actual raid. The British censors agreed that the script revealed nothing of military value, but permission to broadcast live to America continued to be refused. The BBC then taped actual anti-aircraft fire and the sound of bursting bombs and offered the three American networks "punctuation effects" to enliven their broadcasts. The Americans felt that this was deceptive. Finally, during a 2 a.m. nightcap alone with Winston Churchill at Downing Street, Murrow explained his purpose. If America was to enter the war, and Murrow and Churchill thought her entry was essential, the American people would first have to respond emotionally to Britain's plight. The sound of real bombs as they fell on London, Murrow argued, would help arouse America. Churchill agreed, and soon the first night came when Americans heard on their radios a direct attack on London: "I'm standing on a roof-top looking out over London. Off to my left far away in the distance, I can see just that faint red angry snap of anti-aircraft bursts against the steel-blue sky...the lights are swinging over in this direction now. You'll hear two explosions. There they are! That was the explosion overhead not the guns themselves." In order to play fair with the competing

American networks and newspapers in London, the BBC insisted that there should be no exclusive story for any newspaper or network. Murrow learned to respect the BBC and the feeling became mutual. But this was not always the case with American broadcasters who arrived in London.

On the morning of 13 July 1944, Captain Glenn Miller was asked to report to Maurice Gorham, in charge of relations between the BBC and the American forces. The Glenn Miller Band, whose purpose was to bring American music to the Allied Armed Forces in England and to the British public, had just been carried live by the BBC. Gorham, surrounded by several BBC executives, told Miller that the BBC had received complaints from British listeners in remote reception areas saying that they could only hear the band's louder passages. There were times, during the band's softer music when listeners thought the BBC had gone off the air. "And so, Captain Miller," Gorham concluded, "I must insist that you keep your volume constant at all times." Miller tried to explain that the contrasts in volume were an integral part of his band's style, and that much of the music was played soft deliberately. The BBC might have been experts in world-wide transmissions, but that did not give their officials the right to imagine that they were experts in music—and least of all in the music of the big modern band. Miller knew that his playing of "In the Mood" had been an overnight success with the British public. His personal pride and impatience clashed with the pompousness of some BBC officials, and resulted in the BBC's cancellation of all future broadcasts of his band. British listeners, bitterly disappointed, bombarded the BBC with complaints. English newspaper editorials strongly condemned the decision, but neither side gave way.

The Langham Hotel. Built in 1864 for £300,000 in the style of a Florentine palace, the Langham with six hundred rooms, including many private suites, was the first of London's grand Victorian hotels. Exiled royalty, aristocracy, statesmen, artists, musicians and writers all stayed here. Conan Doyle used the Langham in a number of his novels. In 1940 during the Blitz, the 38,000 gallon water tank on the roof was hit and flooded the hotel. The BBC took over the building and now uses it for offices.

After the Civil War one of the first American guests at the

Langham was Henry Wadsworth Longfellow, who had just received an honorary degree from Cambridge University. During his two-week stay, beginning 28 June 1868, the 61-year old poet was heaped with honors, including a dinner at the hotel for three hundred guests with William Gladstone as speaker. *The Song of Hiawatha* and *The Courtship of Miles Standish* (1858) were top sellers in England where Longfellow's mild romanticism, gentleness, sweetness and purity appealed to a vast Victorian public. His income in England was enormous. The publisher George Routledge paid £1,000 for rights to *The New England Tragedies,* a long dramatic poem about persecution in 17th-century New England. Longfellow was received in a private audience by Queen Victoria, met the Archbishop of Canterbury and saw his good friend Charles Dickens. He had his portrait photograph taken by Elliot and Fry at 55 Baker Street. Before leaving for the continent he went to the Isle of Wight for a rest. "I slept for the first time under a roof of thatch," he wrote to Senator Charles Sumner. From his cottage at Shanklin he called on Tennyson before leaving for Paris on 23 July 1868.

Bret Harte stayed at the Langham in April 1879. The author of *The Luck of Roaring Camp* toured England giving lectures. He began at the Crystal Palace on Sydenham Hill where his share of the modest receipts came to $75, continued on to Birmingham and Harrogate before finishing at Glasgow. He then returned to Crefeld in Prussia, where he was U.S. Consul. A few years later he moved permanently to LANCASTER GATE.

46   Joshua Bates, born in Weymouth, Massachusetts, worked in the counting house of William Gray, a wealthy New Englander, who chose him to go to Europe as his agent. He arrived in London in 1817 at the age of 29, and joined the English banking house of John Baring nine years later. The House of Baring was the leader among those merchant bankers known as "American houses" and played a major role as intermediary between the British capitalist and the American entrepreneur. Bates worked at the Baring offices at 8 Bishopsgate Street (the bank is still there) where he directed daily commercial operations with "great nerve, self-possession and self-confidence, with prudence and in the main, good judgement." Over the next thirty-four years, he met every American of importance coming through London and frequently entertained them here in this magnificent Adam house or in his country home in Sheen, near Richmond-on-Thames. In 1852 he donated $100,000 for the building of the Boston Public Library. Five years later, he remarked that he had left Weymouth with five dollars in his pocket and was now worth $4 million. He visited America occasionally, but preferred England, where he died in 1864.

66   Royal Institute of British Architects. Frank Lloyd Wright accepted the Sir George Watson Chair for 1939—the award went one year to an Englishman and the next to an American and its purpose was to serve the better acquaintance of British and American culture. The honorarium was $2,500, and the lecturer was free to give as many or as few lectures as he chose at any English university. Wright chose the University of London but was persuaded to speak here in the new hall. His four lectures, entitled *An Organic Architecture: The Architecture of Democracy,* were published in 1941 by Lund Humphries.

98   Charles Francis Adams and his family moved here from MANSFIELD STREET in the second year of the Civil War. Adams's lonely task was to prevent England from recognizing the South. The American president Abraham Lincoln was seen by the English as fit at best to be a small-town mayor. Henry Adams, his father's secretary, recalled that London "created a nightmare of its own, and gave it the shape of Abraham Lincoln." Confederate victories in July 1862 under a new general, Robert E. Lee, heralded by the *Times,* led the British secretary for foreign affairs, Russell, to write to Palmerston, the prime minister: "I agree with you that the time is come for... the recognition of the independence of the Confederates." But three days later in Antietam, Maryland, Lee's invasion of the North was stopped and Lincoln issued the Emancipation Proclamation. In London, Adams was quick to point out the implication: recognition of the Confederacy would be a vote for slavery. When the incredible news of the Union victory at Vicksburg reached England in August 1863, the Adams family happened to meet Robert Browning at church where the poet revealed his joy and congratulated the Americans. "Luckily there was nobody at hand to mark the impropriety," the poet later confessed. Meanwhile England continued to sell arms to the Confederacy and up in the Mersey shipyards, four armor-plated cruisers were being built for use by the South. Adams had been objecting for fourteen months, and on 5 September 1863, his letter to Lord Russell began with a remark which later became famous: "It would be superfluous in me to point out to your lordship that this is war." Three days later the British government, who had understood the consequences of Vicksburg, issued orders cancelling the sale. Adams had finally established his own position and that of the Union at the Court of St. James. In 1864, the Adams family moved to 5 Upper Portland Place which served as the American Embassy until 1866.

Princes Gate, South Kensington Map F

14   J.P. Morgan gave this house to the U.S. government to be used as an embassy residence, and Joseph P. Kennedy and his family lived here from 1 March 1938 to 22 October 1940. Before leaving Boston, Rose Kennedy received a memo from the State Department describing the house:

> There are eight bedrooms, two single and six double. All appear to be well furnished. For the servants there are thirteen bedrooms, nineteen beds. There are eight baths and three servants' baths. There are mattresses and springs for all beds. In 1931 the Department paid $506.52 for 68 blankets. There are no bed linens; no towels of any kind; no bath mats. The only dining room silver consists of 4 solid silver sauceboats. There is a sewing room which does not appear to be equipped with a Government sewing machine.

The lack of a government sewing machine was more than made up for in this lovely six-story house overlooking Kensington Gardens. There was a magnificent lift, a large fancy cage that went up and down majestically; it was run excitedly the first afternoon by children Bobby and Teddy until the inevitable showdown took place. Since the eleven Kennedys outnumbered the eight bedrooms, and since they were able to make do with fewer than nineteen servants, they used one floor of staff bedrooms for the children and for guests. The staff, headed by a butler, were British. From Boston they brought over a nurse, a governess and a cook who kept the family supplied with "creamed chicken, strawberry shortcake and Boston cream pie." William Randolph Hearst lent them a number of paintings from his castle in Wales. The second weekend in April, the new American ambassador and his wife were invited to spend a weekend at Windsor Castle; the other guests were Prime Minister and Mrs. Neville Chamberlain, Lord and Lady Halifax (he was the new foreign secretary) and the queen's sister, Lady Elphinstone, and her husband. In their suite in one of the towers, with furniture upholstered in red damask, the Kennedys were served sherry by a servant in full livery and a peruke. When he had left, as they gazed across Windsor Park, Mr. Kennedy turned to his wife and said, "Rose, this is a helluva long way from East Boston."

At Princes Gate, their guests included Charles Lindbergh and his wife Anne Morrow, Mr. and Mrs. Henry Luce, and Rose Kennedy's parents. One day her father quietly helped himself to a number of engraved ambassadorial invitation cards. He filled them in with the names of his cronies in Boston inviting them to tea at the embassy five days later and mailed them—they would get the cards the day of the tea. He felt that it was a huge joke, but soon discovered that it was far from being shared by his son-in-law. On 4 May 1939 King George V and Queen Mary were dinner guests. That morning detectives from Scotland Yard came and interviewed the staff, afraid that a member of the IRA might have been taken on as an extra for the evening. The Kennedys' English butler assured the police that his staff "had all served at Buckingham Palace." No further questions were asked. Conversation during dinner centered on the coming trip to the United States by the king and queen. After dinner the gathering watched two Walt Disney cartoons and *Goodbye Mr. Chips.*

The Kennedys became close friends of Neville Chamberlain, and thoroughly endorsed his policy of appeasement of Hitler. Kennedy described the British prime minister as a man "touched with genius." When Chamberlain signed the Munich Pact that surrendered much of Czechoslovakia to the Nazis and promised Europe "peace in our time," Mrs. Kennedy recorded in her diary: "We feel that a new psychology for settling issues between countries has been inaugurated and that henceforth war may be out of the question." Her optimism was echoed in the *Times* which also supported Chamberlain. But eighteen months later, in the spring of 1940, Kennedy was one of the first to prepare himself for what he correctly saw as the coming air attacks on England. He rented the Dodge family's seventy-room country home, 25 miles from London at Sunningdale, close to Windsor. As soon as the London Blitz began, Kennedy sent his family back to Boston. (The J.P. Morgan house is now owned by the Royal College of General Practitioners.)

49   (49 Princes Gate stands a hundred yards down Exhibition Road on the East side.) James McNeill Whistler created the Peacock Room here in 1876. The British art collector Frances Leyland had bought this roomy Victorian house and appointed the celebrated British architect Norman Shaw to oversee the renovations. The dining room was assigned to Thomas Jeckyll, whom Leyland told to use floral-embossed Cordovan leather on the walls which he had purchased at great expense. Jeckyll was also to focus attention on the only painting intended for the room, Whistler's *Princess from the Land of Porcelain*. As Leyland was about to return to his shipping business in Liverpool, Whistler complained that the room had an oppressive feeling to it and that the red flowers on the dark leather clashed with the *Princess*. He suggested a touch of color here and there to lighten the leather. Standing in the hallway, the two men concluded a hasty gentlemen's agreement: Whistler would make the necessary changes, and Leyland dashed off to catch his train. In sole possession of the house, Whistler began covering the leather with an elaborate pattern of gold and blue peacocks. As the work progressed, he became feverish with enthusiasm, and was soon arriving at seven o'clock in the morning and leaving exhausted late at night. He told friends: "It grew as I painted. And towards the end I reached such a point of perfection—putting in every touch with such freedom—that when I came around the corner where I had started, why, I had to paint it over again...the harmony in blue and gold developing, you know, I forgot everything in my joy." At the end of six months, the room, his room, was ready. On 9 February 1877, while Leyland was laboring in Liverpool, Whistler, master of the Peacock Room, gave an open house. Printed invitations went to critics and people of importance. Leyland's name was nowhere mentioned. One uninvited guest quietly appeared. Thomas Jeckyll, whose painstaking labor Whistler had been asked to harmonize with, stood and gazed in astonishment. Nothing of his work remained. He stumbled home in grief. Whistler was euphoric with the success of his reception. The normally hostile *Times* was captivated: "The whole interior is so fanciful and fantastic, and at the same time so ingenious and original in motive as to be totally Japanese." Everyone in London loved it. But when Leyland returned from Liverpool to Princes Gate, he was speechless with anger: The room had been destroyed. "Ah," said Whistler in a moralizing tone, "you should be grateful to me. I

have made you famous. My work will live when you are forgotten."
"What happened to my leather?" Leyland almost shouted. "Your
Spanish leather," answered Whistler as if the shipping magnate
didn't understand, "is beneath my peacocks." Whistler set his fee at
2,000 guineas; but Leyland paid him £1,000. Professionals were
paid in guineas, and workmen were paid in pounds. Leyland knew
that this would sting, and he was right. But it was Whistler who
triumphed. In 1904 the entire Peacock Room was moved to the
Freer Gallery in Washington, D.C.

Princes Street, Hanover Square Map C

8   The poet Longfellow with his wife and two young ladies
from Boston took lodgings here on 20 May 1835. Aged 28, he had
just been chosen to succeed George Ticknor as professor of modern
languages at Harvard and was on his way to spend a year in
Germany. He called on the well-known publisher Richard Bentley
who agreed to publish his first prose work *Outre-mer: A
Pilgrimage Across the Sea,* reminiscent of Irving's *Sketch Book.*
Longfellow spent his days purchasing books or working in the
British Museum, joining the ladies in the evening. On Saturday 30
May Thomas Carlyle called and invited the four Americans to take
tea with him that evening. Longfellow, who had just bought
Carlyle's *Life of Schiller,* was honored by the invitation. They
found their host tall and awkward in his appearance, "but as soon
as he began to converse his original mind beamed forth," noted
Clara Crowninshield, who accompanied the Longfellows. Like the
many Americans who would visit 24 Cheyne Row over the
following forty-six years, they discovered that Mrs. Carlyle was as
entertaining as her husband only more modest. Before the
Longfellows sailed for Hamburg on 8 June they visited
Westminster Abbey, which made no impression on Longfellow,
who little imagined that half a century later he would be the first
American to have his bust in Poet's Corner.

Queen's Gate Terrace Map G

18   Charles Eliot Norton, his wife and children spent five
years in Europe, beginning in England in July 1868. Founder and
coeditor of the *Nation,* Norton, 41, knew everyone. After staying
with Charles Dickens at Gads Hill in Kent, the Nortons took a

country house nearby and moved into town in the autumn. Here their friends included Darwin, Ruskin, Browning and Carlyle. They lunched with John Stuart Mill where the conversation turned to the appalling poverty in England. Mill, who had been an M.P. for three years, felt that the evils in England were not beyond legal remedy, and that the rich ruling class had a sufficient sense of responsibility to introduce reform. Norton disagreed. For him the inequality was such that the question was whether the nation was soon "to decline into a state of chronic decrepitude or to be redeemed by a more or less violent revolution" which would restore vigor to the classes arrayed against each other. He published this argument in an article, "The Poverty of England," in the *North American* for July 1869. Accompanied by his wife, he had lunch with George Eliot and her companion George Lewes in their house at St. John's Wood—socially a daring act since Lewes, although separated, was still legally married. Ladies used to read *The Mill on the Floss,* but they did not call on the author. The Nortons moved to Switzerland in May 1869. Upon their return to America four years later, Norton became professor of fine arts at Harvard, a post he held for twenty-five years during which he became a world-famous art historian.

Queen Victoria Street

(11)   Edison Telephone Company. Thomas Edison sent his 19-year-old nephew, Charles Edison, an excellent electrician, and Edward H. Johnson, his business partner, to London in January 1879 to help run his new company. British backers had put up £100,000 initial capital and company headquarters had been opened in nearby Cannon Street. Both the Bell and the Edison companies in England were competing for a franchise from the British Post Office, authorizing the establishment of telephone wires and exchanges. The first chalk receivers made brave sounds but they had bugs in them; back in Menlo Park, Thomas Edison and his assistants were putting in eighteen-hour days to solve the problem. On 15 March 1879, Charles Edison gave a successful demonstration, with the Prince of Wales and Prime Minister Gladstone speaking over the Edison telephone before an admiring public. The *Times* described Edison's receiver as a "microphone-receiver" or "loud-speaking telephone," far superior to Bell's. The *Standard* reported that "every inflection of the voice is audible."

Skilled men were urgently needed in London to install and operate the private telephone lines that businesses were demanding. British workmen were found to be far too conservative to start learning something as new as the telephone, and Edison was forced to advertise in New York. He gave aptitude tests to sixty applicants and selected twenty; they were trained in Menlo Park in a month and sent to Queen Victoria Street to start work. But there were a few employees taken on in London; among them was a lanky red-haired 23-year-old Dubliner, whose job it was to convince Londoners to let the company put insulators and poles on their roofs to carry the telephone wires. His name was George Bernard Shaw. Shaw provides us with a magnificent sketch of perhaps the first group of American workmen ever seen in England:

Whilst the Edison Telephone Company lasted, it crowded the basement of a huge pile of offices in Queen Victoria Street with American artificers. These deluded and romantic men gave me a glimpse of the skilled proletariat of the United States. They sang obsolete sentimental songs with genuine emotion; and their language was frightful even to an Irishman. They worked with a ferocious energy which was out of all proportion to the actual result achieved. Indomitably resolved to assert their republican manhood by taking no orders from a tall-hatted Englishman whose stiff politeness covered his conviction that they were, relatively to himself, inferior and common persons, they insisted on being slave-driven with geniune American oaths by a genuine free and equal American foreman. They utterly despised the artfully slow British workman who did as little for his wages as he possibly could; never hurried himself; and had a deep reverence for anyone whose pocket could be tapped by respectful behavior. Need I add that they were contemptuously wondered at by this same British workman as a parcel of outlandish adult boys, who sweated themselves for their employer's benefit instead of looking after their own interest? They adored Mr. Edison as the greatest man of all time in every possible department of science, art and philosophy, and execrated Mr. Graham Bell, the inventor of the rival telephone, as his Satanic secretary; but each of them had (or pretended to have) on the brink of completion, an improvement on the telephone, usually a new transmitter. They were free-souled creatures, excellent company: sensitive, cheerful and profane; liars, braggarts and hustlers; with an air of making slow old England hum which never left them even when, as often happened, they were wrestling with difficulties of their own making, or struggling in no-thoroughfares from which they had to be retrieved like strayed sheep by Englishmen without imagination enough to go wrong.

Barely a year later Edison was asked by his English associates if he would sell his share in the English company. He asked them what they would offer. They cabled back: "Thirty thousand." Edison thought that $30,000 was a fair sum and accepted. When the draft reached his bank, Edison was surprised to find that it was for almost $150,000. The English had, of course, meant pounds.

Radnor Place Map G

2   James Russell Lowell spent the summer of 1887 here. The 68-year-old had returned to London where he enjoyed basking in his literary reputation, dining with celebrities such as William Gladstone and visiting his favorite resort, St. Ives. The big event in London was the silver jubilee of Queen Victoria which Lowell witnessed amidst "wonderfully good-natured and orderly" London crowds. The British empire was at its height and fully represented in the parade where Indian, African and Arab princes on horseback provided a glimpse "of the Arabian Nights and of Moorish Spain, their jewelled turbans flashing in the sun." They rode with such admirable ease and looseness of joint, Lowell told his daughter, that their European competitors looked like waxwork figures from Madame Tussaud's. Their noble composure and superiority seemed to vulgarize all the people near them. Coming from a conservative New Englander, this was quite a compliment. Lowell himself had even splurged upon decorations—his grandchildren would be glad to hear, he wrote, that he had festooned his balcony with Chinese lanterns for the sum of eighteen shillings.

Rathbone Place

Edward Bancroft, born in Westfield, Massachusetts, arrived in London at the age of 25 and settled here on the corner of Rathbone Place and Charlotte Street. He studied medicine, wrote on scientific subjects, and published *Remarks on the Review of the Controversy between Great Britain and Her Colonies* (1769), becoming friends in London with Benjamin Franklin. When the three American comn.issioners—Franklin, Silas Deane and Arthur

Lee—began work in Paris in 1776, they soon found Bancroft, who spoke fluent French, extremely useful. For a modest sum, he worked as secretary. He served as interpreter between Deane and Beaumarchais when the first secret contract was signed in September 1776 to ship French arms and supplies to America. But unknown to them, Bancroft had already agreed to work as a spy for the British. During the next seven years, he passed to the British copies of every secret American letter, document and plan, which went through Paris. In 1777, the French foreign minister, Vergennes, after a stormy meeting with the British ambassador in Paris over the clandestine shipment of French arms to America, complained that the British knew more about what was going on in French seaports than the French authorities. This was correct, and it was thanks to Bancroft. He revealed the entire secret negotiations which led to the Franco-American alliance in 1778. He frequently prevented instructions from Congress from ever reaching the American commissioners in Paris. He befriended John Paul Jones. Given his intimate knowledge of American plans, he even gambled in stocks on the London Stock Exchange. Journeying back and forth between Rathbone Place in London and Franklin's residence in Passy, Bancroft was never suspected by his fellow Americans. The French, astonished by the British awareness of their secret discussions, were soon convinced that there was a traitor among them, but they thought it was Arthur Lee and they asked him to leave France in 1779. Working under the assumed name of Edwards, Bancroft's pay of £400 a year was soon raised to £1,000, as he became the most successful spy for the British during the war. He was promised the post of regius professor of divinity at King's College (now in Columbia University) when New York was returned to British control. This was the only agreement that did not go according to plan, but Bancroft lived peacefully in England on a generous pension until his death in 1820. His treachery was not uncovered until 1891.

Regent Street Map C

(19)   Richard Henry Dana arrived in London on 14 July 1856 and moved here two days later. "I have a chamber in the rear that looks out on Wren's old church of St. James, Piccadilly, with its clock, and its bells that strike the quarter hours faintly, as if tired out with years." A graduate of Harvard Law School, the immense success in England of *Two Years Before the Mast* gave Dana the entrée to London society, where he soon became one of those Americans dazzled by the spectacle of the British aristocracy. He dined at the Lord Chancellor's with six other lords present and noted in his journal:

> The style of manners with all these noblemen is simple and unostentatious. Calmness is aimed at, and self-possession, and great (apparent, at least) consideration for the feelings of others. The economy of the dinner is so arranged that no guest shall be obliged to ask another guest for anything on the table, and no questions need to be put by the Master or Mistress of the house to any guest, as to anything to be eaten or drank. All is done by servants, who pass everything, and move, and speak in a low tone, so as not to interrupt conversation, or divert attention. It is a complete triumph of Art.

Back in America, active in politics, Dana helped found the Free-Soil Party. In 1876 he sought appointment as minister to England, but his confirmation was refused by the U.S. Senate.

(264)   James Fenimore Cooper, leaving his family in Paris, arrived in London on Tuesday, 18 June 1833. He put up at Steven's Hotel at 18 New Bond Street and took an apartment here two days later. He had come with the manuscript of *The Headsman* to do the proofreading as the pages came off the press. The offices of his publisher Richard Bentley were just around the corner at 5 Burlington Street. Cooper was sometimes brash when it came to dealing with the English. Afraid of being slighted, he saw rebuffs where none was intended. Just such an incident took place the first day he called on Bentley, who had already published *The Prairie* and *The Heidenmauer.*

> Called at Bentley's. He was busy. Wrote a note saying that I would call at eleven. Before leaving the house, he came in and I told him my name. He begged me to go into another room, without even saluting me, and retired himself. I told the young man to give Mr. Bentley my note and walked off. On reaching the hotel found his card! This is the only way to bring John [Bull] to his senses. At *one* called and found him all I could wish. He gave me *my* price; and we begin to print immediately, to publish in September.

Cooper spent mornings reading and correcting page proofs followed by a comfortable lunch. At the Piazza Coffee House in Covent Garden Cooper and a friend enjoyed "gray soup, Salmon,

Boiled ham and peas, potatoes, Cheese, a plate of indifferent cherries, two pints of porter, and a pint of claret. Bill eighteen shillings or four dollars." Having spent five years before the mast, he liked to drop in to the New England Coffee House on Threadneedle Street behind the Royal Exchange, where American sea captains gathered; here he heard the latest news from home and they told good stories. One afternoon he came across Captain Champlin, who had brought the Cooper family over on the *Hudson* seven years earlier. After a few pints of porter, the two men walked down to the docks in the rain where they went over the captain's new ship. When the weather was fine, Cooper visited the sights taking notes. Like most republicans, he was fascinated by kings and queens. He waited for more than an hour at the gate of St. James's Palace to see William IV come out in his carriage. When the king finally appeared, accompanied by the Duchess of Gloucester, neither of them acknowledged the crowd, who stood in silence. Cooper noted: "I never saw less apparent communion between a Sovereign and his people."

By the end of July, Cooper had finished the proofs and returned to Paris to fetch his family for what he called "le grand départ." After a series of emotional farewells—the Coopers had spent almost seven years in Paris and their five children spoke fluent French—they reached London on 28 August. While the family went sightseeing and worried about the outbreak of cholera in the city, Cooper supplied revisions and new prefaces for *The Red Rover, The Water-Witch* and *The Borderers* in Bentley's Standard Novel Series. The task done, their seven years in Europe over, on 28 September 1833, the Coopers boarded the *Samson* bound for New York, feeling both apprehensive and joyful.

309   Polytechnic of Central London, founded in 1839. Among Americans who have taught here was Ezra Pound, who began on 21 February 1909. The syllabus read:

A Short Introductory Course of Lectures
on the Development of Literature in Southern Europe
will be given by
Ezra Pound, M.A.
(Sometime Fellow in the University of Pennsylvania)

The fee was seven shillings and sixpence for the six lectures, the introductory lecture being free. He covered, amongst other subjects, the search for the essential qualities in literature and dic a of the great critics—Plato, Aristotle, Dante, Coleridge, De Quincey, Pater and Yeats. The lectures were a success and Pound gave twenty-one new lectures beginning in October 1909.

Regent's Park Map A

With barely a Londoner astir, two hours before sunrise, John James Audubon would take his favorite walk from his studio on GREAT RUSSELL STREET through Bedford Square up the Tottenham Court Road to watch the birds in Regent's Park. He disliked London, but alone in the park before daybreak was the closest he could come to the forests of America. One January morning in 1828, failing to find any waterfowl, "I raised my eyes towards the peaceful new moon," he recorded, "and to my astonishment saw a large flock of Wild Ducks passing over me; after a few minutes a second flock passed...two flocks of Wild Ducks, of upwards of twenty each. Wonderful indeed!" After a year in London, Audubon began to be well known for his collection *Birds of America* which was gathering subscribers. One morning in the park Audubon met Nicholas Vigors, the first secretary of the Zoological Society of London, in company with Captain Edward Sabine, mathematician and Fellow of the Royal Society, who had just returned from an expedition to the Arctic:

> I went to the Gardens of the Zoological Society which are at the opposite end of Regent's Park from my lodgings. The Gardens are quite in a state of infancy; I have seen more curiosities in a swamp in America in one morning than is collected here since eighteen months; all, however, is well planned, clean, and what specimens they have are fine and in good condition. As I was leaving I heard my name called, and turning saw Mr. Vigors with the famous Captain Sabine, a tall, thin man, who at once asked me if among the Eagles they had, any were the young of the White-headed Eagle, or as he called the bird *Falco leucocephalus*. Strange that such great men should ask a woodsman questions like that, which I thought could be solved by either at a glance. I answered in the affirmative, for I have seen enough of them to know.

Rosebery Avenue Map B

Sadler's Wells. In the beginning was a medicinal well. Thomas Sadler built a "Musick House" in 1683 as a side attraction with rope dancers, jugglers, clowns and acrobats. The next two centuries saw theater, boxing, and ice-skating, followed by opera and ballet. The Sadler's Wells Ballet moved to Covent Garden in 1946. The present theater is used by foreign and touring companies, and the original well can still be seen under a trap door at the back of the stalls.

On Easter Monday, 3 April 1820, John Howard Payne took over management of the "House" and to the "spectacular and pantomimic" added serious drama. He kept the traditional three-part program of pantomine, drama and farce, but he also introduced new foreign plays, such as Schiller's *The Robbers,* to an unsophisticated English public. He played in each of the dramas, but unfortunately his enthusiasm and ability as an actor did not prevent a financial disaster and he was forced to resign by October. The following month, he published a valedictory in the third person, declaring: "All his losses will be met with cheerfulness if he shall find as the result of his exertions that he has succeeded in elevating Sadler's Wells Theatre beyond a mere vehicle of amusement, by... those means of improvements in Literature and Life from which the Stage derives its Dignity and Value." Cheerfulness notwithstanding, seven weeks later he was committed for debt to Fleet Prison on LUDGATE HILL.

Royal Exchange

New York Coffee House, 7 Sweeting's Alley, "near the Royal Exchange." Frequented by merchants, brokers and sea captains, the house provided meals, beds, mail services, American newspapers and a place to meet. The *Morning Chronicle & London Advertiser* of 3 May 1783 advertised: "Any Gentleman who may be inclinable to lend from £700 to £1,000 for six months, may meet with advantageous terms, and undoubted real security, by directing for A.B. at the New York Coffee House in Sweeting's Alley. Jews, Swindlers, etc. need not apply." The New York Coffee House was first mentioned in 1759 and closed in 1839. The site is now covered by the paved area in front of the east end of the exchange.

Washington Irving, 22, arrived in London on 26 October 1805 and put up here with a friend, John Gorham of Boston. He told his brother William, jestingly, that rather than feeling upon arrival "bone of their bone and flesh of their flesh," all that he had heard about the English character rushed to mind—haughtiness, illiberal prejudice, reserve, rudeness, insolence, brutality and knavery. But these ideas were whimsical, he wrote, and wore off in a day or two. After a few days, the two young men found lodgings in NORFOLK STREET.

Russell Square

(62)   Imperial Hotel. The original highly ornate Victorian hotel with Winter Garden and Turkish Baths of glazed Doulton Ware opened in 1911. It was replaced by the new Imperial Hotel in 1969.

Thomas Wolfe arrived in England on 5 November 1924 and moved into the Imperial Hotel the next day. He had given up his instructorship of English at New York University and had come to Europe for a year. He promptly wrote to the editor of the *Asheville Citizen* to try to sell them a weekly newsletter: "I arrived in London on Wednesday after an amazing voyage, and I am now lost in the beauty and mystery and fascination of this ancient and magnificent city." He ended his letter, written on his twenty-fourth birthday, with optimism: "I would to God I might be twenty-four forever. This is a magnificent adventure and the world is opening like an oyster." Alas, the pages of the *Asheville Citizen*, his hometown in North Carolina, did not wish to share this "magnificent adventure," and after three weeks of walking the "queer, blind, narrow, incredible, crooked streets of the city," Wolfe moved to Paris.

Russell Street, Covent Garden

Hummum's Hotel. Early in May 1873, Thomas Edison and his assistant took rooms in this modest hotel. The 26-year-old inventor worked eighteen hours a day and usually lived on coffee and American pie. At the hotel he was fed "nothing but roast beef and flounders," until, he recorded, his imagination "was getting into a coma." He was apparently saved by the discovery of a French pastry shop in High Holborn where he filled up daily, and his imagination "got all right." He had come to England to demonstrate his new telegraph to the British Post Office, who was unable to transmit for more than fifty miles. He set up the receiving end at the Telegraph Street headquarters, while his assistant went up to Liverpool 219 miles north and began sending messages. Transmitted at over a hundred words per minute, they came through with an imprint "as clear as a copper plate," Edison recorded. He was then asked if, with his system, he thought he could get a greater speed through submarine cables. "Let's try it," he said and 2,200 miles of cable stored underwater in tanks at Greenwich were put at his disposal from 8 p.m. until 6 a.m. "This just suited me as I preferred night-work," Edison recalled. "I got my apparatus set up and then to get a preliminary idea of what the distortion of the signal would be, I sent a single dot, which should have been recorded upon my automatic paper by a mark 1/32 inch long. Instead of that it was 27 feet long." Neither Edison nor anyone else at the time knew anything about induction. Edison spent six frustrating and inconclusive weeks in London before returning to Menlo Park, New Jersey. "The English are not an inventive people," he said on being asked his impressions, "They don't eat enough pie." As for the British Post Office, they eventually adopted another variant of his system. Edison always believed that they had taken what they needed from him without paying anything, but this was never proved.

St. George Street, Hanover Square

(12A) Royal Cambridge Hotel. Thurlow Weed, journalist and political leader, took rooms here on 6 December 1861. He had come to London at the request of Abraham Lincoln in order to help "disabuse the English mind of the idea that the northern people or the federal government had provoked, or were responsible for, the Rebellion." While he was on his way to England, the British ship *Trent* had been stopped and boarded and two passengers, Confederates Slidell and Mason, forcibly taken off by a U.S. warship and carried to a prison in Boston. Thus, when Weed arrived, he found all of England in an uproar, with 8,000 troops being prepared for passage to Canada, and many clamoring for war. He immediately called on the American minister, Charles Francis Adams, son of John Quincy Adams, who advised him that Lincoln had no choice but to release the two southerners immediately and to apologize to Great Britain for having violated her neutrality. If America hesitated, he said, England, her honor insulted, would go to war. Weed then called on his friend George Peabody at his bank on Old Broad Street. There he found a number of English and American merchants assembled, panic-stricken by the thought of a war. American stocks and state securities had already fallen dramatically. Weed secured an interview with the British foreign secretary, Lord Russell, for the following morning. It began badly. Weed referred as delicately as he could to the impressment of American seamen by the British, pointing out that America had submitted to more than 6,000 violations of its flag before resorting to war in 1812. Russell suggested that if Slidell and Mason were released, the danger of war might be averted. Weed replied that if the request were made in a friendly spirit, he was sure that President Lincoln would comply. Their meeting had taken place at Pembroke Lodge in Richmond Park, which had been granted to Russell by Queen Victoria. Afterwards, Lady Russell escorted Weed into the gardens to a spot called Henry VIII's mound, from where it is possible to see St. Paul's Cathedral on the one side and Windsor Castle on the other. She told him that he was standing on the exact spot where Henry VIII had stood watching for a signal from the dome of St. Paul's church announcing the execution of Ann Boleyn. Weed obviously did not look too reassured by this charming anecdote, and Lady Russell told him quietly that Queen Victoria and Prince Albert were most anxious that amicable relations be maintained between the two countries. Relieved, Weed rode back to Hanover Square. On 26 December 1861, news reached London that the "Trent Affair" had been settled. Stocks went up. Then came the report that the two Confederate commissioners were again on their way to England. "Up went the stocks again," recorded Weed.

(24)   Nathaniel Hawthorne and his family moved into their "temporary nest" on 6 September 1855. This was his first visit to London and he passed the days wandering through the city, sometimes alone and sometimes with his children. In the evening he kept his journal, obviously with an eye to publication (*English Note-books*). Hawthorne was appalled by the squalor in which the poor lived. The ginshops, or spirit-vaults as they were called, were set off with "the magnificence of gilded door-posts" on every street corner in the East End of London. Ragged children came "with old shaving-mugs, or broken-nosed teapots" to get "a little poison" for their parents. "Inconceivably sluttish women" entered the gin shop at noon, standing at the counter stirring up misery and jollity together, and "quaffing off the mixture with a relish." The men lounged there all day drinking as long as they had "a halfpenny left." Hawthorne could not condemn these sad revellers for he had

Lindbergh and the Prince of Wales.
The Prince stands on a stair as he refused to appear
in a photograph with a man taller than himself, 1927. (See page 128.)

Mrs. Wallace Simpson in her flat in Bryanston Court where she frequently entertained the Prince of Wales.
(See page 111.)

King Edward VIII reading his abdication speech.
10 December 1936.
(See page 85.)

*Ambassador Joseph Kennedy leaving the Houses of Parliament
after listening to Mr. Chamberlain's speech,
24 August 1939. (See page 210.)*

no better consolation to offer them, they needed such fiery stimulant to lift them a little way out of "the smothering squalor" of their lives. The butchers' shops presented no such fattened carcasses as Englishmen loved to gaze at in the market, no stupendous halves of mighty beefs, or muttons ornamented with carved bas-reliefs of fat on their ribs and shoulders, but "bits and gobbets of lean meat, selvages snipt off the steaks, tough and stringy morsels, bare bones smitten away from joints by the cleaver; tripe, liver, bullocks' feet, or whatever else was cheapest and divisible into the smallest lots." It was a melancholy spectacle, Hawthorne recalled, when an overladen coal cart passed through the street and a handful fell onto the mud, to see half a dozen women and children scrambling for the treasure trove, "like a flock of hens and chickens gobbling up some spilt corn." Such was the misery of their squalid rooms that the poor of London used the sidewalks and the middle of the road as their common hall. Courtships, quarrels, plot and counter plot, family difficulties or agreements were constantly discussed or transacted "in this sky-roofed saloon, so regally hung with its sombre canopy of coal-smoke." It was enough to make a man doubt the existence of his soul—for if these poor wretches were to have no immortality, what claim, asked Hawthorne, could one make for one's own?

(25)   John Singleton Copley lived here with his family from 1783 until his death in 1815. Five doors up from St. George's church, toward Hanover Square, the new house was "elegant and well furnished." In its center was a large high room with skylights which was used for the display of paintings.

One of Copley's first commissions was for a full-length portrait of John Adams, who sat in December 1783 and paid a hundred guineas. The following June, Adams wrote to his son, John Quincy, "Desire Mr. Copley to get a Frame made for my picture and give him the Money. The Frame should be made, to take to pieces, so that it may be removed to the Hague or to Boston, in time. Thus this Piece of Vanity will be finished. May it be the last." The following month, Abigail Adams called and found the portrait to be "a very good likeness" and "a most beautiful picture." Adams was apparently in little hurry to hang his portrait, for it was only brought to Boston by John Quincy Adams in 1817. Copley was next commissioned by the famous London engraver and printmaker, John Boydell, to do *The Death of Major Pierson* (now in the Tate Gallery). In 1781, French troops invading Jersey were beaten in a counterattack led by young Major Francis Pierson, who was killed just as victory was assured. Once again Copley included actual portraits of the participants set in a battle scene of brilliant color, clamor, violence and confusion. Londoners loved it.

Copley, at 45, was at the peak of his career. The Corporation of the City of London wished to commission a painting of *The Siege of Gibraltar,* commemorating the repulse of the Spanish fleet by the British garrison in 1782. Benjamin West was a strong candidate, but Copley was picked. He promised to finish the painting (his largest at 18 feet by 25 feet) in two years. In 1785 George III asked him to paint his three youngest daughters. The portrait was shown at the Royal Academy the following year. A review in the influential *Morning Post* began: "So, Mr. Copley, is this the fruit of your long studies and labours?... Is it because you have heard that *fine feathers* make fine birds, that you have concluded *fine cloaths* will make fine *Princesses?* What delightful disorder! Why you have plucked up harmony by the roots, and planted confusion in its stead! Princesses, parrots, dogs, grapes, flowers, leaves, are each striving for pre-eminence, and opposing with hostile force, all attempts of our wearied eyes to find repose." Copley had combined portraiture and genre to produce a scene from everyday life which would characterize the Romantic painting of the coming Victorian era. But the British public and critics were far from ready for such innovation, and his reputation began to decline with this attack. He struggled on with his mammoth *Siege* which he finally finished in 1790, six years later than promised. Once again he chose not to exhibit in the academy but showed the work privately. He rented "a magnificent Oriental tent" 84 feet long, which he had set up in Green Park. But the Duke of Bolton and other residents from nearby Arlington Street complained that the tent interfered with their view. Copley was forced to move the tent several times until he was saved by an amiable George III: "Push it up nearer to my Wife's house—she won't complain." (The house was Buckingham Palace.) In spite of its aura of heroism and several excellent individual portraits, the *Siege* was melodramatic and unconvincing.

In 1792, Benjamin West—still bitter over Copley's commission for the *Siege*—was elected president of the Royal Academy. The two Americans, once friends and then competitors, ended as enemies. Copley's jealousy of West became almost pathological, affecting both his judgment and his painting. He spoke of returning to Boston but law suits with engravers of his work prevented him. With the outbreak of war between England and France at the end of the century, business declined and painters were the first to suffer. A few years earlier, Copley had sold land overlooking Boston for £7,000, but in time Beacon Hill became a chosen residential area and the land became worth some £100,000. A London diarist, commenting upon the painter's "dejected appearance," attributed it to his "ruminating" over his missed opportunity. Copley kept at his easel but when in 1811 a young Samuel F.B. Morse called upon the former master, he described him as "very old and infirm... his powers of mind have almost entirely left him; his late paintings are miserable; it is really a lamentable thing that a man should outlive his faculties." Copley, 77, died of a stroke here on 9 September 1815. (Today the site of Copley's house is occupied by the Caxton Publishing House.)

St. James's Palace Map C

St. James's Palace was built by Henry VIII. "A goodly manor," it had four courts: the Ambassadors' Court, Friary Court, Engine Court and Colour Court—this last, approached through the gatehouse flanked by its octagonal turrets, is the only large part of the original building to survive. St. James's Palace was one of the principal residences of the kings and queens of England for over three hundred years.

The first American minister to be appointed to the Court of St. James was John Adams. He described his presentation on 1 June 1785 in a detailed letter to John Jay:

> At one, on Wednesday, the master of ceremonies called at my house [Bath Hotel, Piccadilly], and went with me to the secretary of state's office in Cleveland Row, where the Marquis of Carmarthen received me... after a short conversation upon the subject of importing my effects from Holland and France free of duty, Lord Carmarthen invited me to go with him in his coach to Court.
>
> When we arrived in the antechamber, the *oeil de boeuf* of St. James's, the master of the ceremonies met me and attended me, while the secretary of state went to take the commands of the King. While I stood in this place, where it seems all ministers stand upon such occasions, always attended by the master of ceremonies, the room very full of ministers of state,

lords, and bishops, and all sorts of courtiers, as well as the next room, which is the King's bedchamber, you may well suppose I was the focus of all eyes. I was relieved, however, from the embarrassment of it by the Swedish and Dutch ministers, who came to me, and entertained me in a very agreeable conversation during the whole time. Some other gentlemen, whom I had seen before, came to make their compliments too, until the Marquis of Carmathen returned and desired me to go with him to his Majesty. I went with his Lordship through the levee room into the King's closet. The door was shut, and I was left with his Majesty and the secretary of state alone. I made the three reverences,—one at the door, another about half way, and a third before the presence,—according to the usage established at this and all the northern Courts of Europe, and then addressed myself to his Majesty in the following words:

"Sir, The United States of America have appointed me their minister plenipotentiary to your Majesty, and have directed me to deliver to your Majesty this letter which contains the evidence of it. It is in obedience to their express commands, that I have the honor to assure your Majesty of their unanimous disposition and desire to cultivate the most friendly and liberal intercourse between your Majesty's subjects and their citizens, and of their best wishes for your Majesty's health and happiness, and for that of your royal family. The appointment of a minister from the United States to your Majesty's Court will form an epoch in the history of England and of America. I think myself more fortunate than all my fellow-citizens, in having the distinguished honor to be the first to stand in your Majesty's royal presence in a diplomatic character; and I shall esteem myself the happiest of men, if I can be instrumental in recommending my country more and more to your Majesty's royal benevolence, and of restoring an entire esteem, confidence, and affection, or, in better words, the old good nature and the old good humor between people, who, though separated by an ocean, and under different governments, have the same language, a similar religion, and kindred blood.

I beg your Majesty's permission to add, that, although I have some time before been intrusted by my country, it was never in my whole life in a manner so agreeable to myself."

The King listened to every word I said, with dignity, but with an apparent emotion. Whether it was the nature of the interview, or whether it was my visible agitation, for I felt more than I did or could express, that touched him, I cannot say. But he was much affected, and answered me with more tremor than I had spoken with, and said:

"Sir, The circumstances of this audience are so extraordinary, the language you have now held is so extremely proper, and the feelings you have discovered so justly adapted to the occasion, that I must say that I not only receive with pleasure the assurance of the friendly dispositions of the United States, but that I am very glad the choice has fallen upon you to be their minister. I wish you, Sir, to believe, and that it may be understood in America, that I have done nothing in the late contest but what I thought myself indispensably bound to do, but the duty which I owed to my people. I will be very frank with you. I was the last to consent to the separation; but the separation having been made, and having become inevitable, I have always said, as I say now, that I would be the first to meet the friendship of the United States as an independent power. The moment I see such sentiments and language as your prevail, and a disposition to give to this country the preference, that moment I shall say, let the circumstances of language, religion, and blood have their natural and full effect."

Adams had every reason to have been satisfied with this reception. But, the seasoned diplomat John Jay warned, while the king's speech and manner "was indeed true, we must be cautious what consequences we draw from it."

St. James's Place Map C

16 Stafford Hotel. James Thurber and his wife Helen spent June and July 1955 here, after spring in France. Thurber was famous in England and he enjoyed the attention. The newspapers loved him. He appeared on television with the editor of *Punch,* who "seemed more nervous than I was," chatted with J.B. Priestley, had tea with one of his early admirers, T.S. Eliot, and spent an afternoon being interviewed by Kenneth Tynan, that "brilliant and amusing young critic of the *Sunday Times*." There was something about England, Thurber wrote, that kept its writers alive to a ripe old age and he was thinking of settling down here. He was about to be taken to meet Walter de la Mare, aged 84; Somerset Maugham, 81; H. M. Tomlinson, 82, and Eden Philpotts who, noted Thurber, was still writing for British television at the age of 92. He couldn't meet Max Beerbohm, 86, as he was off in Italy. In America, Thurber continued, most male writers failed to reach the age of 60 or, if they did, had nothing more to say, although they said it anyway.

The Thurbers returned to the Stafford Hotel for the summer of 1958. "It is easier to write in London than in New York," he told a friend. He had spent the previous six weeks working on his book about Harold Ross, the editor of the *New Yorker.* "We are going away for two weeks to finish the goddam Ross book—maybe Helen told you that she is writing a novel about me called *By Ross Possessed.*" He published an article in *Punch* on the perils of typo and garble with examples such as "Don, give up the ship."

Thurber's final visit to England was in May 1961, when he received an invitation to speak at the Harvard Business School. In his letter declining, written from the Stafford Hotel, he explained, "I am now in Europe and in the fall expect to be in Jeopardy." He died three months later.

(33)   James Fenimore Cooper and his wife took a small house here on 5 March 1828. "We had a tiny drawing-room, quite plainly furnished, a dining room, and three bedrooms for a guinea a day," wrote Cooper. "The people of the house cooked for us, went to market, and attended to the rooms, while our own man and maid did the personal service. I paid a shilling extra for each fire, and as we kept three, it came to another guinea weekly."

Living close to St. James's Palace, Cooper liked to watch the horse guards march "with a fine band on horseback" from their barracks to the palace. Outside the palace, Ambassadors Court was crossed by Stable Yard. "There is simple good sense, not to call it good taste, that distinguishes the English from their more ambitious kinsmen, our worthy selves, in all matters connected with names," wrote Cooper, who as a writer appreciated the lack of pretentiousness in the English use of language. In America "stableyard" would surely be "stadium" or "gymnasium"—if, indeed, it escaped being called "Campus Martius." While he admired the English nannies with their charges in Green Park, which was open to the public, and the English ladies riding in St. James's Park, where only the aristocracy was allowed, "the outdoor glory of the day" was won by the coachmen of London. "Figure to yourself, the dignity of a portly man of 50, with a sky-blue coat laced on all its seams, red plush breeches, white silk stockings, shoe buckles as large as a muffin, a smug wig, a shovel-nosed hat edged with broad gold lace, and a short nose of his own as red as a cherry, and you will get some idea of these dignitaries."

Cooper was also busy finishing *Notions of the Americans.*

"Your Father writes very hard," Mrs. Cooper assured her daughters in Paris. "He gets up early, and sometimes writes until he becomes so nervous that he can hardly keep his hand still." Near the end of their visit, Mrs. Cooper confided to her sister, "Lord Lansdowne, Lord Spencer, The Duke of Devonshire, Lord Grey and many *minor* folks have given him dinners and parties—so that he has had an excellent opportunity of seeing English society; he does not like it much." In a letter to a friend in New York just before leaving London, Cooper noted that he had dined with all the Whigs, "who are certainly the most talented part of the aristocracy...though London contains a great many highly intelligent and well-bred men...there is no place like Paris for manners." The Coopers left London on 28 May 1828 and arrived back in Paris two weeks later.

St. James's Street

(80) Thatched House Tavern. A fashionable tavern opened in 1705, it was frequented by Swift and served as a meeting place for the Dilettanti Society. On 26 March 1774, twenty-nine Americans met here to protest the proposed closing of the port of Boston in retaliation for the Boston Tea Party. Two weeks earlier Lord North had told Parliament that he thought that "the inhabitants of the town of Boston deserved punishment." The Americans, several of whom were lawyers, spent the evening drawing up a petition for presentation to the House of Lords.

In their petition, the signers saw themselves as "intitled to the Rights of natural Justice, and to the common Law of England, as their inalienable Birthright." They understood that "no man shall be comdemn'd unheard; and that according to Law, no person, or persons, can be judged, without being call'd upon to answer, and being permitted to hear the Evidence against them, and to make their defence." They were much concerned by a "Bill of Pains and Penalties" which was about to be inflicted on the town of Boston, without the town having been apprised of the accusation brought against it or permitted to hear the evidence or to make its defense. The closing of the port of Boston, the petition argued, would "restrain many thousands of his Majesty's Subjects, from subsisting themselves and their Families, by their usual Employments; that it will Punish the Innocent for the Guilty." They concluded by trusting and praying that such an honorable house would not deprive even "the meanest Individual the Prevelage of hearing, and controverting, the Evidence against him; and maintaining his Innocence."

It was a conservative appeal, moderate in tone, based on law. What the signers did not say was that the reaction to the closing of the port of Boston would be one of anger and bitterness, driving hitherto moderates into the ranks of the rebels. No one was more aware of the arrogance, and finally the foolishness, of the British government than the men assembled in the Thatched House Tavern that evening. Lawyers and merchants for the greater part, none of the petitioners wished for war. The petitioners included Stephen Sayre, raised on Long Island, a graduate of the College of New Jersey and now a merchant in London; William Lee, from Virginia, merchant, diplomat and born troublemaker; Arthur Lee, his brother; Benjamin Franklin; Ralph Izard, future senator for South Carolina; Hugh Williamson, a doctor who had witnessed the Boston Tea Party and had carried the news to London; Thomas Barker, merchant and lawyer in Edenton, North Carolina; John Boylston, wealthy Bostonian merchant; Philip Neyle, lawyer, killed in the siege of Charleston in 1780, and Edward Bancroft from Westfield, Massachusetts, writer and inventor, the most successful spy for the British during the Revolution; Edward Fenwicke from South Carolina; Thomas Pinckney, brother of Charles, from South Carolina; Thomas Bromfield, merchant from Boston; Joshua Johnson, tobacco dealer from Annapolis; John Ballendine, Virginian, in London proposing construction of canals and locks on the Potomac River; John Williams, inspector general of the Boston customs, married to the niece of Franklin; Henry Laurens, from Charleston, South Carolina, future president of the Continental Congress. There were twelve additional signers.

The petition was presented to the House of Lords two days later on 28 March 1774; the Record Office docketed: "Petition of Stephen Sayer and others, Natives of America, praying that the Boston Port Bill may not pass into a Law. 28th March 1774. Presented and order'd to lie on the Table." A similar petition was addressed to the House of Commons and another to George III.

They were a mixed group in the Thatched House Tavern that long evening. But they forgot their personal interests and antagonisms in their desire to protest to the British government about the closing of the port of Boston. The next morning, a somber Henry Laurens wrote to his son John, "If Lord North succeeds in his present attempts... his Ambition will be enflamed and require new subjects. Ambition is assuredly the hidden Spring of his Proceedings.... He may possibly fix the Badge of Slavery upon the Sea Coast, but this will hasten the beginning of Independence."

St. Leonard's Terrace, Chelsea Map F

20   Ruth Draper took a house here for the summer of 1926. She began her summer season in London with a command performance at Windsor Castle before King George V and Queen Mary and their fifty guests from the Royal Ascot house-party. She told a friend, "I did ten sketches—the King roared." Before she returned to London she was presented with a diamond and ruby pendant. She opened at the Garrick Theatre to packed houses for she was now known throughout England. She no longer took a bus to the theater but was driven there and back in a Rolls Royce. But success had its price. She was frequently lonely and told a friend, "I didn't meet one fellow performer. That's the funny part of music-hall life, you just do your turn and go home." When she performed for two nights in Birmingham, she returned by plane: "It was nothing less than sublime! My own little machine—a great war hero as a pilot—perfect flying conditions—sunset gray clouds too wonderful—cost only 25 guineas and my manager paid half!" It took an American to fly from Birmingham to London in 1926!

(25)   Grosvenor House. Carson McCullers arrived at Southampton on board the *Queen Elizabeth* on 4 August 1951, unexpectedly accompanied by her husband. He had been undergoing a disintoxication cure in Doctors' Hospital in New York City which he had left for the day to see her off. Having said goodbye, he wandered about the ship and, although possessing neither passport nor money, he decided to stay on board. In Southampton the British immigration authorities would not permit him to land, but the British poet David Gascoyne who had come to meet McCullers, appealed to them along with the American ambassador. The authorities finally relented and allowed "the husband of England's prominent literary visitor" to stay for a week. It was a mistake—the couple had no sooner settled into Gascoyne's large luxury flat in Grosvenor House than they started to drink. Carson McCullers, 34, famous thanks to *The Heart Is a*

Lonely Hunter and *The Member of the Wedding,* began a round of luncheons, cocktail parties and dinners given in her honor. Her host or hostess soon found her a demanding guest, welcome upon arrival but, as Elizabeth Bowen discovered, once ensconced, "a terrible handful." John Lehmann, the English poet and publisher, gave a dinner for her and Tennessee Williams. He was particularly struck, he wrote afterwards, by the tender and affectionate consideration Tennessee showed her. "He knew exactly how to handle his erratic and brilliant friend, and revealed an impressive side to his character of which I had, I confess, not been fully aware before." At another dinner, McCullers became attracted to the very beautiful American wife of her English publisher, Katherine Hammond Cohen. A psychiatrist, Dr. Cohen was immediately sensitive to the frail young writer's infirmities and needs and offered to try to help her. McCullers's left arm was partially paralyzed. After a week at St. George's Hospital, where first she recuperated from the effects of the parties, Dr. Cohen examined her and found no organic reason for the paralysis. Her patient suffered from "hysterical paralysis," and she proposed trying to cure her through hypnosis. McCullers, interested in anyone who was interested in her, agreed to the treatment. Dr. Cohen felt that alternating periods of rest, hypnosis, exercise and work would relieve the atrophied muscles and eventually make the writer whole again. But McCullers was unable to respond to the hypnosis, and was even more upset by her doctor's refusal to become more emotionally entangled with her. She found that she was unable to work during her ten weeks in London and, suffering from a new sense of rejection, she returned home at the end of October.

St. Martin's Lane Map D

Duke of York's Theatre. Charles Frohman introduced many leading American actors and actresses to British audiences while he was manager of this theater from 1897 until 1915. He did away with the statues of heroes such as Shakespeare and Garrick which haunted the foyer of every London theater, and replaced them with large photographs of his live American stars: Maude Adams, Ethel Barrymore, Leslie Carter, John Drew, Otis Skinner and William Gillette. One of his first big successes at his new theater was *The Girl from Up There,* with Edna May. Frohman employed the best-known and highest-salaried producer in London, Dion Boucicault, son of the famous playwright, and embarked on a series of impeccable productions, not all of which made money. On 27 December 1904, *Peter Pan* opened for the first time in England here at the Duke of York. Written by Frohman's friend James M. Barrie, it was revived every year at Christmas time. Frohman was known as an exceptionally fair man whose word was his only contract. He enjoyed working in England where he felt that the theater had a dignity and distinction lacking in America. He said that he would rather make £15 in London than $15,000 in New York. Yet he did not have to worry. As early as September 1901, for instance, he had five different plays running in London at the same time. He spent part of every season in London living in the same suite overlooking the Thames at the Savoy Hotel, where one of his favorite dinner guests was Mark Twain. In 1913 he leased what was perhaps the finest suite of theatrical offices in London in Trafalgar House in WATERLOO PLACE. Two years later he went down with the *Lusitania*.

St. Paul's Cathedral Map E

Chauncey Depew, chairman of the New York Central Railroad, was admiring the tomb of the Duke of Wellington when he fell into conversation with the verger, who told him that of the many Americans who visited the cathedral the most remarkable was Colonel Robert G. Ingersoll:

> He was quite inquisitive and wanted to know all about Wellington's tomb. I told him that the duke's body was first put in a wooden coffin, and this was incased in steel; that this had made for it a position in a stone weighing twenty tons and over that was a huge stone weighing forty tons. He gave me a slap on the back which sent me flying and exclaimed: "Old man, you have got him safe. If he ever escapes cable at my expense to Robert G. Ingersoll, Peoria, Illinois, U.S.A."

Martin Luther King, Jr. preached his favorite sermon, "The Three Dimensions of a Complete Life," here on the evening of 6 December 1964. Four thousand people crowded the cathedral and the crypt where loudspeakers carried his message. By chance Malcolm X was also in London, so King devoted one of his press conferences to minimizing the differences between American blacks. He also spoke on South African racial tyranny at the City

Temple, where he was introduced by Canon John Collins of St. Paul's Cathedral. King spent three days in London before flying on to Oslo to receive the Nobel Peace Prize.

St. Paul's Churchyard

(6)   St. Paul's Coffee House and Hotel. Dr. Oliver Wendell Holmes put up here on 20 May 1834. It was Sunday and after the gaiety of a Sunday in Paris the 30-year-old Holmes found the dreariness of the sabbath in London not merely severe but repulsive. He went to Westminister Abbey where he heard the Bishop of Gloucester preach "a stupid sermon." Monday was an improvement when he visited St. Thomas's Hospital to see Mr. Green operate. A few nights later he attended the theater at Covent Garden where he was impressed by "a nice fresh looking girl, blonde and rather pretty," seated in the royal box. She was the 15-year-old Princess Victoria, heir to the throne of the British empire. As for her uncle, King William IV, he looked like "a retired butcher." The father of the future chief justice of the United States asked forgiveness of his reader, explaining: "I have a disposition to tartness and levity which tells to the disadvantage of the royal living, but it is accidental and must be forgiven."

St. Thomas's Street Map E

Guy's Hospital. The hospital was founded in 1721, and among the expenses for upkeep was £20 paid, in 1735, to a man for killing the bugs which were found to lodge in the wooden bedsteads. As a result iron bedsteads were introduced. Cold, hot and vapour baths were added in 1780. Beginning in the 19th century, discipline among staff and patients was tightened. Rule V stated: "If any patient curse or swear or use any profane language or lewd Talking, and it was proven on them by two Witnesses, such patient shall for the first Offense lose their next Day's Diet, for the second offence, lose two Day's Diet, and the third be discharged." Among the staff were Richard Bright, known in 1827 for his work on the kidneys (Bright's disease); Thomas Addison, who recognized the disease of the adrenal glands in 1855 (Addison's disease), and Thomas Hodgkin, who discovered "a peculiar enlargement of the lymphatic glands and spleen" (Hodgkin's disease). The most famous of the surgeons was Astley Cooper who, at the age of 21, had been appointed "Demonstrator of Anatomy." In 1799 Guy's became the first London hospital to appoint a dental surgeon.

Many American medical students and doctors trained here and at St. Thomas's Hospital which was just across the road. Students were at liberty to attend lectures and operations at both hospitals. In 1859 the site of St. Thomas's was acquired for London Bridge Station and the new hospital was built on Lambeth Palace Road overlooking the Thames. William Baynham from Caroline County, Virginia, arrived to begin medicine just in time for the War of Independence. He remained in London and, after studying anatomy and surgery at St. Thomas's, was appointed assistant demonstrator to Dr. Else. He was "to superintend the anatomical theatre and dissecting room, prepare the bodies for his public demonstrations, make preparations for the museum, and to instruct the pupils in the arts of dissecting, injecting, making anatomical preparations etc." His salary was £98 a year. In 1785 he returned to Virginia where he practiced in Essex Country until his death in 1814.

James Jackson from Boston, future professor of medicine at Harvard, arrived in London in September 1799 and put up at the London Coffee House on Ludgate Hill opposite St. Paul's. After having called upon the American minister Rufus King, he registered at Guy's. He took a room "at the house of a hatmaker in St. Saviour's Church Yard," a two-minute stroll from Guy's, and served as a "dresser" at St. Thomas's while at Guy's he studied under Astley Cooper. Like all medical students at the time, Jackson attended lectures at other teaching hospitals in London. In his *Memoirs,* he recalled: "Vaccination had been introduced about the time I commenced my studies, but the practice had not been extensively adopted at the day, even in England. Dr. Woodville was physician of the St. Pancras Smallpox and Inoculation Hospital, where he attended to the subject of vaccination." Jackson paid ten guineas for his course with Woodville. He returned to Boston in August 1800 where he cooperated with Benjamin Waterhouse in carrying out smallpox vaccinations in Massachusetts, using vaccine imported from England.

John C. Warren from Boston became a "dresser" at Guy's and also studied under Cooper. He wrote to his father on 8 December 1799, "The people here look for facts; they trust no theory, but experiment is the only creed. Go to Edinburgh for theory." Warren became friends with Jackson while at Guy's and later the two men helped found the Massachusetts General Hospital where he was the first in America to operate for strangulated hernia.

❧

William Gibson, from Baltimore, Maryland, received his M.D. from Edinburgh in 1809 and came to Guy's to work under Cooper. He returned home and enjoyed a distinguished career as professor of surgery at the University of Pennsylvania.

❧

Edward Reynolds graduated from Harvard in 1811 and studied with Abernethy and Cooper in London. He went on to Paris to work with Dupuytren and Bichat. He became interested in ophthalmology and upon his return helped establish a dispensary in Boston which later became the Massachusetts Charitable Eye and Ear Infirmary. By the 1830s, Paris began to replace London as a medical training center for Americans thanks to men such as Dupuytren, Bichat, Velpeau, Laennec and Roux. Equally important, social life for a young medical student in Paris was light and gay, in Victorian London it was solemn, purposeful and dull.

❧

Alexander H. Stevens got his medical degree from the University of Pennsylvania in 1811 and sailed to Europe carrying official dispatches during the War of 1812. His ship captured by the British, Stevens was imprisoned at Plymouth, Devon. Upon his release, he came to London and worked under Astley Cooper at Guy's. When he returned to America, he became professor of surgery in the College of Physicians and Surgeons of New York and helped found the New York Academy of Medicine. He later edited an American edition of Cooper's *Surgery*. Cooper, by then the leading surgeon in England, had been knighted—a tall, good-looking man with charming manners, he enjoyed the incredible annual income of £20,000.

❧

John Wagner graduated from Yale in 1812 and served as "dresser" to Cooper for three years at Guy's. He then went to Paris where he worked under Dupuytren. He returned home to Charleston, where he was elected to the chair of pathological and surgical anatomy in the Medical College of the State of South Carolina.

Shaftesbury Avenue Map D

Shaftesbury Theatre. Fred Astaire and his sister Adele opened here in *Stop Flirting* in 1923. Their nervousness on the opening night increased after the first act which drew merely polite applause. But their numbers "Whichness of the Whatness" and the "Oompah Trot" brought endless encores and the evening ended in triumph. The critics described them as "dancers of genius," the *Evening Star* finished its praise by saying that "Adele could dance the depression out of an undertaker." The *Times* said that "they typify the primal spirit of animal delight that could not restrain itself—the vitality that bursts its bonds in the Garden of Eden... they are as lithe as blades of grass, as light as gossamer." The *Pall Mall Gazette* discovered that "they neither look nor behave like ordinary dancers... all temperament and intelligence, their final shoulder-to-shoulder gallop not only brings the house down but is one of the funniest things of its kind." Fred Astaire and his sister began to feel at home in London as they walked to work every evening from the Savoy Hotel. The Prince of Wales came to ten performances, and Adele danced frequently with him at parties. Fred Astaire was delighted with his valet George who disregarded all h's in his speech and also in his writing. One evening the star noticed a strange code written on the upper right corner of the large dressing-room mirror, "AT ERE":

"George, now will you please tell me what the hell that means?
"It's your 'at, Sir."
"Well, what about my hat?"
"I didn't want to forget to take it with me for your entrance, Sir, I
wanted to remind myself that the 'at was 'ere in the room."

The show ran for eighteen months and ended only at the request of the two dancers, who were afraid that they might be forgotten back home. As the SS *Homeric* docked in New York, their agent came on board and began outlining the plot for *Lady, Be Good.* He produced two contracts which they signed on their steamer trunk lid while waiting for the customs officers. With a new joint salary of $2,000 a week, they had not exactly been forgotten.

Tallulah Bankhead was walking down Shaftesbury Avenue at the ripe old age of 21 when she happened to glance up, and read with astonishment the words in electric lights over the theater's marquee:

Tallulah Bankhead
in
"Conchita"

She knew that she had a major role in what turned out to be a most mediocre play, but this was the first time that she had ever seen her name up in lights—it was the finest sight in London, in England and probably in the world. During the last week of rehearsals she circled the block repeatedly to read the magic announcement and "dragooned acquaintances into this grand tour." It was 1924, her second year in London, and it was followed by six more happy ones before she left for Hollywood.

Sherwood Street Map C

Regent Palace Hotel. Thomas Wolfe took a room here for nine shillings and sixpence at midnight on 3 April 1935. His room was small, cold, cramped and cheerless, but he had "the best night's sleep in weeks." After breakfast the following morning in the Louis XVI salon, he returned to his room where he wrote:

> A gaudy, glittery, and, I thought, horribly uncomfortable place filled with Nottingham butchers and their wives or Stenographers—and Leeds, or Birmingham, or Manchester 'Erbs and 'Alfs and Charlies down for a bit of a spree, y'now, with baggy flannel trousers, and brown tweed coats, and very snooty, bored, casual ways—blimey, now almost as good as a bloody bleeding Cambridge bloke—the fixed pitiable deep-rooted snobbery of lower class England.

He returned to the hotel that evening:

> Had two drinks in gild-gold-splendor lounge of Regent Palace—eagerness of Nottingham butchers with broad bottomed wives in evening clothes—great elegance going gradually to vulgarity—"the gentleman's very eloquent and very charming address"—descending to "You don't know who Epstein is." "Of course I now 'oo Epstein is."
> "Nah yer down't—Yer been talkin' 'ere all night about 'is theory of relativity an' you can't tell us what 'is theory o'relativity *is*."
> "Relativity—I'll tell you what it is—Relativity!—I know a *proper* man when I sees one—Now some folks lookin' at yer head, my friend, my think that yer was *bald*—but *me? Nah-h!* When I looks at yer head I sees a fine 'ead o' 'air. *That's* relativity.

American writers in England have persisted in their attempts to reproduce regional accents and particularly cockney, generally with lamentable results by English standards. Thomas Wolfe, who was raised in Asheville, North Carolina, failed here to reproduce a convincing northern accent, but the result was, perhaps unintentionally, excellent cockney.

Sloane Court West Map F

25 Captain Glenn Miller and his sixty-two musicians arrived in London on the night of 29 June 1944. The band had crossed over in six days on the *Queen Elizabeth,* where they had given seven to eight shows each day to the 17,000 troops who filed 2,000 at a time into the main ballroom. Miller, who had flown over, met the ship when it dropped anchor in Scotland's Firth of Clyde. The band and their leader arrived in London to hear the sirens announcing a buzz-bomb attack by the German pilotless planes; it was the last London blitz. Sgt. Johnny Desmond, the singer, went to the roof of Sloane Court to get a closer look: "I had the crazy feeling that as long as I could see a bomb, it couldn't hurt me." Most of the band spent a sleepless night in the underground shelter in Sloane Square, where they found the air foul. Two days later, after endless hours trying to telephone, Miller succeeded in getting two buses to move them to Bedford, a small county town sixty miles northeast of London and three miles from a U.S. air force base. The week after they moved, 25 Sloane Court suffered a direct hit; twenty-six people were killed and seventy-eight others were dug out of the building. In Bedford, they took over a pottery factory, lined the brick walls with hundreds of burlap bags and turned it into a studio which they named "8-H" in honor of the huge NBC studio in New York City from which Toscanini and the NBC Symphony used to broadcast. The band gave seventy-one concerts in five months to American military bases all over England. In Bedford they played for the townsfolk at the Corn Exchange (still standing), which they nicknamed Lombardo Hall. They came to London once a week to play at the Queensbury All Services Club (Old Compton Street). Glenn Miller was killed in France in 1945 in an airplane crash.

Sloane Street Map F

(62) James McNeill Whistler joined his sister and her

husband Seymour Haden here in 1858. At first, Haden, a wealthy 40-year-old doctor and amateur painter, was enthusiastic over the arrival of his 23-year-old impecunious brother-in-law who had just finished his studies in Paris. The two men went sketching together along the banks of the Thames. They even did joint etchings such as *Trees in the Park,* incised in Kensington Gardens: Haden did the trees and Whistler the girl standing among them. Many years later after they had quarreled, a proof of the etching brought a high sum at an auction as Whistler had written on it: "Legs not by me, but a fatuous addition by a General Practitioner." One of the first things Whistler did upon arrival in London was to invite his penniless Parisian friends, Alphonse Legros and Henri Fantin-Latour to come and stay here in fashionable Sloane Street; their sojourn was not a success. Whistler rented a studio in NEWMAN STREET but used this prestigious address to see potential customers.

75   Cadogan Hotel. Sinclair Lewis and his wife took a room here in June 1921. At 36, Lewis had just achieved success with *Main Street.* In England he was seen sympathetically as a critic of American provincialism. Lewis, who hailed from Sauk Centre, Minnesota, could finally indulge himself in handmade suits from Savile Row, waistcoats, spats, silver-headed cane, monocle and, for the countryside, plus fours. But the English soon found his garrulity tiresome. Rebecca West wrote of their first meeting: "His talk was wonderful, but after five solid hours of it I ceased to look upon him as a human being." Lewis asked Arnold Bennett wistfully why it was that he could talk to him and not to H.G. Wells. "Because he is too self-conscious," Bennett replied. Lewis's enthusiasm for English writing began to wane; after meeting "the million Bright Young Authors in England," he told H.L. Mencken that he felt comforted about the artistic future of America. Mencken was delighted and urged him to write an article about the "collapse" of literary England, an offer Sinclair wisely declined. He preferred meeting men such as the young socialist Harold Laski, who had just begun teaching at the London School of Economics, where Lewis went to talk with the students about America. After two weeks in London, Lewis decided to move to the countryside and settle down to work on *Babbitt,* much of which was written in England. He rented Bell House in Bearsted, near Maidstone in the heart of Kent. In this "utterly charming half-timbered Elizabethan cottage," Lewis worked daily from 9 a.m. until 4 p.m., when tea was served by a "perfect English maid," and then took a long walk. Close to the common and the village tavern, surrounded by hop fields and woods and just a few miles from the softly rising North Downs, Lewis complained to Alfred Harcourt, his publisher, that Bearsted was "almost too peaceful a spot for writing.... This is a lazy country. It gets into your blood." Yet within six weeks he had written 75,000 words. He made one journey up to London to talk about a stage version of *Main Street,* the New York opening being imminent. At the end of September, he and his wife left for Paris.

Southampton Street Map D

22-25 Formerly the Covent Garden Hotel. Woodrow Wilson spent July 1896 visiting England, his first trip abroad. He had been overworking in America and had come down with nervous indigestion and what he described as a "derangement of the bowels." His wife Ellen had insisted that he go abroad alone. The colleges of Cambridge struck him as "beyond measure attractive," while simply walking across the lawns of Balliol College in Oxford was "enough to take one's heart by storm." He noted the tutorial system, which he later adapted for Princeton. Of all the landscapes he saw, his favorite was the River Wye, where he sat on a grassy bank near Tintern Abbey and read Wordsworth. In London he met the British historian James Bryce and invited him to lecture at Princeton. He confessed to Ellen, "I have been long in the National Gallery, and all the while the feeling was strong upon me to sadness that the Rembrandts, Rubenses, Reynoldses, Gainsboroughs, Turners, Titians and the rest *belonged to you,* and that I was a selfish thief to take sight of them without you." But Wilson obviously recovered from such feelings of guilt for he thoroughly enjoyed England and, when he returned in 1899, again alone, he stayed in this same hotel just off Covent Garden.

Spring Gardens

This was the site of a pleasure-ground laid out in the 17th century. Little by little it was encircled by mansions, one of which served as a Huguenot chapel. In the following century the chapel became known as the "Great Room" and was used as an exhibition room and museum.

John Singleton Copley rented the "Great Room" in the first week of May 1781 to show his large history painting (7 1/2 feet by 10 feet) of *The Death of the Earl of Chatham* (now in the Tate Gallery). Barely three years earlier, on 7 April 1778, in the House of Lords, the 70-year-old earl heard the Duke of Richmond urge the withdrawal of British forces from the American colonies. Chatham rose and answered, but collapsed at the end of his speech and died a month later. During the next two years, Copley completed the individual portraits of the fifty-four lords who had witnessed his collapse, and placed them kneeling or standing in a dramatic semi-circle around the stricken man. The death scene was recent in time, local in place, and realistic in presentation—Copley had succeeded in combining history with portraiture. The picture created almost the shock of a photograph, and Copley's success was enormous. During the first six weeks, over 20,000 people paid one shilling each to see the painting. During the height of this public acclaim, Copley made a disturbing discovery. In painting *The Death of Chatham,* he had moved in political waters which he did not understand. By honoring Chatham, he had given offense to the opposition, which included powerful men in court and in Parliament. The painting, though admired by all, was bought by none. Twenty-five years later, in desperation, Copley sold it by raffle. Twenty individuals put up £100 each. The man who won it, Alexander Davidson, then promptly announced that he would not take less than £5,000 for it.

Stable Yard, St. James's Palace Map C

Lancaster House. Built between 1825 and 1841, it was owned by the Duke of Sutherland and was known as Stafford House. Given to the nation in 1913 and renamed Lancaster House, it was the site of the Coronation Banquet for Elizabeth II in 1953. It is now used for government receptions and conferences. On the first floor were the state rooms—the drawing room, the music room and the Great Gallery, with works by Raphael, Tintoretto, Titian, Velasquez, Rubens, Van Dyck, Watteau and others. Queen Victoria was often a guest, once commenting to Lady Sutherland, "I have come from my house to your palace." It was a center for Whigs and Liberal politicians, and William Garrison the abolitionist was entertained here.

Harriet Beecher Stowe was guest of honor at a luncheon on 8 May 1853. The Duke of Sutherland, Lord and Lady Shaftesbury, Lords Palmerston, Granville and Russell, Mr. Gladstone and others applauded when the Duchess of Sutherland presented her with a superb gold bracelet, made in the form of a slave's shackle and bearing the inscription: "We trust it is a memorial of a chain that is soon to be broken." *Uncle Tom's Cabin* was one of the most sensationally successful books in Victorian England, selling three times as many copies as in America. A modest Mrs. Stowe had arrived in London to discover "Uncle Tom's pure unadulterated Coffee," "Uncle Tom's improved flagelots," "Uncle Tom china," "Uncle Tom's unshrinkable woolen stockings," while humble eating places, pastry shops and dry-goods emporiums all traded under the name of Uncle Tom. But this was nothing compared to the theater, where the Adelphi ran *Slave Life or Uncle Tom's Cabin;* the Great National Standard, *The Slave's Life in America;* the Royal Victoria *The Fugitive Slave.* At Christmas, the Drury Lane's pantomine, normally Cinderella, was *Uncle Tom's Cabin or the Horrors of Slavery,* while at the Royal Pavilion Circus, Mrs. Cook as Eliza rode fearlessly in "the escape" and performed other noteworthy feats bareback. Parodies proliferated and even ballet companies got in on the act. Everyone made money. On stage, Americans were portrayed as coarse and noisy with expressions such as "Waal, I calc'late," and other supposed Yankeeisms dear to British hearts. There was such an Uncle Tom mania that the critic of the *British Army Despatch* complained bitterly: "On the stage, this work...now electrifying an Adelphi audience, is doing a mischief which a century cannot repair. Let the Lord Chamberlain [British censor] look at *this.* We are playing the part of the despot and the priest. What have we to do with the internal affairs of the American Republic!"

The Strand Map D

Savoy Hotel. In 1889 Richard D'Oyly Carte opened a hotel adjoining the Savoy Theatre, with Cesar Ritz as manager and Auguste Escoffier as chef.

When World War I broke out in August 1914, all shipping was immediately commandeered to ferry troops. For the 150,000 or more American tourists in Europe, most of whom streamed to England, the summer holiday turned into a nightmare. Banks were closed. They found themselves penniless, frequently unable to obtain hotel rooms, or steamer accommodations home. At the Savoy, stranded Americans formed a committee and persuaded Herbert Hoover to head it. Hoover and his committee, many of them engineers from his London office, set up offices in the reception rooms which the hotel provided rent free, together with tables and chairs. With desks manned by American volunteers, they called American firms in London and borrowed cash from company safes. With this money they exchanged a limited number of pounds for each tourist at the normal exchange rate of $4.85. To those tourists, especially students, who ran out of money, they loaned ten shillings per day. Twelve American businessmen guaranteed an account of $1 million with the British Treasury which began to supply cash against American paper money, including personal checks. During six weeks beginning early in August, the American committee helped some 120,000 Americans get back home and paid out over $1,500,000—its loss in bad checks or unfulfilled pledges of repayment was less than $300. The entire operation, Hoover recalled, had sometimes been enlivened by gales of laughter. A young lady from Lansing, Michigan, lost her five trunks en route to London. She cabled her daddy who cabled back $5,000. As she replaced her trousseau in London, she had the packages sent to the Savoy. There was a mix-up at the hotel and as the new clothes arrived they were immediately handed over to Mrs. Hoover and the other American ladies, who distributed them free to destitute women and children arriving from the continent. Among the more colorful American tourists was a Wild West show which had been caught in Poland. Twelve Indians and ten cowboys, penniless but in full regalia, made it to the Savoy where they bivouacked in the lounge. The hotel management used their personal influence to get them on board a ship—any ship. One lady demanded a written guarantee that the ship on which she traveled would not be torpedoed by a German submarine—the committee obligingly wrote one out for her. Thanks to these modest beginnings, Herbert Hoover, a mining engineer and consultant, was asked to head the Commission for Relief in Belgium, and began a career as a public servant which eventually led him to the White House.

⚭

William Saroyan first came to London in 1935, staying at a cheap hotel down "a desolate street" near Russell Square close to his English publisher, Faber and Faber. Aged 27, he had just published *The Daring Young Man on the Flying Trapeze* and was on his way to the Soviet Union. He took a liking to the Strand and vowed that when he became successful, he would stay at the Savoy Hotel. He did so several years later. In 1944, as a private in the U.S. army stationed in England, he convinced the Office of War Information that he should be permitted to write a novel to enhance Anglo-American relations (his *The Time of Your Life* had already won a Pulitzer Prize in 1939). He was allowed to live in the Savoy Hotel at his own expense where, in Room 360 overlooking a narrow alley to the Strand, he produced *The Adventures of Wesley Jackson* in thirty-eight days of non-stop writing. According to Saroyan, the manuscript fell into the hands of "a Hollywood major" who said that the book should not ever be published and recommended that the author be shot. *The Adventures of Wesley Jackson,* a loosely knit, whimsical account of the experiences of a Saroyanesque army private, was brought out by Harcourt, Brace in 1946.

When Edna Ferber stayed here in April 1945 while on a writing assignment, her first breakfast consisted of two mushrooms on a slice of toast (there was strict rationing: in the top restaurants, it was the time of the "escalope de spam"). Suddenly there was a knock on the door and, to her astonishment, there stood Alfred Lunt in his dressing-gown carrying a small basket. It contained two fresh eggs which the waiter promptly took and had boiled. Lynn Fontaine and her husband were playing in *Love in Idleness* at the Lyric Theatre, where their faithful admirers from the countryside would crowd about the stage door after the performance and give them small presents of fresh eggs, fruit, vegetables, English cream and butter—items totally unavailable in London.

Tennessee Williams stayed here in June 1948. He wrote to friends in Venice, "To really appreciate Italy fully you should come to London first. Christ, what a dull town and what stuffy people!" But he admitted that the theater people "have really been awfully sweet." He was glad that Gore Vidal and Christopher Isherwood were there. He had come to England to watch rehearsals of *The Glass Menagerie* with Helen Hayes at Brighton, and had gotten along poorly with the director John Gielgud from the start. The three delivered a broadcast talk on the BBC—the script, supposed to be a conversation, had been prepared in advance and Williams told a friend, "They have given Gielgud all the bright things to say." Helen and himself, he complained, being Americans, were allowed only the most innocuous comments. Williams hoped that he would be able to ad-lib with a remark such as "Oh, John, is it true that you are wanted by the vice squad of New York?" In July the play opened on the HAYMARKET.

The Savoy Hotel has been home to many millionaires and Hollywood stars. Jay Gould, Cyrus McCormick, Charles Dawes, Lucius Boomer and William K. Vanderbilt all had one thing in common besides money—they all ordered breakfast no later than 7 a.m. Those who ordered breakfast later or simply skipped it include Laurel and Hardy, Jimmy Durante, Errol Flynn, Clark Gable, Gene Autry, James Stewart, Edward G. Robinson, Gloria Swanson, Bob Hope, Bing Crosby, Paulette Goddard, John Wayne, Danny Kaye, Ava Gardner.

Savoy Theatre. Paul Robeson opened here in *Othello* on 19 May 1930. The all-star cast included Maurice Browne as Iago, Sybil Thorndike as Emilia and Peggy Ashcroft as Desdemona. There was controversy before the opening night, certain Shakespearian enthusiasts claiming that the Moor was a black Arab and not of Negro stock. Robeson, a singer, was far more concerned about his lack of acting experience, and spent days rehearsing with Sir Frank Benson, the famous Shakespearian actor. The opening night was a huge success, with twenty curtain calls and a brief speech by Robeson. The critic of the *Times* followed Robeson's Othello "with increased pity and fear, sympathy and repulsion, hope and dread." His portrayal contained "tranquil dignity and a melancholy infinitely sad...a sadness that never lifts from the stage, growing as the tempest of fury, scorn and hatred draws to its full, possessing our minds and giving a kind of noble plainness to the tragedy." It was an Othello "pulsating with life," carried by Robeson's "rich and resonant" voice. His fame brought him to the pages of the British *Who's Who.* (He did not achieve recognition in *Who's Who in America* until 1976, the year of his death.) After touring England with *Othello*, he played the giant stoker in

Eugene O'Neill's *The Hairy Ape* at the Ambassador Theatre and in 1933 opened at the Piccadilly Theatre in O'Neill's *All God's Chillun Got Wings.*

100   Simpson's on the Strand. Opened in 1818 as "a home for chess," it later became known as the Grand Cigar Divan because the chess players sat on divans or sofas. (As you enter Simpson's you can see on the right in the hall one of the original billboards.) Thirty years later, John Simpson, a caterer, added his services. Simpson's became known for roast beef and saddles of mutton sliced and served in what was at the time a novel fashion. Richard H. Dana, author of *Two Years Before the Mast,* dined here on 17 July 1856:

> Dined at six o'clock at Simpson's, Strand, where I had a piece of a joint of roast mutton. The joint is kept hot, and under cover is rolled to your table on a small stand upon castors, the cover taken off, and with the nicest skill and care, a hot slice is cut for you, with your due portion of fat, and the cutting is so done that the juice of the meat runs into, and lies in the hollow of the meat, and not into the dish, and thence it is served out by a spoon. It was by far the best serving and eating of mutton I ever knew, and how civil the waiters are, how well trained—"Thank-you, Sir," "If you please, Sir,"—at all proper occasions.

(142)   Ralph Waldo Emerson took "a good sitting room and chamber" on 2 March 1848, at John Chapman's American bookseller and publisher. One of his first visitors was his old friend Thomas Carlyle. The two writers discussed the recent civil disturbances in Paris and the repercussions in England where mobs had smashed shop windows. "London has too many glass doors to afford riots," Emerson observed, "every street window is full of wealth." He found that of the newspapers the *Times* had "taken the best tone on the subject, as they had no sympathy or respect 'for poor Louis Philippe'." Indeed, Emerson was so enthusiastic over what he called "the best English literature by far," that he felt there should be a little club of neighbors at home who should subscribe to the *Times* newspaper.

Emerson had come to England in the hope of giving a series of lectures, but a month after his arrival he admitted to his wife that he had not earned a single pound. "The universal anxiety of people on political and social dangers makes no favorable theater for letters and lectures," he explained. He was obviously happy going to constant dinner parties "with the best people." His letters brim with titles. He enjoyed being recognized and meeting famous people such as Dickens and Chopin. As for Tennyson, he told his wife, "he has a great deal of plain strength about him, and though cultivated, is quite unaffected. Take away Hawthorne's bashfulness, & let him talk easily & fast & you would have a pretty good Tennyson."

For all his New England rusticity, in London Emerson promoted himself to the hilt. On 6 June 1848 the *Times* advertised his six lectures "On the Mind and Manners of the Nineteenth Century" to begin that day at the Literary and Scientific Institution, 17 Edwards Street, Portman Square. In his final lecture entitled "Natural Aristocracy," after describing "the man without duties," Emerson asked, "Who can blame the peasant if he fires his barns?" Lord Morpeth who was among the listeners called on Emerson here on the Strand and said that he hoped he would leave that passage out if he gave the lecture again. The two men "had a most plain and faithful talk quite in the fashion of the Concord study," which ended with Morpeth inviting Emerson to dinner. The entrance fee to each lecture was five shillings, so there was little danger of the working class attending (five shillings was the weekly wage for a maid for eighty hours' work). Emerson had been led to believe by his friends that he would earn £200 but received only £80. Before leaving England, he visited Stonehenge, Salisbury Cathedral and Winchester. When he got back to London in August, he was relieved to get the chance to give three lectures in Exeter Hall for 35 guineas, "in order to pay my passage home in the steamer."

Adelphi Theatre. Joseph Jefferson, actor and strolling player, opened here in *Rip Van Winkle* on Monday 5 September 1865. Jefferson, 36, had spent the four years of the Civil War acting in Australia and had stopped in London on his way back to New York. Here he ran across the Anglo-Irish plawright, Dion Boucicault, who was famous for his adaptations. When Jefferson told him that he needed work and hoped to repeat his 1859 New York success in *Rip Van Winkle* in London, Boucicault offered to rewrite the drama and Jefferson accepted. The dramatist heightened the "fairy-tale" elements of the play while Jefferson infused the character with human tenderness and dignity. The new play ran for 170 nights here at the Adelphi. With the prospect of playing other major roles and touring England, Jefferson took lodgings at 5 Hanover Street, Hanover Square, where he was joined by his children. But no other role brought him as much success, and for the next fifteen years back in America Jefferson performed this version of Rip Van Winkle almost exclusively.

Stratford Place Map C

7 Martin Van Buren, the American minister-designate, arrived in London on 13 September 1831 and put up at Thomas's Hotel at 25 Berkeley Square, moving to Stratford Place a few days later. Having presented his credentials to William IV, he left on a tour of England accompanied by the secretary of the legation, Washington Irving. Among the sites they visited was Newstead Abbey, Lord Byron's ancestral home, where Irving gathered material which he later used in *The Crayon Miscellany*. Once Van Buren had taken over the running of the legation, Irving resigned and spent much of the winter here on Stratford Place completing *The Alhambra*. In December Van Buren received the embarrassing news that his nomination as minister to Great Britain had been defeated in the Senate by one vote, cast by John C. Calhoun. For the British government this was simply proof of the incompetence of the machinery of the American administration. Van Buren, thoroughly humiliated, kept silent, while Irving furiously complained of the injury done "to our national character by this reckless act of party violence." Early in the spring of 1832 Van Buren returned to Washington where he became vice-president under Andrew Jackson.

Suffolk Street, Pall Mall East

(15)   Garland's Hotel. Opened in the 1840s, this elegant and discreet hotel numbered among its patrons Harriet Beecher Stowe and Henry James. Beginning in 1894, Bernard Berenson used to stay here during his many visits to London.

Walter Lippmann took rooms here on 9 July 1914. His first book, *A Preface to Politics,* had just been published in England and he was stopping in London to round up writers for the *New Republic* before going on a walking tour in the Swiss Alps. Thanks to Graham Wallas, the English political scientist and psychologist who had taught him at Harvard, Lippmann met the Fabian Society founders, Beatrice and Sidney Webb, and George Bernard Shaw.

He enjoyed the hit of the season, *Pygmalion,* and asked Shaw if it was true that one could really discover where people came from by their speech as Henry Higgins had done. "Of course," Shaw replied and launched into a multivoiced conversation with himself in a variety of accents corresponding to different counties in Ireland. The 25-year-old American was taken aback when he asked the dramatist what he thought of Freud to discover that Shaw was not in the least interested in the new theories of psychoanalysis; he wanted to talk about sports cars, just having bought one. Finding Lippmann remarkably mature for his years, H.G. Wells introduced him to his latest mistress, Rebecca West. Lippmann was enchanted by her and signed her up to write cultural articles for the *New Republic* on whatever interested her. Indeed one quarter of the articles in the first year of the new review came from Lippmann's contacts in England. Lippmann loved London, and his only real disappointment was Ezra Pound, whom he found an "unhealthy, neurotic, infinitely conceited person and pretentious to the point of exasperation."

Oddly enough, though he argued about socialism and the new society with English friends until the early hours of the morning, it had not occurred to Lippmann to think about political realities. On 28 July he set off for Switzerland via Brussels, where to his amazement he discovered the train station in chaos and the banks closed. Austria had declared war on Serbia, Germany was threatening Russia, and when he tried to get a ticket to Zermatt he was told that the Swiss borders had just been closed. He finally made it back to London, where he attended an anti-war meeting in Trafalgar Square interrupted by crowds booing and singing "God Save the King." In his diary that night he noted: "I was overcome with a general feeling of futility, a sense that fighting had to be, and the sooner the better." The Webbs, who had so impressed him upon his arrival, simply said to him, "We don't form opinions on foreign affairs," and suddenly, they and their Fabian friends seemed terribly irrelevant. On the evening of Tuesday 4 August 1914, as he stood on the terrace of the House of Commons overlooking the Thames, Parliament declared war on Germany. He realized that his concern with local problems and progressive socialism was outside any meaningful international framework. That evening was his initiation into a lifelong preoccupation with foreign affairs. He finally managed to get a passage back to New York on 17 September.

*Broadcaster Ed Murrow in front of All Souls Church
and the BBC during World War II.
(See page 205.)*

*King George VI, the Queen and Winston Churchill,
inspecting the bomb damage of a wing of Buckingham Palace.
(See page 35.)*

*Winston Churchill and General Eisenhower
who received the Freedom of the City of London,
12 June 1945. (See page 129.)*

Rainbow Corner,
the American servicemen's club
on Shaftesbury Avenue just off Piccadilly, 1944.

Frank Lloyd Wright stayed in the Garland Hotel in 1939. He found "the old place delightful. English homeliness and quaint ugliness." The hotel was destroyed by bombs in 1943.

Tedworth Square, Chelsea Map F

23 Mark Twain and his family moved here on 3 October 1896. A quiet square, it was only a brief stroll from the fashionable artists' and writers' residences on Tite Street and Cheyne Walk, and they took a four-floor red brick corner house for five and a half guineas per week. The 61-year-old author had barely arrived in England when he learned of the death of his daughter Susy. Griefstricken, he spent the winter nursing his sorrow here in Chelsea—one of the villages of London, as he called it. He rose at 4 or 5 a.m. and wrote compulsively for hours to shut out the visions of his dead daughter. One day he called on Henry James in Kensington who, remembering that Twain had been the first author to submit a typewritten manuscript to a publisher, explained that he too was learning to dictate directly to a "typewriter," as typists were then called. Twain had spent the past year lecturing all over the world in order to pay off debts of $200,000 after the failure of the Paige typesetting machine. He began writing *Following the Equator* describing his travels, but found it hard to concentrate. One day, a reporter from the New York *Journal* showed up at Tedworth Square with two cablegrams which he read to Twain. One read: "If Mark Twain dying in poverty, in London, send 500 words;" the other: "If Mark Twain has died in poverty send 1,000 words." An interview with him appeared in New York a few days later. "Of course, I am dying," Mark Twain had smiled grimly, "But I do not know that I am doing it any faster than anyone else. As for dying in poverty, I had just as soon die in poverty here in London as anywhere. But it would be a little more difficult, because I have got quite a number of friends, any of whom would be good for a month's provisions, and that would drag out the agony a fairly long time."

Slowly his grief subsided. He enjoyed walking unnoticed among the colorful denizens of Chelsea whom he liked to call "Shakespeare People." His notebook for 18 February 1897, reads: "Brilliant morning (very rare). Some of the people looked glad to be alive. But many not. Walked an hour in the King's Road, as usual, between Markham Square and the Chelsea Polytechnic—back and forth. Shakespeare people all on hand as usual." In the summer of 1898, he and his family moved to Switzerland before settling for the winter in Vienna.

Temple Map D

Inner Temple, 1 Crown Office Row. Sinclair Lewis and his wife returned to London in October 1923. They settled in Mayfair in the Hotel Curzon and Lewis, eager to get back to work on *Arrowsmith,* took what he called an "office" here just off the Strand. He wrote to his father:

> I have an office, in which to write, in, of all charming places, the Temple—the old, enclosed part of London (reminding one somewhat of an American college campus set down with its quiet courts and gardens right in the busiest part of London) in which the lawyers have their offices. I'm in the comparatively new building—only two hundred years old—but right near is the round Norman Church, built in about 1100, when the Knights Templars, the Crusaders, had their houses here. Dr. Johnson, Lamb, Goldsmith and countless other famous authors have lived and written here.

Upon his arrival in London, Lewis received a cable from New York saying that his publisher and friend, Alfred Harcourt, had accepted an offer of $50,000 for the serial rights to *Arrowsmith,* since it was the highest serialization sum he had ever known. Lewis finally took "a rather charming house—just on the borders of Kensington and Chelsea," 58 Elm Park Gardens, where he and his wife spent the winter. They were neighbors of Bertrand Russell, who was standing for Parliament, and Lewis took it upon himself to join the campaign. He gave a number of speeches which were commented on acidly by the British press as interference in internal politics. His writing went well, but his personal life did not—Lewis drank and argued with his wife incessantly. They returned to New York in late spring of 1924.

Temple Place, the Strand

Howard Hotel (rebuilt in 1975). Louis Armstrong and four friends took rooms here early one Friday morning in 1932. Why he had suddenly decided to come to Europe is not clear. In *Horn of Plenty*

Robert Goffin says that one day John Collins drove out to Los Angeles and said, "I've just signed us up for Europe." Armstrong had replied, "Swell, if I ain't got my divorce by the time we leave, I'll get it in France." Preparation for the tour was almost non-existent, but they did have an agreement to play for a fortnight at the Palladium on ARGYLL STREET. When they arrived at Paddington station on the 12:25 a.m. boat train from Plymouth, the five travelers were met by Dan Ingman of the *Melody Maker,* a London music publication. There was one large man with a cigar in his mouth, Ingman recalled, who turned out to be Johnny Collins, accompanied by his wife and another lady. "The big surprise was the other couple, a young-looking and charming black girl and a small, slight fellow wearing an enormous white cap and long biscuit-coloured coat. I believe he had on a purple suit, too." The small fellow turned out to be Louis Armstrong. The band did not have hotel reservations and, as Ingman telephoned hotel after hotel giving the number of flamboyantly dressed guests and their color, excuse after excuse came until the five Americans began to show dismay. Finally the exclusive Howard Hotel accepted them. The following evening, Armstrong was guest of honor at a dinner party at the Ambassador Hotel in the West End. Those present included Billy Cotton, Ray Noble, Henry Hall, and Spike Hughes. Most were bandleaders. Once the word was out that the young American trumpeter was in London, the Howard Hotel was besieged by musicians who sat in the hall or joined Armstrong in his bedroom to listen to a few lusty bars. Before the week was out, the Americans were politely asked to leave.

Throgmorton Street Map E

27   Drapers' Hall, first mentioned in 1425, was destroyed in the Great Fire, rebuilt and again damaged by fire in 1772. Today, only the court dining room with its fine plaster ceiling and the clerks' office remain. The present garden with its mulberry trees is but part of the original Drapers' Gardens, which stretched as far as the London Wall. The Drapers, thanks to the wool industry, were among the richest liveries in the City, providing over a hundred lord mayors.

On Wednesday afternoon, 28 July 1784, Abigail Adams, accompanied by her young American friend, Charles Storer, visited the Hall and described it to her sister as:

a magnificent eddifice at the end of which is a most beautifull garden surrounded by a very high wall, with four alcoves and rows of trees placed upon each side of the walks: in the middle of the garden is a fountain of circular form in the midst of which is a large swan, out of whose mouth the water pours, and is conveyed there by means of pipes under ground. Flowers of various sorts ornament this beautifull spot: when you get into these appartments and others which I have seen similar, you are ready to fancy yourself in Fairy land.

Tite Street, Chelsea Map F

In the 1870s and 1880s, Tite Street was almost an American enclave with, among others, James McNeill Whistler, John Singer Sargent, Romaine Brooks and Edwin Abbey living and working here. Oscar Wilde lived at number 64 and when one morning he saw the famous actress Ellen Terry going to sit for her portrait in Sargent's studio he noted, "The street that on a wet and dreary morning had vouchsafed the vision of Lady Macbeth in full regalia magnificently seated in a four-wheeler can never be as other streets: it must always be full of wonderful possibilities."

31 and 33   John Singer Sargent settled at number 33 in the summer of 1885 in the studio above Whistler. Aristocratic, cultured and urbane, the 29-year-old American painter had given up working in Paris where his portrait of Madame Gautreau had created a scandal. With no prospect of sitters in London, Sargent accepted an invitation from Edwin A. Abbey, the illustrator, to join fellow American artists in a tiny village in the west of England with the somewhat incongruous name of Broadway. There he met Frank Millet, painter and writer for *Harper's* magazine, and he painted his daughter Kate and another girl dressed in white pinafores lighting lanterns in the garden at twilight. Entitled *Carnation, Lily, Lily, Rose,* it was exhibited at the Royal Academy in 1887 and enjoyed a major success. It was purchased by the academy for £700. Meanwhile, Whistler having moved, Sargent took over his ground-floor flat, which consisted of one large studio with narrow halls leading to a dining room and a bedroom. He lived here for the rest of his life. His friend from his Paris days, composer Gabriel Fauré, frequently came to stay, and Sargent gave parties here where his music was heard for the first time in England. Years later he provided the same help to Percy Grainger.

On 29 December 1888 Sargent was present at the opening

night of *Macbeth* at Henry Irving's Lyceum Theatre. The moment that Ellen Terry made her entrance as Lady Macbeth, Sargent knew that he had to paint her. A year later she posed here, and *Ellen Terry as Lady Macbeth* was purchased by Henry Irving and hung in the foyer of the Lyceum Theatre. In 1890 he was commissioned to paint a series of murals, *The History of Religion,* by the Boston Public Library. This not only gave him a guaranteed income, but assured wealthy Americans visiting London that his portraits would also be a good investment. And working on murals was a pleasant change after constant portraits.

In the Royal Academy Exhibition of 1898, Sargent caused a sensation with his portrait of the dealer Asher Wertheimer. The intensity of the expression conveyed a wealth of knowledge about the individual—his Jewish background, the source of his apparent wealth, a certain craftiness of which the subject himself was aware, a self-admitted keenness, but also showed pathos and sufficient humor for Wertheimer to see himself for what he was. Henry Adams saw the portrait in Tite Street and noted: "Sargent has just completed another Jew...Wertheimer, a worse crucifixion than history tells of." Over the next decade, Sargent did a total of twelve canvases of the Wertheimer family. By the late 1890s, his fee for a portrait was one thousand guineas and the list of applicants just as long. In February 1899, an exhibition of his work was opened in Copley Hall in Boston—a one-man show of ninety-four portraits and landscapes, plus drawings, which was almost unheard of in America. Bostonians were delighted, considering Sargent one of their own, although he had spent but a few seasons working there. In London, one of Sargent's oldest friends, Henry James, remarked, "Sargent grows in weight, honor and interest—to *my* view." It was a safe assessment.

Sargent now required more space. He took the house next door, number 31, and had a small archway knocked through. He converted the entire second floor of the new house into a studio, and also rented a larger studio in nearby Fulham Road. After Queen Victoria's death in 1901, his American friend Edwin Abbey was asked to do the coronation picture of her successor. During a sitting with the Prince of Wales, Abbey was astounded when the prince asked him how much Sargent earned. Abbey replied, with truth, that he did not know. The prince countered, "Do you suppose it's ten thousand?" "More like twenty," Abbey ventured. "My God!" replied the heir to the British throne, "I wish I had twenty thousand pounds a year!"

The following year Sargent returned to Boston to continue work on the Boston Public Library murals. As usual, he was besieged by requests for portraits, and spent an uncomfortable two weeks in the White House painting an impatient Theodore Roosevelt. Home again in Tite Street, Sargent, now the foremost portrait painter in England, resumed work. Charles Eliot, President of Harvard, sat, followed by Joseph Pulitzer, who began by asking Sargent what his methods were. He suggested that the painter would probably "study me by just talking, conversing and generally summing up my character," during the first sitting. Sargent replied quickly, "I paint what I see"—the days when he made friends of new sitters was long gone, now he knew that every portrait he painted made an enemy. The truth was that Sargent, 50, was beginning to tire of portraits. Formerly he used to try for that delicate balance that would please both himself and the sitter; now he cared less and less about the feelings of the sitter. On the first Sunday of April before the annual show of the Royal Academy, the public would throng to his studio to see which portraits he was going to show, thus revealing those he had chosen not to show. Tite Street would be crowded by the chauffeur-driven motor cars of Lady Randolph Churchill, the Edens and the Asquiths. In 1907, the prime minister, on behalf of King Edward VII, asked Sargent if he would accept a knighthood. The painter declined respectfully on the basis that he was an American citizen. On 6 May 1910, the king passed away and lay in state at Windsor. A royal messenger arrived at Sargent's studio with the request that he do a drawing of the dead king. He agreed, but at the same time let it be known that he would do no more portraits in oil. As a result the prices of his paintings began to rise. When his personal collection of paintings was auctioned off at Christie's after his death, the 237 lots fetched £170,000. It was a far cry from his early days in London when he had been asked to do a portrait of Robert Louis Stevenson, and had had to borrow £5 to pay for his train fare down to the writer's home in Bournemouth.

Sargent devoted many of the last fifteen years of his life to impressionistic landscapes in watercolor, many of them done in the Tyrol and in Venice. He spent a considerable time in Boston finishing his murals at the library. On 14 April 1925, after a pleasant evening at his sister's in London, he walked home along the embankment to Tite Street. In bed, he read from Voltaire's

Dictionnaire Philosophique before going off to sleep; he died during the night.

(35) White House. The original White House built for Whistler was ready in October 1878 but by then, at the end of his suit for libel against Ruskin, the painter was bankrupt. He nevertheless moved in with his model Maud and, unable to afford giving dinners, gave Sunday breakfasts instead. Guests included Henry James who described his host as "a queer little Londonized Southerner," who painted abominably. (Later, when Whistler became highly successful, James revised his opinion.) James came for the buckcakes and to enjoy other guests such as Lily Langtry, the newest mistress of the Prince of Wales. To Whistler, "Jersey Lily" was the most beautiful woman he had ever seen and he did an *Arrangment in Yellow* of her. On 18 September 1879 the White House and its effects were auctioned off by his creditors. In a final stroke of irony, the house was bought for £2,700 by Harry Quilter, the *Times* art critic who had been a witness for Ruskin against Whistler.

(42) Chelsea Lodge. Edwin A. Abbey bought this house toward the turn of the century. Born in Philadephia, he studied at the Pennsylvania Academy of Fine Arts before becoming an illustrator for *Harper's*. At the age of 26, he was sent to London to gather materials for his illustrations to Robert Herrick's poems. He took a studio at 54 Bedford Gardens and also began work for the important London magazine *Graphics*. Little by little he settled into the comfortable life of the successful artist in London, where his friends soon included Whistler, Sargent, Oscar Wilde and Henry James. In December 1889 the first of a series of essays on the comedies of Shakespeare by the English writer Andrew Lang appeared in *Harper's,* each illustrated by Abbey. The series ran for six years during which Abbey's 132 drawings established him as America's foremost illustrator. Henry James observed that Abbey had "enlarged the idea of illustration." Abbey married a Vassar graduate and moved into Chelsea Lodge at the foot of fashionable Tite Street, where there was also room for his studio. At the end of the day, friends dropped in freely; one evening Whistler discovered Mark Twain here and the two talked through the night.

Now wealthy, Abbey turned more and more to painting, in which also enjoyed great success. In 1890 he began his *Holy Grail* frieze for the Boston Public Library which he had visited with John

Singer Sargent. The two huge paintings, each 90 feet of life-sized figures involving scaffolding, costumes, armor, casts and models, took four years. Abbey exhibited them first in London with a brochure vetted by Henry James before shipping them to Boston. He then agreed to do the murals for the rotunda of the dome of the new Pennsylvania state capital building in Harrisburg. While visiting the new building he received an honorary doctorate from the University of Pennsylvania and met President Theodore Roosevelt at the White House. He enjoyed the trip, but felt there was something philistine about America and was glad to return to Chelsea. In 1902, Edward VII chose him to do the official canvas (9 feet by 15 feet) of his coronation. The king proposed that he be knighted, but Abbey politely declined, pointing out that he was American. He became president of the local Artists' Cricket Club, which held an annual dinner here at Chelsea Lodge. In 1911, he was found to have cancer. Abbey was brought home and carried up to his second-floor studio where he could see his *Valley Forge* mural ready for Harrisburg. He died on 1 August.

Torrington Square, Bloomsbury

(67)   Margaret Sanger took a top-floor "bed and breakfast" room here in December 1914. There was one bathroom in the house which cost an extra shilling to use. Like all boarding houses at the time, each bedroom contained a low tub for washing which was usually kept under the bed. In her autobiography, Sanger recalled, "Every morning about 7 came a knock, and when I opened the door I discovered a midget jug of hot water outside. I was supposed to break the ice on my large pitcher, mix the two, and pour all into my tin tub, the back of which rose behind me like a throne." Within a month, Sanger was stricken by the first digestive upset she had ever had. She saw an American doctor who immediately asked her if she had been drinking English coffee. "Yes," she replied. He warned her never to drink coffee in England and to take only tea. In less than a week she was better.

The 31-year-old former nurse was under indictment from an American court for sending her *Family Limitation* birth-control pamphlets through the post. Rather than risk prison, she left her children with women friends in New York, took the train to Montreal, obtained a false Canadian passport and sailed for England, where she disembarked under the name of Bertha

Watson. In spite of the cold she felt at home in Bloomsbury, and on her second evening attended a lecture on Nietzsche, "the most splendid and understandable rendering of Nietzsche" she had ever heard. A few days later she was invited to tea at the home of Dr. and Mrs. C.R. Drysdale, the English champions of birth control, who "hugged me and took me to their hearts." On 13 December, she noted in her diary her decision to leave her husband: "Today, I have cast the die. I have written Bill a letter ending a relationship of twelve years." As for the children, they'd manage somehow. Thanks to the Drysdales, she met Havelock Ellis, whose seven-volume *Studies in the Psychology of Sex* had made him a world authority. They became close friends. He advised her to go to Holland where birth control was openly discussed, and where the rates of infant mortality and women dying in childbirth were a third those of the United States. She left for Amsterdam in January 1915.

Tothill Street

This street takes its name from "Tothill Fields" which once lay between Westminster Abbey and Millbank. Bridewell Prison, built here in 1618, served as a model for Hogarth in *The Rake's Progress.* It was torn down in 1885 and the site covered by Westminister Cathedral.

John Trumbull, charged with high treason, was brought here on 20 November 1780. The 24-year-old son of the governor of Connecticut, he had served briefly as an aide-de-camp to Washington in 1775, and had pleaded guilty to having served in the rebel army. He was also accused of corresponding with the enemy, namely Benjamin Franklin's grandson in Paris. Since he had resigned from the rebel army in 1777 and had been given permission to come to England to study art, his status under the law was not clear and over the months his case became an embarrassment to the British government. The new prisoner immediately appealed to his teacher Benjamin West for help. West, a fellow American, promptly went to Buckingham House where he assured the king that Trumbull's behavior had been exemplary and that his devotion to painting had left no time for political intrigue. The king promised that in the worst possible event of the law, Trumbull's life would be safe. West hurried to Bridewell Prison to deliver the comforting news, where he discovered that the prisoner's lot was not as desperate as he had feared. The keeper, formerly butler to the Duke of Northumberland, had the manners of a gentleman and conducted the prison accordingly. Trumbull left a fine sketch of his incarceration:

> The building which bears the name of Tothill-fields Bridewell, was a quadrangle of perhaps two hundred feet—an old and irregular building—the house of the keeper occupying one angle and part of a side; the entrance, turnkey's room, tap-room, and some space for prisoners, and a small yard, another side; the female apartments and yard occupy the third; and the fourth was little more than a high brick wall. Besides the yards, a pretty little garden was enclosed within the wall; all windows looked upon the interior of the square. Its situation was behind Buckingham House, towards Pimlico.
>
> After the first shock, during which I cared not where I slept, or what I ate, I hired from Mr. Smith, the keeper, one of the rooms of his house, for which I paid a guinea a week. It was a parlor on the ground floor, about twenty feet square; the door opened upon the hall of the house, at the foot of the stairs, and was secured by a strong lock and bolts. Two windows looked upon the yard, and were also firmly secured by strong iron bars. The room was neatly furnished, and had a handsome bureau bed. I received my breakfast and dinner,—whatever I chose to order and pay for, from the little public house, called the *tap*. The prison allowance of the government was a penny-worth of bread, and a penny a day; this I gave to the turnkey for brushing my hat, clothes and shoes. Besides these comforts, I had the privilege of walking in the garden. Every evening when Mr. Smith went to his bed, he knocked at my door, looked in, saw that I was safe, wished me a good night, locked the door, drew the bolts, put the key in his pocket, and withdrew. In the morning, when he quitted his own apartment, he unlocked my door, looked in to see that all was safe, wished me a good morning, and went his way.

Trumbull was free to receive visitors. Gilbert Stuart called frequently, nicknamed him "Bridewell Jack," and painted his portrait. Using a fellow prisoner as a model, Trumbull did a number of studies of the male nude dated "Tothill Fields, 1780" (now in Fordham University, New York). He also finished his copy of *St. Jerome* (now in Yale University Art Gallery). Charles Fox, leader of the opposition to Lord North, called, followed by Edmund Burke. The result was bail with sureties of £400 put up by West and John Copley on the condition that Trumbull leave the country within thirty days and not return until peace was restored.

John Trumbull was released on 12 June 1781 and sailed first to Amsterdam and then home to Lebanon, Connecticut.

Tower of London Map E

Henry Laurens of South Carolina was imprisoned here from 6 October 1780 until 31 December 1781. The former president of the Continental Congress had been chosen in 1779 to negotiate a treaty of friendship and commerce with Holland and to arrange a loan of $10,000,000. He sailed from Philadelphia on the *Mercury* which was captured by a British man-of-war on 3 September. Fearful that his official papers would be discovered, he threw them overboard in a sack, but the sack floated and was retrieved by the British who arrested him. The good treatment he received from his captors changed the day he was escorted into London.

Laurens was examined before the Privy Council where his claim of diplomatic immunity was refused. He was sent to the Tower under "suspicion of treason committed at Philadelphia and on the high seas," and lodged in the house of a warden, James Futerell. The Futerell family went out of their way to make his incarceration bearable—Laurens later left them a legacy in gratitude. But permission to walk in the Tower grounds was rarely granted, and the health of 56-year-old Laurens declined rapidly from lack of exercise. The few visitors permitted found him "very ill, emaciated and bitterly invective against the people for his harsh treatment." Laurens passed the long hours reading the best seller of the day, Gibbon's *History of the Decline and Fall of the Roman Empire*. He was bothered by the presence of a fellow prisoner in the Tower, the celebrated Lord George Gordon, whose Protestant followers had just rioted in their attempts to secure repeal of the Catholic Relief Act. Gordon was anxious to talk, but Laurens tried to avoid him for fear of being seen as a sympathizer. Laurens was troubled most of all by what he felt was indifference on the part of Congress to his imprisonment—due to strict British censorship, he was unaware of the efforts of Benjamin Franklin in Paris to secure his release. In August 1781, his cause was taken up by Edmund Burke, who suggested a pardon, but Laurens refused on the basis that this implied guilt. With the surrender of General Cornwallis at Yorktown in October 1781, the War of Independence was virtually over and Laurens was eventually released on bail after fifteen months' imprisonment. "Thus terminated," wrote Laurens, "a long, and to me an expensive and painful farce."

263

❧

Nathaniel Hawthorne brought his family to see the Tower in September 1855. The entry price of sixpence a head included a visit to the armory and crown jewels. He particularly enjoyed the yeomen of the guard, or beef-eaters, "dressed in scarlet coats of antique fashion, richly embroidered with golden crowns, both on the breast and back, and other royal devices and insignia: so that they looked very much like the kings on a pack of cards, or regular trumps."

❧

Late on the afternoon of Friday 8 June 1917, an extraordinary event took place at the gate of the Tower—sixty-seven American soldiers, in a column headed by Captain George Patton and preceded by the band of the London Honorable Artillery Company, marched under the Bywater Tower and around the White Tower to the applause of the British troops who lined the walls. It was the only occasion on which foreign troops ever marched into the Tower, except as prisoners. The Americans, part of the 188 men and civilians who made up the vanguard of the American Expeditionary Force under General John Pershing, had been assigned to quarters in the Tower. That evening at 10 p.m. the 32-year-old Patton was asked by the picket officer (the Officer of the Day) if he wished "to take the keys." Patton happily accepted, thinking that it was a quaint English expression for going out to take a drink. They only had half-an-hour before the pubs closed. To his surprise (and dismay) they proceeded with due solemnity to the guardhouse:

> We saw the guard lined up under the ancient colonade with No. 1 sentinel stalking up and down before them. Presently a lantern appeared approaching the guardhouse. No.1 challenged: "Halt! Who comes there?" to which the lantern replied: "The Keys." No.1 answered: "Whose keys?" The lantern replied: "King George's keys." To which No.1 exclaimed: "God Bless King George." The guard then presented arms, and the Officer of the Day called "Amen." No. 1 then called "Advance keys, all's well."

Patton was astounded to learn that the ceremony of the keys had been taking place every night for seven hundred years. On the evening of 12 June, he and his men packed before leaving for France the following morning. They were given a magnificent farewell dinner and Patton finally got his drink, many more than he had expected. The British officers insisted on staying up and celebrating with toast after toast and song after song until the American departure at 4:30 a.m.

Trafalgar Square

(4)   Morley's Hotel was built in 1831 at the junction of Charing Cross Road and the Strand. With a hundred bedrooms, it was one of the foremost older hotels. It became South Africa House in 1921.

Henry Stevens, born in Barnet, Vermont, a Harvard graduate, came to London in 1845 for two or three years, as an agent for several eminent American book collectors. A year later, he met Anthony Panizzi, chief librarian at the British Museum, who asked him if he "would sweep America for us, as you have done [here] for America." For Stevens, 26, the offer was a turning point. Except for regular visits to America to search for books, he stayed in London until his death in 1886.

Stevens lived in Morley's Hotel from 1848 until his marriage six years later. He continued to conduct his business here, thus avoiding paying the considerable taxes levied on bookstores, an advantage which sat heavy with his fellow book dealers. He spent many evenings "in the pleasantest way imaginable" in this large cosmopolitan hotel dining with Thackeray, Tom Taylor the playwright, C.R. Leslie the painter, Richard Doyle the caricaturist, George Peabody the financier and, on Sunday 25 November 1849, with Herman Melville who had come to England to sell the manuscript of *White Jacket*.

In his early days in London, Stevens worked out of the bookstore of fellow American Obadiah Rich at 12 Red Lion Square and out of George P. Putnam's American Literary Agency at 6 Waterloo Place. In 1848, Stevens made his most spectacular purchase while on a visit to America: the library of George Washington. He paid $3,000 for 460 volumes and some 750 pamphlets. His father wrote to him: "The purchase of Washington's library for the British Museum is really wicked, it ought not to go out of the government." Stevens, deferring to his father and, more important, not wishing to alienate potential American customers, sold the collection instead to the Boston Athenaeum.

One day, in 1850, Stevens received a visit from the son of a tailor who claimed to have important American documents. Like all buyers of manuscripts, Stevens was frequently approached by modest individuals who thought they had found incredible treasures which invariably turned out to be worthless. Skeptical, but nevertheless intrigued, Stevens accompanied the young man to a room above a St. James's tailor where he discovered 3,000 manuscripts of Benjamin Franklin. They had been brought there in 1790 by Franklin's grandson, William Temple Franklin, who had rented a room above the tailor with the intention of publishing them. At least one document had been trimmed to use as a sleeve pattern. Stevens had the manuscripts bound in blue morocco in sixty volumes which, together with the purchase, cost him over £1,000. Three years later, he offered them for $25,000 to Congress who refused. They finally acquired them in 1881 for $35,000. But Stevens had withdrawn one item from the Franklin manuscripts, feeling perhaps that it was too precious to entrust to Congress. It was a letter of Franklin dated 6 June 1745 on "Why a Young Man Should Choose an Old Mistress." (Today it is owned by the City of Chicago.)

During the forty years Stevens worked in London, he procured over 100,000 books for the British Museum, making the American collection there the best in the world at the time.

Henry James arrived in London on a dismal Sunday evening, 28 February 1869. With Cambridge and America behind him, James, 26, was beginning the Grand Tour unaware that London would become his home for twenty years and a place of return for two decades after that. Homesick on this first evening, he was cheered by the warm fire in the coffee-room where the heavy mahogany furniture gleamed in its light. To his mother he complained about the musty bedroom where the large four-poster bed was lit up luridly by a candle rather than gaslight. Morley's lacked the comforts, he felt, of Boston's Parker House. After a few days, he discovered that London, in spite of its slums and squalor, dirt and darkness, had an air of magnificence about it. "The place sits on you, broods on you, stamps on you," he told his sister, "It is anything but a cheerful or a charming city. Yet it is a very splendid one. It gives you, here at the West End and in the city proper, a vast impression of opulence and prosperity." While searching for lodgings he encountered the landladies of London, "hard-faced, garrulous ravening creatures encrusted with a totally indescribable greasy dingy dowdiness." But he chanced upon a Mr. Fox, who soon became his butler, landlord, valet, guide, philosopher and friend in HALF MOON STREET.

Vauxhall Gardens

Vauxhall Gardens used to lie on the south bank of the Thames opposite the Tate Gallery. First opened in 1660, they were popular for two centuries. The main walks were lit at night by hundreds of lamps. There were also dark walks with windings and turnings so intricate that "the most experienced mothers often lost themselves in looking for their daughters." Boswell commented, "Vauxhall Gardens is peculiarly adapted to the taste of the English nation; there is a mixture of curious show, gay exhibition, musick, vocal and instrumental, not too refined for the general ear."

John and Abigail Adams, Thomas Jefferson and John Jay were among the many Americans who wrote of their visits, but the best description was left to us by 21-year-old Yale graduate, Samuel Morse, who came here in September 1811:

> The moment I went in I was almost struck blind with the blaze of light proceeding from thousands of lamps and those of every color. In the midst of the gardens stands the orchestra box in the form of a large temple and most beautifully illuminated. In this the principal band of music is placed. At a little distance is another smaller temple in which is placed the Turkish band. On one side of the gardens you enter two splendid saloons illuminated in the same brilliant manner. In one of them the Pandean band is placed, and in the other the Scotch band. All around the gardens is a walk with a covered top, but opening on the sides under curtains in festoons, and these form the most splendid illuminated part of the whole gardens. The amusements of the evenings are music, waterworks, fireworks, and dancing.
>
> The principal band plays till about ten o'clock, when a little bell is rung, and the whole concourse of people (the greater part of which are females) run to a dark part of the gardens where there is an admirable deception of waterworks. A bridge is seen over which stages and wagons, men and horses, are seen passing; birds flying across and the water in great cataracts falling down from the mountains and passing over smaller falls under the bridges; men are seen rowing a boat across, and, indeed, everything which could be devised in such an exhibition was performed.
>
> This continues for about fifteen minutes, when they all

return into the illuminated part of the gardens and are amused by music from the same orchestra till eleven o'clock. They then are called away again to the dark part of the gardens, where is an exhibition of the most splendid fireworks; sky-rockets, serpents, wheels, and fountains of fire in the greatest abundance, occupying twenty minutes more of the time.

After this exhibition is closed, they again return into the illuminated parts of the gardens, where the music strikes up from the chief orchestra, and hundreds of groups are immediately formed for dancing. Respectable ladies, however, seldom join in this dance, although gentlemen of the first distinction sometimes for amusement lend a hand, or rather a foot, to the general cheerfulness.

In a few minutes the chief orchestra ceases and is relieved in turn by the other bands, the company following the music. The Scotch band principally plays Scotch reels and dances. The music and this course of dancing continue till about four o'clock in the morning, when the lights are extinguished and the company disperses. On this evening, which was by no means considered as a full night, the company consisted of perhaps three thousand persons.

The gardens were closed in 1859 but not before seven "farewells" had been held.

Vigo Street

(2)   Charles Sumner arrived in London on the evening of 31 May 1838 and put up at the Tavistock Coffee House on the "Great Piazza," Covent Garden, before taking digs here on the corner of Regent Street. After five months in Paris, he had decided to take a steamer from Calais and approach London via the river. The next morning, on entering the Thames bordered by "smiling villages," he witnessed a continuous stream of vessels for eighty miles until the last five miles, where "the banks were literally lined with ships, their black hulls in gloomy array, and their masts in lengthening forests." Sumner saw what few Americans ever saw—the incredible wealth of shipping of 19th-century England. In his first letter from London written the following morning he told his brother that Paris had taste and art, London, "wealth and business." That evening he attended Drury Lane and found it "dull and tasteless" after the wonders of the Paris opera. A graduate of Harvard Law School and future lecturer there, he had come to

London to see "society, men, courts and parliaments." Thanks to letters of introduction from Justice Joseph Story of the U.S. Supreme Court, he spent most of his ten months in England observing the daily application of the law from murder trials at the Old Bailey to county squires sentencing local poachers. He sat on the bench at Westminster Hall, and accompanied the judges on the western circuit to Winchester, Salisbury and Exeter. By the time he left England, he felt that he had mastered English practice and English circuit life. He admired the "heartiness and cordiality" of the English bar; "they are truly a band of brothers," he concluded, "and I have been received among them as one of them."

Villiers Street, the Strand

(27)   Gilbert Stuart moved to a house where Charing Cross Station now stands early in 1777. Talented, indolent and without funds, the future painter appealed to Benjamin West: "Pitty me Good Sir, I've just arrived at the age of 21 an age when most young men have done something worthy of notice and find myself ignorant without bussiness or friends, without the necessarys of life so far that for some time I have been reduced to one miserable meal a day and frequently not even that...." The reply was a gift of several guineas and an invitation to come to his home on NEWMAN STREET. West recognized Stuart's talent, took him on as a student and later as an assistant, giving him access to supplies, large studios, models, pictures to study and books to read. The daily contact with West also provided him with the discipline he lacked.

Under West's sponsorship, Stuart showed his *Portrait of a Gentleman* in the 1777 Royal Academy Exhibition. Over the next five years he participated regularly in these exhibitions, gaining confidence and minor commissions under the watchful and benevolent eye of his master. He also enjoyed the companionship of John Trumbull from Connecticut, whom West had also accepted as a student. In January 1782 Stuart received a visit from a trim, handsome Scotsman, William Grant, who had come to sit for a life-size portrait. That morning it was almost as cold in the studio as outside and Stuart, who had discovered that his client enjoyed skating, suggested that they warm up by taking a spin on the frozen Serpentine in Hyde Park. Upon returning to the studio, Stuart proposed that he paint Mr. Grant skating. The result was his memorable *Portrait of a Gentleman Skating* (now in the National Gallery of Art, Washington, D.C.). In a cool harmony of gray, black and white with touches of red in the background, arms folded as he glides, the skater evokes an allegorical image of winter, hugging his body against the cold. In the Royal Academy exhibition that May, the picture was a sensation. Years later Stuart observed that he was "suddenly lifted into fame by a single picture." With West's advice that he could now set out as a portrait painter in his own right, Stuart took a house just across the road from his mentor.

Waterloo Place Map C

(6)   George P. Putnam, 27, accompanied by his charming young American wife, arrived in 1841 to establish the London office of the New York publishing house Wiley & Putnam. The young couple's cottage at 6 Mornington Row just off Regent's Park soon became a meeting place for writers and European liberals exiled from the continent. Dinner guests included Charles Dickens, Washington Irving, Edwin Forrest the actor, George Peabody the banker, Tom Thumb, Mazzini the Italian patriot, Anthony Panizzi the librarian of the British Museum, Louis Napoleon later Napoleon III, and numerous Polish exiles. Henry Stevens, bookseller, lived with the Putnams for two years until he moved to Morley's Hotel in TRAFALGAR SQUARE.

Putnam first opened his offices at 7 Amen Corner, 36 Paternoster Row and, in 1844, moved here to Waterloo Place where his business became known as the "American Literary Agency." Herman Melville's elder brother made arrangements with Putnam for the American publication of his brother's first .book, *Typee*. Putnam returned to New York in 1848 where he founded G.P. Putnam's Sons and launched *Putnam's Magazine*.

George Catlin rented modest rooms in 1849. The 53-year-old widower, desperately in need of money, returned to London haunted by his earlier success at Egyptian Hall in PICCADILLY. He had spent the previous four years in Paris where his gallery of 600 portraits of North American Indians had drawn many spectators but few buyers. Here, just off Pall Mall, Catlin had a studio and just sufficient showroom space into which he crowded enough Indian paintings and other materials to lure some viewers at a shilling each. In April 1851, he made an agreement with Sir Thomas Phillipps to paint fifty-five copies of his original pictures for £2 each. It was the same year that he did the series of 167 beautifully executed pencil drawings entitled *Souvenir of the North American Indians,* which is today in the New York Public Library. Financial salvation lay with Congress, or so Catlin hoped. In the 1852-53 session, a bill for the purchase of the George Catlin Indian Gallery came to a vote. On the floor of the Senate, Daniel Webster described the paintings as "more important than all the other drawings and representations on the face of the earth." But that was not sufficient for Congress and the bill was defeated by one vote. Catlin, sure that the bill was going to pass, had borrowed heavily against his only asset, the paintings. Now his creditors closed in like prairie wolves. By chance, one creditor, Joseph Harrison, owner of the Harrison Boiler Works in Philadelphia, the largest locomotive building concern in the world, was passing through London on his way home from Russia. He paid off the principal debts against the Indian Gallery and had the paintings crated quickly and thrust on the first ship for Philadelphia. Catlin's three daughters were taken back to Jersey City by relatives while he returned to a small hotel room in Paris. Catlin returned to America in 1870 where he died two years later, destitute, still unsure as to what would happen to his collection. The original "Catlin Indian Gallery" which had been stored in a loft in the boiler works in Philadelphia was presented to the Smithsonian Institute by the heirs of Joseph Harrison.

11   Trafalgar House. Charles Frohman leased a suite of six rooms here in 1913 from which he ruled over his empire of West End theaters. Between his first play in 1896 and his death in 1915, he produced 125 plays and musicals in London. He brought over such typically American dramas as *The Great Divide, Brewster's Millions, Alias Jimmy Valentine, A Woman's Way, On the Quiet* and *The Dictator.* One of his delights was to call on his dramatist friend James M. Barrie on Adelphi Terrace. It was an atmosphere he loved. John Galsworthy lived above, actor and dramatist Harley Granville Barker lived below, while George Bernard Shaw lived just across the street. When Barrie wanted to notify Shaw that Frohman was with him, he would throw bread-crusts against Shaw's window-panes. In a few moments the sash would fly up and out would pop the familiar grinning bearded face. On one occasion Shaw yelled across: "Are you inviting me to a feast, Barrie—are you casting bread upon the troubled waters or is it just Frohman?"

Waterloo Road Map D

Old Vic Theatre. Ruth Gordon played the role of Mrs. Pinchwife in William Wycherley's *The Country Wife* here in October 1936. Miss Gordon, an established American actress at 40, had accepted the three-week engagement as she wanted the chance to play opposite Edith Evans, whom she described as "the unmatched actress of Restoration comedy." She found rehearsals unnerving, for when Edith Evans went through her scenes with Michael Redgrave, all the stage hands and the students of the Old Vic repertory school sat and watched, whereas when it was her turn the stage hands returned to their work and the students drifted away. When she had received the offer in New York, the idea of an American actress playing a well-known English comical role before an English audience seemed an exciting challenge, but as she sat in the cold, dark, empty theater and watched Evans's flawless rehearsal, she began to regret her own bravado. All she needed was the comment made in all sincerity by the director Tyrone Guthrie, "To me, you're not funny. This part *has* to be funny. The play won't go if it isn't." To which she answered lamely, "I was funny in Westport." She still remembered that exchange thirty-five years later and noted in her memoirs how awful it was to describe "how funny you *were.*" On the opening night, Gordon had only one wish—to be back in New York. In her first scene alone, she was in bed, and got out to look for her slippers. "Find things under the bed," Tyrone Guthrie had said. "Look for more and more. They'll think you're looking for the pot, but fool them. *Let* them think so: *you* get lost in other things." As Mrs. Pinchwife first she found a slipper, then an orange (laughter), then another orange (more laughter), then she crawled under the bed and the audience knew what she had found—she came out with a deck of cards (lots of laughter). At the end of the scene, there was major applause. With her confidence regained, the evening went superbly. At the final curtain, as they took bows, Edith Evans spoke briefly then, suddenly, it was Ruth Gordon's turn. She began by explaining very seriously to the audience that she had only made one speech before and that was when the theater had caught fire. The English audience collapsed in laughter and then into applause, and a startled Ruth Gordon discovered that they had found her "madly witty."

Wellington Court, St. John's Wood

(30)   Mark Twain and his family lived here in May 1899. Since the apartment was too small for a writing room, his publishers, Chatto and Windus, gave him space in their own offices at 110 St. Martin's Lane. Everyone in London wanted Mark Twain to dinner and at the Savage Club he responded to the toastmaster by observing, "I was sorry to hear my name mentioned as one of the great authors, because they have a sad habit of dying off. Chaucer is dead, Spenser is dead, so is Milton, so is Shakespeare, and I am not feeling very well myself." At the White Friars Club dinner held for him on 16 June 1899 in the huge banquet room of the Hotel Cecil, there were two hundred guests, including the American ambassador, Joseph H. Choate, and the senator-elect from New York, Chauncey Depew. Toward the end of his speech, addressing himself to his two fellow Americans, Twain commented, "You will notice that while we are absent there is a pleasing tranquility in America—a building up of public confidence. We are doing the best we can for our country, and we never serve it to greater advantage than when we get out of it." The English journalists and editors found that far funnier than did Choate and Depew.

The creative years of Mark Twain, now 65, were drawing to a close. The rich vein of American experience he had been mining for forty years had been used up, but he continued to write articles. Christian Science had made its appearance in England and his article, "Christian Science and the Book Of Mrs. Eddy," appeared in *Cosmopolitan* (October 1899). It produced such a furor that the editor sent Twain an additional $200 above the agreed price. "I cannot help feeling rather inordinately proud of America for the gay and hearty way in which she takes hold of any new thing that comes along," he replied, "many an ass in America is getting benefit out of X-Science's new exploitation of an age-old healing principle...let them call it by whatever they choose, so long as it does helpful work among the class which is numerically vastly the largest bulk of the human race, i.e. the fools, the idiots, the pudd'nheads." It was rumored in the summer of 1900 that he was going home. At the annual banquet of the Royal Literary Fund, Twain confirmed the rumor, adding, "I am now on my way to run for the presidency."

Wellington Square, Chelsea Map F

32   Thomas Wolfe, 25, took the whole first floor consisting of "two rooms, a bedroom and an ample sitting room" early in August 1926. His rent was being paid by his 45-year-old friend Aline Bernstein, a successful stage designer, who had just returned to New York—his affair with her lasted for eleven years. He was writing some 3,000 words a day on what was to become *Look Homeward, Angel.* His lurid fantasies of "fame, wealth, and honor have become," he told a friend, "if not less modest, more mature." Such maturity was nowhere evident in his behavior, however. Drunken brawls, insulting behavior with apologetic letters written the next afternoon, alternated with days of work and self pity. On 4 October he moved from Chelsea to 57 Gower Street in Bloomsbury where he had "a huge room; much furniture; red curtains on my bed; plaster statues under glass, engravings of the Crimean War." At the end of the month he left for Oxford, visited Germany and sailed back to New York in December.

Wellington Street Map D

The Lyceum. This large room for concerts and exhibitions was built in 1771. It was sometime a theater, a circus, and in 1802 it housed Madame Tussaud's first London waxworks exhibition. Its finest years were from 1871 until 1900, when Henry Irving played Shakespeare with Ellen Terry as his leading lady. Today it is a dance hall.

Americans were frequent visitors. On Saturday, 22 May 1790, Gouverneur Morris recorded in his journal:

> At five go to the Lyceum to view the large Lincolnshire Ox. It is truly a wonderful Creature, now seven years old, nineteen Hands high and three feet four Inches across the Hipps. It is at the same Time the best formed and cleanest limbed Ox that I ever beheld, indeed a Model as to Form and in Size a Prodigy. The Length is about ten feet. He is estimated at 2,800 lbs for Beef and Tallow. According to my little Judgment on Subjects of this Sort I think that his Beef, Hide and Tallow will weigh above 3000 lbs. He is to be sold in a Day or two, the Owner having too much to attend to as he says to continue here for the Purpose of exhibiting him. I tell him that he had better have him killed as much for the Show and spare the Expence of feeding and attendance upon the Beast.

A New Departure.

THE

"MATTHEWS"

American

Soda ..

Fountain

"The National Beverage of America is fast becoming England's Favorite."

For Dispensing PURE, HEALTHFUL and PALATABLE Aerated Beverages of Superior Quality.

ALL OUR FOUNTAINS are fitted with the famous "MATTHEWS" SYRUP SYSTEM, by means of which the required quantity of Syrup is drawn from GLASS TANKS, and is AUTOMATICALLY measured into the tumbler WITHOUT COMING IN CONTACT WITH METAL AT ANY TIME, thus insuring ABSOLUTE PURITY. Insist on having your Soda Water from the Matthew's Glass Tank Fountains.

American Soda Fountain Company,

BOSTON. NEW YORK. PHILADELPHIA. CHICAGO. LONDON.

Stiles Limited, SOLE BRITISH REPRESENTATIVES,

OFFICES, SHOW ROOMS AND WORKS:

72-74, GRAY'S INN ROAD, HOLBORN, LONDON, W.C

Advertisement
in Bancroft's guide to Americans residing in London,
1902.

AMERICAN DENTAL INSTITUTE,
LIMITED.

E PLURIBUS UNUM.

LONDON
- 55, ST. JAMES'S STREET (Near Piccadilly).
- 34, THURLOE SQUARE, S.W.
- 1, FRANCIS STREET, VICTORIA STREET, S.W.
- 50, FINSBURY SQUARE, E.C. Corner of Finsbury Pavement.

LIVERPOOL: 50, RODNEY STREET.
MANCHESTER: 10, ST. ANN'S SQUARE.
BRIGHTON: 123, KING'S ROAD.
BOURNEMOUTH: THE SQUARE, NEXT DOOR TO HUGH KING'S.
KINGSTON-ON-THAMES: 25, HIGH STREET.

The advantages of the Institute are the special facilities ensured for successfully undertaking every branch of genuine American Dentistry.

SPECIALITIES:

The construction of ordinary artificial Teeth, which are scientifically and artistically made.

The various methods of "Crown Bar and Bridge Work," including the permanent adjustment of Artificial Teeth without plates or wires.

The preservation of Teeth too far decayed to be filled, and the tightening of loose ones.

Contour Work, or building up Teeth with Gold.

Painless treatment.

Fees Moderate, Uniform and Consistent with the Ordinary English Charges, and always arranged beforehand.

Hours of Attendance, 9 till 6 o'clock. No Fees for Consultation.

The privacy of the most refined Dental Practice observed throughout the Institute.

XXXVI

*Advertisement
in the Langham Hotel guide to London,
1901.*

Edwin Booth and Henry Irving opened in *Othello* on 2 May 1881 with Booth in the title role and Irving as Iago. Ellen Terry played Desdemona. The London critics hailed the production as a triumph. On 10 May Booth and Irving exchanged roles and, while critics appreciated the challenge, they agreed that the first casting was the best. The two men nevertheless alternated roles until the play closed on 16 June. It would have been one of the happiest theatrical experiences in Booth's life had it not been for his "domestic misery" at the hotel on BERKELEY STREET where his wife was dying. The following year, Booth returned to London. He opened in *Richelieu* for a six-week run at the Adelphi Theatre and on 8 July was honored by a midnight gala supper given by Irving here at the Lyceum. Besides a large number of English actors, dramatists and critics, Booth's American friends included the editor of the *Atlantic Monthly* Thomas B. Aldrich, and the New York drama critic Lawrence Hutton. The party "with no ladies present" broke up at dawn and Booth was "conveyed to his hotel" by William Winter, drama critic for the New York *Tribune*. He awakened the following afternoon at 2:30 p.m., "feeling quite decent." He thanked Winter and added, "Have not the faintest shadow of recollection anent last evening beyond the fact that the table was luxurious, the lager cold, and the spirits warm."

Westbourne Grove Terrace, Bayswater

(6)   Louisa May Alcott took "a pleasant little room" on 10 June 1865 in Mrs. Travers's lodging house, where she enjoyed "plain living, and for society, Mrs. T. and daughter, two sisters from Dublin, and ten young men—barristers, clerks, ministers and students. A guinea a week." Alcott, aged 32, had enjoyed her stay in AUBREY ROAD, but here she was finally alone and independent. She started by exploring Furnival's Inn, where Dickens had begun to write her favorite, *Pickwick Papers;* dropped in at the Saracen's Head Tavern, and went to St. Paul's where Ralph Nickleby set his watch. On 2 July she called on the publisher George Routledge who paid her five guineas for the privilege of printing *Moods,* her first novel. Routledge was encouraging and told her that he would consider her next novel, quite unaware that it was to be, three years later, the best-selling *Little Women.*

Westminster Map D

Westminster Abbey. James Fenimore Cooper was one of many Americans to enjoy the abbey. When he read the names of Shakespeare, Milton and Ben Jonson on the tombstones in Poet's Corner, he felt a thrilling of the nerves. The chapels of the abbey were filled with impressive monuments, while Poet's Corner, close to the entrance, was a sort of modest vestibule, where the creative spirits, wrote Cooper, "as if entering one by one, and finding good companions already assembled, had stopped in succession to enjoy each other's society." He admired the Chapel of Henry VII, but felt that most of the much-talked-of monuments lacked simplicity and distinction. They told their stories badly. Half-jokingly and half-seriously, he described how the heads of Washington and other American officers had been broken off the bas-relief of Major John André's tomb. "Why have they done this?" Cooper asked the guide. "Oh! sir, plenty of evil-disposed people get in here. *Some American* has done it no doubt." Cooper concluded: "So you perceive we are not only accused of hanging our enemies, but of beheading our friends!"

Washington Irving spent the month of May 1842 in England, ensconced in the Little Cloisters, "one of the interior buildings connected with the Abbey." He was on his way to take up the post of minister plenipotentiary to the Spanish Court in Madrid. His quarters, a monkish nest, "a perfect old curiosity shop, furnished with all kinds of antiquities... quaint old furniture, the walls hung with ancient armor, weapons of all ages," were in stark contrast to the newest technology which had brought Irving to England. Having made little progress off the Irish coast, Irving had transferred from his sailing ship to a steam packet bound from Cork to Bristol where he stepped ashore the following morning. He had then traveled to London by train and was impressed by the superiority of the British railways:

> These rail roads have altered the whole style and course of traveling in England. You fly through the country rather than ride. We were about four hours traveling a distance of one hundred miles: and such admirable vehicles. I sat as comfortably cushioned and accomodated as in my old Voltaire chair at the cottage. The rail roads too are so well finished that you experience none of the jarring and vibration that are felt in ours.

Irving, now 59, was presented to Queen Victoria, whom he found short of stature but well formed and well rounded. Her appearance was agreeable and intelligent, her eyes "light blue with long light eye lashes." She acquitted herself in her receptions with great grace and even with dignity. Her cousin Prince Albert whom she had married two years earlier was "a tall, elegantly formed young man, with a handsome prepossessing countenance." It was said that he was frank, intelligent, manly and accomplished. The young couple was obviously attached to one another, wrote Irving; "It was rare to see such a union of pure affection on a throne."

A few days later Irving sat next to his old friend, the Irish poet Robert Moore, at the Literary Fund dinner presided over by Prince Albert. In spite of the "very splendid dinner," Irving was agitated by the knowledge that as a guest of honor he would be asked to speak. He received very warm and prolonged cheering but confided later to his sister, "I felt as if I would never attend a public dinner again." He was much happier as a simple spectator at Queen Victoria's fancy dress ball where 2,000 people were arrayed in "rich historical, poetical or fanciful costume," based on the visit of Anne of Brittany to England. Here reality mingled with fiction, "Royalty represented royalty, and nobility represented nobility." There was no tinsel or stage trumpery, added Irving, but "a blaze of diamonds beyond anything I had ever seen." The young queen was evidently fatigued by her royal robes "and especially by a crown of gold, which weighed heavy on her brow and to which she was continually raising her hand to move it slightly." Before the evening was over, he was obviously proud that Prince Albert had spoken to him, "in excellent English," Irving noted. Irving left in June for Madrid.

Court of Exchequer, Westminster. The new avant-garde Grosvenor Gallery opened in May 1877 as a rival to the staid Royal Academy. Whistler exhibited *Nocturne in Black and Gold: The Falling Rocket,* his impression of fireworks at the Cremorne Gardens in Chelsea. John Ruskin, the Slade Professor of Art at Oxford, wrote a review in which he chastised the owner of the gallery for displaying such a painting and not protecting a purchaser, and added: "I have seen, and heard, much of cockney impudence before now; but never expected to hear a coxcomb ask two hundred guineas for flinging a pot of paint in the public's face." Whistler sued Ruskin for libel. The trial opened at 10 a.m.

on Monday 25 November 1878 at the Court of Exchequer in the shadow of the Houses of Parliament. The 150 seats for the public were quickly filled. To the disappointment of both public and plaintiff, Ruskin did not appear but was represented by a prestigious law firm who had assembled an imposing array of artists and fellow critics as witnesses. While Whistler enjoyed the support of many well-known painters, none wished to appear in a suit against the leading art critic in England and perhaps in Europe. On the witness stand, Whistler faced Sir John Holker, the attorney general:

> Sir John: Did it take much time to paint the *Nocturne in Black and Gold?* How soon did you knock it off? [Laughter]
>
> Whistler: How long did I take to "knock off" that Nocturne? As well as I remember about a day. I may have put a few more touches to it the next day if the painting were not dry. I had better say, then, that I was two days on it.
>
> Sir John: The labor of two days, then, is that for which you ask two hundred guineas?
>
> Whistler: No. I ask it for the knowledge of a lifetime. [Applause]

The jury found for Whistler, but awarded him only symbolic damages of one farthing. Costs were divided, and Whistler's legal fees for his day in court came to a total of £845. It was not an enormous sum in itself, but he had just finished building his own house and studio, the White House, in TITE STREET, which he had not yet paid for. Furthermore, during the year between Ruskin's article and the trial, he had sold almost nothing. With debts mounting to £4,644, and assets of only £1,824, Whistler, 44, was bankrupt. Everything he owned was seized—house, paintings, etchings, Japanese cabinets and pianoforte. Two days before the sale of 16 September 1879, Whistler took the train to Venice.

Palace of Westminster, Houses of Parliament. On 3 February 1766 Benjamin Franklin was ordered to attend the House of Commons which was sitting as a committee of the whole (members of the Commons and Lords sitting together) to hear witnesses concerning the Stamp Act.

Before bringing in the Stamp Act the previous year, Lord Grenville had told the American colonial agents resident in London that he wished to make the act as little inconvenient to the

Americans as possible. He did not want to send stamp officers from England to America, but preferred that discreet and reputable persons be chosen in each province. He called for names. Franklin suggested his friend John Hughes for Pennsylvania and Jared Ingersoll for Connecticut. This turned out to be one of Franklin's few errors while representing American interests abroad, but it was a serious one. He had misjudged his countrymen and had not expected them to resist the Stamp Act so violently. Disagreeable as it was, he felt it better to submit to it and then work for its repeal. His enemies in Philadelphia accused him of helping to frame the act himself and of receiving money for recommending his friends as officers. There was even talk of setting fire to his new house on the south side of Market Street between Third and Fourth. Franklin's wife sent their daughter Sally away, and had her brother and a nephew bring guns. She wrote to London, "We turned one room into a magazine. I ordered some sort of defence upstairs." It was obvious that the quiet voices of reason which Franklin, in London, had hoped would prevail back home had not been heard.

The Stamp Act had been designed to raise £60,000 a year to help offset the £350,000 cost of maintaining British troops on the frontier. The colonists had shown their unwillingness and inability to provide their own defense, thus the act seemed to the British as necessary as it was equitable. Country squires, appalled by the national debt, had heard that the colonies were now rich and felt that they surely owed gratitude to the mother country which had just defended them against the French. The Stamp Act was the first direct tax levied by Parliament upon the American colonies. American arguments of no taxation without representation were, according to the British, subterfuge—hiding the real truth, which was that the Americans did not wish to pay for their own defense.

Benjamin Franklin was summoned to Parliament on 3 February 1766 and ten days later he came to the bar to answer the questions of the House about America. He was on the stand for two hours. He pointed out that Americans already paid heavy taxes. The frontier counties, having been ravaged by the enemy, were impoverished and paid little but the coastal cities paid proportionally more. As to the practicality of the Stamp Act, Franklin explained that frequently such long distances were involved in America that many would have to travel miles to purchase the stamps they needed, "spending perhaps £3 or £4 in order that the Crown get sixpence." The questioners returned to the major cities:

"Do you not think the people of America would submit to pay the stamp duty if it was moderated?"

"No, never, unless compelled by force of arms."

"Can anything less than a military force carry the Stamp Act into execution?"

"I do not see how a military force can be applied to that purpose."

"Why may it not be?"

"Suppose a military force be sent into America, they will find nobody in arms; what then are they to do? They cannot force a man to take stamps who chooses to do without them. They will not find a rebellion; they may indeed make one."

British merchants were concerned that a boycott of British goods would result if the Stamp Act were imposed. The final question was now put to Franklin:

"What used to be the pride of the Americans?"

"To indulge in the fashions and manufactures of Great Britain."

"What is now their pride?"

"To wear their old clothes over again until they can make new ones."

It was Franklin's finest hour. Any past errors or misjudgments on his part were more than compensated for by this performance. The Stamp Act was repealed eight days later.

Westminster Bridge Road

Astley's Amphitheatre. Philip Astley, a man with the "proportions of a Hercules and the voice of a senator," left the British cavalry in 1768 and received his horse as a farewell gift. He gave open-air equestrian displays before erecting a canvas-covered ring near Westminister Bridge which he called the "Royal Grove." After a fire in 1794, he rebuilt it as Astley's Amphitheatre. Clowns, including Grimaldi, acrobats, conjurors and equestrians appeared. Sword fights and exotic dramas were also presented. In *Sketches by Boz*, Charles Dickens, who loved Astley's, described how everything there was "delightful, splendid and surprising." Astley's, popular with Americans, closed in 1893.

On Monday evening, 10 May 1790, Gouverneur Morris noted in his journal that he had gone that afternoon "to Astley's which is I think the best Theater I have seen in London and the best performer in it is a Horse. The Equitation is indeed wonderful but I observe that Music seems to be an essential Part of it, for the Horse gallops in perfect time and that enables the riders to perform Feats which to be believed must be seen."

Whitehall Map D

War Office. It was here that General John Pershing met General Sir William Robertson, chief of the imperial general staff, on 11 June 1917. Billeted with his staff at the Savoy Hotel, Pershing was leading the vanguard of the American Expeditionary Force and spending eight days in London before going on to France. He arrived at the War Office from Buckingham Palace where he and the American ambassador had lunched with King George V. The British monarch had told his guests that together, the American and British were "fighting for the greatest cause for which peoples could fight. The Anglo-Saxon race must save civilization." There was no mention of the French, Pershing noticed. During his meeting over tea with General Robertson he was soon bombarded with questions. What was the size of the American army? When would it arrive? Could America send a "large number of destroyers" to save the shipping fleets from German submarines? Given the close cooperation already existing between the British and American naval forces, Robertson suggested that American troops might be immediately integrated into existing British units to replace British soldiers killed or wounded. There would be no language problems, no barriers of any type, he explained, merely brothers fighting side by side. Pershing politely pointed out that the American plans were for American forces to fight alongside their British and French allies, to cooperate fully, but to retain their individual identity. He did not add that his first act upon arrival in Paris would be to visit Lafayette's tomb; he had been quite unprepared for the active dislike of the French shown by several senior British staff. At the end of their talk, Pershing felt somewhat uneasy—it was almost as if the British had forgotten that during the revolution the French had been the Americans' allies. He left Whitehall for the Houses of Parliament where he met the minister for munitions, Winston Churchill. It was a fine afternoon, Churchill was all charm, and the two men talked amiably on the terrace of Parliament, that long balcony siding the Thames. When they got to the issue of the American need of heavy artillery and ammunition, Churchill offered British equipment. Pershing thanked him, but said that the American army was probably going to adopt the French type of artillery. Churchill, a statesman, revealed no sign of hurt pride. During his stay in London, Pershing learned two unexpected but valuable things: to handle newspapermen with the same politeness and ease as he had seen British officers do, and· diplomacy.

Whitehall Court Map D

2   Royal Horseguards Hotel. This large eight-story building put up in 1884 in French Renaissance style contained many clubs, of which only one now remains, the Farmers' Club. In January 1948 Thornton Wilder took a room with a sweeping view over the Thames in what was then the Authors' Club. That tireless letter-writer and celebrity-collector, Lady Sibyl Colefax, gave him a luncheon at the Dorchester with Michael Redgrave, Peter Ustinov, Pamela Brown (foreign affairs editor of the *Economist*) and the Hamish Hamiltons. Wilder attended rehearsals of *The Skin of Our Teeth,* directed by Laurence Olivier, before its opening in Australia. He met the undergraduate head of the Oxford University Dramatic Society, Kenneth Tynan. Each impressed the other. Depressed by the food rationing and the general atmosphere in postwar London, Wilder hurried to the "sumptuous food" and the welcome of actor-producer Louis Jouvet in Paris.

Woburn Walk Map B

5   William Butler Yeats lived here from 1895 until 1919. Writers attending his Monday evening "at homes" included George Moore, John Masefield and Rupert Brooke. In 1913, Robert Frost was introduced here by Ezra Pound. During the candlelit evening, as Yeats talked on with Pound stretched out casually on the floor at his master's feet, the Irish poet seemed much older than his 48 years, talking, Frost recalled, as if all his work lay behind him. His conversation meandered through the realms of ghosts and little people. Frost wanted to ask him if he believed in fairies, but decided that it was not the moment. Indeed, he appeared so wrapped up in his own memories that at the end of the evening Frost felt that he had failed to establish any rapport with the poet he had so long admired. He returned here twice, but the hoped-for friendship never materialized.

Acknowledgments and Picture Credits

P. 240 from *The Notebooks of Thomas Wolfe,* edited by Richard S. Kennedy and Paschal Reeves. Copyright 1970 The University of North Carolina Press. Reprinted with permission.

Cover, Streets of London and Maps of London: *London in the Nineteenth Century, Illustrated by a Series of Views from Original Drawings, by Thomas H. Shepherd, with Historical Topographical and Critical Notices.* London: Jones, 1829.

Following page 24

1. Royal Commission on the Historical Monuments of England. 2 (top), 2 (bottom), 3 (top), 3 (bottom), and 4 (top). Guildhall Library, City of London. 4 (bottom) The Metropolitan Museum of Art. All rights reserved, The Metropolitan Museum of Art.

Following page 48

1. Royal Commission on the Historical Monuments of England. 2. New York Public Library Picture Collection. 3 and 4. Guildhall Library, City of London.

Following page 76

1. Crawford Theater Collection, Yale University Library. 2. Theatre Arts Library, Harry Ransom Humanities Research Center, The University of Texas at Austin. 3 (top). The Illustrated London News Picture Library. 3 (bottom). Theatre Arts Library, Harry Ransom Humanities Research Center, The University of Texas at Austin. 4. Royal Commission on the Historical Monuments of England. Insert. Theatre Arts Library, Harry Ransom Humanities Research Center, The University of Texas at Austin. 5. The Bettmann Archives/BBC Hulton. 6. Photography Collection, Harry Ransom Humanities Research Center, The University of Texas at Austin.

Following page 100

1. The Photo Source. 2. Photography Collection, Harry Ransom Humanities Research Center, The University of Texas at Austin. Permission granted by Angus McBean. 3. The Photo Source. 4. Royal Commission on the Historical Monuments of England. 5 and 6. The Photo Source.

Following page 118

1. Photography Collection, Harry Ransom Humanities Research Center, The University of Texas at Austin. 2 and 3. Royal Commission on the Historical Monuments of England. Insert. The American Museum in Britain, Bath. 4 (top) and 4 (bottom). Royal Commission on the Historical Monuments of England.

Following page 140

1 (top). By Courtesy of Birmingham Museums and Art Gallery. 1 (bottom). "Queue outside Mr. Sargent's" (1908), by Max Beerbohm, from Evan Charteris's *John Sargent,* 1927. 2. Collection of American Literature, The Beinecke Rare Book and Manuscript Library, Yale University. 3. Photography Collection, Harry Ransom Humanities Research Center, The University of Texas at Austin. 4. Dorothy Thompson Collection, George Arents Research Library for Special Collections, Syracuse University.

Following page 162

1, 2 and 3. The Illustrated London News Picture Library. 4. Photography by Britain on View Photographic Library (BTA/ETB).

Following page 192

1 (top), 1 (bottom), 2, 3 and 4. Royal Commission on the Historical Monuments of England. 5. The Bettmann Archive/BBC Hulton. 6. Royal Commission on the Historical Monuments of England.

Following page 224

1. Lindbergh Picture Collection, Yale University Library. 2. The Bettmann Archive. 3. UPI/Bettmann Newsphotos. 4. The Photo Source.

Following page 252

1. CBS Photography. 2. Royal Commission on the Historical Monuments of England. 3. The Photo Source. 4. The Bettmann Archive/BBC Hulton.

Following page 274

1. Bancroft's *Americans in London,* 1902. 2. *The Langham Hotel Company Guide to London,* 1901.

Index

Americans are in boldface.

Melville, Herman, 71-2, 265, 270
Mencken, Henry Lewis, 242
Meredith, Burgess, 198
Meredith, George, 17, 62
Mielziner, Jo, 57
Mill, John Stuart, 8, 214
Millay, Edna St. Vincent, 139-40
Miller, Glen, 207, 241
Miller, Henry, 71
Miller, Joaquin, 188
Millet, Frank, 256
Milnes, Richard Monckton, 9, 133
Monro, Harold, 34, 92
Monroe, Harriet, 17, 142, 149
Monterey, Carlotta, 19
Montgomery, Bernard Law, 33
Moore, George, 41, 60, 84, 282
Moore, Robert, 277
Morgan, John Pierpont, 101, 210
Morgan, Junius Spencer, 101
Morgan, Lewis Henry, 43-4
Morpeth, Lord, 44, 250
Morris, Jonathon, 195
Morris, Gouverneur, 49, 152-4, 274, 280-1
Morrow, Anne, 94, 211
Morse, Samuel, 65-6, 173, 182, 199, 227, 267
Mott, Lucretia, 120
Mountbatten, Louis, 129
Mulgrave, Baron, 75
Mumford, Lewis, 15
Muni, Paul & Bella, 56-7
Murray, John, 56, 67, 105, 117
Murrow, Edward R., 30, 97, 131-2, 198, 205-7
Murrow, Janet, 131
Museums and galleries
 —British Museum, 20, 43, 122, 129, 185, 187, 213, 265-6
 —Colnaghi's, 186-7
 —George Catlin Indian Gallery, 201-2
 —New Gallery, 41
 —Spring Gardens, 13
 —Storran, 4-5
 —Tate, 68
Mussolini, 143

Napoleon, 11, 12, 182, 200
Napoleon III, 270
Nash, John, 34, 45

Nathan, George Jean, 42
Nation, 213
Nelson, Horatio, 13, 184
New Republic, 252
New Yorker, 5, 34, 55, 131
Neyle, Philip, 232
Nicolson, Harold, 115
Nightclubs and casinos
 —Crockford's, 60
 —400 Club, 60
 —Colony Club, 60
 —Rector Club, 38
 —Talk of the Town, 71
Nixon, Richard, 133, 197
Noble, Ray, 255
North, Lord, 124, 231, 232
Norton, Charles Eliot, 130, 168, 213-4

O'Hara, John, 59-60
O'Neill, Eugene, 19
O'Shea, Kitty, 87
Oakley, Annie, 99, 205
Oliver, Frederick S., 67-8
Olivier, Laurence, 157, 282
Orwell, George, 57

Paine, Thomas, 153, 163-4
Palmerston, Lord, 141, 209, 245
Panizzi, Anthony, 265, 270
Parks
 —Green, 9, 21, 226, 230
 —Hyde, 9, 11, 124, 152, 154
 —Regent's, 54, 220
 —St. James's, 35, 198, 230
Parnell, Charles Stewart, 87
Patton, George, 264
Paulding, James K., 50
Payne, John Howard, 49-50, 65, 116, 168-9, 221
Peabody, George, 100-2, 146, 154-5, 179, 197-8, 223, 265, 270
Peale, Charles Willson, 36, 47, 48, 193
Peale, Rubens & Rembrandt, 193
Peel, Robert, 202
Penn, John, 136, 153
Penn, Mrs. John, 48
Penn, Thomas, 77, 195
Pennell, Elizabeth R., 41
Pennell, Joseph, 41

Maps of London

Exeter Exchange, Strand, 1829

MAPS
OF
LONDON

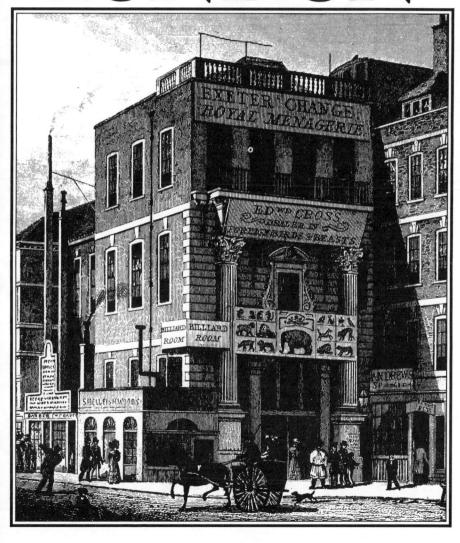

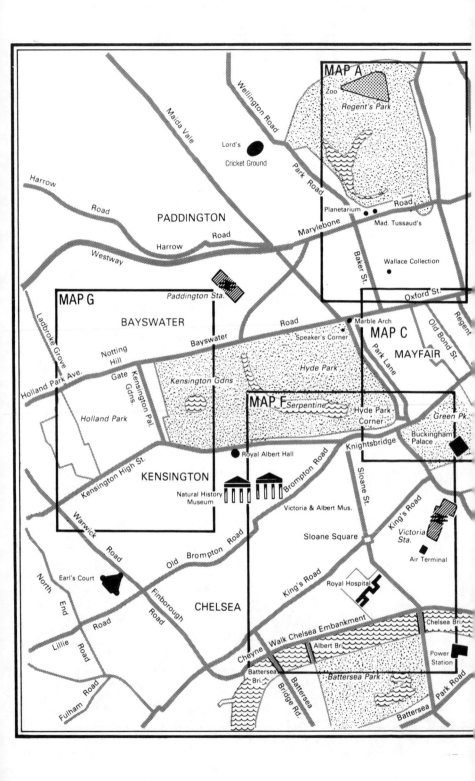

MAP A

Zoo

Regent's Park

Lord's
Cricket Ground

Wellington Road

Maida Vale

Park Road

Harrow

Road

PADDINGTON

Harrow Road

Road

Westway

Planetarium

Marylebone Road

Mad. Tussaud's

Baker St.

Wallace Collection

Oxford St.

MAP G

BAYSWATER

Paddington Sta.

Ladbroke Grove

Holland Park Ave.

Notting Hill Gate

Bayswater Road

Speaker's Corner

Marble Arch

MAP C

Regent St.

Old Bond St.

MAYFAIR

Park Lane

Kensington Pal. Gdns.

Kensington Gdns.

Hyde Park

Holland Park

Serpentine

MAP F

Hyde Park Corner

Green Pk.

Buckingham Palace

Kensington High St.

KENSINGTON

Royal Albert Hall

Knightsbridge

Sloane St.

Natural History Museum

Brompton Road

Victoria & Albert Mus.

King's Road

Victoria Sta.

Warwick Road

Old Brompton Road

Sloane Square

Air Terminal

North End Road

Earl's Court

Finborough Road

CHELSEA

King's Road

Royal Hospital

Lillie Road

Fulham Road

Cheyne Walk

Chelsea Embankment

Albert Bri.

Chelsea Bri.

Power Station

Battersea Bri.

Battersea Bridge Rd.

Battersea Park

Battersea Park Road

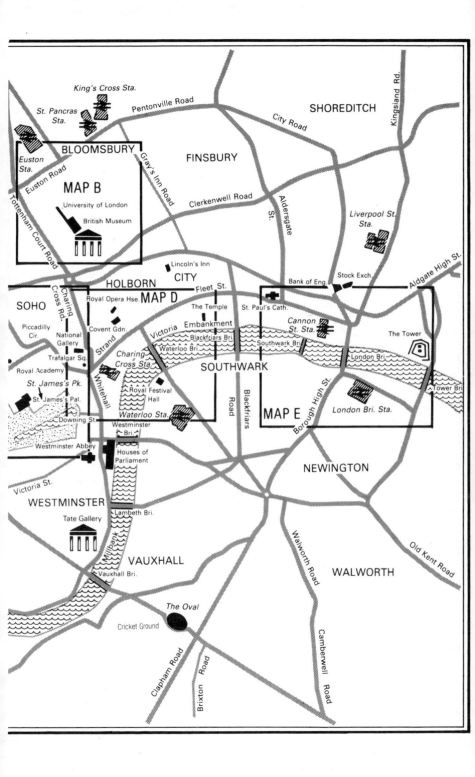

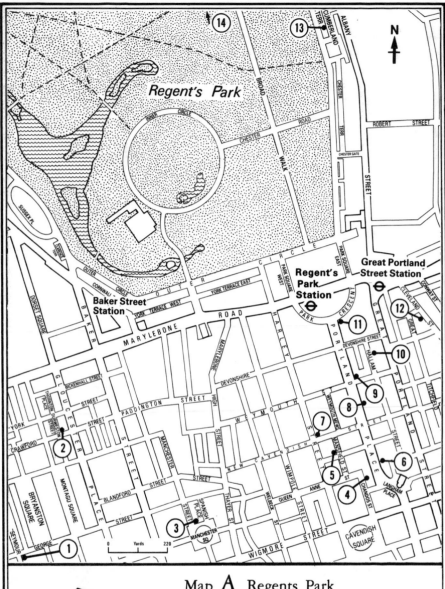

Map **A** Regents Park

1. Simpson 5 George St
2. Eliot 18 Crawford St
3. Bingham Manchester Sq
4. Irving 3 Chandos St
5. Adams 5 Mansfield St
6. Murrow, Miller Portland Pl
7. Bingham 62 Harley St
8. Bates 46 Portland Pl
9. Wright 66 Portland Pl
10. Murrow 84 Hallam St
11. Adams 98 Portland Pl
12. Morse, Leslie
    141 Cleveland St
13. Simpson
    16 Cumberland Ter
14. Audubon
    Regents Park Zoo

Cumberland Terrace

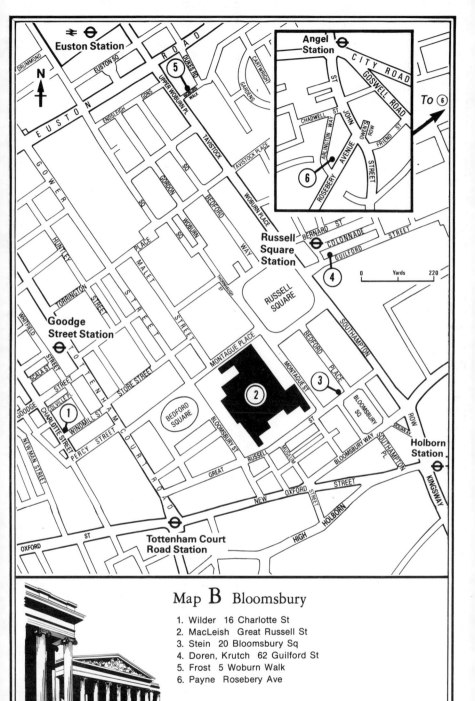

Map B Bloomsbury

1. Wilder 16 Charlotte St
2. MacLeish Great Russell St
3. Stein 20 Bloomsbury Sq
4. Doren, Krutch 62 Guilford St
5. Frost 5 Woburn Walk
6. Payne Rosebery Ave

British Museum

Map **C** Mayfair

1. Selfridge 400 Oxford St
2. Eisenhower 20 Grosvenor Sq
3. Kennedy Grosvenor Sq
4. Winant 7 Aldford St
5. Steinbeck Park Lane
6. Eisenhower 47 Grosvenor Sq
7. Adams 9 Grosvenor Sq
8. Van Buren 7 Stratford Pl
9. Grant 17 Cavendish Sq
10. Cushman 92 New Bond St
11. Fitzgerald, Gordon, Donovan,
    Hopkins, Eisenhower,
    Goldberg 51 Brook St
12. Kellogg Curzon St
13. Millay 41 Hertford St
14. Hughes Hamilton Pl
15. Steinbeck 116 Piccadilly
16. West, Adams, Jay, Tom Thumb,
    Wilson Buckingham Palace
17. James 7 Half Moon St
18. Wilson Half Moon St
19. T. Roosevelt, F. Roosevelt,
    Twain, Lindbergh 21 Dover St
20. Hutchinson 149 New Bond St
21. Wolfe 25 Hanover Sq
22. Longfellow 8 Princes St
23. Pound 309 Regent St
24. Armstrong, Ellington,
    Berlin Argyll St
25. Stuart 3 New Burlington St
26. Berenson 14 Old Bond St
27. Fairbanks, Pickford Piccadilly
28. Thurber 16 St James's Pl
29. Stowe Stable Yard, St James's Pal
30. Adams St James's Pal
31. Lewis 10 Bury St
32. Thurber 5 Albany Crt Yrd
33. Wolfe Sherwood St
34. Draper 80 Pall Mall
35. Choate 1 Carlton House Ter
36. Hay 5 Carlton House Ter
37. Emerson, James 107 Pall Mall
38. Frohman 11 Waterloo Pl
39. Hayes, Cushman,
    Williams 6 Haymarket
40. Kerouac 39 Coventry St

Buckingham Palace

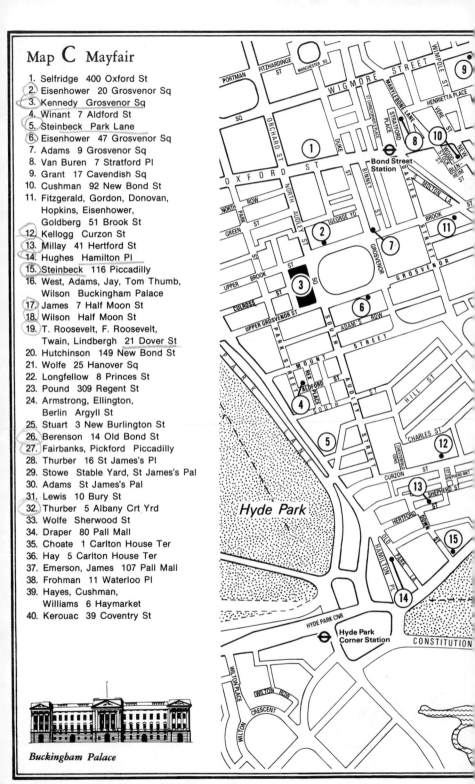

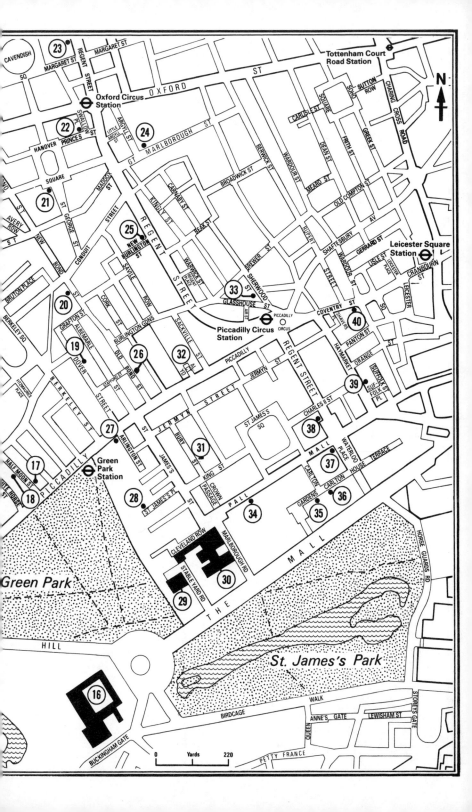

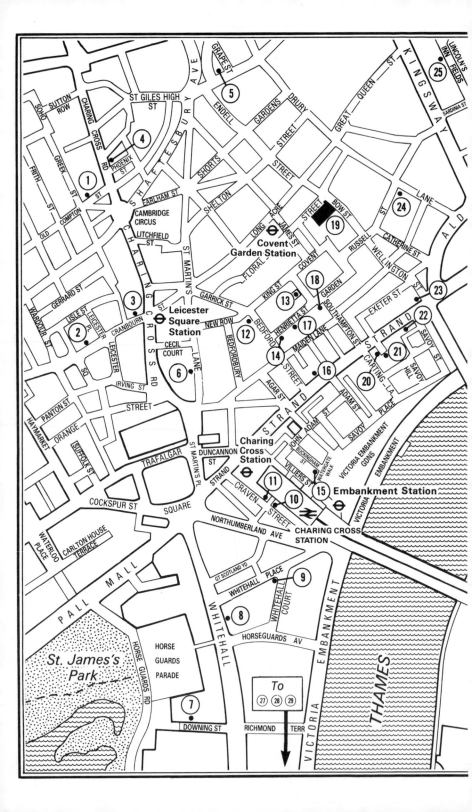

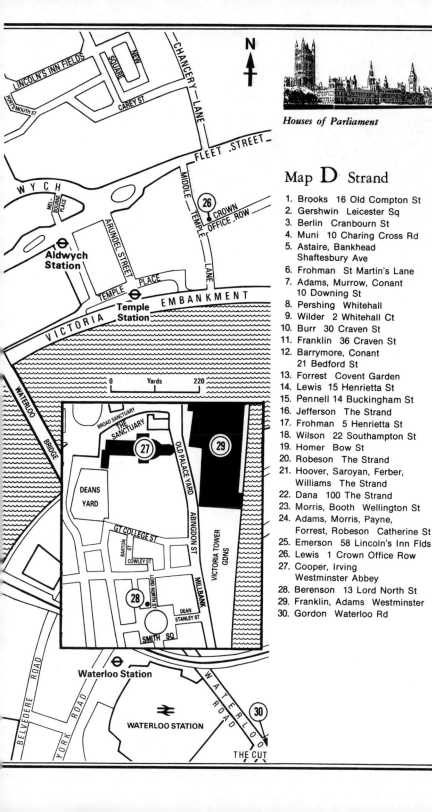

N

Houses of Parliament

Map D Strand

1. Brooks 16 Old Compton St
2. Gershwin Leicester Sq
3. Berlin Cranbourn St
4. Muni 10 Charing Cross Rd
5. Astaire, Bankhead Shaftesbury Ave
6. Frohman St Martin's Lane
7. Adams, Murrow, Conant 10 Downing St
8. Pershing Whitehall
9. Wilder 2 Whitehall Ct
10. Burr 30 Craven St
11. Franklin 36 Craven St
12. Barrymore, Conant 21 Bedford St
13. Forrest Covent Garden
14. Lewis 15 Henrietta St
15. Pennell 14 Buckingham St
16. Jefferson The Strand
17. Frohman 5 Henrietta St
18. Wilson 22 Southampton St
19. Homer Bow St
20. Robeson The Strand
21. Hoover, Saroyan, Ferber, Williams The Strand
22. Dana 100 The Strand
23. Morris, Booth Wellington St
24. Adams, Morris, Payne, Forrest, Robeson Catherine St
25. Emerson 58 Lincoln's Inn Flds
26. Lewis 1 Crown Office Row
27. Cooper, Irving Westminster Abbey
28. Berenson 13 Lord North St
29. Franklin, Adams Westminster
30. Gordon Waterloo Rd

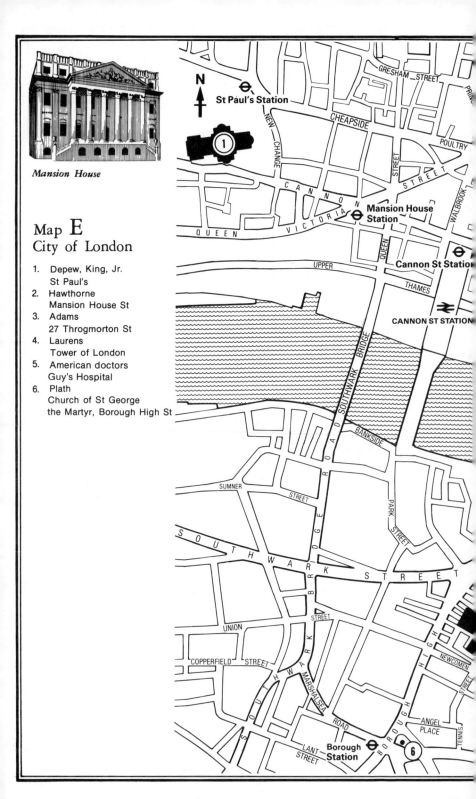

Mansion House

Map E
City of London

1. Depew, King, Jr.
   St Paul's
2. Hawthorne
   Mansion House St
3. Adams
   27 Throgmorton St
4. Laurens
   Tower of London
5. American doctors
   Guy's Hospital
6. Plath
   Church of St George
   the Martyr, Borough High St

St Paul's Station

GRESHAM STREET

CHEAPSIDE

POULTRY

NEW CHANGE

CANNON

VICTORIA

QUEEN

STREET

WALBROOK

Mansion House Station

QUEEN

UPPER

THAMES

Cannon St Station

CANNON ST STATION

SOUTHWARK BRIDGE ROAD

BANKSIDE

SUMNER STREET

PARK STREET

SOUTHWARK STREET

UNION STREET

COPPERFIELD STREET

SOUTHWARK BRIDGE ROAD

MARSHALSEA ROAD

HIGH STREET

NEWCOMEN STREET

ANGEL PLACE

TENNIS

LANT STREET

Borough Station

BOROUGH

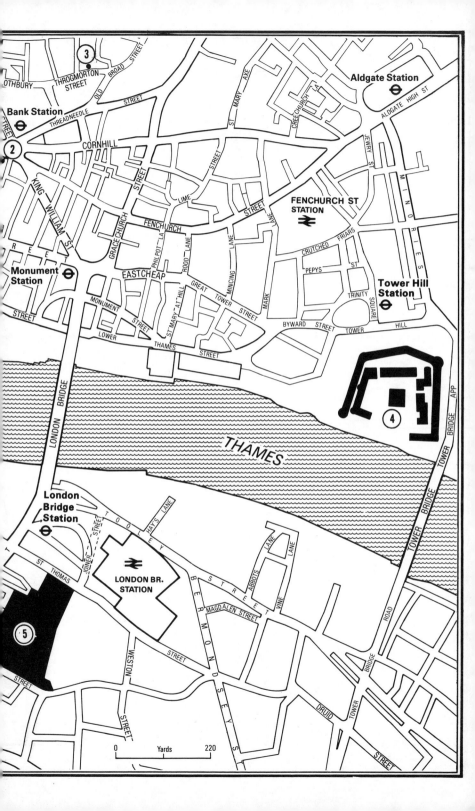

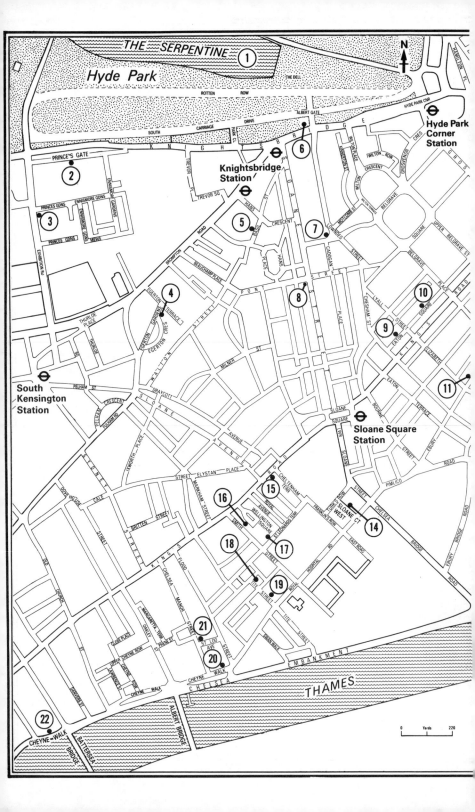

23 Tedworth Square

Map F Chelsea

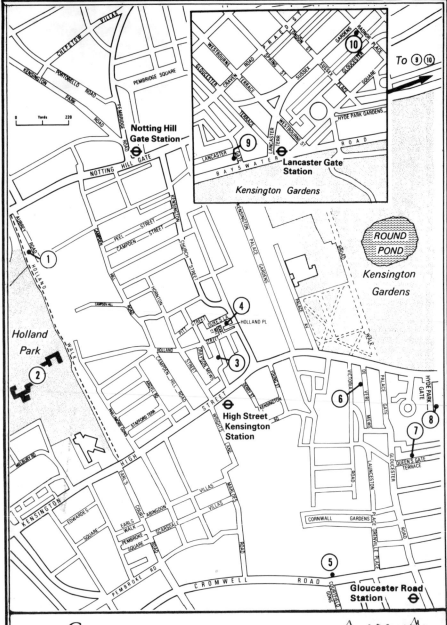

Map G Kensington Gardens

1. Alcott Aubrey Rd
2. Cooper Holland Park
3. Pound, Williams
   10 Kensington Church Walk
4. Pound 5 Holland Pl Chmbrs
5. Harland 144 Cromwell Rd
6. James 34 De Vere Grdns
7. Norton 18 Queens Gate Ter
8. Hoover 39 Hyde Park Gate
9. Harte 109 Lancaster Gate
10. Lowell 2 Radnor Pl

Holland House